P(G

Figures of
Life and Death
in Medieval
English Literature

Figures of
Life and Death
in Medieval
English Literature

PHILIPPA TRISTRAM

Paul Elek London

First published 1976 by
ELEK BOOKS LIMITED
54–58 Caledonian Road
London N1 9RN

Copyright © 1976 by Philippa Tristram

ISBN 0 236 40063 0

Printed in Great Britain by
Latimer Trend & Company Ltd Plymouth

In Memory
of
my parents
E. W. and Eileen Tristram

Contents

Plates

The Horseman of Death. *frontispiece*
Les Très Riches Heures du Duc de Berry, f. 90 v. Jean Colombe, late fifteenth century, Musée Condé, Chantilly.

between pp. 146 and 147

1 Plague.
Les Belles Heures de Jean Duc de Berry, f. 74. Limbourg brothers, early fifteenth century. Cloisters Collection, Metropolitan Museum of Art, New York.

2 The Pride of Life.
Smithfield Decretals, 10 E IV BM, f. 251 v., f. 252, f. 254, f. 259 v. Late fourteenth century, British Library.

3 (a) Nature at her Forge and
(b) Venus Assaulting the Tower of Shame.
MS Douce 195, f. 114 v., f. 147 v. *Le Roman de la Rose*, late fifteenth century. Bodleian Library, Oxford.

4 Chaucer's Squire.
Ellesmere MS of *The Canterbury Tales*, Henry Huntington Library, San Marino, California.

5 Langland's Pride.
MS Douce 104, f. 24. *Piers Plowman*, C Text, 1427. Bodleian Library, Oxford.

6 Zodiac Man.
MS Canon Misc. 248, f. 42. Early fourteenth century. Bodleian Library, Oxford.

7 Youth Succeeds to Age.
Hours of Catherine of Cleves, M-p. 180. *c.* 1440. Guennol Collection, Pierpont Morgan Library, New York.

8 Lamech, Adolescens and Cain.
Visconti Hours, LF 70. Belbello da Pavia, early fifteenth century. Biblioteca Nazionale, Florence.

9 The Three Ages, January and May.
Alabaster of the Adoration of the Magi, *c.* 1350. Church of the Holy Trinity, Long Melford.

10   The Wheel of Life.
     A cycle of the four ages in ten stages. MS Arundel 83, f. 126 v. *c.* 1330.
     British Library, London.

11   Jupiter, Mars and Venus.
     MS Fairfax 16, f. 14 v. Chaucer's Minor Poems, *c.* 1450. Bodleian
     Library, Oxford.

12   The Great Dead.
     MS Bodley 263, f. 7. Frontispiece to Lydgate's *Fall of Princes*, 1440–50.
     Bodleian Library, Oxford.

13   Janus as Youth and Age.
     Les Belles Heures de Jean Duc de Berry, f. 2. Limbourg brothers, early
     fifteenth century. Cloisters Collection, Metropolitan Museum of Art,
     New York.

14   (a) January and (b) February Warming.
     MS Bodley 614, f. 3, f. 4. Mid twelfth century. Bodleian Library,
     Oxford.

15   (a) April and (b) May.
     MS Douce 24, f. 2 v., f. 3. *c.* 1300. Bodleian Library, Oxford.

16   (a) January and Aquarius and (b) May and Gemini.
     MS Douce 144, f. 6, f. 10. 1407. Bodleian Library, Oxford.

17   Two-Faced Fortune, Philosophy, the Muses and Boethius.
     MS Douce 298, f. 1. *c.* 1400. Bodleian Library, Oxford.

18   Open-Eyed Fortune.
     From a drawing by E. W. Tristram of a thirteenth-century mural in
     Rochester Cathedral. Victoria and Albert Museum, London, E. 488–1915.

19   Blindfold Fortune.
     MS Douce 332, f. 58. Late fourteenth century. Bodleian Library, Oxford.

20   Renaissance Fortune.
     Copper engraving, attriubuted to Baccio Baldini. Biblioteca Nazionale,
     Florence.

21   The Contemplation of Death.
     St Jerome with skull and marginal emblems of resurrection. Grimani
     Breviary, f. 751 v. Late fifteenth century. Biblioteca Nazionale Marciana,
     Venice.

22   Lazarus.
     MS Auct. D. 4. 4., f. 243 v. 1370–80. Bodleian Library, Oxford.

23   Animate Corpse.
     The corpse of Diocrès cries out, at the moment of burial: 'I have been
     justly accused in the judgement of God.' Les Belles Heures de Jean Duc
     de Berry, f. 95. Limbourg brothers, early fifteenth century. Cloisters
     Collection, Metropolitan Museum of Art, New York.

24   'Drery Dethe'.
     MS Douce 322, f. 19 v. 1550–75. Bodleian Library, Oxford.

25   The Three Living and the Three Dead.
     Codex Harley 2917, f. 119. Fifteenth century. British Library, London.

Acknowledgements

I am grateful to the following for permission to reproduce the illustrations: Biblioteca Nazionale, Florence (Plates 8, 20); Biblioteca Nazionale Marciana, Venice (Plate 21); Bibliothèque Nationale, Paris (Plate 28); Bodleian Library, Oxford (Plates 3, 5, 6, 11, 12, 14, 15, 16, 17, 19, 22, 24, 26, 34, 35); British Library, London (Plates 2, 10, 25, 27, 36); Huntington Library, San Marino, California (Plate 4); Metropolitan Museum of Art, New York (Plates 1, 13, 23); Musée Condé, Chantilly (frontispiece); National Monuments Record, London (Plates 9, 29, 30, 31, 32); Pierpont Morgan Library, New York (Plates 7, 33); Victoria and Albert Museum, London (Plate 18).

Preface

I am indebted to my parents for a childhood whose brightest colours were medieval; to Gervase Mathew who, in his inspiring direction of a post-graduate essay connected with this subject, renewed that original delight; and to David Moody, to whom I owe the confidence to pursue that theme more extensively. I am most grateful to Elizabeth Salter, for her illuminating criticisms of the book's material and of its structure; to Philip Brockbank, for his patient scrutiny of its prose; to Helen Houghton, for her attentive scholar's eye, and to Ann Douglas, for her editorial care and kindness. All have helped me to enjoy the company of Life and Death (even its grimmer members), and I hope that the finished book may transmit something of their creative impulse.

Introduction

' "Ich shal daunce ther-to; do al-so thow, suster!" ' Peace enjoins Righteousness, as Christ descends to conquer Death in Langland's dramatization of the Harrowing of Hell. ' "Thou art ryght dronke!" ' Righteousness retorts. ' "Leyvest thou that yon light unlouke myghte helle?" ' The reply tendered by her sister elucidates the presence, throughout medieval literature, of the various company of Life and Death:

'Ho couthe kyndeliche with colour discrive,
Yf alle the worlde were whit, other swan-whit alle thynges?
Yf no nyght ne were, no man, as ich leyve,
Sholde wite witerly what day were to mene.'[1]

Readers of its literature are apt, like Righteousness, to regard the Middle Ages as a period in which the 'quiet hierarchies' of religious orthodoxy flourished in a world innocent of 'dynamically interacting polarities'.[2] The figures of Life and Death, which play so prominent a part in medieval writing, offer dramatic evidence to the contrary. They reflect the many colours that merge to form the 'swan-whit' world of faith, and they urge the necessity of darker understandings to a full comprehension of the meaning of day.

These figures are sometimes actual personifications—such as Youth, Nature, Fortune—and at others, themes or motifs—the Seasons, the Ages, the Dance of Death. All dramatize the 'dynamic polarities' of Life and Death, but most can vary their colours and serve in either company. Youth may, on the one hand, express the perfection of temporal life, and thus relate to Christ; or, on the other, represent the Pride of Life whose prototype is Lucifer. Age, normally the embittered precursor of Death, may sometimes personify the fulfilment of Old Testament history. Life and Death themselves have no constant values, for

---

unlouke unlock   *kyndeliche* properly   *discrive* describe   *witerly* for certain

Death is sometimes God's messenger, at others his enemy; whilst Life, in its temporal aspect, may signify spiritual death, or, in its eternal dimension, the soul's immortality. These paradoxes enrich the literature of the Middle Ages, for the 'quiet hierarchies' of Righteousness would hold less interest for us if they were not so arduously won from the various world that Peace describes.

The figures which compose the company of Life and Death can be found throughout the literature of the Middle Ages, though they appear far more frequently from the middle of the fourteenth century. I have confined myself largely to English writing, since a European scope would be unmanageable; but because it would be impossible to understand these figures fully without some knowledge of their origin or context in those great French and Italian works which influence England, and in the art, the thought and the history of the time, considerable reference is made to this wider setting. Since in English writing these figures are not confined to particular authors or genres (although they may develop particular characteristics in either), I have drawn upon a variety of sources, some of which could scarcely be described as 'literary'. It might be objected, as Wind has done in relation to painting, that 'the commonplace may be understood as a reduction of the exceptional, but . . . the exceptional cannot be understood by amplifying the commonplace'.[3] Yet the commonplace, whilst being so radically developed in great literature that its antecedents become scarcely distinguishable, may yet, in its humbler context, illuminate some aspects of the major work which are particularly those that reveal its greatness. A concern with the commonplace need not reduce the great to the conventional; it may restore meaning to the conventional and make manifest the distinction of the great.

It is useful to recall Ruskin's observation in *The Stones of Venice*:

This is the glory of Gothic architecture, that every jot and tittle, every point and niche of it, affords room, fuel and focus for individual fire. But you cease to acknowledge this, and you refuse to accept the help of the lesser mind, if you require the work to be all executed in a great manner.[4]

The figures of Life and Death express their 'individual fire' in the niches, crockets and corbels of ordinary writing; but it is the unending dialogue between them which sustains the 'great manner', both of the major works of the later Middle Ages in England, and of the profound insights of medieval civilization which those works express.

I

The Figures' Context

The clarity with which the later Middle Ages portray the companies of Life and Death is a result of the particular context in which they are developed. Relevant aspects of this context in history and art are late in date and relatively local; for the figures of Life and Death are chiefly developed (though not invented) in the years 1350–1500, under the pressure of particular events which come to trouble the great design, notably war, plague and economic depression which afflict the countries of western Europe during that period. The origin of these figures in Christian thought asks to be considered first, however, for it extends back to the earliest years of Christianity, thus spanning many centuries and countries. The philosophers of the Middle Ages built upon their predecessors with a consciousness less perceptible in medieval poets and artists, whose pious and often ignorant regard for historical figures tends to turn them into household myths. But it is impossible to read Aquinas, Ockham or Scotus without being referred, specifically and continually, to the thought of Aristotle and Plato, of Augustine and Boethius, of Anselm and Abelard. When medieval philosophers thought through their predecessors they preserved them as an inescapable part of Christian intelligence.

These structures of thought were, moreover, to some extent common to all Christendom, so that, in matters of belief at least, there is some continuity between the simplest poetry of the Middle Ages and its most complex philosophy. The teaching of the Church upon the soul and its future did as much as the poetic imagination to establish the figures of Life and Death. But it is too easy to speak as though each medieval Christian was an aspect of a single orthodox mind, for orthodoxy was itself the result of many centuries of debate. Because Christianity had no doctrine of the soul, 'Christian theologians', as Pelikan remarks, 'must look beyond Scripture and tradition for the content of their ideas about the soul and about the shape of death.'[1] The geography of the afterlife, which now seems so permanent a part of Christian belief, was developed over many centuries: Hell and the Harrowing of Hell, Purgatory and

Limbo, are all relatively late developments in Christian thought. Indeed, the immortality of the soul was still matter for debate in the sixth century, and the geography of the afterlife of course depends in part upon the acceptance of this doctrine.

By the fourteenth century such beliefs were relatively well established. Notions entertained by the early fathers of the transmigration or pre-existence of the soul, or of its mortality, had been excluded. Nevertheless, a distance exists between accepting a belief in an afterlife, and imagining the afterworld that it necessitates; Purgatory and Limbo, the latter never a very precise area in Christian thought, represent, for example, an endeavour to mitigate the effects of a justice made eternal. Moreover, the attempt to envisage these states, not as conditions of the soul, but as actual places, inevitably sent the imagination in search of prototypes. Otherworldly visions of a pagan past were drawn upon, the more naturally since Christian teaching on the afterlife owed a great deal to pagan thought in any case.[2] Dante's dependence upon Virgil in his exploration of Hell and Purgatory is multi-faceted.

Where men became preoccupied with the destiny of the soul, paradox and contradiction were in consequence frequent. The later Middle Ages are characterized in any case by doubt, and belief is often defined only when it is threatened. The teaching of the Catholic Church has never, one must remember, been established as a body defined for all time; additions have constantly been made to its doctrine, even if these represent the formalization of beliefs already generally accepted. This capacity for continued growth can be a strength, but it should at least modify the notion of monolithic, unalterable unity. That is why the nineteenth and twentieth century tendency to regard the Middle Ages as a period of harmonious belief is so misleading, for this view has its origin in the nostalgia of an age of doubt for a supposed age of faith.

The relevance of Christian beliefs about the afterlife to the literature of Life and Death is obvious enough, but medieval thought had its effect upon poetry in ways less specific though equally profound. I do not mean to imply that the connection between literature and thought was an intimate one, especially at the close of the Middle Ages. In the schools the study of literature and the exegesis of biblical texts had parted company in the twelfth century: John of Salisbury laments the separation in his *Metalogicus*, a defence of the Arts of the Trivium; whilst in the early fourteenth century the humane Richard de Bury feels compelled to supply a detailed answer to the question, *Quare non omnino negleximus fabulas poetarum* (Why we have not altogether neglected the stories of the poets).[3] For reasons to be touched upon later, the status of literature became too humble to merit serious attention. But, if the connection between philosophy and literature was not intimate, the former did in more general ways influence the latter. For the poets of the later Middle

Ages, the *Consolatio Philosophiae* of Boethius is, for example, a seminal work. A central text in the schools, it is thoroughly known by Chaucer, though his actual translation at times reveals an imperfect grasp of both language and argument; but the work is alluded to and cited by many who have clearly never read the original at all, for their commonplaces have only a marginal connection with the text to which they are confidently attributed. In addition, however, to this direct popularization of medieval thought, the idea of man which its thinkers present, and their notion of art, have relevance to the development in literature of the figures of Life and Death.

The image of man in the Christian mind from Augustine until the end of the Middle Ages can be clearly distinguished from that of the Renaissance. For the medieval Christian, man is forever overshadowed by God, even if that shadow is protective. The relation is always of creature to creator, and, although the creature is perfectable, he is so only through the creator's mediation. Furthermore, the paradigm of his perfection is Christ, and the ideal is therefore unattainable, for no human being can achieve divine manhood. One consequence, relevant for the literature of Life and Death, of this humble and relative conception of man, is the absence of tragedy, for tragedy elevates the human protagonist at the cost of the divine. Within an eschatological scheme, damnation neither can be elevated, nor salvation be regarded as tragic. A second consequence is the recurrent debate over freewill and necessity which dominates the literature of the later Middle Ages. For if the creature is invariably subordinated to the creator, the extent of his freedom is inevitably called into question; both salvation and damnation may be beyond his control. The Renaissance, while retaining much of the medieval notion of God, nevertheless recovers faith in man. He is, for example, no longer represented as the helpless victim of Fortune, but as an independent and even sovereign being; the medieval wheel to which the great are bound to rise and fall with its inevitable motion, not of their own volition, is replaced in the Renaissance by a sailboat with man at the tiller[4] (Plates 17, 18, 19, 20).

The conception of man which dominates the Middle Ages is connected with its attitude to the created world; for just as man, necessarily imperfect, is continually aware of his subordination to divine perfection, so the world which he inhabits lies also under the shadow of the celestial. Christian theology, even after the recovery of Aristotle, remains dominantly Platonic, and particularly in its retention of the notion of perfect form. The Platonic idea connects on the one hand with the philosophical debate over universals which dominates the schools from the twelfth to the fourteenth centuries; on the other, it relates to the popularity of the allegoric or figural in medieval literature. Here, if anywhere, can be found the genesis of the figures of Life and Death, for an abstract can be more confidently delineated than an individual. In this view each created thing in the apparently substantial world is no more than a sign, an intimation of what its perfect form would be. The medieval realist (in a sense contrary to our own use of the word) regarded the notional perfect form as the only true reality, an abstract which the human mind could never discover in the world, but only imagine. Even when, in the fourteenth century, the so-called nominalism of Ockham came to replace the moderate realism of the twelfth and thirteenth centuries, the result was not to restore substance to the created world, but to emphasize even more radically the gulf that divided the divine idea from its fallen creation.

These of course are large generalizations, and it is important to emphasize that none of them stood without debate in the Middle Ages. Each period within that large epoch had distinctive approaches to these problems. Augustine, for example, does not exhibit that *contemptus mundi* which characterizes so much writing in the later Middle Ages; he accepts that death is the punishment for sin, but the prospect of mortality does not render this world contemptible. The antithetic figures of Life and Death serve instead to emphasize the beauty of the world:

Neque enim Deus ullum, non dico Angelorum, sed vel hominum crearet, quem malum futurum esse praescisset, nisi pariter nosset quibus eos bonorum usibus commodaret, atque ita ordinem saeculorum tanquam pulcherrimum carmen ex quibusdam quasi antithetis honestaret.[5]

(For God would never have created anyone, human, I mean, not angel, whom he knew beforehand would be evil, had he not also known what good use to make of them, thus adorning the course of history, by means of these antithetic figures, like a most beautiful song.)

The beauty of the world, if within certain limitations, is powerfully felt in his writings. In *De Trinitate* he enumerates its best-loved features— landscape, fertile farms, well-run houses; the body and the necessities of life which it enjoys; the attributes of the human heart (and riches too, because they make for ease); the skies, with their luminaries (including angels); speech and song (if their burden is sufficiently profound):

Quid plura et plura? Bonum hoc et bonum illud: tolle hoc et illud, et vide ipsum bonum, si potes; ita Deum videbis.[6]

(Why continue? This good and that good: take away this and that and see the good itself if you can; then you will see God.)

This account is in no sense renaissance; it is distinctively medieval. A response is encouraged only to that which is morally good, and this is itself seen merely as a veil, radiant with his brightness, over the face of

God. But neither has this passage the savage desolation which characterizes much of the writing of the later Middle Ages. The fourteenth and fifteenth centuries, with some notable exceptions, have lost this early Christian assurance. Man becomes a helpless figure, capable, in Ockham's estimation, of discovering very little by the operation of intelligence. A great gulf is fixed between reason and faith; the area of free choice grows smaller, and the elect, for the orthodox Bradwardine, are predetermined by grace, not merit. The bright face of God is no longer glimpsed through creation, for the deficiencies of the created world are not indications of perfection to come, so much as tokens of separation and dissolution.

The position at the close of the Middle Ages is succinctly expressed by Panofsky: 'The common denominator of these new currents is, of course, subjectivism—aesthetic subjectivism in the case of the poet and humanist, religious subjectivism in that of the mystic, and epistemological subjectivism in that of the nominalist.'[7] Thus the climate that destroys the confidence of scholastic thought is one that nourishes literature, for, whilst the Church had always willingly employed the arts as aids to divine worship, its distrust of the individual voice had long led it to hold those arts in minimal esteem, especially in their secular form. Although the early Church was nourished by Neoplatonic rather than Platonic thought, the Middle Ages, unlike the Renaissance, did not distinguish clearly between the Platonic disdain and the Neoplatonic admiration for poetry. Thus Philosophy contemptuously banishes the tragical muses from Boethius' cell as *meretriculas* (courtesans) and *Sirenes usque in exitium dulcis* (Sirens charming all the way to ruin). Music as song has her place in the *Consolatio*, but her function is distinctly menial: she is *laris nostris vernacula*, Philosophy's household slave.[8]

This attitude to poetry, characterized at best by condescension, at worst by contempt, is representative of most medieval thinkers and many poets. From the scholastic point of view, poetry is *infima inter omnes doctrinas* (the most humble of all forms of teaching). Even Aquinas, who allows that *est autem naturale homini ut per sensibilia ad intelligibilia veniat* (it is however natural to man to achieve understanding by way of the senses), sees poetry as an indulgence wholly inferior to reason:

Poetica utitur metaphoris propter repraesentationem, repraesentatio enim naturaliter homini delectabilis est. Sed sacra doctrina utitur metaphoris propter necessitatem et utilitatem.[9]

(Poetic art uses metaphors in the interests of representation, for a delight in representation is natural to man. But sacred teaching uses metaphors because they are necessary and useful.)

Art of any kind is seen as a subordinate activity; it is an imitation by the creature of the divine art of God's creation. As such, Aquinas will often draw upon it for analogies, but, significantly, he has recourse more often to architecture than to painting or poetry: the criterion is almost purely one of social utility, for architecture has a superior value in expressing solidarity and progress.

There are of course some noted exceptions to these generalizations. The interconnection of poetry and philosophy is vigorously affirmed by John of Salisbury, whose attitude, and the ebulliently sexual metaphor which expresses it, anticipates the English Renaissance by some four centuries. Having described *illa dulcis et fructuosa conjugatio rationis et verbi* (this sweet and fruitful coition of reason and language), he continues:

Ut hostis omnium publicus merito censeatur, quisquis hoc, quod ad utilitatem omnium Deus conjunxit, nititur separare. Mercurio philologiam invidet, et ab amplexu *Philologiae* Mercurium avellit, qui eloquentiae praeceptionem a studiis philosophiae eliminat.[10]

(He deserves to be rated a public enemy who strives to put asunder what God, for the common profit, has joined together. He who banishes the teaching of eloquence from philosophical study, envies Mercury the possession of Philology, and tears him from her embrace.)

This connection between language and reason, literature and philosophy, is affirmed in every line of the *Divina Commedia*, and is explicitly stated by Boccaccio:

Dico che la teologia e la poesia quasi una cosa si possono dire, dove uno medesimo sia il suggetto; anzi dico più: che la teologia niuna altra cosa è che una poesia di Dio.[11]

(I say that theology and poetry may virtually be identified where they share the same subject; I go further still: that theology is nothing else than a poetry of God.)

For the continent, however, Dante and Boccaccio are Renaissance figures. It must not be forgotten that English medieval literature begins to flourish only when the Renaissance is already established in Europe. Chaucer is a reader of Dante, 'the wise poete of Florence', of Boccaccio, and of Petrarch, 'the lauriat poete/. . . whos rethorike sweete/Enlumyned al Ytaille of poetrie'.[12] Yet, although he draws heavily upon their poetry, and particularly upon Boccaccio's, he remains a medieval, not a renaissance, figure.[13] English literature has to wait until the sixteenth century for its true emancipation from scholastic condemnation. Though it may have its own distinctive character, achieving, sometimes unconsciously, its own unorthodox vision of life and man, this vision is always tentative.

No English poet ever affirms with Dante's assurance that poetry itself may be the instrument of a man's salvation.

The context provided by medieval thought for the figures of Life and Death is necessarily far-reaching, but English history and art, whilst owing much to the continent, are surprisingly self-contained. Historical events may grow out of the past and their repercussions extend into the future, but their connections with both are much less perceptible to a contemporary eye. It is only relevant, therefore, to touch on those events in England between 1350 and 1500 which seem to be vividly present in the literature of Life and Death. This is to ignore a great deal that is crucial to the history of Christendom at that period, but the insularity of England at that time results from ignoring it. It is effectively separated from Europe by the Hundred Years' War, and its life, in every respect, continues at a different tempo.[14] When, for example, the Church in Europe is riven by the Avignon papacy, the Great Schism and wave after wave of heresy followed by persecution, England is troubled only (and then after a time-lapse) by Wycliffism and Lollardy, highly parochial forms of the same infection.

But the foremost event in this context, the advent of bubonic plague, of course affected Europe as well as England (Plate 1). It reached Sicily from the East in October 1347, and gradually spread through the whole of the European mainland, arriving in England towards the end of the following year. It was to recur at intervals of approximately ten years for the remainder of the Middle Ages, but its first occurrence, now known as the Black Death, was undoubtedly at once the most severe and the most shocking. The history of histories of the Black Death could form a subject in its own right: during the eighteenth century it received only casual mention, but came, in the nineteenth, to be invoked as the compendious explanation of all those changes which mark the close of the Middle Ages—the break-up of feudal society, the waning influence of the Church, that growth of national and religious independence which was to lead both to the Renaissance and the Reformation. In our own time historians have grown sceptical: they question both the scale of mortality and the extent to which it initiated, rather than promoted, change. On the first count, scholars have pointed out that medieval statistics tend to rhetoric; whilst on the second much careful research has indicated that virtually all those social, economic and moral changes once attributed to the Black Death can be traced back well before its advent. The sharp economic decline which affected the whole of Europe from about 1300, can, for example, probably account in part for falling levels of population, for decay in agriculture, and for the consequent erosion of the feudal system, all of which were once attributed to the plague alone.[15]

'Acceleration' certainly differs from 'origination', but it can be equally dramatic, and the scale of the disaster and its impact should not be understated in the interests of that distinction. Even the sober statistics of modern scholarship put the death toll somewhere between 25 and 40 per cent; when one reflects that such percentages reflect the scale of mortality in a *single year*, one can understand why medieval observers spoke with a despair so absolute. Thus a friar, John Clyn, a Minorite of Kilkenny, writes in 1349:

I, as if amongst the dead, waiting till death do come, have put into writing truthfully what I have heard and verified. And that the writing may not perish with the scribe, and the work fail with the labourer, I add parchment to continue it, if by chance anyone may be left in the future and any child of Adam may escape this pestilence and continue the work thus commenced.[16]

Moreover, a disaster on such a scale can cause a change in degree so great that it becomes virtually synonymous with a change in kind; evidence of incipient social change may be found before the plague, but the events of 1348 may not only precipitate, but through their violence alter, the nature of that change. One small example may clarify the point. The famous challenge of Tyler in the Peasants' Revolt of 1381—'When Adam delved and Eve span,/Who was then the gentleman?'—is not a new one. It can be found, to choose one of many instances, in a poem attributed to Rolle, who died of plague in 1349: 'When Adam dalfe, and Eve spane . . . Whare was than the pride of man?'[17] These lines are the conventional warning of the Church to the rich—that all men are equal; but the plague, in its indiscriminate attack on all orders of society, made this dramatically evident. The spectacle of the open grave pits, in which rich and poor alike were levelled in a grotesque and ugly death (Plate 1), turned an injunction to reform for the afterlife into a demand that the rich should reform this life; the admonition of the Church against pride became the battle cry of a rebellion against privilege.

This stark and recurrent catastrophe inevitably left its mark on the sensibility of the time. The suddenness of the onslaught, the arbitrariness with which it struck, the impossibility of explaining in any rational way how the infection was carried, led to a supposition that the disease was the instrument of divine vengeance. That notion, moreover, received support from the Old Testament, where God afflicts not only their enemies, but his chosen people too, with plagues; and even the New implies the conclusion that sickness is a punishment for sin, when Christ enjoins the lame man he has healed, 'Sin no more, lest a worse thing come unto thee.' The alternative, to treat disease as the product of chance, was even less desirable, because, as Deaux remarks, 'it suggests a world of chaos and anarchic natural forces far more unacceptable even than the terrors of a cosmos ruled by a jealous, but reasonably consistent, God.'[18] Yet the belief in divine vengeance must, as much as anything, have contributed to that decline in human confidence which marks the end of the Middle Ages. Man was no longer the special creation of God, made to share in his perfection, but a criminal creature who merited his punishment, the ugly humiliation of the visible grave pit.

There are, in Middle English, no vivid descriptions of the plague to match, for example, the opening of the *Decameron*; even the chronicles of those monastic houses which lost most of their members record that fact with surprising brevity and restraint. But Boccaccio's account, in which the Death severs even the closest of human bonds, so that wives abandon their husbands, parents their children, must reflect events which became horribly commonplace throughout Europe.[19] If the plague receives little vivid mention in England, relative at least to the scale of the disaster, it was probably because, as Manzoni observed of a later epidemic, the magnitude of its misery 'went not only beyond the bounds of what could be remedied, but also, one might say, beyond the bounds of what could be pitied'. Under-emphasis does not mean absence of impact, but the reverse: the greatest accounts of the plague are works of fiction. It does, nevertheless, receive constant, if not elaborate, mention in the literature of the period, and is inescapably a part of life. It is, for example, often referred to in the C text of *Piers Plowman*, and almost always as a punishment for sin:

> Reson reverentliche by-for al the reame
> Prechede, and provede that thuse pestilences
> Was for pure synne, to punyshe the puple. (Ps. VI, ll. 114–16)

The social disorders of the time are seen both as cause and effect of this visitation. The art and literature of the period dwell upon the decaying corpse in much the way that the eye must have dwelt in fact; and always to remind the viewer that, in the face of death, all human purposes become vanity. The imagination less often glimpses the face of God in the created world, and natural objects are less apt to intimate perfection than to signify mortality. Yet the omnipresence of death can as often inspire the febrile gaiety of *carpe diem*, as induce the sobriety and repentance of a *memento mori*.

If this period is dominated by the fear of pestilence, it is equally threatened by that of war. The Hundred Years' War with France began a decade before the first outbreak of plague, and continued well into the fifteenth century. The civil Wars of the Roses effectively commence with Richard II's deposition in 1399, and continue until Henry VII's defeat of Richard III at Bosworth in 1485. Virtually the entire period is thus dominated by these two wars, yet they have a very different effect upon the imagination of the time. The Hundred Years' War, under Edward III and Henry V, though not in the reign of Henry VI, is on the whole positively regarded. Its image is chivalric and heroic; death, challenged on the battlefield, enhances life. The fine poem of the Chandos Herald, celebrating the Black Prince, touches this strain continually:

> Là veoit-hom maynte baniere
> Pointe de fyn or, et de soye;
> Et là, si le vrai Dieux m'avoye,
> Englois estoient tout à pez
> Com cils qui furent afaitez
> De combatre et entalentez.[20]

(There many a banner could be seen, embroidered with fine gold and silk; and there, God knows, were the English afoot, like men eagerly straining to fight.)

Though it did considerable damage to the English economy, this war, across the channel, did not scar the land itself; rather it provided the nation with unity and purpose—Shakespeare did not invent Henry IV's notion of 'busying giddy minds with foreign quarrels'. But the civil wars, affecting the nation both physically and economically, present a very different image, of disorder and decay, of a death that is ignoble, not heroic. The poets of the earlier period may lament the absence of the kings in France, but their tone, on the whole, is one of patriotic fervour. Civil disorder, in contrast, is regarded as disaster, and praise is given only to those who will restore prosperity and peace in England. The change this represents in the attitude to death is an important one: in the heroic conception a man may advance confidently to his reward in a future life; but when death loses its heroism, the continuity between life and afterlife is ruptured by the agnostic spectacle of physical mortality.[21]

The Arthurian sentiment of Edward III and Henry V is an indication of the romanticism that surrounded the war with France. They were not the first English kings to make political capital of the Round Table, once Geoffrey of Monmouth (in his *Historia Regum Britanniae*, written c. 1135) had firmly established this influential structure of pseudo-history.[22] Henry Plantagenet, as Haskins observes, has been 'accused of encouraging Arthurian romance as a literary basis for a new British imperialism', and Kendrick describes how his grandson was named Arthur, in the hope that he would prove to be 'a predestined instrument of the revival of the Arthurian glories related in the British History'.[23] But it would be wrong to suggest that the Arthurian sentiment of Edward III and Henry V was merely expedient. The story was so deeply rooted in the English sensibility of the Middle Ages that when,

in the reign of Henry VII, Polydore Vergil, a devoted but also candid
Anglophile, dismissed it as fiction in a few lines of his *Anglica Historia*,
he met with an outraged reception.[24] The oath to create a Round Table
for his knights, taken by Edward III in 1344, was a means of asserting
that war was still a supremely honourable profession.[25] Henry V revived his ancestors' nostalgia for chivalry in an age that was more
bourgeois than feudal, and recovered, if only temporarily, a heroic
notion of death. When he himself died in France, his body was carried
from Paris to London in a vast funeral procession of knights in black
armour, their lances reversed, whilst his coffin was preceded by his
horse wearing the insignia of Arthur on its harness. The event is surely
more suggestive of romantic sincerity than political acumen.[26]

But death in civil war is allowed no heroism. Like the plague, the
Wars of the Roses are seen as a punishment for the corruption of the times.
In the troubled reign of Richard II, Chaucer, in his poem 'The Former
Age', looks wistfully back to an improbable period in which men lived
in harmony with themselves and the natural world; whilst the anonymous *Mum and the Sothsegger* explicitly attacks the disruption caused
by Richard's rule. The king is surrounded by flatterers, the followers of
Mum, who conceal from their monarch the true condition of his subjects, and the dreamer searches vainly for a 'sothsegger', a speaker of
truth: 'Now, Richard the redeles, reweth on you-self,/That lawelesse
leddyn youre lyf, and youre peple bothe.'[27] Wycliff too inveighs against
civil unrest, and much fifteenth-century poetry laments discord at home
and the absence of the kings in France. The double image of war is
focussed in Lydgate's prayer to St Thomas of Canterbury when, in the
same verse, he both beseeches the saint to intercede 'For Knyghtes,
Squyeres, and yomen for the werre,/In al juste Title make hem to pre-
vaile' and, at the same time, asks St Thomas to 'Pray Iesu stynt blood-
shedynge and Bataile'.[28]

The position of the Church, on war as on other issues in the period,
remained ambiguous. As in this instance, religious poetry can both
attack the depravity of the times and lend expedient support to secular
rulers. This ambiguity is of course generally operative in Christian
thinking, but it also reflects at this period the pressure under which the
Church lay. Although only a retrospective view can salute Wycliff as the
herald of the Reformation, it is nevertheless true that a new religious
spirit is abroad in the England of the late Middle Ages. 'The trauma of
the Black Death', as Deaux remarks, 'revived old antagonisms, and, by
creating situations in which the authority of the traditional hierarchies
was tested and found wanting, aroused latent individualism.'[29] There
are no dramatic confrontations between religious and secular authority,

---

redeles devoid of counsel

as there were on the continent, but whilst the English kings in Europe speak with a conservative voice on ecclesiastical matters, they make quiet inroads at home on the authority and possessions of the Church. Similarly, whilst there are no dramatic heresies (on the scale, for example, of that of the Free Spirit in France), it is nevertheless an age of religious debate, and of increasing independence in matters of conscience.[30] In the fourteenth century, religious biography, absent in devotional works of the thirteenth which are anonymously directed, begins to appear; and the author of a work such as *The Cloud of Unknowing* speaks with an individual voice for the inward life and private virtue. His religious sensibility is simple, ardent and direct, in contrast with the continual ecclesiastical controversy which characterized his period.[31] This retreat, however orthodox its inception, led inevitably to the unorthodox, since it bypassed the whole structure of the Church.[32] Thus, in the fifteenth century, *The Book of Margery Kempe*, whilst it is in one sense merely a public version of religious intensities already known in the fourteenth, marks, in another, a distinct step towards the unorthodox: the individual voice no longer speaks inwardly to the heart, but pronounces its outward claim to the attention of all men. Even amongst the highest dignitaries of the Church, Margery Kempe met as often with reverent acceptance as with condemnation, and this in itself is a sufficient indication of the uncertain spiritual temper of the time. If pride is the sin of kings, envy, as Gower observes, is that of clerics:

> And so to speke upon this branche,
> Which proud Envie hath mad to springe,
> Of Scisme, causeth forto bringe
> This newe Secte of Lollardie,
> And also many an heresie
> Among the clerkes in hemselve.[33]

When the Church itself was riven by dissension, its temper became didactic and even vindictive. To minds already oppressed by plague and civil war, it offered little reassurance in the hope of an improved afterlife.

Although from many points of view the age repeatedly offers itself in negatives, there are exceptions. The fifteenth century also saw a good deal of quiet wisdom, and even of pre-renaissance humanism. *The Dicts and Sayings of the Philosophers*, a compendium of the wisdom of the ancients which is characterized by a tone of measured forbearance and secular sagacity, found five different translators or revisors, four of them prominent figures, in the third quarter of that century. Moreover, Caxton's edition of Earl Rivers's translation was probably the first book printed in England in November, 1477.[34] Palladius' work on husbandry, a peaceful fourth-century verse treatise on the seasons and their appropriate agricultural labours, was translated in time of civil strife and pestilence, probably by a monk in one of the garden-loving religious houses of Colchester.[35] Early in the century, at the Carthusian priory of Mount Grace in Yorkshire, Nicholas Love produced his own rendering of the *Meditationes Vitae Christi*, a tender thirteenth-century work of 'devoute ymaginaciouns' which he offers as a corrective to Lollard doctrine.[36] Significantly, all these works are translations, as if only the past could provide consolation adequate to present ills. Yet Lydgate, in the monastery at Bury, composes an admirably equable 'Dietary and Doctrine for the Pestilence':

> Who will been holle & kepe hym from sekenesse
>   And resiste the strok of pestilence,
> Lat hym be glad, & voide al hevynesse.
>   Flee wikkyd heires, eschew the presence
>   Off infect placys, causyng the violence;
> Drynk good wyn, & holsom meetis take,
>   Smelle swote thynges & for his deffence
> Walk in cleene heir, eschewe mystis blake.[37]

The image of the later Middle Ages, in art as well as literature, is thus a varied one, but it must be admitted that the prevailing impression is dark. Yet most of those themes related to Life and Death which are generally taken to characterize the later phase (after 1350)—the emphasis on corruption and mutability, on the sufferings of man and those of Christ as man—can all be found earlier. As in so many other cases, they are tendencies which the Black Death does not initiate, but which it certainly brings into prominence, and even renders into obsessions. But the seeds of obsession can be glimpsed, for example, in the fragment of a manuscript preserved in Worcester Cathedral Library, and dating from the twelfth century. It contains a grim meditation upon the text *Homo Putredo et Filius Hominis Vermis*, in which the poet sees life as a process of continual decay, and is led to the nihilistic cry: 'wo me that ic libbe,/that aeffre mine lif dawes thus longe me ilesteth.'[38] (Woe is me that I live, that ever the days of my life should last so long.) The *Meditationes Vitae Christi* are, as already mentioned, the work of a serene spirit, yet, in the early fourteenth-century rendering of Robert Manning of Brunne, they contain many of the emphases which characterize late medieval religious art and lyric poetry. The vision of Christ and Mary, despite its humanity and pathos, betrays a sense of the macabre; the emphasis is no longer upon Christ's nobility but upon his wounds. He is brought naked before Pilate at dawn on a chill day; the flagellation and nailing to the cross are described in agonizing detail, and after the burial Mary, with a human rather than an orthodox gesture, clings desperately to the tomb.[39] The only quality that distinguishes these meditations from subsequent writing and art is their didactic fidelity to the Gospels. The alteration in fifteenth-century treatments of the Passion is largely one of tone, from emotion with a point to make to emotion for its own sake. This alteration is, for example, strikingly registered in the Lamentation of the Virgin in the early fifteenth-century Rohan Book of Hours where the attention is firmly centred upon the grim spectacle of death and grief; it is similarly captured in Marian laments such as this:

> O woman, woman, wel is the,
> Thy childis cap thu dose upon;
> thu pykys his here, be-holdys his ble,
> thu wost not wele when thu hast done.
> But ever, alas! I make my mone
> To se my sonnys hed as hit is here;
> I pyke owt thornys be on & on,
> ffor now liggus ded my dere son, dere.[40]

Traditions are, however, continued in the literature of the late fourteenth and early fifteenth centuries in a way that is less true of art. In the visual area 1348 does mark a distinct break. This is due partly to the fact that the economic effects of the Black Death did more to disrupt artistic than literary activity, so that English literature begins to flourish as English art begins to decline. In 1348 the art of manuscript illumination had reached its peak in England, but for twenty years after that date few manuscripts were produced, and when, towards the end of the century, the art was again revived, its inspiration came from abroad (as can be seen in the Anglo-Italian styles of the Bohun manuscripts), and its recovery was short-lived.[41] In the case of roof bosses, which were increasingly common at the close of the Middle Ages, the disruption caused by the plague is clearly indicated by the cessation of all work on the great series at Norwich until the close of the fourteenth century.[42] The position in wall painting is not much better; although there is no decline in the best work—to the fifteenth century is owed the great scheme in Eton College chapel—in the poorer churches few extensive schemes were undertaken after 1350, and the paintings which are executed show a decline in quality.[43]

But while manuscript and decorative art declined, architecture modestly prospered. To build in time of stress was to provide necessary employment and to capitalize on low building costs. At home the building of

---

dose put   *pykys* comb   *ble* appearance   *liggus* lies

St Stephen's chapel at Westminster is continued, despite the plague, without interruption or change of style, whilst abroad the great cathedral at Milan is actually begun shortly after the Black Death. It is possible in England to give a continuous history of the development of Perpendicular style, despite the disasters that occurred in the years of its growth; and although the greater simplicity of that style, when compared with the Decorated which it gradually replaced, may indicate the retrenchments which fostered its development, it is nevertheless an architectural achievement in its own right.[44]

The development of the Perpendicular style is at least a reminder that the dark picture often presented of the late medieval sensibility in the visual arts is, as in literature, not without relief. But an injustice may also be done if the dominantly negative aspects of late medieval sensibility, which may be particularly illustrated in tomb sculpture, are dismissed merely because they are negative. Émile Mâle, the famous French historian of medieval art, who does little to disguise his prejudice in favour of the sensibility of the high Middle Ages, exemplifies this attitude. The dead on the tombs of the thirteenth century are, as he points out, young, handsome, transfigured, already suited to participation in eternal life (Plate 29); the makers of these effigies, far from fearing death, seem almost to love it, whereas those at the close of the fourteenth century come suddenly to see it as a thing of horror.[45] The distinction is in itself perfectly valid—the typical effigy of the fifteenth century does not idealize the human body. Instead the two-tiered tomb becomes representative: here the body, often realistic in age and feature though dignified by its robes of office, surmounts a grim *en transi*, a representation of the corpse in the process of decay as it lies in the coffin beneath: 'Whare was than the pride of man?' (Plate 32). But if the stylistic distinction is right, Mâle's discrimination may be open to question. The virtue of modesty, *pudeur*, with which he credits the thirteenth-century effigies, is a significantly limited term for what he feels to be lacking in the sensibility of the later Middle Ages. These tombs have a force and relevance of their own, a less serene and ideally Christian sense of the meaning of death, but also a more vigorous and more human one. As Panofsky says, they do not merely reveal 'the general preoccupation with the macabre'; they also express a 'feeling for the collective'.[46]

Criticisms similar to those of Mâle have been offered of the other arts of the period. Cave regards some roof bosses as frankly coarse in their carvings, and cites the example of a man at stool, juxtaposed with a representation of the Five Wounds.[47] Wall painting abounds with depictions of the Three Living and the Three Dead, in which three living men, often princes, encounter three animate skeletons who warn them of their approaching end. Of more than fifty examples of the subject recorded in the last century, nearly half have been destroyed because they gave offence to Victorian parsons. Paintings of the Seven Deadly Sins, often admittedly grotesque, have in many cases met a similar fate. 'The thirteenth-century painter', Caiger-Smith remarks, 'was decorating a church: his fifteenth-century counterpart was trying to compel devotion.'[48] The murals of the early Middle Ages, with their confident connected schemes in nave and chancel, certainly express an age of healthy religious faith; it is an art of celebration. By contrast, fifteenth-century painting is both technically inferior and imaginatively disturbed. The effort to crystallize faltering belief begets a literalism which often makes that belief merely ludicrous. Yet this disturbance is in some respects a sign of vitality. Realism and romanticism, comedy and nihilism, didactic hectoring and pagan ebullience are constantly juxta-posed. The period of breakdown is also one of new beginnings.

The same vital paradoxes are evident in the literature of the time, especially in the lyric and the drama. In one vein, Dunbar writes:

> Now all this tyme lat us be mirry,
> And sett nocht by this warld a chirry;
> Now, quhill thair is gude wyne to sell,
> He that dois on dry breid wirry,
> I gif him to the Devill of hell.

On another occasion, with similar phrase but contrasting mood, he advises:

> Man, pleis thy makar and be mirry,
> And sett not by this warld a chirry;
> Wirk for the place of paradyce,
> For thairin ringis na covettyce.[49]

Very few writers—the *Gawain*-poet is the pre-eminent exception—exhibit a confident religious faith, and even in his case one may feel that this assurance is the product of inward illumination, analogous with that of the mystics, rather than the reflection of an outward confidence. The sacrifice of the Mass is, in *Pearl*, less an occasion for public worship than for the private reassurance that the prince into whose keeping his pearl, or child, has fallen is personally present in the visible world: 'For I haf founden hym, bothe day and naghte,/A God, a Lorde, a frende ful fyin.'[50] Chaucer and Langland, though in quite different ways, are un-doubtedly religious men, but Langland's poem is an endeavour to give life to a letter that is felt to be dead, and Chaucer's religious sense is largely separate from what his imagination can discover. Where the *Divina Commedia* is the actual instrument of Dante's salvation, Chaucer

---

wirry choke   *ringis* reign

attempts to save his soul by rejecting 'the tales of Caunterbury, thilke that sownen into synne' and many other works which, because of their dubious moral character, he regards as 'my giltes'.[51] Certainly the retraction has its precedents,[52] and it is possible to conclude that Chaucer did not repent so fully as Boccaccio, who atoned for the 'giltes' of the *Decameron* with the heavy penance of *De Casibus Virorum Illustrium*. Yet it would be mistaken to conclude that Chaucer's Retraction, because conventional, was insincere, for the existence of such a custom is in itself evidence of the rift that was felt to exist between the sacred and the profane. It is we who wish to opt for the profane at the expense of the sacred; for Chaucer, though their claims are in opposition, each has its validity. There are no serene answers in the later Middle Ages, but it is precisely this uncertainty that gives fibre and life to literature.

This is not to deny that much writing, especially in the fifteenth century, which is often regarded as a hiatus between Chaucer and Shakespeare, is routine and uninspired. Nevertheless, without arguing for the quality of some works of the period as one justifiably could, a documentary value can certainly be claimed for the mass of the mediocre.[53] It is a period in which creative writing becomes progressively more aware of its own value and centrality. This assurance has little in common with renaissance pride in art as the distinctive achievement of man—no claim, for example, is made to originality; for the notion of individual creation is foreign to the Middle Ages in all forms of intellectual activity: 'the search for truth in any full or absolute sense [was] beyond the scope of all human enquiry.'[54] In some ways, this modesty was intensified by the scepticism of the later Middle Ages, and especially so in the field of thought; but the loss of universality, which spelt the end of scholastic philosophy, in many ways led to an increase of confidence in literature.[55]

The attention given to literature by the schools had, in any event, been always either historical or practical in nature before its exclusion; its models were Roman, its purpose was to instruct in the arts of grammar and rhetoric. When Oxford University was founded, the vernacular was not its language.[56] Although the potential of English, as a literary language particularly, was already well developed at the time of the Conquest, it was gradually displaced thereafter, for most formal purposes, by Latin and French. In law, for example, Latin became the language of the courts during the reigns of the two Williams, and in the mid-twelfth century Old English laws were translated into French, although it was much less developed as an instrument for their expression. When, in the fourteenth century, English is reinstated, this appears to be partly a result of the Black Death.[57] John Trevisa, in his 1387

---

sownen tend to, make for

rendering of Ranulph Higden's chronicle, records the complaint of the author (d. 1364) that in England 'Chyldern in scole, agenes the usage and manere of al other nacions, buth compelled for to leve here oune longage and for to construe here lessons and here thinges a Freynsch, and habbeth suthe the Normans come furst into Engelond.' Trevisa himself comments: "Thys manere was moche yused tofore the furste moreyn, and ys sethe somdel ychaunged'; he further remarks that where children are no longer taught French in school, they learn their grammar more quickly, but are at a loss when they go abroad, for 'childern of gramerscole conneth no more Frensch than can here lift heele'.[58]

The position of English as a literary language is far more complex; it seems never to have fallen wholly into desuetude, yet, as the speech of the cultivated, it generally yields pride of place to Latin and French. No English writer creates his language with the conscious pride and deliberate artifice of Dante, but Dante's aim was ideal, for he was inspired by the notion of a perfect language, the inheritance of Adam, spoken and understood universally until the catastrophe of Babel when man's pride was punished by the formation of different tongues.[59] Chaucer does not attempt to discover this perfect language, but he does impose a certain order and consistency on the diversity of contemporary English, and is anxious that the integrity of his text should be preserved, for, at the close of *Troilus and Criseyde*, he writes:

> And for ther is so gret diversite
> In Englissh and in writyng of oure tonge,
> So prey I God that non myswrite the,
> Ne the mysmetre for defaute of tonge.   (ll. 1793–6)

His endeavour is clerical rather than visionary, but *Troilus and Criseyde* is clearly a poem written for the cultivated, and Chaucer's concern for his 'litel bok' suggests a confidence in the durability of the English vernacular.

Moreover, the fifteenth century in England marks in literature a growing sense of individuality, and the consciousness of a strictly English tradition. Earlier writing is not without these characteristics, for at the beginning of the thirteenth century, Orm emphasizes both his identity and his Englishness: 'Icc thatt tiss Ennglissh hafe sett, Ennglisshe menn to lare,/Icc wass thaer thaer I crisstnedd wass Orrmin bi name nemmnedd.' He is also concerned for the integrity of his text, in all its idiosyncracy: 'Annd whase wilenn shall thiss bocc efft otherr sithe writenn,/Himm bidde icc thatt he't write rihht, swa summ thiss boc him taechethth.'[60] In the fourteenth century such attributions gradually

---

moreyn plague   *lift heele* left heel   *whase wilenn shall* whoever shall wish
efft otherr sithe on another occasion

increase, though it is significant that the *Gawain*-poet should remain anonymous; that the figure of Chaucer as dreamer, scholar and pilgrim should be a fiction, and that 'Will' in *Piers Plowman* should be personification as well as Christian name. But in the fifteenth century many minor poets name themselves firmly—Metham and Ashby are examples[61]—whilst Lydgate and Hoccleve describe their own persons and histories,[62] and Lydgate offers a defence of the art itself.[63] Certainly the pilgrim Lydgate in *The Siege of Thebes* is modelled upon Chaucer's fictional traveller in *The Canterbury Tales*, but where Chaucer conceals his true identity from the Host, Lydgate responds to a similarly disparaging address with the direct reply: ' "my name was Lydgate/Monk of Bery, nygh fyfty yere of age" ' (ll. 92–3).

The cult of individuality is not, of course, an unmixed blessing, but it is perhaps the necessary consequence of a properly high valuation of literature. The related tendency, to set an individual work in a context that is now strictly English, is even more significant. The great writers are no longer remote, possibly unread, figures such as Homer and Virgil; nor are they, as in Chaucer, French or Italian predecessors—Machaut, de Lorris and de Meun; Dante, Petrarch and Boccaccio. Fifteenth-century writers attribute their inspiration to English figures, always to Chaucer, and commonly to Lydgate and Gower. This change is movingly registered at the close of the century in Dunbar's 'Lament for the Makaris', a poem which is clearly medieval in its sense of mortality, and as clearly modern in its high regard for the 'makaris' and in its celebration of an insular, even domestic, tradition:

> I se that makaris amang the laif
> Playis heir ther pageant, syne gois to graif;
> Sparit is nocht ther faculte;
> *Timor mortis conturbat me.*
>
> He hes done petuously devour,
> The noble Chaucer, of makaris flour,
> The Monk of Bery, and Gower, all thre;
> *Timor mortis conturbat me.*[64]

Thus the poets of England themselves become figures of Life, Death, and enduring Life.

---

makaris makers *laif* rest *graif* grave *petuously* piteously

B

II

Youth and its Mentors

Juventus est causa spei propter tria: . . . objectum spei . . . est futurum et arduum et possibile . . . Juvenes enim multum habent de futuro et parum de praeteriti. Et ideo, quia memoria est praeteriti, spes autem futuri, parum habent de memoria, sed multum vivunt in spe. Juvenes etiam, propter caliditatem naturae, habent multos spiritus; et ita in eis cor ampliatur. Ex amplitudine autem cordis est quod aliquis ad ardua tendat. Et ideo juvenes sunt animosi et bonae spei. Similiter etiam illi qui non sunt passi repulsam, nec experti impedimenta in suis conatibus, de facili reputant aliquid sibi possibile. Unde et juvenes . . . sunt bonae spei. Duo etiam istorum sunt in ebriis.[1]

(Youth is ground for hope for three reasons: the object of hope is future, difficult and possible. The young are much involved with the future and little with the past. Thus, because memory is of the past and hope of the future, they have little memory but live much in hope. Secondly the young, because of their warm nature, are high-spirited and thus great-hearted. It is from greatness of heart that a man attempts the difficult. Therefore the young are full of courage and good hope. Thirdly, those who have not suffered repulse, nor encountered frustration in their efforts, easily assume that something is possible for them. Thus the young too are of good hope. Two of these characteristics can also be found in drunkards.)

Youth, who leads the company of Life, also reflects the dualities of medieval response to the temporal world. His own delight in life and its riches is invariable, but his pleasure may be seen, on the one hand, as an appropriate response to God's bounty, a spiritual virtue; or, on the other, as a seduction of the soul by the temporal, and therefore a vice. Aquinas' attitude to Youth, expressed above, is, like Chaucer's to the Squire, a nicely middle-aged blend of irony and sympathy: experience perceives the limitations of innocence, but finds its naïveté less irritating than disarming. In the Middle Ages (even more than today), a realism so tolerant is, however, exceptional; for the most part the young are alternately idealized and disparaged, and condemnation is apt to outweigh commendation.

These dualities of attitude inevitably have their human root, for the idealization of Youth may reflect nostalgia for past joys and missed opportunities, as in Chaucer's Franklin; whilst envy and incomprehension, the antagonisms of different generations, may, as in the case of the Reeve or the Merchant, promote condemnation. But the mistrust of Youth has also, in the Middle Ages, sources more profound than subjective frailty, for it is rooted in the theological notion of man's fallen nature, and thus receives the sanction of religion. As a representative figure of Life, Youth comes to reflect the religious suspicion of the merely natural, the purely temporal: confidence in the first is, for example, misplaced, because innocence and experience are not synonymous. As Augustine remarks: *Ita imbecillitas membrorum infantilium innocens est, non animus infantium.*[2] (Thus the innocence of children is in the feebleness of their limbs, not in the infant purity of their souls.) Since temporal life is only an imperfect reflection of the eternal, its representative figure can at best only point men beyond it; and, at worst, may distract them from their only true pursuit, the salvation of their souls. The second attitude is particularly marked in the later Middle Ages, where the uncertain temper of the time sees the exuberance natural to Youth, and his immersion in the moment, as expressing an illusory confidence in natural life which is synonymous with spiritual death. The positive figure of Youth is fully developed before the Black Death in the idealizing mode of romance; but his negative counterpart, the Pride of Life, comes increasingly to dominate him thereafter, nurtured by the didactic genre of miracle and morality play. It is true that, as the drama develops, life may sometimes spring to its own defence, and literary delight in the roistering Pride of Life defeat the sober censure that surrounds him. But this is a secular pleasure, without theological sanction; whilst the qualities of romance Youth—beauty, hope and energy—receive their due of admiration from the Church: *pulchrum est idem bono sola ratione differens*[3] (the beautiful is the same as the good, differing only in mode).

The dualities polarized in Youth and the Pride of Life are explored more insistently in their mentors, Venus and Nature. Youth is the springtime of man and the season of love, and it is in his sexuality particularly that man faces the theological divide between animal and spiritual, temporal and eternal. Under the vigilant guardianship of Nature, Venus may promote procreation, and thus be all very well in her place; but more usually she gets out of hand, and induces the animal in man to commit those sins of the flesh that are death to the soul. In consequence, she is normally viewed with suspicion, and becomes a negative figure, where Nature is more often positively regarded; Venus marks a declension into the purely physical world, where Nature, though busied mundanely in her workshop where she repairs the physical ravages of Death (Plate 3a), has as her context the stars and their cosmic order.[4] It is Nature's strength that she can bridge that rift in created life between flesh and spirit, but this resource itself precipitates problems almost as insistent as those that surround Fortune.

The romance figure of Youth,* like that of Nature, can also, though in a simpler way, mediate flesh and spirit; but he is far from being merely 'natural'—on the contrary, he is as highly civilized as his creators can make him. When body and soul are harmonized in him, it is through the perfection, not the mere *donnée*, of Nature. The 'child' of the romances, a title significantly denoting a youth of gentle birth,[5] whilst enjoying a certain pristine innocence, exhibits virtues which are the product of secular Christian culture. The asexual innocence of Floris and Blancheflour—'The children lovyd togeder soo/They myght never parte a twoo' —has little in common with the warm animal innocence of a Greek romance such as Longus' *Daphnis and Chloe*.[6] The pastoral idyll, which derives more directly from such originals, appears late in the fifteenth century, and as a supplement to chivalry.[7] Yet the 'great heart' of Youth has in earlier medieval romance at least one capacity in common with the Greek: the power to restore unities which an older generation has fractured. The virtues necessary to this task—of physical courage and spiritual initiative—also characterize Arthurian story, which is thus attracted to the romance form from the chronicles where it originated. *La gloire des princes pend en orgueil et en haut peril emprendre*[8] (the glory of princes depends on pride and the undertaking of great peril). This characteristic, so close to the Pride of Life, yet acclaimed as virtue, is finely expressed in the high chivalric tone of *Le Prince Noir* where the hero's virtues are identical with those of the romance protagonist; life models itself upon art, and art upon life:

> Tant fut cil Prince de hautesce
> Qu'il volt toutz les jours de sa vie
> Mettre toute son estudie
> En tenir justice et droiture.[9]

> (This Prince was so full of pride that he wished, all the days of his life, to devote himself wholly to maintaining justice and right.)

A high regard for Youth, it will be noted, depends in part upon a heroic attitude to Death; and as this confidence declines in England, under the impact of disease, civil disorder, and clerical denunciation, the romances lose their original ballad-like purity, becoming more dis-

---

* For illustrations of the idealized figure, see Plates 9 (the youngest of the Magi), and 13, 15a and b, 16b—as seasonal figures.

cursive and finally religiose in tone.[10] Chaucer registers this transition in *The Knight's Tale*, where he clearly responds to the heroic, yet treats the profession of arms with considerable scepticism: the Temple of Mars does not (like Arcite's funeral pyre) reflect the heroism of Crécy, but the petty anarchy which warfare begets:

> Ther saugh I first the derke ymaginyng
> Of Felonye, and al the compassyng;
> The crueel Ire, reed as any gleede;
> The pykepurs, and eke the pale Drede;
> The smylere with the knyf under the cloke;
> The shepne brennynge with the blake smoke;
> The tresoun of the mordrynge in the bedde;
> The open werre, with woundes al bibledde;
> Contek, with blody knyf and sharp manace.   (ll. 1995–2003)

The stories of Alexander, so popular in the fifteenth century, labour with all the sagacity of Age to impress upon the mind of Youth the vanity of conquest,[11] where the romances of the thirteenth and early fourteenth centuries attribute wisdom only to the young, as the prerogative of innocence, not experience. In the early romances, Youth resorts to arms with simplistic confidence, assured, like the Chandos Herald, that prowess will uphold the justice and integrity of warlike deeds; and because these are confined to the individual 'quest', they avoid those complexities of social implication which occur in the wider context of the battlefield.

This pristine figure of Youth is, as a result, more commonly found in those romances which are not connected with Arthurian tradition, or only obliquely so. They may, like *Floris and Blancheflour* (*c.* 1250), be set in scenes as exotic as Babylon, or, like *King Horn* (*c.* 1225), in the familiar land of the listeners; but in either case they share an integrity of tone and incident not subordinated to other purposes, which might be defined as one of ballad-like simplicity, of ritual triteness. They may, like the opening lines of *King Horn*, be awkward and uncertain in diction:

> A sang ihc schal you singe
> Of Murry the Kinge.
> King he was biweste
> So longe so hit laste.
> Godhild het his quen;
> Faire ne mighte non ben.
> He hadde a sone that het Horn,
> Fairer ne miste non beo born.[12]

Contek Conflict   *biweste* in the west country   *So longe so hit laste* all his life

At their best, however, that directness and economy can promote a clarity of gesture, a simplicity of speech, which more sophisticated literature cannot parallel. When Emaré's husband, in the romance *Emaré* (c. 1400), is reunited with his son, the latter's simple, ritual action expresses a discovery of the spirit:

> He toke hys hond at the grece ende,
>   And fayre he helpe hym yn;
> And sayde, 'Syr, yf your wyll be,
> Take me your honde and go wyth me,
>   For y am of yowr kynne.'[13]

This vision is gone from most romances of the fifteenth century; the elaboration, enumeration and repetition in verse like that of *The Squire of Low Degree* (late fifteenth century) alters the perception; for, where nouns and adjectives dominate verbs, the emphasis falls on material acquisition, not spiritual quest:

> 'Your basenette shall be burnysshed bryght,
> Your ventall shal be well dyght;
> With starres of golde it shall be set
> And covered with good velvet.
> A coronall clene corven newe,
> And oystryche fethers of dyvers hewe.'[14]

In the verse of *Emaré* verbs are more conspicuous than nouns; Youth is not possessive, but active, and seeks spiritual, not material, fulfilment.

The story of each early romance need not be related, for the course followed nearly always adheres to the same paradigm: the hero and heroine are born for one another and to a high inheritance, but separation from kindred necessitates a long and arduous journey before, eventually and inevitably, they arrive at the rediscovery and renewal of that original bond. Such tales do not ask to be read as more than tales, but they certainly permit it: their clarity and compact literalness is that of archetypal significance. They can, for example, be legitimately read as the assertion of Youth against Age. The older generation, of 'Murry the Kinge' and 'Godhild his quen', either by fortune or by fault, severs connection with its children. Horn is kidnapped by pagan raiders; Degaré is abandoned by his mother who seeks to conceal the rape that robbed her of her virginity; Emaré, rejecting her father's proposal of an incestuous marriage (a proposition authorized by the Pope) is set adrift at sea, and later abandoned to the sea again, this time with her own

---

grece grace　　*basenette* light steel headpiece　　*ventall* visor　　*coronall* circlet on helmet
corven carved

child, at the instigation of a wicked stepmother.[15] But the Youth of the romances, in Aquinas' definition but without his scepticism, embraces the impossible undertaking and succeeds; his innocence confidently encounters all human and natural hazards, and his ultimate triumph is assured. It is this aspect of the genre, its revolutionary potential, that the author of *Gamelyn* (mid fourteenth century) develops in a tale that is an early precursor of Robin Hood, for the idealism and energy of Youth here oppose the corrupt adult world with a totally different notion of social justice.[16]

In the earlier romances, however, Youth possesses a charismatic or spiritual power of imaginative rather than social significance; one which, as I have suggested, expresses a faith in the cultivation of the spirit, rather than in the natural man, the unspoilt human creature. The child of such stories is nobly born, and even when his dignity of birth is concealed from him, as in *Sir Perceval of Galles* (*c.* 1350), his innate nobility reveals itself. Perceval, raised in a semi-savage state in the woods, by a mother who wishes to preserve him from the chivalric life that destroyed his father, encounters three of Arthur's knights with a courage, if not with a diction, which reflects his descent:

> 'I sall sla yow all three
> Bot ye smertly now telle mee
> Whatkyns thynges that ye bee,
>   Sen ye no goddes are.'[17]

The qualities of these romance heroes are not simply physical, for bodily and spiritual attributes are profoundly connected, to a point where they become virtually interchangeable. Beauty and strength, innocence and hope, become aspects of the same good: innocence is beauty, beauty strength, strength is hope and hope innocence. It is not surprising that there should be a traffic between the legends of the saints and the tales of romance, that the journeys of the figure Shakespeare named Pericles should become a chapter in the tale of Mary Magdalen, that the adventures of Amis and Amiloun should be assimilated to the story of St Pelagius.[18]

Although in these early romances the forces of evil are often pagan, the heroes always Christian, they are nevertheless, when concerned with Youth, neither didactic nor overtly moral in nature: thus Chaucer's sophisticated story of Constance, told by the Man of Law, and the naïve romance of *Emaré* which is contemporary with it, share substantially the same story; but Chaucer's is clearly a didactic tale, exemplifying in its adult heroine the virtue of constancy, where the youthful Emaré (whose name, like Degaré, means 'lost'), inhabits a world of less specific and thus more spacious imaginative significance. The nature of the youthful romance hero and heroine is given, their final arrival assured; but the outcome of their actions is hidden, the course of their journey, over so many seas to so many strange lands, is unplotted. The assurance with which they reach their goal, and the coincidences which help them on their way, thus suggest a mysterious and unseen guidance. *The Man of Law's Tale* has only anecdotal connections, and its incidents are exempla. *Emaré*, like Shakespeare's *Pericles*, is a journey of the spirit, and has at once the inconsequential form of a life as it is lived, and the unity that a life can be seen to have when it is complete.

Emaré has been described as 'a poem which is generally agreed to be of poor quality'.[19] One might demur at that, for in the context of romance it should surely not be rated so low; but that is to admit that the context, with a few exceptions, is not one of great literature. A popular genre may, however, possess potential which it takes a genius to realize, and the romance figure of Youth, whose naïveté is both attractive and limiting, may develop unexpected profundity in the hands of more sophisticated writers. Chaucer's Sir Thopas and his Squire, the *Gawain*-poet's treatment of Youth in *Sir Gawain and the Green Knight*, develop in quite distinct ways the potentialities of the romance figure. Chaucer's attitude is sceptical and realistic; the naïve aspirations of romance do not engage his imagination, though the motives that generate its idealism do. The *Gawain*-poet has much more sympathy both with the genre and the figure: he develops, explores and relates where Chaucer analyses.

Chaucer's criticism of the dream of Youth which the romances portray has both validity and wit when expressed in the parodic *Tale of Sir Thopas*. He registers, for example, that preoccupation with things which later declines into the inert convention already noted in *The Squire of Low Degree*:

> His jambeux were of quyrboilly,
> His swerdes shethe of yvory,
>   His helm of latoun bright;
> His sadel was of rewel boon,
> His brydel as the sonne shoon,
>   Or as the moone light. (ll. 875–80)

But if this is valid comment upon much romance literature, particularly that which betrays its own vision of Youth, it is also a valid comment upon Chaucer, one which he perhaps acknowledges by putting the tale into his own mouth. His genius does not lie in the way of romance perception; the dominant medieval figure does not exemplify all the dominant medieval strengths. The conventional phrase can, as in this

---

jambeux leg armour   *quyrboilly* leather   *latoun* latten (copper and zinc)   *boon* ivory

passage from *Sir Launfal* (late fourteenth century), be an image of spiritual implication for Youth on the threshold of experience:

> All that he hadde before ywonne,
> Hyt malt as snow agens the sunne,
>   In romaunce as we rede;
> Hys armur, that was whyt as floure,
> Hyt becom of blak coloure.[20]

Chaucer's conventional analogies—'as the sunne shoon', 'as the moone light'—are deliberately inert and wittily contradictory. Those in *Sir Launfal* are ritual—'as snow agens the sunne', 'whyt as floure'—and are referred specifically to the context which interprets them—'In romaunce as we rede'. These phrases do not merely describe Launfal's spoils or his armour; they express in substantial terms an event in the spiritual life, for riches are vain in comparison to good faith. The pilgrimage of Youth portrayed in romance is, at its best, a metaphor for the journey of the soul, and here it lies beyond Chaucer's grasp, as spiritual certainties and perceptions commonly do. *The Prioress's Tale* of little St Hugh, martyred by the Jews for singing canticles in their ghetto, is the nearest he ever comes to idealizing the young, and even this is qualified by the anti-semitic crudities of the speaker's narrow delicacies.[21] Chaucer's elaboration of the innocent pathos of children in his rendering in *The Monk's Tale* of Dante's account of Ugolino,[22] suggests that he was deeply moved by that childish innocence which depends upon physical vulnerability; but the innocence of the figure of Youth, a virtue of the spirit, he treats with a friendly scepticism.

Chaucer's personification of Youth, the Squire of *The Canterbury Tales* (Plate 4), is, as his own tale reveals, culpably, not ideally, romantic; yet he is by no means a Sir Thopas, a literary figure of fun. He is a convincing, indeed familiar, representative of Youth, and it is not in fact easy to say precisely where he falls short of the romance ideal. One feels he would indubitably have stood 'in his lady grace', since she would inevitably have complemented him as the romance heroine. But the perspective offered on the Squire is not the grave approbation of one equally young; it has the ironic and affectionate realism of an age more advanced. Thus both the portrait of the Squire and his tale are allowed to move between Youth's own solemn self-estimation, and the comic spectacle which such romantic behaviour may offer to a mature realism. *The Squire's Tale* has no independent being; its life, to an extent unusual even in *The Canterbury Tales*, consists in its dramatization of the speaker. His exercise in arms is actual; he has fought in Flanders, Artois and

---

malt melted

Picardy, if not on his father's scale in the lands of the Crusades. But the cultivation of arms moves readily into that of manners: his qualities as a Squire—of strength, dexterity and humility—are those of a lover; his sleepless nights are a convention of behaviour as much as a romance fiction, and their object, his lady, does not need to be described, for the appropriate phrases should spring to every reader's lips. When the Franklin interrupts the Squire's narrative, his praise, significantly, is for the speaker rather than his tale. The Franklin's ideal of 'gentilesse' is fulfilled by the Squire, whose perfect figure he contrasts with the reality of his own imperfect son.

The point is certainly two-edged: the Squire, like some people, is too consciously set in the mould of fashion; yet his virtues, whilst less than absolute, are more than mere affectation. His innocence is felt in his narration, if with an element of naïveté: it is as clear, for example, that he intends no sexual pun upon the word 'queynte' as that the Wife of Bath, in her *Prologue*, does.[23] His apologies for incompetence—' "Have me excused if I speke amys;/My wyl is good" '—lose some of their grace as his story stumbles from one impasse to another—'And ther I lefte I wol ayeyn bigynne'. Yet the ear, wearied by the tale, may still delight in the teller, for the Squire educates us in his own virtues—in the conviction, for example, that it would not be 'gentil' to reflect upon his deficiencies. His tale has many elements of escapist wish-fulfilment, but no one could deny that its wishes—for a sword that will heal as well as wound, for a mirror to reveal the hidden heart—are generous ones.[24] That odd mixture of idealism, affectation and innocence, that characteristic gravity with which Youth regards himself, still retain their ring of familiar truth.

As his early poems show, Chaucer has much affection for the conventional figure of Youth, but it is the friction between life and art, not the pursuit of art itself, which ultimately engages him.[25] As the pilgrim of *The Canterbury Tales*, an observer in the world of men, his figures of Youth are anything but idealized.[26] Even Aurelius and Absolon, who do most to cultivate the fictional form, are very differently evaluated, and partly because the tellers of their tales, the Franklin and the Miller, do not share the same values. To the Miller, Youth is a healthy joke, to the Merchant and Reeve a sour one; to the Franklin it is romantically nostalgic, to the Wife of Bath a challenge to her vigour. As the Squire remarks of the crowd which admires the magical horse: 'Diverse folk diversely they demed:/As many heddes, as manye wittes ther been.' It is in this acknowledgement of diverse response—a diversity in which we, as readers, are included—that Chaucer registers the complex 'trouthe', not of the ideal of Youth itself, but of man's need for and reaction to it.

The anonymous author of *Sir Gawain and the Green Knight* is, in contrast with Chaucer, more concerned with the 'trouthe' of the ideal as such.[27] Although he in no sense shares the naïveté of the romances, he clearly has more sympathy than Chaucer with the romance imagination, and a much stronger awareness of its spiritual potential. The poem nevertheless has its connections with the literal, for one may sense in it the human and domestic trenchancy of the provincial eye—of the poet, as of Sir Bercilak's *ménage*—scrutinizing the renowned sophistication of the court—whether of London or Camelot.[28] But the realistic view offers only one perspective on Gawain, where it comprehends Chaucer's Squire, for in Gawain are tested the ideals of Arthur's court, which are, by implication, those of civilized Christian society as a whole.[29] As has been said, the romance figure of Youth has little to do with the natural man as such;[30] the Squire's closest approach to the natural world thus lies in the artifice of his dress:

> Embrouded was he, as it were a meede
> Al ful of fresshe floures, whyte and reede.
> Syngynge he was, or floytynge, al the day;
> He was as fressh as is the month of May. (*Pro.*, ll. 89–92)

For Chaucer, that distance between the civilized and the natural is a means of indicating the artifice of the young ideal; but the 'gentilesse' of Gawain must, for his poet, be absolute, for if it is merely relative then it cannot be worth pursuing. For this reason the poem exposes that civilized ideal directly to the hazards of the natural: to the mysterious powers of the Green Knight, to the rigours of the Wirral, to the vigour of Sir Bercilak and, most of all, to the natural impulses of a man's heart—carnal temptation and the will to live.

The aspiration of the poem is thus of a seriousness and profundity which removes it from romance and even from Chaucer; yet, whilst the poet integrates romance elements into a whole that is peculiarly that of his own distinctive imagination, they are not transformed 'out of recognition'. Many of the characteristics of early romance can be recognized—the combination, for example, of courtliness and youth in the figure of Gawain, who is recognized in Sir Bercilak's court as 'that fyne fader of nurture' (l. 919), and as the prototype of Youth: 'The ver by his visage verayly hit semed' (l. 866). His journey, whilst clearly a venture of the spirit, is simultaneously true to the romance path, for he follows no agreed route, yet arrives inevitably at the right time and destination, with no better answer from the Green Knight to his query, ' "where is thy place?" ' than the cryptic rejoinder, ' "That is innogh in Nwe Yer, hit nedes no more" ' (ll. 398 and 404). His character, as defined in the design of the pentangle, is known, but the outcome of his actions is not; just as the year always follows the same course, but 'yeldes never lyke' (l. 498), so this figure of Youth, in romance fashion, conforms to the ideal pattern, but is in action unpredictable. Gawain does not prove flawless, because he accepts the girdle, nor does he restore sundered relationships; but, on a metaphysical level, he does reunite the sundered elements of man's nature, the natural with the civilized, the physical with the spiritual, for he learns through his fall to acknowledge both parts. When on future journeys he rides ' "in renoun" ', the girdle will recall him to ' "The faut and the fayntyse of the flesche crabbed" ' (l. 2435).

The court which Gawain represents can be seen as a society of Youth, with the strengths and limitations which belong to that figure. In the first fit, which describes Arthur's company gathered at Camelot to celebrate Christmas, and recounts the marvellous appearance of the Green Knight and his challenge, both the court and their king are established as young in contrast to their antagonist. The company as a whole is introduced as youthful: 'For al was this fayre folk in her first age' (l. 54), a description which distinguishes them from Sir Bercilak (Gawain's host the Christmas following, who is eventually revealed as the Green Knight), for he is referred to as a 'hoge hathel . . . and of hyghe eldee' (l. 844) and later as 'The olde lorde of that leude' (l. 1124).[31] The contrast indeed is as much one of attitude as of physique, for one may add to those phrases concerning age the description of Arthur: 'He was so joly of his joyfnes, and sumquat childgered' (l. 86), a characteristic which the poet explains as a restlessness of spirit, a desire either to hear of or participate in some adventure, 'in jopardé to lay,/Lede lif for lyf' (ll. 97–8)—all manifestly the characteristics of Youth. Reflecting upon Arthur's boyishness is the challenge of the Green Knight: ' "Hit arn aboute on this bench bot berdles chylder" ' (l. 280). The claims of Arthur's court are those of an unexposed virtue; those of the Green Knight are seasoned, an advantage instantly substantiated by the equanimity with which he accepts decapitation and retrieves his head.

The court of Arthur possesses, of course, no comparable power: ' "Bot thagh my hede falle on the stones,/I con not hit restore" ' (ll. 2282–3), Gawain comments ruefully at the return encounter. The court's capacity, in potential at least, is for spiritual not physical renewal; for the salvation, not of the body, but of the soul. Thus, though the poem does, on one level, dramatize the conventional temporal tensions between the Ages, pitting an untried idealism against the wisdom of experience, on another it extends that confrontation to one between civilized and natural virtue, and thus comes to embrace eternal, as well as temporal, life. The virtues of Arthur's court are as clearly a product of civilization as the *donnée* of Youth, and it is significant that the qualities of which Gawain is representative, which are tested in him and which finally

---

hoge hathel huge man   *of hyghe eldee* in his prime   *leude* people   *joyfnes* youth
childgered boyish   *Lede* Risk   *berdles chylder* beardless children

prevail, should not be martial, as he expected, but courtly. He is asked to prove himself in the bedchamber and the hall, not upon the battle-field. The perfection of the pentangle, which he bears as a device upon his shield, is the ideal of Arthur's court, one in which bodily and spiritual attributes unite in an unending yet integrated design. Yet the five virtues that the pentangle includes—'fraunchyse', 'felawschyp', 'clannes', 'cor-taysye' and 'pité'—have more relevance to social than to martial existence. Moreover, the abstraction, unusual in this poem, of the pentangle itself, and of the language in which it is described, expresses that distance between ideal and act which the poem dramatizes.

The Green Knight, equally, is no simple personification of experience; indeed, his characteristic expansiveness distinguishes him sharply from the narrow materialism of the conventional personification of Middle Age. As John Burrow has pointed out, many motifs are expressed through this figure, and their complex relation greatly contributes to his mystery.[32] It is the more surprising that Burrow should be content to explain his greenness as the colour of Youth, or Death, whilst excluding those con-notations of the natural world which seem to me inescapable.[33] In the final encounter, wielding his axe ominously by the Green Chapel, which so closely recalls the burial mound, one can certainly sense vividly his connection with Death; yet no more vividly than one senses, in that first encounter, where he suffers a blow from his own axe in Arthur's court, the intensity of his connection with natural growth and renewal. One does not need to read the poem as fertility myth to remark the centrality of the confrontation of the civilized with the natural: the point may be cogently made by a comparison of the courts of Arthur and Bercilak, which does not involve the strange greenness of the latter at all. The first, like Gawain's testing, is all interior, whilst its activities are general-ized, public and ritual. The second never loses contact with the winter world outside, and its comforts are in consequence specific, domestic and sensual. Where Guinevere is an emblematic figure, ornately set, 'Dressed on the dere des, dubbed al aboute' (l. 75), so that she gives scarcely any impression of physical womanhood, Bercilak's lady literally emerges from her dress, and is moreover described in an image which recalls the natural world in appropriate winter: 'Hir brest and hir bryght throte bare displayed,/Schon schyrer then snawe that schedes on hilles' (ll. 955–6).

It is thus fitting that Arthur's court should be tried, so unexpectedly, in terms of the civilized world, and not, as Gawain anticipates, in those appropriate to the Green Knight, of stamina and physical prowess; for the real test occurs in the bed chamber, and the final encounter at the

---

fraunchyse generosity *Dressed* Arrayed *dere* precious *des* dais *dubbed* adorned
schyrer more brightly

chapel only makes its outcome explicit. In the context of the 'gay bed . . . cortyned aboute' the virtues of the pentangle are not as easily related as on the field of battle: 'clannes' conflicts with 'cortaysye', 'fraunchyse' and 'pité' with 'felawschyp'. But the test is not merely courtly; the very privacy of its context finds Gawain defenceless against the basic desire for survival which, in a martial setting, he would have been prepared to resist. ' "Bot for ye lufed your lyf; the lasse I yow blame" ' (l. 2368), is the Green Knight's comment. It is Gawain's young idealism that prevents him from mitigating a lapse so natural to Youth, and it is only in his perspective, one curiously close to pride or even pique, that the failure has crucial significance. The encounter with the Green Knight, disproportionately magnified in the hero's apprehensive imagination, becomes disproportionately insignificant when the ultimate test of life and death is transformed into game. As in the earlier romances, a dual perspective, connected with notions of time, is at work in the poem. Events, as they are encountered sequentially by both Gawain and the reader, are anything but playful; they are mysterious, threatening, and potentially tragic. But, once the mystery is removed, the hero, whilst still the most perfect of men, becomes a comic figure from certain points of view as his momentous undertaking reduces itself to play. Yet the poise is a delicate one, for the stakes remain those of life and death, and Gawain is only saved from a tragic end by his own virtue. The laughter of Troilus in the Epilogue to *Troilus and Criseyde* rings more truly at the close of *Sir Gawain*; for in Chaucer that reaction seems to disparage the temporal and terrestrial tragedy on which it looks down, whilst in *Sir Gawain* the two visions of man, comic and tragic, merge together, both remaining within the temporal, both adumbrating the eternal.

The poem, like other romances, does not, certainly, ask to be read as allegory, but it does permit a more than literal reading. It can, for example, be read (though never exclusively) as the pilgrimage of Everyman. The shape of a man's journey is that of his life: seen sequentially, that journey has no predictable direction, only an inevitable close in the encounter, somewhere, sometime, with death. Gawain's journey, however, differs from the pilgrimage of life with its end in the grave because it is enclosed within the regenerative cycle of natural life which renews itself beyond the Winter. That cycle is both echoed in human nature and distinguished from it: the year returns, but men do not return—as Gawain ruefully observes. Yet when he is himself summoned to judgement, he discovers that survival depends, not upon the moment of death, but upon the determining moments of life; his physical survival points to the Christian faith in spiritual immortality, in the regeneration of the soul, a miracle unavailable to the purely natural world. Death, though so much dreaded, may, after all, have little significance; yet because it is the many actions preceding that moment which are decisive, *Sir Gawain* is a poem about the afterlife only because it is so fully a poem about this life.

It is not unusual to find in Arthurian romance the combination of those natural and spiritual energies which are both elements in the conventional figure of Youth, although the former are elsewhere more usually condemned as the Pride of Life. In the heroic tradition, this combination is a necessary metaphor: 'lyke as May moneth flowryth and floryshyth in every mannes gardyne, so in lyke wyse lat every man of worshyp florysh hys herte in thys worlde.'[34] But only the *Gawain*-poet really succeeds in integrating these elements fully. He is in no sense Epicurean, for the sensation of *carpe diem* is absent even in Gawain's reactions; but neither does he go to the other, and more common, medieval extreme of rejection. Earthly delights are given their full value, and a natural movement is established between physical and spiritual joy:

Delectatio enim perficit felicitatem, sicut pulchritudo juventutem.[35]

(Delight makes happiness perfect, as beauty does youth.)

Quia enim, ut Philosophus dicit, *nullus diu absque delectatione potest manere cum tristitia*; . . . illi qui non possunt gaudere in spiritualibus delectationibus transferunt se ad corporales.[36]

(Wherefore, as the Philosopher says, 'no one can remain in sorrow without delight for long'. Those who cannot rejoice in delights of the spirit will turn to those of the body.)

The wisdom of Aquinas is imaginatively realized in the vision of the *Gawain*-poet:

> On the morne, as uche mon mynes that tyme,
> That dryghtyn for oure destyné to deye was borne,
> Wele waxes in uche a won in worlde for his sake;
> So did hit there on that day thurgh dayntés mony:
> Both at mes and at mele messes ful quaynt
> Derf men upon dece drest of the best.   (ll. 995–1000)

Aquinas' description of Youth, quoted earlier, has to do with the real; his remarks upon delight are concerned with the ideal. The early romances understand the second, and Chaucer comprehends the first, but the *Gawain*-poet contains both. There is much responsiveness in his poem

---

mynes remembers *dryghtyn* the Lord *in uche a won* in every dwelling *mele* meal, mealtime *messes* dishes *derf* doughty *dece* dais *drest* served

to the world as it actually is, to its joys and its hazards; and the relative perception that it would be somehow improper for a man to be wholly perfect is a comforting wisdom. But an urgent sense remains, none the less, that all men should aim at total perfection, that only in so doing can they fulfil their dual nature. Gawain, as a figure of Youth, is thus much more than a stereotype; he is the animation of an ideal, a realization of what Youth should be. Yet he does share with the Squire a tendency to take himself too seriously, and he cannot quite sustain, as the poem can, that essential connection between profundity and laughter: it is clear that he has much to learn from the seasoned good sense of Sir Bercilak.[37]

The idealism of Youth may indeed be its danger. To be like God is the temptation of the serpent, the attempt to be God was the cause of Lucifer's fall. The Pride of Life, unqualified by Gawain's saving humility and redemptive imperfection, is the cause of spiritual death. Yet it is that same idealism which, at certain points in the Middle Ages, makes the stereotype of Youth, related to Christ both in age and in aspiration, a figure of the fulfilment of life, both temporal and eternal.

The figure of the Pride of Life* is thus intimately related to that of Youth: it is the dark obverse of a bright coin, the vision of fallen, not of perfectible, nature. The qualities which make admirable the positive figure of Youth are, in this other perspective, precisely those that make the Pride of Life contemptible. The visionary and effective capacities of Youth derive from his immersion in the moment, but the tendency of the Pride of Life to regard the moment as eternal is precisely that which renders him finally blind and impotent. Beauty and position, energy and confidence, all become futile under the threat of time. The King of Life, described in the following verses from the mid fourteenth-century morality play, *The Pride of Life*, is divided by a hair's breadth only from the figure of Youth:

> Of the Kyng of Lif I wol you telle;
>   He stondith first biffore
> All men that beth of flessch and fel
>   And of woman ibore.
>
> He is, forsoth, ful stronge to stond,
>   And is bycomin of kinge,
> Giveth lawis in eche a londe,
>   And nis dradd of no thinge.

---

* For illustrations, see Plates 2a–d, 5, and Youth in 7.

In pride and likinge his lif he ledith,
   Lordlich he lokith with eye;
Prince and dukis, he seith, him dredith,
   He dredith no deth for to deye.

He hath a lady lovelich al at likinge,
   Ne may he of no mirth mene ne misse;
He seith in swetnisse he wol set his likinge
And bringe his bale boun into blisse.[38]

Fearless, joyful, royally descended, he could move with ease into romance, but that he lacks that essential spiritual quality of 'gentilesse': he is an object of dread, as Youth never is, and his delight in life is not generous, but grasping—because it lacks the element of spiritual joy, it has turned the corner into carnal pleasure. When challenged by Death this figure dwindles, where that of Youth comes into its own; a confidence that is merely physical cannot survive the threat of mortality.

Because there is a continuity between his deeds in this world and his assurance of the next, Death is of marginal importance to the heroic figure of Youth; but the Pride of Life 'dredith no deth for to deye', because he arrogantly assumes he is immune to all natural hazards, mortality included. Where Youth is fearless, the Pride of Life is simply unaware of Death's approaching shadow. Nevertheless, his affirmation of the natural man can, despite its folly, make him a dynamic, and hence attractive, figure; and his capacity for pleasure may sometimes be more vivid than his condition of spiritual decay. The ideal figure of Youth is the achievement of the high Middle Ages; the Pride of Life, though so often viewed with medieval suspicion, in many ways anticipates a renaissance confidence in man. Marlowe's Tamburlaine, for example, has little in common with Youth: he has no 'gentilesse', no humility, no self-effacing serenity. His antecedent is clearly the Pride of Life, and even when he is finally forced to admit that 'Tamburlaine, the Scourge of God, must die!' this is not, as in medieval drama, a recognition of vanity and folly, for the play closes with the words: 'Let earth and heaven his timeless death deplore,/For both their worths will equal him no more.'

The Pride of Life thus differs from Youth in certain specific ways. The romance hero is, for example, characterized by humility; he acknowledges the hierarchy of king and God, as Gawain and the Squire do, and recognizes that his endowments are indeed gifts, not personal achievements. The Pride of Life is deluded by the conviction that his capacities are of his own making, that he is omnipotent and permanent—he is, like Tamburlaine, a man who thinks himself a God. The *Speculum Guidonis de Warwyk* makes a revealing connection between the romance

---

mene complain of   *boun* quickly

notion of Youth and the didactic conception of the Pride of Life; for, having achieved the success proper to a hero of romance, Guy takes instruction from the hermit Alcuin, who warns him particularly against the dangers of pride and spiritual death: ' "Thi lyf, man, is cleped liht,/ and thi deth the derke niht." '[39] In the perspective of death, life becomes the day in which Guy must labour, not for renown, but for his salvation; from this point, though he continues to fight, he does so in disguise. The honourable desire of Youth to prove himself is seen as courting the fatal sin of Pride, and only anonymity, the deliberate effacement of the self, can preserve him from spiritual death.[40]

For the Middle Ages pride is the supreme sin: it was the sin of Lucifer, the first to assail Christ and the last to leave him, whilst for men it is the fountain-head of all other sins.[41] It is a sin to which the great and gifted are particularly prone: *Appetitus autem inordinatus boni ardui pertinet ad 'superbiam vitae': nam superbia est appetitus inordinatus excellentiae.*[42] (The inordinate appetite for a good difficult of attainment belongs to the Pride of Life: for pride is the inordinate appetite for excellence.) This definition is simply and succinctly echoed in 'The Mirror of St Edmund': 'Pryde es lufe of unkyndly heghyng.'[43] These formulations may not appear to us particularly damaging, but to Aquinas and his contemporaries *inordinatus* and 'unkyndly' (unnatural) are more powerful words. An impulse which may start as virtue but end by contravening nature, threatens the structure of the medieval world in a way that does not apply to ours; for, in asserting the creature, pride threatens to displace the creator. For the Renaissance, Aquinas' definition could have indicated the virtue of man: 'The striving for the infinite, the inability to stop at anything given or attained is neither a fault nor a shortcoming of the mind; rather, it is the seal of its divine origin and of its indestructibility.'[44] To the Middle Ages, the Faustian offence—an assertion of the individual capacity, a failure to acknowledge dependence on the divine—can end only in damnation. In that perspective, which is reflected in the comic scenes of Marlowe's *Faustus*, the figure in medieval drama is bombastic and ridiculous, closer to comic melodrama (which for Marlowe is only one element) than to tragedy as we would define it. For in the medieval view tragedy is indeed contemptible: *in fine seu exitu est foetida et horribilis; et dicitur propter hoc a 'tragos', quod est hircus, et 'oda', quasi cantus hircinus, idest foetidus ad modum hirci*[45] (its end or exit is fetid and horrible; and on this account it is named from *tragos*, which is a goat, and *oda*, goat song as it were, that is, fetid in a goat's manner). The Middle Ages would certainly have experienced terror if they had seen Marlowe's *Faustus*, but very little pity and no admiration; they would have wasted no tears in lamenting that 'laurel bough' of Apollo 'that might have grown full straight'.

The centrality of this figure to medieval drama of all kinds—mystery, miracle, morality—is none the less striking, even though it is offered as a subject for contempt. If the divine—as God, Christ, or those whose lives reflect Christ—is the protagonist, the Pride of Life is the antagonist. In the four great cycles of mystery plays the Pride of Life appears in the first scene in the person of Lucifer, returns in Herod and Pilate at the climax of the Passion, and is defeated only in the Last Judgement. He can be found at the centre of those plays which do not belong to the cycles: in the miracle plays *The Conversion of St Paul* and *Mary Magdalene* as the youthful Paul himself and as Tiberius Caesar,[46] and in moralities throughout the Middle Ages. *The Pride of Life* is itself a fragment of one such early morality; its King of Life, Dux Moraud in the mid fifteenth-century play of that name, Mundus and Manhood in the early sixteenth-century morality, *Mundus et Infans*, are all related figures and indicate the durability of the prototype.[47] It would in fact be hard to find any medieval play on which the Pride of Life had left no mark, which is conclusive evidence of its dramatic vitality.

The great original of the Pride of Life figure, Lucifer, comes closer in the mystery plays to the renaissance conception than do his descendants, Herod and Pilate. The reason is simple, for Lucifer is shown both in an unfallen state as the brightest of God's angels, and in a fallen, as the ruler of Hell. For the Middle Ages, whilst condemning pride in general, do make distinctions (which can, as in the *Divina Commedia*, be very fine ones), between its appropriate and inappropriate forms. The difference between Cacciaguida's pride in *nobiltà di sangue* (nobility of blood) in the *Paradiso*, and Farinata's family arrogance in the *Inferno*, is chiefly one of tone, for Cacciaguida's vision is comprehensive and flexible, where Farinata's is imprisoned in the rigidities of the self.[48] Representations of Lucifer, as they occur in the mystery cycles, are not of course so subtle, but they draw upon the same tradition of thought.

It is significant that all four of the complete cycles[49] should open with the voice of God proclaiming his omnipotence; his role as creator is thus emphasized, and Lucifer, though the highest achievement of his art, is as clearly a creature:

> Of all the mightes I have made moste nexte after me,
> I make the als master and merour of my mighte,
> I beelde the here baynely in blys for to be,
> I name the for Lucifer, als berar of lyghte. (*YP*, I, ll. 33–6)

Light is the element of the unfallen Lucifer, as it is of the figure of Youth; but he is 'berar of lyghte' only, a 'merour' reflecting God's brightness, not the light itself. Lucifer's sin is to see himself as his own source:

---

beelde make   *baynely* obediently

> I am so fare and bright,
> of me commys all this light,
>   this gam and all this gle.   (*TP*, I, ll. 82–4)

Confident in his own power and self-sufficiency, he moves quickly to the assumption that dominion in heaven is his of right. His beauty and brightness are, for him, synonymous with power:

> I am a thowsand fold
>   brighter then is the son;
> my strengthe may not be told,
>   my myght may no thyng kon.   (*TP*, I, ll. 90–3)

Moreover, he is assured that the moment is eternal, and, as a result, that he is invulnerable: 'Here sall never payne me be pynande' (*YP*, I, l. 72). His personal attributes make him immune from change: 'I am so mightyly made my mirth may noghte mys,/Ay sall I byde in this blys thorowe brightnes of bemes' (*YP*, I, ll. 83–4). The good angels also claim 'lyfe that es lely ay lastande' (l. 77), but because they are 'fede with the fode of [God's] fayre face' (l. 76), not by virtue of what they are in themselves. Their speech is always communal: the operative pronoun is 'we', where Lucifer's words are dominated by the insistent 'I'.

    The act, as distinct from the state of mind, which brings about Lucifer's downfall, is a curiously simple, yet highly symbolic, one—he sits literally in God's seat. This is the final offence of the Pride of Life, to put the self in the place of God.[50] From this point on Lucifer loses all his brilliant attributes, and becomes merely comic and ridiculous. If the unfallen angel has been reminiscent of Youth, the fallen Lucifer recalls Age: 'Now ar we waxen blak as any coyll,/and ugly, tatyrd as a foyll' (*TP*, I, ll. 136–7). It is a reminder that the moment is not eternal, that the fire will burn out and reduce itself to ash, that the attributes of Youth are at the mercy of time; the process of ageing makes visible in man a truth that, in Lucifer, is one of the spirit. But the effect, especially in the York play, is undoubtedly comic, almost slapstick. God's chair is, as it were, pulled from under Lucifer's posterior: 'Owe! what am I derworth and defte.—Owe! dewes! all goes downe!' (I, l. 92). The fires of Hell strike him with unexpected unpleasantness: 'Owte owte! harrowe! helples, slyke hote at es here' (I, l. 97). Not only is evil in no sense admirable; it is not even terrifying. Medieval drama reduces the devil to plebeian domestic joke: 'Ffor fere of fyre a fart I crake' (*LC*, I, l. 81).

    In the case of Lucifer, the comic tone is partly explained by his re-

---

pynande torturing   *lely* truly   *coyll* coal   *foyll* fool   *derworth* precious   *defte* clever
dewes deuce   *slyke* such

moteness; the figure of Herod, belonging to the human world, is never so bright and always more terrifying—the comedy that surrounds him is black, not slapstick. Because he approximates more closely to the earthly ruler, his power of life and death, as in the Massacre of the Innocents, is felt as a real threat. Unlike Lucifer, he is not conquered finally by the direct act of God, but, like man, by the grim figure of Death. At times, as in Lydgate's *Fall of Princes*,[51] he becomes an embodiment of the process of corruption:

> His flessh gan turne to corrupcioun,
> Fret with wermys upon ech partie,
> Which hym assailed bi gret tormentrie:
> His leggis suelle, corbid blak gan shyne;
> Wher vengaunce werkith, a-dieu al medecyne.
>
> Of his seeknesse the stench was so horrible,
> Tawaite on hym no man myhte abide;
> Unto hymsilff his careyn wex odible,
> So sore he was troublid on ech side.   (Bk VII, ll. 213–21)

To be odious to oneself is the ending appropriate to the Pride of Life, which lavishes admiration and affection on the physical perfection of the self. Of all his fallen princes, it is only Herod whom Lydgate sees as an actual disfigurement of his book:

> And for his stori doth this book difface
> With woful clauses of hym whan I write,
> Therfor I caste no mor of hym tendite.   (Bk VII, ll. 243–5)

Despite his close connection with death and corruption, the Herod of the drama nevertheless fully exemplifies his prototype. His speech, according to a long-standing tradition, is characteristically violent and bombastic.[52] He is most impressively realized in the *Ludus Coventriae* which, of all the mystery cycles save Chester, makes the clearest connection between the Pride of Life and Death. The York cycle has a lively encounter between the Magi and Herod, but is faint in the crucial Massacre of the Innocents, whilst in the Towneley plays Herod becomes merely one amongst other evil pagans, all of whom swear by Mahound. The exchange with the Magi in the Chester encounter is similarly subdued, and it is arguable that the very centrality of the notion of the Pride of Life to the Chester and Towneley cycles may render their portrayal of individual figures more stereotyped and less interesting. The Chester Massacre of the Innocents does however achieve a small triumph of per-

---

fret chafed   *suelle* swelled   *corbid* crooked   *odible* odious

ception, for when Herod hears that his own child was amongst the innocent victims, he is transformed into a figure of Age:

> alas! my days be now done.
> I wott I must dye soone,
> for damned I must be.
>
> My legges rotten and my armes;
> I have done so many harmes,
> that now I see of feendes swarmes
> from hell cominge for me.   (X, ll. 418–24)

That illusory trust in the moment is dissolved at a touch, and Herod
discovers, through the death of his own son, that princes, like other men,
are mortal.

In the *Ludus Coventriae* Death is actually personified, and its Herod,
appropriately, is the most vigorous expression of the Pride of Life:

> Of bewte and of boldnes I bere ever-more the belle
> Of mayn and of myght I master every man
> I dynge with my dowtynes the devyl down to helle
> Ffor bothe of hevyn and of herth I am kyng sertayn.
>
> I am the comelyeste kynge clad in gleterynge golde
> ya and the semelyeste syre that may be-stryde a stede
> I welde att my wyll all wyghtys upon molde.   (XVIII, ll. 5–11)

There is much here of the vanity of Youth and of the contemporary
ruler; there is even something of Lucifer in Herod's claim to rule both
heaven and earth—in fact, he out-Lucifers Lucifer. But at the height of
his confidence, established as he thinks by the slaughter of the Innocents,
at the very moment when he claims, 'I was nevyr meryer here be-forn/
Sythe that I was fyrst born' (XX, ll. 164–5), Death joins his triumphant
feast. And Death, although the messenger of God, is significantly another
Pride of Life figure: 'All thynge that is on grownd I welde at my wylle'
(l. 182). In a final analysis, Death alone can claim to be a real success as
the Pride of Life.

By comparison with Herod or Lucifer, Pilate, whilst clearly conforming
to the same stereotype, is rather less commanding; but the fact that the
dramatists chose to cast him in that role is in itself of interest, since other
traditions would have allowed him a more humane rendering. The Pilate
of the Gospels, unlike their Herod, does not obviously lend himself to
a tyrannical persona; the apocryphal *Gospel of Nicodemus*, which proved
so rich a hunting ground for later elaborations of the Gospel story,

---

dynge strike

portrays Pilate sympathetically, as a troubled, responsive and thoughtful man.[53] Yet although, in *The Golden Legend*, de Voragine admits his acquaintance with Nicodemus' account of the Passion, he elaborates for Pilate a quite distinct history, which emphasizes his wickedness and cruelty.[54] Since *The Gospel of Nicodemus* was probably translated into English in the early fourteenth century, and was known very much earlier than that,[55] the dramatists' choice of the dark version was obviously deliberate: the wicked Pilate was obviously thought to be the more dramatic figure, for a drama, that is, of strong outlines, rather than inward subtlety. But the choice may also have been governed, as Kolve suggests of the Towneley cycle, by the desire to put the blame for Christ's death on one single historical character, rather than on humanity in general.[56]

The effect of this, however, is to make Pilate a rather petty figure; his pretensions in the Towneley cycle are much reduced from those of its Herod. He calls shrilly for silence, and his affirmations of power, with their doggerel Latin, reveal the anxious and insecure authority of a town clerk:

> Stynt, I say! gyf men place, quia sum dominus dominorum!
> he that agans me says, rapietur lux oculorum;
> Therfor gyf ye me space, ne tendam vim brachiorum,
> And then get ye no grace, contestor Iura polorum,
>   Caveatis;
>   Rewle I the Iure,
>   Maxime pure,
>   Towne quoque rure,
>   Me paveatis. (XXIV, ll. 10-18)

After the Crucifixion, Pilate reluctantly agrees to dice for Christ's garments, which he feels are his by right; he loses, but claims them in any case. The portrait is entirely reductive, for this Pride of Life is a very petty bourgeois indeed. The pallor of Pilate relative to Herod is further increased by his place in the cycle; for, where Herod has the floor to himself, Pilate's scenes are dominated by the largely silent figure of the condemned Christ, the very antithesis of the Pride of Life. Outside those scenes—in the Conspiracy of the York cycle, for example, or the Resurrection in the Chester plays—he emerges with far more zest and bravado. But it is appropriate enough that, just as Death puts paid to the vaunts of Herod, so Christ, the figure of spiritual life, should subdue the boasts of Pilate.

Lucifer, Herod and Pilate together form a consistent trilogy of Pride of Life figures in the mystery plays, but their similarities are not merely due to their conformation to the same stereotype. Their differences— Lucifer's glory, Herod's mortality, and Pilate's pettiness—are also consistent and have their point. If the link between them is stressed, it is because they conform to the same type of folly; but when, for example, Herod is described as Prince of Purgatory and Captain of Hell,[57] one is also aware that his offence is mortal where Lucifer's is immortal.

A similar claim cannot so easily be made for those other Pride of Life figures who appear sporadically in the mysteries. The Towneley and Chester cycles seem, as I have mentioned, particularly interested in the conception; for Octavian, Anti-Christ and a whole procession of the great and damned appear in the Chester plays, Pharaoh and Caesar in those of Towneley. The play *Mary Magdalene*, which belongs to the genre of miracle rather than mystery, has in its first part a positive cluster of such figures. In addition to the customary trilogy, there is Cyrus, the father of Mary Magdalene and Lazarus, the King of the World, the King of the Flesh, and a 'galaunt' who all conform to type. Even the taverner betrays a characteristic boastfulness:

> I am a taverner wytty and wyse,
> that wynys have to sell gret plente.
> of all the taverners I bere the pryse
> that be dwellyng with-inne the cete;
> of wynys I have grete plente,
>   . . .
> Ther be no better, as ferre as ye can goo.[58]

It is particularly clear in this play that the figure can move all too readily into morality—in the direction, that is, of the personified vice, and away from a complex spiritual and human context. For Mary Magdalene, these are simply the voices of the world from which Christ wins her; they scarcely need to be further distinguished. The pattern of her own conversion is repeated in the second part of her play where the King of Marcylle, the prototype of Pericles, is weaned by her from his own Pride of Life. The Chester cycle, which makes equal play with the figure, and centres itself also in the confrontation between the values of this world and of the next, has, because of its biblical context, a depth of significance which is lacking in the moralities. The religious sensibility is certainly moving towards simplification, but its stark contrasts, especially where they draw on richer traditions, have their own power as an interpretation of the comprehensive span of Christian history.[59]

One can however see, especially in the Chester cycle, that the dramatists' interest in this figure is not purely religious; it has, in a marked form, those aspects of political and social concern which lend the plays vitality and relevance. In the fourteenth and fifteenth centuries the figure of the king assumes a greater centrality than in the earlier Middle Ages, and a telling illustration of this can be found in the sculpture of French cathedrals. In the thirteenth century figures of kings, as distinct from saints or the heroes of the Old Testament, are rarely found, and when they do appear, their inferiority is clearly indicated by their relatively small size, their kneeling position, and their subordinate placing: Louis VII is thus depicted on one tympanum of Notre-Dame, and Saint Louis, with his wife, Marguerite of Provence, kneel, in another, before the Virgin who is seated to the right of her son. In the following century Charles V, the Dauphin Charles VI, and other dignitaries of the time, are sculpted for the cathedral at Amiens to stand beside the Virgin and St John as figures of equal height.[60] The Pride of Life, so often characterized as king or prince, dramatizes the debate which surrounds this increasingly important role of the monarch, for the altered status of the king inevitably results in tension between the authority of the Church and that of the state. One of the great fourteenth-century debates in England centres upon the rival authority of the two swords, and whether the temporal or the spiritual rightly possesses ascendancy.[61] It was of course in the interests of established religion to condemn the aspiring pride of kings, although the reforming (and ultimately heretical) spirit of the times urged that the things of Caesar should be rendered to Caesar. In Wycliff's view, the Church, in enjoying property, betrayed Christ; the king, in so doing, was merely true to his own nature; but this attempt to elevate the Church above worldly concerns succeeded only in subordinating it to the mundane interest, for, paradoxically, the practical consequence of Wycliff's thinking was the subordination of Church to king, as the English Reformation made evident.[62]

It is a further irony that the more elevated 'descending' theory of kingship, the theocratic point of view adopted by Augustine and Aquinas, should become the argument for the Divine Right, in which the king is justified in asserting his authority over both Church and people; for there was, during the Middle Ages, an alternative 'ascending' theory, a populist tradition which saw the king as receiving his authority, not from God, but, more democratically, from his subjects. Whilst the kings naturally advocated the former view, a-natural in origin, whose goal was properly the other world, the growing secular consciousness was drawn to the latter, based on natural manifestations, and concerned with immediate existence.[63] Thus the voice of the oppressed Church joined with that of the suffering poor, so that the language of the pulpit and that of social complaint may, as in the following anecdote, come to coincide:

A certain man as he entered the hall of a nobleman, seeing an ape in front of him dressed up in the silken garments of one of the children, thought it was actually his lord's own son, because it had its back to him at the time. When he was addressing it with due reverence, he discovered that it was an ape that was grinning at him. 'Curse you!' said he to it, 'I thought that you were Jankyn, my lord's son!'[64]

The coincidence of ecclesiastical with popular attitude is clearly marked
in literature of all kinds from the early fourteenth century onwards.
Social and religious concerns tend, as in Langland, to mingle. His figure
of Meed, for example, pertains to the Pride of Life; she even has certain
affinities with the positive figure Liffe in the alliterative poem *Death and
Liffe* which obviously owes much to Langland's influence, and probably
belongs to the early years of the fifteenth century.[65] Even in *Piers Plowman* Meed is not to be condemned out of hand:

> For Mede is moillere, Amendes was here dame;
> Thouh Fals were hure fader and Fykel-tonge hure syre,
> Amendes was hure moder by trewe mennes lokyng.
> With-oute hure moder Amendes, Mede may noght be wedded,
> For Treuth plyghte hure treuthe to wedde on of hure douhteres,
> And god grauntede it were so, so that no gyle were.   (C, III, ll. 120–5)

It is the use to which Meed is put, rather than her actual nature, which
is at fault; and whilst the problem of right usage remains with the king,
the poem assumes both a religious and a social right to instruct the
monarch, one which is even more keenly felt in *Mum and the Sothsegger*,
where Richard II is specifically addressed.[66]

For Langland, as for Dante, the spiritual health of men is inextricably
related to the health of their social condition: the kingdom of God can
only be established on earth if it is first a kingdom of men. Both writers
feel that the Church should not meddle in temporal matters, but both
regard the monarch as their representative, open to their exhortations.
Amongst less exceptional writing, the popularity of the *Secreta Secretorum* (which purports to be advice offered by Aristotle to Alexander, and
is really a manual for acceptable rule) reflects this urgently democratic
tendency;[67] so too do the equally popular stories of Alexander, in which
Darius instructs his conqueror in the dangers of power and wealth,
whilst the Gynosophists and Brahmins show, through their life of nature,
that there are after all unconquerable worlds—those which do not share
the material values on which kingship is based, and cannot be subjugated
because they have nothing to lose. The point is sharply made by the
Gynosophists, to whom the admiring Alexander offers whatever they can
ask; their choice is 'deathlessness', and they mock the conqueror's assumption of might when, perforce, he refuses.[68] Such works, clearly, are
the antithesis of *Tamburlaine*.

The general view of kingship is, however, a less constructive one than
the stories of Alexander suggest. It is striking that the *Gawain*-poet (who
can, for example, treat with humane compassion the lecherous drowned

---

moillere woman (usually a wife)

in the Flood) should devote Section XII of *Cleanness* to the vengeance
awaiting the unrighteous king.[69] The political poems of the time characteristically see only the sharper oppositions: the gaily dressed flatterer
who is favoured by Meed is vicious and encourages war; the poor man,
who receives no favours from her, does not; there is freedom in poverty,
but none in riches.[70] The negative representation of Youth obviously
derives from this attitude to the privileged and, above all, to the ruler.
As in the romances, the Pride of Life is nearly always nobly born and
richly endowed, the sibling, at least, of kings; but because he is a waster
and a prodigal, who squanders both his spiritual and temporal patri-
monies, his noble origins, unlike those of Youth, become cause for
complaint, not complaisance.[71] The social and religious accusations
against him often focus upon the same objects: his typical dissipations
of hunting and hawking, for example, or his affection for fine clothes
(Plates 2c and 5). But in the social view, which sees him primarily as a
waster and thus a danger to the social order, there is often a trace of
sympathy for his attitude of *carpe diem*; whereas in the religious perspective, it is precisely his emphasis upon the moment that constitutes his
danger of damnation.[72]

An exemplum from a sermon of the early fifteenth century is wittily
expressive of the religious view: an angel and a hermit, when walking
together one day, passed a carrion, at which the hermit held his nose,
but the angel didn't; later they met a fair young man in deadly sin,
whereupon the angel held his nose but the hermit didn't.[73] The juxtaposition of Youth and carrion is a popular one; it does not only occur
in the story of Herod in the mystery plays and in various moralities, but
is given individual expression in the debates between Youth and Age,
and in the legend of the Three Living and the Three Dead.[74] The re-
taliation proper to *carpe diem* is *memento mori*.

The late fourteenth century, with some justification, thus conflates
the images of king, profligate Youth and the Pride of Life. As the poet
observes in *Mum and the Sothsegger*, 'ho is riall of his ray . . . light reede
him folwith'; it is no more appropriate for youths of twenty-four to
advise the king than for a cow to hop in a cage.[75] This coincidence of
views, however, outlasts the unfortunate Richard, and is in any case an
established motif quite apart from such specific instances. It can be found
in *The Pride of Life*, where the proud and masterful king, exhibiting all
the brash confidence of Herod, describes himself as 'King of Life', yet
exhibits this power mainly as one of death: 'Nas ther never no man of
woman iborre/Ogein me withstonde that I nold him spille.'[76] *The Interlude of Youth*, written some 150 years later, still retains, in this respect,
the characteristics of the early morality.[77] Youth is a notably empirical

---

ray dress   *spille* destroy

character, involved in a world whose only realities are those of solid objects; the confidence of the quasi-permanent leads him to the un-empirical assumption that he too is everlasting, 'a king eternal', although Charity and Humility finally wean him from this conviction by a description of the passion of Christ.

The extent to which all these portraits of Youth tend to the abstract and conceptual is the more striking when one returns to the affectionate realism of Aquinas or Chaucer. The Pride of Life, though often dramatic and powerful, even attractive, lacks their realistic immediacy. One may turn with relief to the humorous impatience with which Richard de Bury, in the earlier thirteenth century, treats of Youth's carelessness of his beloved books:

Fructus et caseum super librum expansum non veretur comedere, atque scyphum hinc inde dissolute transferre; et quia non habet eleemosynarium praeparatum, in libris dimittit reliquias fragmentorum. Garrulitate continua sociis oblatrare non desinit, et dum multitudinem rationum adducit a sensu physico vacuarum, librum in gremio subexpansum humectat aspergine sali-varum. Quid plura? statim duplicatis cubitis reclinatur in codicem et per breve studium soporem invitat prolixum, ac reparandis rugis limbos replicat foliorum, ad libri non modicum detrimentum.

Iam imber abiit et recessit et flores apparuerunt in terra nostra. Tunc scholaris quem describimus, librorum neglector potius quam inspector, viola, primula, atque rosa necnon et quadrifolio farciet librum suum.[78]

(He does not hesitate to eat fruit or cheese over an open book, or carelessly to carry a cup to and fro, and because he has no alms-bag ready, he drops his remaining crumbs into the books. A continual chatterbox, he never stops arguing with his friends, and whilst he advances a host of empty-headed contentions, he wets the book lying open in his lap with a spray of saliva. Then what? He rests his folded arms upon the book, and by brief study invites a long nap, then in order to smooth out the creases he bends back the margins of the pages, to the book's no small injury. Now the rains are over and gone and the flowers have appeared in our land. Then the scholar we've been describing, a neglecter more than an inspector of books, will stuff his book with violet, primrose, rose and quatrefoil too.)

This tone, of life, not the Pride of Life, can be heard rarely; in Chaucer certainly, and occasionally in Dunbar, but almost nowhere else in Eng-lish medieval literature. Yet it would be a mistake to dismiss the Pride of Life, as Kolve does, because the writers of the cycles have chosen to humiliate the great through caricature.[79] The concept itself is more complex than he suggests, and its centrality to the great Renaissance drama of the sixteenth century indicates that it represents a new depar-ture as much as a decline; Shakespeare's Falstaff, and Jonson's Epicure Mammon, as well as Marlowe's Tamburlaine, owe much to this proto-type. It is true that the Pride of Life is no figure of Everyman; even in

Langland, whose personifications of the Seven Deadly Sins are, for the most part, ale-house characters, Purnele Proute-herte, the first of them all, clearly wishes to be distinguished from the ale-house company as (amongst other things) 'lovelokest to loken on, and lykyngest a bedde' (C, VII, 1. 44). But because the proud are characteristically amongst the great, the condemnation attaching to them is the more absolute. The drama, in its treatment of ordinary men, is not apt to condemn them; even the torturers in the York Crucifixion, preoccupied with fitting the body to the cross, are not the grotesques of cruelty sometimes found in wall painting.[80] They are inefficient craftsmen, completing a job whose terrible significance they do not comprehend; whereas the Pride of Life—Lucifer, Herod and Pilate—are men who know what they do.

If, moreover, the Pride of Life is not Everyman, the concept does derive from, and return to, the generalization, relevant to all men, of contemptus mundi. This connection may be illustrated from that group of poems known as 'Earth upon Earth', of which many variants exist in the Middle Ages, though all conform to one of two main versions.[81] The earliest example of the A version (from MS. Harleian 2253, c. 1325) expresses this contempt succinctly in its savagely ironic sense of man's mortality:

Erthe toc of erthe erthe with woh,
Erthe other erthe to the erthe droh,
Erthe leyde erthe in erthene throh,
Then hevede erthe of erthe erthe ynoh.

In the earliest example of the B version, written perhaps a century later, this warning to Everyman has become an admonition specific to the Pride of Life:

Erthe uppon erthe yet wolde be a kynge,
But how erth shall to erth thynketh he nothyng;
But when erth byddyth erth his dute hom bryng,
Than shall erth fro erth have a peteus partyng.

Erth wynnyth uppon erthe both castellys and towris;
Than sayth erth unto erth: 'This is alle owres'.
But whan erth uppon erth hath byllyd all his bowrys,
Thanne shalle erth for erth suffer sharpe showres.

Erth byldyth uppon erth as molde uppon molde,
And erth goth uppon erth glyttryng alle gold,
Lyke as erth unto erth never goe sholde;
Ann justly than shalle erth go to erth rather than he wolde.

---

droh drew   throh coffin   hevede had   ynoh enough   dute dues

The generalized significance of the A version is, however, returned to in the moralities, *Mundus et Infans* and *The Castle of Perseverance*, both of which characterize the world itself as the Pride of Life, and thus offer their meaning to men in general.[82]

The emotion of *contemptus mundi* is a repellent one—intended of course to be so—and especially to modern taste; because this is the context of the Pride of Life, it is inevitable that a good deal of uninspired moral cliché should be expressed in the figure. Yet the type also expresses the complex religious paradox that man is fallen, mortal, corruptible, earth—but earth made in the image of God. And as the absoluteness of the condemnation intensifies, so the covert delight in life grows stronger, the glittering figures increasingly boisterous and buoyant; the World in *The Castle of Perseverance* offers a real temptation:

> Worthy wytys in al this werd wyde,
>> Be wylde wode wonys and every weye-went,
> Precyous prinse, prekyd in pride,
>> Thorwe this proper pleyn place in pes be ye bent!
> Buske you, bolde bachelerys, undyr my baner to abyde
>> Where bryth basnetys be bateryd and backys ar schent.
> Ye, syrys semly, all the same syttyth on syde,
>> For bothe be see and be londe my sondys I have sent,
>>> Al the world myn name is ment.
>>> Al abowtyn my bane is blowe,
>>> In every cost I am knowe,
>>> I do men rawyn on ryche rowe
>>>> Tyl thei be dyth to dethys dent.   (ll. 157–69)

Nature and Venus, the mentors of Youth and the Pride of Life, express in a wider, more abstract context the dilemmas that surround those two figures; they are the principles, from whose ambiguities spring the confusions of human behaviour. Together they dramatize that same paradox—that man is both less than the beasts, but made in the image of God—but because they are remote from specific aspiration or complaint, they are also more inclusive: they express the search for meaning in human existence. Rather than being offered as answers, Venus and Nature thus tend to promote debate, and the genre in which they most frequently appear is an indication of their ambiguity; for where the positive figure of Youth is the hero of romance, the Pride of Life the villain of the drama, their two mentors appear chiefly in the more suggestive, less clearly evaluative, world of dream poetry. Here the imagina-

---

weye-went pathway   *basnetys* helmets   *on syde* aside   *sondys* messengers
bane summons   *rawyn* behave madly   *rowe* line of persons   *dyth* put

tion is freshly exposed to objects familiar enough in the waking world, events follow each other with a logic that escapes the spectator who continually demands explanation, and the dreamer may emerge from his dream, as Chaucer does in *The Parliament of Fowls*, enlightened chiefly in a sense of new complexities: 'I wok, and othere bokes tok me to,/To reede upon, and yit I rede alwey' (ll. 695–6).

Because Venus is the smaller and subject figure, relating merely to the dilemmas of carnal love, she is often viewed as a temptress, and thus, as mentor, has the ear of the Pride of Life; whilst Nature, who embraces cosmic, not merely human, patterns of behaviour, and marks the continuity between carnal and spiritual, has a closer affinity with Youth. Venus, when she escapes the control of Nature, incites to lechery; the Pride of Life, thus mistaking means for ends, dallies with his paramour in lust, not love. Nature, in directing sexuality towards procreation, enables Youth, for whom human and divine love are continuous, to fulfil God's plan by populating his creation. The medieval suspicion of Venus is not, however, peculiar to a Christian fear of the flesh: her ambiguities are explored much earlier in Plato's *Symposium*, which, in its two Aphrodites, exemplifies two distinct kinds of love, the one 'rightly named common', the other heavenly.[83] The Middle Ages did not know the *Symposium* directly, and would, in any event, have approved only the heavenly, not the homosexual, aspect of the Uranian Aphrodite; this example reveals rather that the dualities of Venus reflect a recurrent human difficulty, pagan as much as Christian, in distinguishing between lust and love.

The contempt for that Venus 'rightly named common' is established for the Middle Ages by the work of Fulgentius, writing in the sixth century, who sees in her fatherhood by Saturn an allegory of lust rising out of excess. His Venus is based upon the Roman Goddess, who in her turn corresponds with the Greek Aphrodite; but he connects 'Saturn' with *saturitas* (satiety), and thus arrives, by a cruder means than Plato's, at his negative reading.[84] Although Venus is rarely 'heavenly' in the Middle Ages, she is usually far more ambiguous than Fulgentius allows. *De Planctu Naturae* of Alanus de Insulis, an extremely influential work of the late twelfth century, established her dual possibilities.[85] If the *Consolatio* of Boethius is the great source book for the treatment of Fortune in the Middle Ages, *De Planctu Naturae* is cited almost as widely in treatments of Venus and Nature. In *The Parliament of Fowls* Chaucer does not bother to reiterate its classic description of Nature, holding a simple reference sufficient:

And right as Aleyn, in the Pleynt of Kynde,
Devyseth Nature of aray and face,
In swich aray men myghte hire there fynde. (ll. 316–18)

Alanus accounts for the double nature of Venus in terms of her lawful and unlawful unions: the former is her marriage to Hymen, God of marriage, and the latter her adultery with Antigamus. In her adulterous vein, she is the destructive deity of Boccaccio's *Teseida*, to whose temple, lit by *nuove fiamme nate di Martiri* (new flames born of martyrdom) the prayer of Palemone ascends; she is his ally only in her enmity towards the chaste, for she has *molti archi a' cori di Diana/. . . appiccati e rotti* (many bows of Diana's company hung up and broken).[86] On the other hand, where chastity means virginity, it may be opposed to Nature's law, as much as to Venus; thus it is possible for the Venus of the *Roman de la Rose* to be seen both as the enemy of the chaste—*Venus, qui torjorz guerroie/Chastée* (Venus, who ceaselessly fights with Chastity)—and as Nature's friend—*'Dame Venus, m'amie'*.[87] Properly subordinated to Nature, Venus promotes the lawful expression of sexuality in marriage and the procreation of children; thus, whilst Love's barons prepare to assault the Castle of Jealousy, Venus, as Nature's general, attacks the Tower of Shame[88] (Plate 3b).

Even in the role of Nature's ally, Venus remains more common than celestial; Chaucer's prologue to Book III of *Troilus and Criseyde* is exceptional in connecting the power of the Goddess with that of Providence, echoing in his lines the verses in which Philosophy celebrates divine love in the *Consolatio*.[89] When, as Cytherea in *The Parliament of Fowls*, she is invoked in the largeness of the skies as a benign influence which promotes fertility not only in man but throughout the created world, this 'blysful lady swete' is curiously disinct, as muse or inspiration, from the Venus enclosed on earth in a 'prive corner' of her own temple.[90] Even in Chaucer, the planetary figure is rarely benign: the Venus of *The Knight's Tale* is based upon the catastrophic deity of the *Teseida*. But the wholly negative view of Venus is, one must add, no more frequent in medieval literature than the wholly positive. DeGuilleville, certainly, creates a Venus who has no redeeming qualities whatever: she is a foul old woman, attached to Gluttony's tail, whose offices are rape, incest and adultery, and who claims the *Roman de la Rose* as her own special literary creation.[91] DeGuilleville, however, is writing from a firmly religious position; secular literature is rarely so decisive, although, as in *De Planctu Naturae*, the scales may well tend to incline against her. For Alanus himself has more to say of her in accusation than defence, and his work opens with the words:

In lacrymas risus, in fletum gaudia verto:
In Planctum plausus, in lacrymosa jocus,
Cum sua naturam video secreta silere,
Cum Veneris monstro naufraga turba perit.
Cum Venus in Venerem pugnans, illos facit illas:
Cunique suos magica devirat arte viros.

(I turn laughter to tears, joy to weeping, applause to complaints, merriment to tearfulness, when I see Nature keeping silent about her secrets, when the crowd perishes shipwrecked by the monster of Venus. When Venus fights with Venus, she makes men into women, and unmans men with her magic art.)

Her enlistment in the service of Nature thus seems, in the human if not in the animal world, to be a complex and ambiguous undertaking; chastity on the one hand, and lechery on the other, both frustrate Nature's purposes. In Lydgate's *Reason and Sensuality*, Diana is positively pedantic in her attack upon her opponent:

> Whos name for to specyfie
> Aftir ethymologye,
> Venus, by exposicion,
> Is seyde of venym and poysoune;
> And of venym, this the fame,
> Venus pleynly took her name.[92]

But the doctrine of *fin' amour*, expressed in the chivalric code, is yet another deviation from the natural order; when Diana praises the ladies of Arthur's court because 'Their choys was nat for lustynesse,/But for trouth and Worthynesse', the poem recognizes that, in the interests of debate, she simplifies the matter when she polarizes the alternatives into love 'Under the yok of honeste,/In clennesse and chastite', and 'Unleful lust'.[93] Venus is a force for good as well as ill; she can elicit virtue as well as vice:

> For hyt ys she the whiche, in soth,
> Kan, whan hir lyst, both nyghe and ferre,
> Pes I-tournen in-to werre,
> And she kan bringe ageyn taccord
> Folke that stonden at discord.
>   . . .
> And thorgh hir myght, which ys dyvyne,
> She the proude kan enclyne
> To lownesse and humilyte,
> And the deynouse meke to be.[94]

Just as Genius praises fecundity in the *Roman de la Rose*, and Emily, both in the *Teseida* and Chaucer's *Knight's Tale*, is converted from her devotion to Diana and the celibate life, so Venus can encourage mankind into more diversely positive, as well as more dangerously destructive, modes of life. Her cultivated garden is not identical with Nature's landscape: the garden of Sir Mirth is not, as Genius points out in the *Roman de la Rose*, the same as the shepherd's park; its appearance of naturalness is deceitful, as Diana explains in *Reason and Sensuality*:

C

> Eke in this gardyn of Deduit
> The tren of kynde ber no fruit,
> Thogh nature hem sustene,
> Ay tendre, fresh, and grene.[95]

Nevertheless, the frustration of Nature can, when under Nature's control, be brought to bear fruit as Diana's bow cannot.

In her capriciousness and mutability, Venus has much in common with Fortune; her instabilities, similarly, may be balanced only when they are seen fully in context—in relation to the natural order in the one case, to the divine in the other. Nature, on the other hand, though sometimes out of temper with the difficulties of her task, is for the most part characterized by the serenity and stability of a being whose place in the divine order is always clear (Plate 3a). If Youth and Nature seem to have much in common, it is because their vision is never confined to this world, or to the littleness of individual satisfactions. This is not to imply, however, that Nature is without her complexities: in her cosmic context she may share in its immutable order, but in her relations with mankind she is often infected by the instabilities of the human condition. As mediator between the two aspects of man, his flesh and his spirit, she focusses the whole problem of that relation.[96] In *The Assembly of the Gods* (often erroneously attributed to Lydgate), Nature pleads for the freedom of her servant 'Gentyll Sensualyte, that hath me servyd long', whilst in *Reason and Sensuality* (so far as one can judge from the poem's unfinished state), she is presented, not as the advocate of Sensuality but of Reason, for the 'ryghte way' is 'the wey of Reson'.[97] The unpredictability of this representative of order may to some extent be explained by a difference in genre, for to assume a genre is to adopt the outlook and the judgement it implies. The Nature of love poetry, as in *The Assembly*, is not the Nature of religious poetry, like *Reason and Sensuality*; thus the first may well favour the senses, where the second opts for the intellect. Even so, these varying attitudes to Nature do reflect the fact that, to the medieval mind, she is essentially a dilemma. What is the relation of man's physical and instinctual being to the life of his soul in its response to spiritual ordinance?[98] Why does man alone stand apart from Nature's rule, in which all other creatures are harmoniously ordered? And if he is included in that order, then to what extent is he a free being, capable of meritorious choice?[99]

In medieval literature, Nature is clearly an abstraction; to meditate upon her is to revolve the problems that abstraction entails. Although the nineteenth century valued the 'naturalness' of Gothic, the romantic notion of nature would have been incomprehensible to the Middle Ages;

Deduit Pleasure

even in Petrarch, who is often regarded as the founding father of that attitude, 'nature cannot be understood, felt, and enjoyed *per se*, but only as a dark or light background for the Ego'.[100] When two centuries earlier, the first Cistercians established themselves in unspoilt countryside, they were in search of an environment conducive to contemplation, in much the same way as the medieval illuminator, who uses the natural world as a background to frame an event of spiritual significance.[101] The natural world as such thus excites little direct attention and no strong sense of affinity; but the intellectual concept of Nature is almost as great an obsession with the medieval mind as is the notion of Fortune.

This preoccupation with the intelligible as distinct from the sensible world is manifested in the detail of medieval language. Middle English employed the word 'kind' in a sense synonymous with 'nature', and from approximately 1300, when 'nature' came into use from Latin through French, until *c.* 1600, when 'kind 'in this sense became obsolete, the two words co-existed with equal currency.[102] If anything, 'kind' possessed the stronger conceptual force when used to mean 'the character or quality derived from birth or native constitution; natural disposition, nature'. Its strength is reflected in Langland's definition, where it is really synonymous, as many of his formative concepts come to be, with God:

> 'Kynde is a creator,' quath Wit, 'of alle kyne thynges,
> Fader and formour of al that forth groweth,   ﹅
> The wiche is god grettest that gynnynge hadde nevere,
> Lord of lyf and of lyght, of lysse and of payne.
> Angeles and alle thyng aren at hus wil;
> Man is hym most lyk of membres and of face,
> And semblable in soule to god, bote yf synne hit make.'   (C, XI, ll. 151–7)

Kind here personified becomes creator both of celestial and of terrestrial worlds,[103] whilst mankind, unless deformed by sin, is, of all his creations, 'most lyk' to this 'Lord of lyf and of lyght'. The definition offered by Wit is, however, a simplification, as Langland knows, for his poem is intensely aware of the difference between the letter and an experiential understanding of its spirit. Wit skates over the dilemmas: that the creator should be a source of pain as well as joy, that man's freedom should seem to consist largely in the power to sin.[104] When Nature's power is seen, as it more commonly is, as sub-celestial only—not co-extensive with that of the creator, but wielded by a figure who is his instrument—these problems intensify. It is also worth noting that both words can imply gender or sex in Middle English, for sexuality is the crux of the problem. To obey the ordinance of Nature and 'do one's kind', means in general 'to enact one's nature', and specifically to 'perform the sexual act'. But to do so was, for many medieval thinkers, to debase the image of God in man by behaving like a beast, an action only redeemed by the procreation of the race.

The medieval figure of Nature is thus largely conceptual; yet, as personification, she is often movingly described. Her appearance, as already mentioned, has consistent lineaments which derive from her representation in *De Planctu Naturae*. She appears to the author, as does Philosophy to Boethius, in the guise of a divinity, recognizably human, but larger than life in her continuity with the divine:

Cujus crinis non mendicata luce, sed propria scintillans, non similitudinarie radiorum repraesentans effigiem, sed eorum claritate nativa naturam prae-veniens, in stellare corpus caput effigiabat puellae.[105]

(Her hair, which shone with its own, not an artificial, light, not presenting an appearance of rays but by its innate brilliance outdoing nature, transformed the girl's head into a body like a star.)

It is this Nature to whom Chaucer refers his readers in *The Parliament*, whom Lydgate recreates in *Reason and Sensuality*:

> Whos here shoon as the sonne bryght,
> That cast aboute swych a lyght,
> So persyng pleynly and so shene,
> That I myghte nat sustene
> To beholde the bryghtnesse
> Nor the excellent fairnesse.
> For up to the sterres rede
> This lady raughte with hir hede.   (ll. 411–18)

Unlike the Philosophy of Boethius, however, Alanus' Nature voices, rather than assuages, complaint. When her laws are in abeyance and Venus reigns, society is destroyed by the monster of sensual lust. The reason of Nature, and the lust of Venus, inevitably oppose each other; only when properly regulated does Venus have her use in insuring the propagation of the species—and this point is made with splendid rationality through the metaphors of grammar and logic.[106] The attitudes of this authoritative Nature, her firmly hierarchical sense, her censure of men for departing from her harmony, are as consistent in medieval English literature as her feminine beauty and her combination of the wisdom of Age with the graces of Youth. Her command is as firm at the close of the Middle Ages in Dunbar's 'The Thrissil and the Rois', as it is in the pages of Alanus or in Chaucer's *Parliament*:

Thrissil Thistle

Scho ordnand eik that every bird and beist
Befoir hir hienes suld annone compeir,
And every flour of vertew, most and leist,
And every herb be feild fer and neir,
As thay had wont in May, fro yeir to yeir,
To hir thair makar to mak obediens,
Full law inclynnand with all dew reverens.[107]

The complaint that, whilst *Omnia certo fine gubernans* (governing all things to one certain end), Nature excludes men alone from her ordered rule, marks another point of contact between Alanus and Boethius, one which is echoed in much medieval literature. Thus in the *Roman de la Rose*, when Nature confesses to Genius, she is careful to absolve the natural world—of seas, elements, plants and animals—from blame; only man, who derives all his blessings, if not his intelligence, from her, opposes her laws:

'et mes sarpenz et mes couleuvres,
tuit s'estudient en mes euvres.
    Mes seus hom, cui je fet avoie
tretouz les biens que je savoie.'[108]

(and my serpents and snakes—all endeavour to do my work. Man alone excepted, to whom I have directed all the blessings I know of.)

In religious poetry this complaint can come to be an expression of *contemptus mundi*, as in this 'Holy Meditation':

Trees bring foorthe, thou woost weel, as I gesse,
Branch, leef, and floure, wyn, oyle, and suche swettnesse,
                        . . .
Of thee kemethe dung, uryne, vomyt and spitting,
Lysse, nyttes, flees, and suche filthy thing.[109]

For Langland's dreamer, however, man's failure in the natural order represents a problem:

Ac that that moste mevede me and my mod chaungede,
Was that ich seih Reson suwen alle bestes
Save man and mankynde; meny tymes me thouhte,
Reson rewelede hem nat, nother riche ne poure.   (C, XIV, ll. 180–3)

Reason here comes to express something like order, not independent ratiocination; paradoxically man, the only creature to possess that faculty, is seen as the least rational. As the dreamer asks Reason:

---

vertew i.e. medicinal   *suwen* follow

'And ther-fore mervaileth me, for man, as in makynge,
Is most yliche the, in wit and in werkes,
Whi he ne loveth thy lore, and lyveth as thow techest?'   (ll. 193–5)

When viewed as a freedom only to depart from the good, man's intelligence does not exalt him above the animals, but debases him below them.

In the religious view, man is not only separated from Nature, but a conformity to her laws does not necessarily promise him an integration of body and spirit. Nature, as Rolle observes, encourages man to love the fairest things, but ordered love enjoins him to love the good.[110] The beautiful and the good do not, for Rolle, coincide as they do for Aquinas, and even when the two are related, the medieval bond of the good with the beautiful subordinates the things of this world to the 'real' or ideal forms of theology and metaphysics.[111] Where the order of Nature is seen by the Middle Ages both as wholly good and wholly beautiful, their sense of determinism is increased; nothing, without jeopardy, can go against Nature, since it is God's creation.[112] But this leads to a further problem, for conformity to the ideal law denies man the freedom of his own reason, whilst departure from it is irrational and reduces him to something less than the animals. Even if he chooses freely to conform, that choice involves uncertainties: in *Reason and Sensuality*, for example, Nature affirms that the world is made for man since he is its microcosm; yet it is precisely the beauties of this world, its sunshine, rivers, mountains, seas and skies which distract the narrator from the path which Nature has advocated, 'For the false, veyn plesaunce/Of thys worldly vanyte'.[113]

These difficulties inhere, however, in the fallen nature of man, rather than in Nature as such. It has sometimes been argued that the notion that the natural world fell with man was current in the Middle Ages, as it appears to have been in England from the Renaissance until the advent of the Romantics. But the crux of that argument—that the pre-lapsarian world was a *tabula rasa*, disfigured by the Fall with the 'warts and wens' of mountains—is certainly not evident in medieval writing.[11] Just as Augustine numbers high mountains, gentle hills and level fields together amongst the good things of the earth which command the affections of men,[115] so for Lydgate 'ful high mountaynes,/The holtis hore and large playnes' are amongst the pleasing vanities of life. The hardships of the natural world may sometimes make it a place of trial for man, as the cold and other dangers of the Wirral are for Gawain but this does not necessarily imply that those dangers are evidence of a comprehensive Fall, for the stormy sea and the wild beasts seeking their food are included by Lydgate in his list of earthly delights. A distinction needs to be made between the concept of Nature, and experience of the natural world: the latter may sometimes be distinctly uncomfortable, but that does not indicate that the former is corrupt.

Part of the reason for that disjunction may be that the medieval mind, in its theoretic vein, looks at the natural world with a Platonic inattentiveness which enables it to find only what it expects to see—a closer congruity with an ideal form than man can achieve. The Fall is thus seen as the means by which man became alienated from that natural order, and a dream of recoverable harmony is reflected in medieval treatments of unfallen existence in Eden. This optimistic and nostalgic myth remains potently specific: a stage direction to Adam, 'Whosoever names Paradise is to look and point towards it', is a telling example of this literalism.[116] References abound in medieval literature to the unfallen Adam's ability to communicate with the animal world, and Christ, as the second Adam, is often credited with the same power. The poet of *Genesis and Exodus* (mid thirteenth century) asserts that only when man sinned did the natural world turn against him.[117] The author of the *Cursor Mundi* (c. 1325) postulates a recovery of this concord between man and beast in face of the mutual catastrophe of the Flood; he describes a similar return to harmony during the Flight into Egypt, whilst he takes the Christ Child's empathy with the natural world as a sign of his divinity.[118]

Arcadia, the secular Eden, extends this ease of natural life to the whole human race.[119] Its innocent simplicities are nostalgically revisited in Chaucer's poem, 'The Former Age':

> Yit were no paleis-chaumbres, ne non halles;
> In caves and in wodes softe and swete
> Slepten this blissid folk withoute walles,
> On gras or leves in parfit quiete.
> Ne doun of fetheres, ne no bleched shete
> Was kid to hem, but in seurtee they slepte.
> Hir hertes were al oon, withoute galles;
> Everich of hem his feith to other kepte. (ll. 41–8)

The golden age of Saturn, the age of innocence, is the classical equivalent to Eden because it is the only period in which man's nature is undivided. Dante's tragic figure of the *gran veglio*, the old man of Crete who symbolizes human history, is rent by a great wound from the neck down; only the golden head preserves the integrity of unfallen man.[120] It is a sign of this divided nature that sexuality becomes complex and guilt-ridden; as the Friend explains in the *Roman de la Rose*, love in the golden age was innocent:

---

kid known *galles* galls (i.e. jealousy)

'Seur tex couches con je devise,
sanz rapine et sanz covoitise,
s'entracoloient et besoient
cil cui li jeu d'amors plesoient.'   (ll. 8401-4)

(Upon beds such as I describe, without rape and without whoredom,
those who pleased to play love's game embraced and kissed each other.)

Instincts honoured in Arcadia are, however, discouraged in post-lapsarian society, and it is in the guilt of the flesh particularly that the divide is most vividly sensed between man and the natural world. To a post-Romantic understanding of the natural, the attitudes to Nature in the Middle Ages may seem dryly scholastic, not to say theological, just as their fear of Venus may savour to us of antique prudery. Certainly in much religious poetry, where these perceptions degenerate into the clichés of *contemptus mundi*, some impatience is unavoidable, but that is partly because its conceptual life has degenerated. In the greatest medieval poetry, it is the dilemmas themselves that attract the literary imagination, not because of their didactic potential, but because such poets take a quite unscholastic delight in the paradoxical and insoluble.

In *The Parliament of Fowls*, the subtlest poem in Middle English on the subject of Venus and Nature, those two figures are at once dilemmas for the mind and the personae of literary convention: the two are fused. Chaucer, as a young poet, in an endeavour to find his appropriate subject, explores the possibilities of dream, which is traditionally peopled with the conventions that literature has to offer; Nature and Venus are two of its characters, and the problems that surround them (as with human figures) compose their fascination. Unlike the scholar-narrator of *Troilus and Criseyde*, this earlier dreamer is more inclined to contemplate the emotional wonders of paradox, than to tease out the dilemmas for their own sake; for he is not so much a poet who seeks to understand life, as one who wishes to chart the great subject of poetry—love.[121] In his search, the dreamer must thus necessarily encounter love's two great abstracts, Venus and Nature; the path by which he arrives at these ladies is worth following, for it expresses a good deal about the place in medieval literature of these two figures of Life.

The speaker's own uncertainty leads him to look first for an answer in literature, namely in the Dream of Scipio; a story calculated to dissuade from earthly, in favour of heavenly, love. Its *contemptus mundi*, however, fails to satisfy its reader: 'For bothe I hadde thyng which that I nolde,/And ek I nadde that thyng that I wolde' (ll. 90-1). The religious view, though not refuted, is treated as irrelevant to the quest, for there is a distance between the experience of life and its vicarious experience in literature. From reading, the narrator moves to dreaming, and what he encounters initially are the conventions of literature—the allegoric gate and the temple of Venus. He reacts to the goddess with appropriate ardour, but, as an intimation of love, she fails to satisfy: 'Forth welk I tho myselven to solace' (l. 297). The world that he enters, of Nature's open 'launde', is again one step nearer to experience, for in the debate of Nature with the birds he is at least more directly in touch with the emotional problem of love. The debate as such does not, however, provide an answer, but only a compromise, when the formel eagle, who cannot choose her mate, is allowed to postpone her decision for another year, thus releasing more humble birds to their less complex mating. The polemic of the parliament is not there for its own sake, demanding an abstract answer: it is an education in feeling, and the dreamer awakes from it ready to look with new eyes, rather than new conclusions, on the waking world of actual experience.

For Chaucer, the theoretic question, whether Venus or Nature, is not merely theoretic, for it approximates more closely to the actuality of feeling than either books or the conventions which derive from them; and the debate is not self-sufficient, for it illuminates only when the mind returns to the world of actual life. The answer for Chaucer, more clearly than for any other medieval English poet concerned with the theme, cannot be the simple abstract of religious ordinance. Bennett speaks appropriately of 'that special kind of *Canterbury Tales* contentment wherein, having seen all varieties of human folly and self-deception, we come to an abiding sense of the worth and purpose of human love, even though we be no whit the nearer to defining or explaining it'.[122] The paradoxes of Nature and Venus are a means of eliciting that variety, and the contentment which results is an answer of a kind (perhaps of the best kind), because it is ambiguously experiential, not lucidly theoretic.

Yet this is not to deny that *The Parliament of Fowls* makes its own poetic evaluation of Venus as against Nature, and of the virtues of Nature herself. Its discriminations are inexplicit, as they commonly are in Chaucer; even in his earliest poetry, it is usually truer to say that he encourages his readers to judge, than that he advances his own judgement. But indications of judgement can be sensed in the whole movement of the poem, for the dreamer is always felt to be advancing, and Nature's 'launde' is one considerable step closer to his object than Venus' temple. The poem's preference for Nature over Venus is clear; it stands squarely in the tradition traceable from Alanus through Jean de Meun, in which Nature, not Venus, is the true source of the knowledge of love.[123] The poem celebrates both the firmly hierarchical order that Nature imposes, and the equally firm law which governs the various company of contentious birds. Yet Nature's rule is not untroubled, as the very fact of the debate and its postponed solution make evident. In face of the formel eagle's refusal to 'serve Venus', Nature can only permit events to take their course: ' "Now, syn it may non otherwise betyde,"/Quod tho Nature, "heere is no more to seye" ' (ll. 654–5). The success of her rule, as in human parliaments, resides in the appearance, rather than in the fact, of democratic decision.

It is interesting that the act of mating should appear to the formel eagle (a devotee, obviously, of Diana) as subservience to Venus, rather than as service to Nature. The perpetuation of the species is a part of Nature's order, not the whole; and even in this part, the sexual act itself is desirable only in the context of its full purpose. In isolation, pursued for its own sake, the act is merely lust, and the claustrophobic atmosphere of Venus' temple is the result of this isolation:

> Derk was that place, but afterwards lightnesse
> I saw a lyte, unnethe it myghte be lesse,
> And on a bed of gold she lay to reste,
> Til that the hote sonne gan to weste.   (ll. 263–6)

The privacy of Venus' activities, her withdrawal from the eye of day, clearly place her in relation to Nature, whose light surpasses that of every other creature, as the clear summer's sun surpasses that of the stars (ll. 299–301). The dreamer himself, delighting in the sight of Venus' bare breasts, and even more in the thinness of the cloth that covers her from the waist down, participates pleasurably in the dalliance, and the lines which describe this have their own beauty. The poem's effect is the more subtle because Venus is not intrinsically condemned; because the limitations of such love emerge chiefly through a comparison with Nature: it is man who lingers in the temple of Venus, and the birds of the ordered animal world who participate in Nature's parliament. Even in that comparison, the poem does not condemn Venus wholly, for it is a frustration of Nature's purpose, albeit a temporary one, that the formel eagle should refuse to enter Venus' service. As Bennett remarks, 'if the dichotomy between the bird-suitors and the human lovers, between the environs of Venus' Temple and Nature's "place so swote and grene", is not absolute, this very indeterminacy provides a hint that some—the ennobling, the unequivocal—aspects of human love are reconcilable with Nature's divine purpose'.[124]

A wholly positive and uncomplicated view of human love is very rare in medieval literature. When it occurs, it tends, like the figure of Youth, to be the product of that early romance faith, not of those stories which are courtly and Arthurian. The love of Lancelot and Guinevere, though not without its virtue, is for Malory a central cause, both of the Round Table's making and of its destruction. In a wider context, love both creates Arthur's fellowship of knights, and develops the rift in it which gives entrance to the baser aspirations of a Mordred—himself, significantly, the child of Arthur's lust. More naïve romances, innocent of such complexities of thought and feeling, see love as a beneficient magic, capable of literal healing: the protective ring of *Ywain and Gawain* can only operate in the context of love; only love, in *Eger and Grime*, can sustain Eger's cure.[125]

Because they establish that movement between humane and divine love which can be traced in the most complex of all medieval poetry—in the continuity between the Beatrice of the *Vita Nuova* and the Beatrice of the *Divina Commedia*—it is unjust to call these romances merely 'naïve'. Nevertheless, Dante wrote truly, *io spero di dire di lei quello che mai non fu detto d'alcuna* (I hope to say of her that which has never yet been said of any woman).[126] English medieval literature certainly has no Beatrice: even the child of *Pearl*, who fulfils a similar role, reflects the relation of father to daughter, rather than man to woman. Nevertheless, the continuity between romance, faith and spiritual vision is sensed not only by the secular imagination, but by the religious also. The medieval preacher likens Christ to a knight, who sets out to restore to the soul her heritage, on condition that she will love, and, if he dies, remember, him.[127] The author of that intimate thirteenth-century manual of instruction for ancresses, the *Ancrene Wisse*, describes the love of Christ through the story of a king, who sustains his beleaguered and ungrateful lady with every means at his disposal, and, when she still refuses his hand in marriage, offers her his life itself, in the hope that, if she cannot love him living, she may find it in her heart to love him dead.[128] The mysterious chivalric lament, 'Lully, lulley, lully, lulley,/The fawcon hath born my mak away', fulfils its meaning when religious impulse adds two final lines, and identifies the bleeding knight: 'And by that bedes side ther stondeth a ston,/"Corpus Christi" wreten theron.'[129]

The imagination of the later Middle Ages may, to a large extent, be dominated by a *contemptus mundi* which, whatever its didactic intention, does much to obstruct the continuity between body and spirit, between this life and the next. It is nevertheless true that nearly all the greatest poetry runs counter to this intention. Chaucer, whilst limiting himself fairly strictly to this life, never holds it in contempt: *The Parliament* is not satisfied with the rejections of Scipio's Dream, where it warms to the conclave of Nature. Langland and the *Gawain*-poet, if less content with this world, assert its value in affirming its continuity with the next: the lost child, when found there, is a pearl of far greater price, whilst in *Piers Plowman* earthly 'kind' may expand to embrace the Creator himself.[130] The separation of body and soul in the grave may cast a retrospective shadow over life; but the Incarnation, in which the divine assumes human flesh, reunites body and spirit; for the flesh that it assumes can survive death itself, and, through that victory, extends to all mankind the promise of ultimate unity.

III

Age and its Perspectives

[Delit] 'est de touz maus la racine,
si com Tulles le determine
ou livre qu'il fist *de Viellece*,
qu'il loe et veust plus que Jeunece,
car Jeunece boute home et fame
en touz periz de cors et d'ame.

    . . .

Jeunece met home es folies,

    . . .

Mes Viellece les en resache.

    . . .

Mes mal emploie son servise,
car nus ne l'aime ne ne prise,
au mains jusqu'a ce, tant an sai,
qu'i la vosist avoir an sai.'[1]

([Lust] 'is the root of all evils, as Tully establishes in the book he wrote *On Old Age*, which he praises and values above Youth, for Youth impels men and women into every peril of body and soul. Youth prompts men to folly, but Age retrieves them from it. But its services are badly received, for no one, so far as I know, loves and prizes Age sufficiently to want it for himself.')

As Reason suggests in the *Roman de la Rose*, a remedy for the follies of Youth can be found in the experience of Age; but, however sound that suggestion, it is likely to go unheeded, since no one appreciates the virtues of the state sufficiently to embrace it voluntarily. The writers of the Middle Ages are certainly not disposed to find, in the perspective afforded by the close of life, that 'long hoped for calm, the autumnal serenity/And the wisdom of age'; whilst the spectacle of personified decrepitude, though invariably admonitory, is as rarely elevating. As the debates between the Ages indicate, the retrospective view of Elde upon Youth is more often the opposition of an irreconcilable point of view, than the constructive, because continuous, succession of experience to innocence.

Age is presented in many ways in the literature of the Middle Ages: it can be an inward state of vexed reflection, or an outward spectacle, sometimes macabre, sometimes comic; it can, on the one hand, be a prototype of Death, or, on the other, the realization of God's plan in human history. Only in the last instance does it express that 'long hoped for calm', and even there this derives from the fulfilment, not of personal life, but of an impersonal destiny: thus Simeon, receiving the child Jesus in his arms, rejoices for mankind as a whole, 'Lord, now lettest thou they servant depart in peace, according to thy word: for mine eyes have seen thy salvation.' But to lives which are merely personal, Elde is a condition which fearfully marks the wastage of years, not their completion. The figure of Elde in *The Parlement of the Thre Ages*, whose craven prayers are dictated by a narrow self-concern, gives this attitude vivid expression:

> The thirde was a laythe lede lenyde one his syde,
> A beryne bownn alle in blake, with bedis in his hande;
> Croked and courbede, encrampeschett for elde;
> Alle disfygured was his face, and fadit his hewe,
> His berde and browes were blanchede full whitte,
> And his hare one his hede hewede of the same.
> He was ballede and blynde, and alle babirlippede,
> Totheles and tenefull, I telle yowe for sothe;
> And ever he momelide and ment and mercy he askede,
> And cried kenely one Criste and his crede sayde,
> With sawtries full sere tymes, to sayntes in heven;
> Envyous and angrye, and Elde was his name.
> I helde hym be my hopynge a hundrethe yeris of age,
> And bot his cruche and his couche he carede for no more.[2]

The Parlement itself belongs to the latter half of the fourteenth century, but this figure is not the creation of those post-plague years. Harley MS 2253 contains an 'Old Man's Prayer', which cannot be later than *c.* 1310; yet it is not unlike Dunbar's 'Meditation in Winter', written at the close of the fifteenth century.[3] Horror of age is expressed much earlier, in the Worcester Fragment, dating from the latter half of the twelfth century, and in a grim description of the ageing in the thirteenth-century *Cursor Mundi*.[4] One could, of course, go further back (as Reason does) without postulating a connected tradition: Horace, in the *Ars Poetica*, compares Age very unfavourably with the other periods of man's life, whilst the Elegies of Maximian, which became so popular in the Middle Ages, represent Elde both as a warning to Youth, and as

---

laythe lede ugly man   *lenyde* bent   *beryne* knight   *bownn* dressed   *babirlippede* thick-lipped   *tenefull* querulous   *momelide* mumbled   *ment* moaned   *sawtries* psalms   *sere* sundry   *hopynge* opinion

a state intrinsically contemptible and vindictive.[5] The following verse concludes a free thirteenth-century paraphrase of a Latin original:

> Iich may seien alas,
> That ich I-boren was;
> I-lived ich have to longe.
> Were ich mon so ich was,
> Min heien so grei so glas,
> Min her so feir bihonge,
> And ich hire hevede bi the trasce
> In a derne place,
> To meken and to monge;
> Ne sholde hoe nevere at-witen
> Min helde ne me bifliten,
> Wel heye I shulde hire honge.[6]

It is thus as the inheritor of a long tradition that Age stands first in the company of Death: his condition of physical decay anticipates the grave; he is a living reminder, in the temporal world, of man's mortality. If the Pride of Life is, for the later Middle Ages, the prototype of spiritual death, then 'babirlippede Elde' is its physical equivalent. A contemporary reader may find his harsh treatment at the hands of medieval writers more acceptable than their rejection of the boisterous Pride of Life, but both are equally the product of a dichotomy between body and spirit; for, where the second is free, the first is tied to temporality and corruption:

Anima autem, ad quam pertinet spiritualis nativitatis et spiritualis aetatis perfectio, immortalis est: et potest, sicut tempore senectutis spiritualem nativitatem consequi, ita tempore juventutis et pueritiae consequi perfectam aetatem; quia hujusmodi corporales aetates animae non praejudicant.[7]

(The soul, however, to which belongs a spiritual birth and a spiritual prime, is immortal: it is capable of spiritual birth in bodily age, and of achieving its prime in the years of youth and childhood, because the ages of the body do not determine those of the soul.)

As in his definition of the Pride of Life, Aquinas' words can move readily into a renaissance context, but their spirit cannot; for achievement in the body is for him clearly distinct from accomplishment in the soul.

The difference between medieval and renaissance attitude may be vividly illustrated by their distinct emphasis in tomb sculpture. The typical tomb of the later Middle Ages stresses the rift between body and

---

heien eyes   *ich hire hevede bi the trasce* I had theirs by the locks   *derne* secret
meken abase   *monge* maul   *at-witen* blame   *helde* age   *bifliten* chide

spirit by placing the grim *en transi* of the decaying corpse beneath the serene effigy of the clothed body lying in state. This dichotomy can only be bridged by the figure of the resurrected Christ, for the corpse itself— and, by implication, the whole of its earthly life—is reduced to the pitiable anonymity of common mortality, and depends for any future being totally on the mercy of its redeemer (Plate 32). The Renaissance reverses this development, transforming the body from *en transi* to *au vif*, but this apparently living figure does not, as in the early Middle Ages, seem to participate in eternal life (Plate 29), for the eternity to which it looks is that of undying fame, the prize of mortal achievement; that troubled hope for the soul's futurity is bypassed by a confidence in this life, not fulfilled in the expectation of heaven.[8] In *The Duchess of Malfi* (l. 1612–13) Bosola gives the Duchess an ironic account of this transition:

> DUCH. Why, do we grow phantasticall in our death-bed?
> Do we affect fashion in the grave?
>
> BOS. Most ambitiously: Princes images on their tombes
> Do not lie, as they were wont, seeming to pray
> Up to heaven: but with their hands under their cheekes,
> (As if they died of the tooth-ache)—they are not carved
> With their eies fix'd upon the starres; but as
> Their mindes were wholy bent upon the world,
> The selfe-same way they seeme to turne their faces.[9]   (Plate 31)

In the later Middle Ages and the Renaissance alike, Age and the Pride of Life are seen to have their connection; but in the former they are figures of physical and spiritual Death, in the latter, as in *Tamburlaine*, they testify in physical form to the perpetuation of a man through his achievements. The later view no doubt has more to recommend it to modern consciousness; but it must not be forgotten that the Renaissance, whilst restoring a confidence in this life, also restricts itself to the insights that this life affords.

It must, however, be admitted that the didactic impulse, which does so much to create the figure of Elde, affords few perspectives of the Resurrection: his sense of life is restricted and grudging, whilst his apprehension of Death serves to close, not to cleanse, 'the doors of perception'.[10] The preacher's stress upon the impotence and vanity of Elde is an effective deterrent to sin, where an emphasis upon the serenity and wisdom that years afford would, as de Meun's Reason remarks, prove an ineffective invitation. The failure of the body is thus allowed to throw a dark shadow over all worldly ambition, and moral decay is shown as the inevitable accompaniment of physical degeneration.[11] The characteristics of Elde depicted in *The Parlement* typify the figure in most other medieval literature, whether comic or serious in tone. Even the retrospect of Age upon the past (which, though less frequently found, permits a more subtle exploration of the condition than the outward spectacle) is more commonly one of vindictive disillusion than of experiential wisdom.[12]

This is to some extent true even of Henryson's *Testament of Cresseid*,[13] which, in the late fifteenth century, exhibits in many respects a humanistic sensibility; it is the more striking that the figure of the ageing poet, which introduces and sets the tone of the narrative, should remain so typically medieval. The 'doolie sessoun' in which the poem is written is both a literal season of bitter (though uncertain) weather 'in middis of the Lent', and also the period of declining life, of abstinence and repentance appropriate to 'ane man of age'. Lacking the readily kindled blood of Youth, the poet, a sometime devotee of Venus, retreats from the cold Winter's sky in which she reigns, to the security of his little room and its substitute comforts. He mends the fire, to provide the physical warmth his body lacks, tosses down his dram 'my spreitis to comfort', and resorts to a book—Chaucer's *Troilus and Criseyde*—to provide vicarious experience of the love of which he is no longer capable, and, in old man's fashion, 'To cut the winter nicht and mak it schort'. It is an endearing scene, but its attractive humanity should not disguise its connection with the confession of Lust in *Piers Plowman*:

> 'Ich lay by the lovelokeste, and loved hem nevere after.
> Whenne ich was old and hor, and hadde lore that kynde,
> Ich had lykynge to lauhe of lecherous tales.'   (C, VII, ll. 192–4)

Henryson's reading of Chaucer has, however, a further and more serious purpose: it is the retrospect of Age upon life, an endeavour, paralleling Cresseid's own, 'to remember and learn from the past'.[14] Unlike Chaucer's Troilus, Henryson and his Cresseid achieve their valuation of those things that life treasures in *this* world; theological and human judgements thus combine, as they fail to do in Chaucer's other-worldly epilogue. Nevertheless, as that sentence implies, the purpose of the retrospect remains medieval in that it has more to do with the life to come than with the achievement of the life lived. Cresseid's suffering and Henryson's age are redeemed by no sense of earthly fulfilment, but only by the opportunity that retrospect allows of repenting the vanity of temporal life as a condition of final salvation: 'Ane doolie sessoun to ane cairfull dyte/Suld correspond and be equivalent.'

The figure of Elde, if tending towards darker emotions than the contemplation of Age, and lacking its subtlety, is nevertheless dramatically versatile and conceptually commanding, with a range which extends

---

doolie dismal   *cairfull* painfull   *dyte* written work

from the basely human to the gravity and grandeur of the great Christian archetypes. Without for the moment exploring those two extremes, for the typical figure is modified in both, one can offer a general description of Elde, whose characteristics, despite the figure's range, are remarkably consistent. As a human, if generalized, figure—distinct, that is, from an abstract prototype of Death—the physical incapacities of Age are given their appropriate mental equivalents. The decline of the senses is especially emphasized, partly because physical and moral qualities readily blend at this point; but this emphasis is intensified by its relation to the signs of death, a theme which recurs in lyric poetry, and is lengthily described in medical treatises.[15] A world reduced to crutch and couch is a narrow one; bodily decay and decay of temper go hand in hand. It is no surprise that Langland should personify Avarice as an old man:

> And thanne cam Coveytise, can I hym noughte descryve
> So hungriliche and holwe sire Hervy hym loked.
> He was bitelbrowed and baberlipped also,
> With two blered eyghen, as a blynde hagge;
> And as a letheren purs lolled his chekes,
> Wel sydder than his chyn thei chiveled for elde;
> And as a bondman of his bacoun his berd was bidraveled.

(B, V, ll. 188–94)

Paradoxically, the assumption that the decline of the senses entails a moral decline is an implicit admission of the importance of sensual life. When, in one late medieval lyric, a bird laments that Age has bereft her of the four feathers of youth, strength, beauty and riches, one is reminded that the loss of the first three leave her with nothing 'to make her riches pleasant'.[16]

If the characterization of Elde is often reductive, there is, nevertheless, potential authority in the conception. When the realities of the Ages are dwelt upon, as in *The Parlement*, the figure of Elde emerges poorly from the contrast with Youth; yet it is Elde who describes the Nine Worthies, in a speech which seems intended to generalize the disputes of the three Ages of Man to a consideration of the three Ages of human history; his voice is thus given a final weight in the general retrospect of the poem, if not in one's immediate response to its participants. The authority with which Elde is invested derives, as in this instance, from predicament rather than personality: though characteristically so fearful of Death, his position on the brink of the grave assimilates him to his object of terror, and confers on him something of his master's authority.

Hervy i.e. a covetous man   *bitelbrowed* with prominent brows   *Wel sydder* Even now
chiveled trembled   *bidraveled* slobbered

The sermon's exemplum of the old man on his deathbed, forsaken by those closest to him who are interested only in their inheritance, is a commonplace throughout the Middle Ages (Plate 7): if a man is loved on account of his worldly goods, it is like the love of a hosteler—he is welcomed on arrival, but forgotten once the bill is paid.[17] Such instances are reductively domestic, but the same preacher's conclusion—'dethe and poverte hath new frendes'—can develop from a crabbed reflection on human nature, into the profound and moving loneliness of Everyman, summoned by Death to his 'longe iourney':

> Alas! I may well wepe with syghes depe!
> Now have I no maner of company
> To help me in my iourney and me to kepe;
>
> . . .
>
> The tyme passeth. Lorde, helpe, that all wrought!
> For though I mourne it avayleth nought;
> The day passeth, and is almoost ago.
> I wote not well what for to do.[18]

Everyman is dramatized purely through this predicament, rather than any individualized character, for the isolation of the protagonist is the dreaded familiar of every human heart; he is genuinely 'every man' in his journey to the grave.

This play, like the contemplation of Age, internalizes the condition; when it is externalized, as an adumbration of each man's death, a constant reminder to spectator or reader that it is his eternal, not his temporal, condition that is of ultimate significance, Elde becomes, as in *Piers Plowman* and DeGuilleville's *Pilgrimage*, the ally and messenger of Death itself.[19] Langland's personification of Elde has, in an abstract form, all the human characteristics of Age delineated in his Avarice; but this does not prevent him from figuring appropriately in the apocalyptic Vision of Anti-Christ, where 'Elde the hore was in the vaunt-warde,/ And bar the baner by-fore Deth, by right he hit claymede.'[20] As so often in *Piers Plowman*, the personified figure and the inward state are inextricably connected, and the grandeur of Death's standard bearer can mingle with the personal lament of the ageing Will, which is yet a lament for all human decay:

> And of the wo that ich was yn, my wif hadde reuthe,
> And wisshede wel witerlyche that ich were in hevene.
> For the lyme that she lovede me for, and leef was to feele,
> And a nyghtes nameliche, when we naked were,
> Ich ne myghte in none manere maken hit at heore wille,
> So Elde and hue hit hadde a-feynted and forbete.   (C, XXIII, ll. 193–8)

---

vaunt-warde vanguard   *witerlyche* truly   *a-feynted* enfeebled   *forbete* beaten down

The dramatic range of this figure can be vividly illustrated from Chaucer, whose poetry contains both the characterized figure of Elde, in the Reeve and the Merchant,[21] and its movement into a prototype of Death in the Old Man of *The Pardoner's Tale*. Significantly, Age in the first (its characterized) form is in Chaucer a teller, like Youth, not a character in a tale: it is an attitude of mind, splenetic, defensive, disappointed and vindictive, which colours the tale subsequently told. Yet neither the Reeve's story nor the Merchant's dramatizes the narrator in quite the way that the Squire's does; both their tales have more intrinsic coherence and grasp upon the attention of the audience. Appropriately enough, the youthful romance imagination is self-engrossed and self-delighting, fully engaged in personal presentation; by contrast, the imagination of Elde is jaundiced with the self, and strains to engross the audience in its composite disillusion: didactic and human propensities coincide. The Reeve's grudge against the Miller, which prompts him to tell his tale, is not merely professional; it is the resentment of impotence and fading powers at the presence of robust vigour and pleasure: ' "for thogh oure myghte be goon,/Oure wyl desireth folie evere in oon." '[22] His tale, so comparable with the Miller's in form, event and point, is thus quite different in tone and in impression. The Miller's bawdy story is funny, as a tale told in a pub might be; its vigour is a form of inebriation which disarms prudery. But substantially the same tale, told in a different context, can be merely disgusting: the Reeve, whose substitutes for vigour are ' "Avauntyng, liyng, anger, coveitise" ', the ' "foure sparkles [that] longen unto eelde" ', tells a tale that is repellent. It is not merely that the Miller's sexual slapstick is transformed into an enervated salaciousness, but that this view extends to the whole of life: ' "For sikerly, whan I was bore, anon/Deeth drough the tappe of lyf and leet it gon." '[23] This is recognizably the preacher's perspective; but for Chaucer it is clearly that of a restricted and pitiable sensibility.

The Merchant's tale of January and May is, like the Reeve's, much more than a gloss upon the text that ' "wedded men lyven in sorwe and care" '; because the Merchant's notion of the married man is reduced to that of January, unequally matched with a much younger wife, that union itself becomes an expression of senility. Although the teller denies that his tale is autobiographical—' "but of myn owene soore,/For soory herte, I telle may namoore" '—his voice permeates his narrative; the reference of one of his characters, Justinus, to the Wife of Bath, enforces that point.[24] As with the Reeve, a dislike of the condition of Age becomes a distaste for life in general. One line in *The Squire's Tale*, 'Diverse folk diversely they demed', curiously echoes the Merchant's lines,

---

Avauntyng Boasting *sparkles* little sparks *sikerly* certainly

'Diverse men diversely hym tolde/Of mariage manye ensamples olde';
but where the Squire allows for all varieties of human opinion, and concludes his couplet, 'As many heddes, as manye wittes ther been', the
Merchant allows only for one, that of Justinus, who echoes his own
opinion:

> 'Preyse whoso wole a wedded mannes lyf,
> Certein I fynde in it but cost and care
> And observances, of alle blisses bare.'[25]

The Old Man of *The Pardoner's Tale* is, in contrast, an emblematic
figure, and the tale which includes him is in no sense personal; it is a
sermon, whose impersonal authority reaches to the heart (and thence to
the pocket) of everyman. Its story of the three rioters and death is not
elevated, but its immediate conviction and relevance gives its subject
authority, as the inescapable destiny of all men. The cosmic cold of
Saturn's voice, the astrological prototype of Age in *The Knight's Tale*,
bites less deeply than the chill of the Old Man's speech, which is closer
to contemplative than vindictive Elde in its quiet personal ring. The
position of the three young men resembles an early version of the Faustus
story, in which Faustus sells his soul to the Devil on condition that he
receives three warnings of the imminence of Death to allow him time
for repentance; each time the warning is offered in the form of an old
man, a sight so familiar that Faustus fails to register its significance.[26]
The Pardoner's three youths are similarly impervious to the three warnings that come their way—the corpse of their contemporary, the presence
of pestilence, and their encounter with the Old Man himself. They are
distinctly Pride of Life figures, confident in the moment, anticipating a
future of ' "myrthe and jolitee" ', who, in words proper only to the
Christ of the Harrowing of Hell, commit the King of Life's blasphemy
in regarding Death as a corporeal enemy whom they can destroy: ' "He
shall be slayn, he that so manye sleeth." '[27] When the proudest of the
three challenges the Old Man—' "Why lyvestow so longe in so grete
age?" '—he receives a reply whose quiet chill blinds him to its relevance:

> 'For I ne kan nat fynde
> A man, though that I walked into Ynde,
> Neither in citee ne in no village,
> That wolde chaunge his youthe with myn age;
> And therfore moot I han myn age stille,
> As longe tyme as it is Goddes wille.
> Ne Deeth, allas! ne wol nat han my lyf
> Thus walke I, lyk a restelees kaityf,
> And on the ground, which is my moodres gate,
> I knoke with my staf, bothe erly and late,
> And seye "Leeve mooder, leet me in!" ' (ll. 721–31)

The skeleton in Holbein's Dance of Death, who helpfully supports Age by the elbow as he steps down into his grave, is the answer to this Old Man's prayer (Plate 28b).

The three rioters, with some justification, accuse the Old Man of being Death's spy; for, as the tale reveals, death has no personified being, but is the inevitable end which awaits each man. By centring on the figure of Age, and denying the existence of the abstract figure of Death— Chaucer never portrays one—the Pardoner makes death the more terrifying in its omnipresent invisibility. This terror is increased by the presence of the Pardoner himself in the tale. Exceptionally, for the Middle Ages, none of Chaucer's pilgrims is either wholly ideal or absolutely contemptible; even the Pardoner, though traditionally numbered amongst the 'rogues', has redeeming qualities. Yet that particular quality which the tale makes most apparent—his considerable religious and psychological insight—intensifies both the darkness of his character and the dark perceptions of his address. When his affective appeal to the heart is redirected to the pocket, thus leading the Host to indulge in that blasphemy which the sermon has warned against, the Pardoner himself becomes an example of the Pride of Life, another impervious rioter who ignores the clear adumbrations of death and judgement which his own insight has afforded the pilgrims.

The typical figure of Age is thus fully explored in Chaucer, though one of its extremes—that of Christian archetype as in Simeon—is characteristically absent from his writing. The other extreme, the comic figure which has not yet been discussed, is predictably frequent; for it is easy to see how the personification of Elde, when used in the less than serious context of many of Chaucer's characters and tales, can move readily into a figure of fun. Even didactic poetry may verge close to humour, as do these lines from a fifteenth-century lyric:

> For than wole no thing us availe
> but oure bedis and oure crucche,
>
>   .   .   .
>
> & than wole sijknes us assaile
> Til it hath made us lijk a wrecche,
> & than may we do no greet traveile
> But summtyme grone, & sumtyme grucche,
> And sumtyme clawe for scabbe & icche;
>
>   .   .   .
>
> God sende us paciens in oure olde age![28]

The realism of this description transforms it from the darkly sober into the grimly humorous; when this impotent figure is juxtaposed with that of Youth, as it so often is in the January and May situation of unequal marriage, then the theme has clear comic potential. The savage tone of *The Merchant's Tale* can moderate into the warmer humour of the Miller's

John and his Alisoun, or the Wife of Bath and her youthful Jankyn.
The credulity of John, in believing Nicholas's prophecy of a second Flood,
and his anxiety to preserve his beloved Alisoun from its waters, prevents
him (like January) from perceiving his wife's unfaithfulness; in *The
Merchant's Tale* this is, however, an additional ironic twist, whilst it
appears, in the Miller's, as a fortunate turn of events.[29]

It is significant that, in its frequent references to Noah, *The Miller's
Tale* should clearly draw upon the drama's tradition of a comic and aged
Noah, for the cycles contain many examples of comic Elde, the more
surprisingly since these same characters may fill exalted roles in Christian
history. Not only Noah, on whose virtue the survival of the whole
human race depends, but Joseph, the foster-father of Christ himself,
are often presented as garrulous, plaintive dodderers. The versatility
of Elde's potential is here graphically illustrated, for Noah and Joseph
both bridge its extremes of triviality and elevation (Plate 9). Noah, as
a crucial figure in Old Testament history, both looks back to Adam and
prefigures Christ, and the dignity of such a figure is sufficiently acknowledged in the funniest play of them all, that of the Wakefield master.
There is nothing laughable in Noah's dialogue with God:

> NOE. A! benedicite! what art thou that thus
> Tellys afore that shall be? thou art full mervelus!
> Tell me, for charite, thi name so gracius.
> DEUS. My name is of dignyte and also full glorius
>   To knawe.
> I am god most myghty,
> Oone god in trynyty,
> Made the and ich man to be;
>   To luf me well thou awe.[30]

This is Noah in his typological role: the domestic and actual Noah,
persuading his unwilling shrew of a wife abroad the ark, cuts a very
different figure. The measured, antiphonal exchange of the deity and
humanity's representative, alters into the ding-dong of domestic discord:

> UXOR. . . . wifis that ar here,
>   ffor the life that thay leyd,
>   Wold thare husbandis were dede,
>   ffor, as ever ete I brede,
>   So wold I oure syre were.
>
> NOE. Yee men that has wifis, whyls they ar yong,
> If ye luf youre lifis, chastice thare tong:
> Me thynk my hert ryfis, both levyr and long,

---

ryfis splits   *levyr* liver   *long* lungs

To se sich stryfis wedmen emong;
 Bot I
As have I blys,
shall chastyse this.
 UXOR. Yit may ye mys,
  Nicholl nedy! (*T*, III, ll. 392–405)

The language of these plays, even in the hands of the Wakefield master, often contrasts poorly with the cosmic range of their conception; but there can be little doubt that the dramatists themselves do add to that range in ways that are not always implicit in the Scripture and its tradition. The movement between the pettiness of man's everyday being and the sublimity of his eternal role is their characteristic and distinguished creation.

The comedy of Joseph has, however, a more complex theological history than that of Noah. The early Church, perhaps aware of the danger of his being taken as the actual father of Christ, gives him only a minor role; his cult does not develop until the twelfth century, and remains local until the fifteenth.[31] The stress placed in the Apocrypha upon his age, his chastity and his surprise at Mary's pregnancy, no doubt represents a determination to exclude the possibility of actual paternity (Plate 9): thus, in the *Protevangelium* Joseph refuses his miraculous election as Mary's husband, 'saying: I have sons, and I am an old man, but she is a girl: lest I became a laughing-stock to the children of Israel'.[32] Kolve has suggested that his comic role in the mysteries reflects a related desire to present him as an inadequate father for Christ, and Huizinga remarks that the figure of Joseph becomes increasingly caricatured as, in the later Middle Ages, that of the Virgin becomes correspondingly exalted.[33] Certainly the sober opinion of the Knight of the Tour Landry seems comic—to our eyes at least: 'God wished that she should marry that saintly man Joseph, who was old and upright, for God wished to be born in wedlock, to comply with the current legal requirements, to avoid gossip.'[34]

Whatever the cause, its result in the drama is the creation of a classical January and May situation, played out with a delicacy of sentiment which humanizes the relationship of Joseph and Mary, without impairing the elevation of their role. The *Ludus Coventriae* elaborates through a number of plays the surprise of Joseph at Mary's pregnancy, and their innocence of carnal intercourse.[35] The inspiration of this cycle is, however, chiefly doctrinal, and although it may achieve its own dramatic triumphs (as in The Woman Taken in Adultery), the full quality of the relationship of Joseph and Mary is more finely caught in the rather more conventional Flight into Egypt of the York Cycle:

MAR. Allas! Joseph, for grevaunce grete!
Whan shall my sorowe slake,
For I wote noght whedir to fare.
JOS. To Egipte talde I the lang are.
MAR. Whare standith itt?
Fayne wolde I witt.
JOS.   What wate I?
I wote not where it standis.
MAR. Joseph, I aske mersy,
Helpe me oute of this lande.
JOS. Nowe certis, Marie, I wolde full fayne.

    . . .

MAR. Joseph, full wo is me,
For my dere sone so swete.
JOS. I pray the Marie, happe hym warme,
And sette hym softe that he not syle,
And yf thou will ought ese thyn arme,
Gyff me hym, late me bere hym awhile.
MAR. I thanke you of youre grete goode dede.[36]

Feminine plaintiveness, obstinacy, unreason, sentiment and dependence, meet in Joseph a mixture of restrained irritability and protective tenderness. In this domestic scene, the comic figure of an old man fostering another's child becomes one of the finest creations of late medieval religious sensibility.

In all the various roles hitherto described, Elde makes many appearances in the later Middle Ages; but his most serene characterization, as the fulfilment of human life, is relatively rare in literature. Art, on the other hand, is clearly much attracted to this presentation of Age: many magnificent figures of Joseph and the prophets can be found in cathedral sculpture, and, on the plane of common humanity, Calendar illuminations of January and February often show Age enjoying those comforts— fires and feasting—appropriate both to the season and to his time of life (Plates 13, 14a and b, 16a). The literary examples which follow belong, however, to elevated rather than ordinary human life, for the notion that the actual condition of Age could be one of serenity and appropriate beauty seems almost wholly absent. Though professions of tenderness and respect for the old are not infrequent, their tone is rather one of compassion for the weak than of veneration for the wise.[37]

Nevertheless, a number of scriptural figures are endowed with a fullness of years which has no hint of comedy. This may, in most cases, be no more than a reflection of biblical statement; yet there is some additional suggestion that Lamech and Simeon are emancipated from the folly of old men because, unlike Joseph and Noah, they are con-

---

happe wrap up   *syle* drop

ceived almost totally in their historical or figurative roles.[38] The curious
interlude between Lamech and Adolescens in the *Ludus Coventriae*
Play of Noah is a case in point[39] (Plate 8). The Flood itself, with a
traditionally comic Noah and Wife, does not close that chapter of human
history with sufficient finality; one's sense is, on the contrary, of irrepressible human continuity. By shifting into a different and more
abstract convention, in order to represent the destruction of the first
age, in the person of Cain, at the inadvertent hands of blind Age mis-
guided by the eyes of Youth, the dramatist, with some intellectual skill,
reminds his audience that the mystery cycle is at once that of human
history and of divine design: when Age, in despair at this unconscious
murder, destroys Adolescens, the meaningless cycles of human action
are cogently contrasted with the significance of God's continuum.[40]

Simeon, whose recognition of Christ marks another stage in the development of historical time and spiritual fulfilment, also represents the
old order which gives place to the new as the child grants him his
dimittis—those words which become the prayer of the Church over the
body of every Christian. The Simeon of the Towneley Plays is presented
as a dramatically aged figure, 'So old on lyfe know I none':

> Myn ees are woren both marke and blynd;
> Myn and is short, I want wynd;
> Thus has age dystroed my kynd,
>   And reft myghtis all;
> Bot shortly mon I weynd away;
> what tyme ne when, I can not say,
> ffor it is gone full many a day
>   Syn dede began to call.   (XVII, ll. 33–40)

The speech has all the characteristics of Elde, but it is free from vindictiveness, and manages, though narrowly, to avoid comedy; its simple
language succeeds in conveying the weariness of a figure burdened not
only with his own years, but with those of history. The Herod play of the
Digby collection, whose Simeon affirms that, through the Harrowing of
Hell, God has come 'To chaunge thynges that are transitory', completes
the possibilities inherent in the Gospel story.[41] The epoch of the old
law receives from the new that fresh life which sets a period to man's
mortality; in asking for death, Simeon now pleads for eternal life. The
fall of Herod marks the failure of the body—'my legges ffalter, I may
no lenger stande'; but it is closely followed by Simeon's confident
affirmation of the Incarnation: 'ffrom the sterrid hevyn, lord, thu list
come down/In-to the Closett of a pure virgyn.' When the old man takes

---

marke dim

the child in his arms, his homely joy lifts the burden of age: 'My spretes Ioyen, thou art so amyable,/I am nat wery to loke on thi face.' This Simeon, once the child has come, wastes no words on the detail of physical decay; such speeches are appropriate only to the wicked who, like Herod, can look for joy only in this life. The death of the body has lost its importance for the old man, so certainly are his eyes fixed upon the 'dwellynge [Christ] shalt purchase,/brighter than berall outher clere cristall'.[42]

It is the condition of mortality that makes Elde despicable or comic; as such, the figure is a comment merely upon the physical condition of man. The fact of physical decay, when generalized as an insight into human history, can, it is true, have a tragic nobility; but I can find no example in English literature at all comparable with Dante's *gran veglio*, whose curiously sculptured body is a monument to the ages of humanity, but whose living tears are the sources of those rivers which water Hell. This figure stands in Crete, within Mount Ida, *che già fu lieta/D'acqua e di fronde* (which once was glad with water and with leaves), but is now *diserta come cosa vieta* (deserted like a forbidden thing).[43] These lines express the temporal fate of humankind, where the great archetypes of English literature represent man's eternal context in God's plan. Nature is, for example, sometimes described as very old, but she is rarely repellent for that reason; indeed, when her role as minister of divine order is affirmed, her appearance of perennial youth expresses her fulfilment, within time, of God's timeless design.[44]

This duality of response could be generalized to the conception of Age as a whole. The medieval sensibility, with reason, is acutely conscious of bodily imperfection, and is, in consequence, prone to see life as a process of continual decay. Egeus' verdict in *The Knight's Tale*— ' "This world nys but a thurghfare ful of wo,/And we been pilgrymes, passynge to and fro" '—is that of Age, though it can be taken as a comment of a kind on the whole Canterbury journey.[45] But it is a comment of only *one* kind, applying to man's physical nature and temporal being, seen in a somewhat jaundiced perspective. There is a contrary type of observation, which, though less frequent, can see men, not as passing through time to the grave, but out of time into eternity: that is the spiritual meaning of pilgrimage. The first and negative perception is one of which a great poet like Langland can be acutely conscious; his awareness—in the abstract, in the flesh and in the heart—of the miseries of Age has already been illustrated.[46] Nevertheless, Piers himself is shown to age before he sets off on the pilgrimage to Truth:

'For now ich am old and hor and have of myn owene,
To penaunces and to pilgrimages ich wol passe with othere;
For-thi ich wolle, er ich wende, do wryten my byquyste.'

(C, IX, ll. 92–4)

Piers' will divides the things of time from those of eternity; his soul is given to God, his goods to his wife, and his body to the Church, which, mediating temporal and eternal, will care for his 'caroyne' until the general Resurrection. Christ did not live to suffer the indignities of Age, but Piers, who comes to represent his human nature, embraces the close of man's life, and redeems it by indicating its true purpose. To be 'old and hor' is not the end, but a new beginning: it is the time appointed to set out on the pilgrimage to Truth and to eternal life.

The perspectives of Elde receive their fullest expression in writing concerned, either implicitly or explicitly, with the Ages of Man. Reason's conviction, in the *Roman de la Rose*, that *Jeunece met home es folies . . . Mes Viellece les en resache* (Youth prompts men to folly, but Age retrieves them from it), often provides the impulse for works either structured around the perspectives of the Ages, or concerned to debate their separate merits. Youth, involved in the moment, inhabits a world whose horizons are restricted to the temporal; Elde, with the wisdom of experience behind him, the prospect of eternity before him, is in a position to achieve insights of more permanent value, because they are detached from ephemera. In his little poem, 'The Prais of Aige', Henryson makes this subject an old man's song:

> Wythin a garth, under a rede rosere,
> Ane ald man, and decrepit, herd I syng;
> Gay was the note, suete was the voce et clere:
> It was grete joy to here of sik a thing.
> 'And to my dome,' he said, in his dytyng,
> 'For to be yong I wald not, for my wis
> Off all this warld to mak me lord et king:
> The more of age the nerar hevynnis blis.'[47]

The music, however, has more gaiety than the words, ' "False is this warld, and full of variance" '; Aige may claim ' "The state of youth I repute for na gude" ', but Youth, as de Meun's Reason notes, is apt to make the same riposte to Elde. The world does not seem false to those who can still enjoy it, and this tension is vividly present in many works concerned with the Ages of Man. The imagination rejoices in Youth, and finds it far easier to present Elde as a deterrent and fearful warning, than as a perspective that opens upon wider horizons. Writers are thus more prone to present the views of different generations as an opposition of irreconcilable points of view, than as complementary and necessary stages in the journey towards 'hevynnis blis' (Plates 7, 13, 14a).

In the Ages of Man Elde is in consequence more often seen as the ally of Death and the antithesis of Youth and of Life, than as the completion of temporal, in preparation for eternal, existence. When the Ages are reduced to two, they become opposed voices in a debate which can reach no conclusion; they are the vexed polarities of a mutable world. The opening verses of Henryson's 'Ressoning betuix Aige and Yowth' are an instance of this opposition.[48] Where Yowth sings a 'sang that richt sweitly was sett: "O yowth, be glaid in to thy flowris grene" ', Aige inverts that refrain (in the inscription on his breast, for his voice is hoarse): ' "O yowth, thy flowris fedis fellone sone." ' In such confrontations, Youth and Elde can never agree: Youth, at the zenith of Fortune's wheel, believes, like Pride of Life, that the moment will last forever; Elde, at its nadir, can see only that all things are transitory and end in death (Plate 10). Youth's opposition elicits the narrowly temporal aspect of Elde: in Henryson's 'Ressoning', unlike his 'Prais of Aige', the old man loses his heavenly song. On the other hand, when paralleled with the four seasons or the twelve months of the year, the Ages can participate harmoniously in the natural cycle, which causes the plant to bud, to flower, to fruit, and finally to fade (Plate 10). One can sense this possibility even in the opposed refrains of Henryson's debate, for the spring of the flower and its fall belong to a continuous cycle. This sense of connection, underlying opposition, is subtly rendered when Aige and Yowth come finally to be heard as aspects of a single voice, for the closing lines of the poem affirm that perception:

> Of the sedullis the suthe quhen I had sene,
> Of trewth, me thocht, thay triumphit in thair tone:
> 'O yowth, be glaid in to thy flowris grene!
> O yowth thy flowris faidis fellone sone!'

The truth of the inscription is recognized, but it does not become exclusive, and if the poem does not offer the celestial perspective of the old man singing beneath the rose tree, it at least suggests that the Ages of Man do not mark meaningless stages in decline, but compose between them a natural harmony.

Henryson's poetry is written near the close of the fifteenth century, but the essence of his 'ressoning' can be found almost three centuries earlier, in *The Owl and the Nightingale*, one of the finest of early English poems, written *c.*1200.[49] Because the birds are identified with the seasons, the Owl with Winter, the Nightingale with Spring or Summer, the poem is primarily a seasonal debate, and is more appropriately discussed in that context.[50] But the birds have an obvious relation to Age and Youth, and whilst their seasonal relationship touches one aspect of Henryson's 'ressoning', the harsh croak of the Owl and her gloomy sentiments, the

---

fellone desperately   *sedullis* inscription

sweet song of the Nightingale and her delight in life, as clearly touch upon the other. The theme of the Ages could be readily paralleled in other early literature, and although, as in so many other instances, its darker aspects tend in the later Middle Ages to receive more stress than its bright ones, its essentials do not alter.[51]

A division of the Ages into the three periods of Youth, Middle Age and Elde can also occur in debate, as in *The Parlement of the Thre Ages*; but the triad is more commonly used for purposes of pattern or structure where they stress connection rather than opposition. The number three is, of course, charismatic, and the division into Ages a ready way of establishing diversity in unity: thus the three Magi, a popular subject both in art and literature, are often represented as young, middle-aged and old (before they become, instead or as well, white, yellow and black); so too are the Three Living and the Three Dead of the popular late medieval legend, where the corpses may mockingly echo, in the stages of their corruption, those distinct steps in their journey towards the grave which are depicted in the Living (Plates 9 and 25). In literature the pattern afforded by the three Ages may be used as an incidental motif, or as the structure of an entire work. Malory affords an example of the first, when Gawain and his two brothers are paired off with three ladies:

Aboven thereby was the hede of the streme, a fayre fountayne, and three damesels syttynge thereby. And than they rode to them and ayther salewed othir. And the eldyst had a garlonde of golde aboute her hede, and she was three score wyntir of age or more, and hir heyre was whyght undir the garlonde. The secunde damselle was of thirty wyntir of age, wyth a cerclet of golde about her hede. The thirde damesel was but fiftene yere of age, and a garlonde of floures aboute hir hede.[52]

It may be significant that, where the youngest lady wears perishable flowers, the middle-aged wears gold, and the eldest combines the perishable with the durable in her golden garland: nevertheless, one feels it is fortunate for Gawain that the oldest brother gets the youngest lady. The pattern here offered by the three Ages is satisfying, a characteristic of works secular rather than religious; thus the author of *The Prose Life of Alexander* observes soothingly:

Barnehed rejoyse it in sympilnesse, youthede in presumptuosnes, And grete elde in stabilnes. For wha will luke efter wysdome in a childe, In a yunge man stabillnes, or in an alde man wildenes?[53]

This sense that the Ages have complementary qualities, appropriate to the several stages of life, is largely absent from religious writing; where its authors see connections between the Ages, their unity is based upon the observation that all periods of life are, in their different ways, equally sinful:

Youth is but 'a day *of drirines*, because *muche filth, care and soroo is in it*': Middle age is 'a day *of besines*, because much toil and tribulation is in this middle-life': Old age is 'a day *of hevynes*, because great penalty, *soroo and seknes* is in this ultimate end'.[54]

When the three Ages are used, not as incidental motif, but as structure, this distinction between religious and secular writing still holds. A short lyric, like Lydgate's 'Prayer in Old Age',[55] may be composed around the sequence of the Ages, whilst a work on the scale of *The Knight's Tale* may use them as an integral form. Though a secular work, *The Knight's Tale* takes a grim view, on the whole, of human life; nevertheless, the Ages are seen to have complementary virtues, not merely differing vices as in Lydgate's poem. For all his tranquilly contemplative tone, the ageing monk of Bury regards youth as a period of 'grevous gyltes' and 'insolent outrage'; his 'mydle yeris,/When lust with fors was fresh' were equally 'Fer fro vertu, contrarye to resoun'; and if he is no longer equally sinful, this appears to be largely because he has lost the power to sin: 'Whenne febylnesse hath crokyd bak and chyne,/Currage and blode appalle, and wexe colde.'[56]

The division of the Ages into four (Plate 10) generally occurs on analogy with the seasons, into six on the model of the canonical hours, and into twelve when paralleled with the hours of the day or the months of the year. The distinction into seven is less obvious; it may derive from a neat division of man's allotted span of three score years and ten into its seven decades, and be reinforced by its theological charisma, expressed in the seven virtues and vices. The lower numerical distinctions of the Ages —into two, three or four—occur far more frequently in literature than the higher—into six, seven and twelve; the latter are most frequent in didactic writing, because their potential is expository rather than dramatic. Certainly the seven Ages of the morality play, *Mundus et Infans*, have an expository clarity, but prove inert as a structure for drama; and this criticism may hold true even in poetry, in 'The Mirror of the Periods of Man's Life' for example.[57] Another poem, included in the collection which contains 'The Mirror', and entitled 'This World is but a Vanitee', employs the twelve Ages much more succesfully, in a didactic sense.[58] Those divisions of the Ages which connect with the various natural cycles—with the seasons, the hours whether canonical or diurnal, and the months of the year—have, however, a more positive potential than those which do not. It is striking that Lydgate, who, when writing of two or three Ages, whether in a religious or in a secular vein, is so negative in tone, can give a very different impression when linking the stages of man's life to the due passage of the day, and the unhurried procession of the canonical hours:

> Tryste is not best that cometh afforne his tyme,
>   Ner hasty clymbynge to grete possession.
> Nexte Phebus upryste the next oure is prime,
>   And mydday folewuth by iyste succession.
> Caste weel thyn houres by revolucyoun,
> Dethys horlage wul not passe his tyde,
>   Be-war that complyne, preferre not his sesoun,
> He hastuth wele that wysely can abyde.[59]

This poem is aptly named 'A Ditty upon Haste', for, taken in due measure, the Ages complement each other and compose a sum of tranquil wisdom; when their succession is seen as a part of the diurnal course, of man's little waking day, even 'Dethys horlage', though not to be anticipated, loses much of its terror, becoming 'that complyne', the protective prayer which guards the Christian soul from the perils of night.

As will already be apparent, the Ages of Man come to mirror more intricate distinctions and connections within the large stages of human life. In the *Convivio*, for example, Dante distinguishes four Ages and sees in each certain characteristic connections:

La prima è *Adolescenza*, che s'appropria al *caldo* e all' *umido*; la seconda si è *Gioventute*, che s'appropria al *caldo* e al *secco*; la terza si è *Senettute*, che s'appropria al *freddo* e al *secco*; la quarta si è *Senio*, che s'appropria al *freddo* e all' *umido* . . .

E queste parti si fanno simigliantemente nell' anno, in *Primavera*, in *Estate*, in *Autunno* e in *Inverno*. E nel dì ciò è infino alla *Terza*, e poi fino alla *Nona*, lasciando la *Sesta* nel mezzo di parte, per la ragione che si discerne, e poi fino al *Vespro* e dal Vespro innanzi.[60]

(The first is Adolescence, which connects with the hot and moist; the second is Youth, which connects with the hot and dry; the third is Age, which connects with the cold and dry; the fourth is Senility, which connects with the cold and moist. And these parts occur similarly in the year, in Spring, in Summer, in Autumn and in Winter. And in the day—that is, up to Terce, and then up to Nones, omitting Sext between these parts, for an obvious reason, and then up to Vespers, and from Vespers onwards.)

There is little distinction between Dante's scheme and that of the Pythagoreans, nearly two thousand years earlier; they did not, of course, make the connection with the canonical hours, but their matching of the Ages with qualities and seasons is identical.[61] If the Middle Ages did little to alter this scheme, they did elaborate it in certain ways, and a pattern of planetary influence, first established by Arab writers in the ninth century, is of some importance (Plate 6). The humours, which the Pythagoreans associated with the Ages, seasons and qualities, of blood (sanguine), yellow bile (choleric), black bile (melancholic), and phlegm (phlegmatic), were further paralleled with Jupiter, Mars, Saturn and the Moon or Venus[62] (Plate 11). Dante apart, many medieval writers began their cycle with the phlegmatic nature, and ended it with the melancholic, thus yielding this general scheme:

Season	Age	Planet	Disposition
Spring	Boyhood	Venus	Phlegmatic
Summer	Youth	Jupiter	Sanguine
Autumn	Middle Age	Mars	Choleric
Winter	Age	Saturn	Melancholic

In his 'Pageant of Knowledge' Lydgate thus connects the influence of the planets with the disposition of the Ages they govern:

Satourn disposith to malencolye,
　Iubiter reiseth men to hih noblesse,
And sturdy *Mars* to striff, werre, and envye,
　　　　　. . .
The *moone* mutable, now glad, and now drepyng,
　And gery *Venus*, ful of newfangilnesse.

'The *sangueyn* man', he says, 'hath hardynesse', is generous and loving: 'The *fflewmatyk*' is, however, slow, depressed, white-faced and rudel spoken; 'The *coleryk*' subtle, deceitful, lean, yellow, very bad tempered and thoroughly wasteful; whilst the '*malencolik*' is malicious, deceitful, and ill-humoured. The possibilities, sanguine men apart, are not particularly cheering, and the refrain of his 'Pageant'—'Fewe men be stable heer in ther livyng'—comes as no surprise.[63] One can detect here ample reason for the opposition of the Ages, and the arbitrarily mutable world constructed between them, through which a man can choose no secure path since his nature is externally determined. But the association of the Ages with the seasons and the elements (water, air, fire and earth, respectively), can also be made to point to the harmonious sum of the parts of a man's life, because they form the constituents of a cycle at once natural and necessary.

Since contention is less cheering than harmony, it seems preferable to examine first those debates in which the Ages oppose each other, and to conclude with those in which they are seen as complementary. Of the form of debate, Chambers remarks: 'English literature, indeed, had had from Anglo-Saxon days a natural affinity for the dialogue form, and presents side by side with the translated *débats* others—*strifs* or *estrifs* is the English term—of native origin.'[64] The debate is traditionally a form of political controversy, conducted between two types or personified abstractions, in which the decision may sometimes be referred to an arbiter. *The Owl and the Nightingale* and *Winner and Waster* both invoke referees, but in neither does that really serve to settle the question. In the earlier poem, the two disputants agree to consult one Master Nicholas, but the dreamer awakes before they find him; in the later, the argument is referred to the King, but here, though his sentences on Winner and Waster are clear enough, his judgements of them are not, and his impartiality is moreover very questionable.[65] Ambiguity, even in cases such as these, does suggest that the debate form was intended to maintain incompatible points of view rather than to resolve them, and although the attractiveness of Youth may encourage a modern reader to take his side, this seems to run contrary to the medieval rules of the game: it is the poise between points of view, not the victory of one side over the other, that calls for remark in such poems.

The difficulty of deciding between Winner and Waster is enforced by the medieval equation of the sin of prodigality with that of avarice.[66] Superficially, Waster may seem the more attractive of the two, especially when he argues:

'With oure festes and oure fare we feden the pore;
It es plesynge to the Prynce that paradyse wroghte;
When Cristes peple hath parte hym payes alle the better
Then here ben hodirde and hidde and happede in cofers,
That it no sonn may see thurgh seven wyntter ones.' (ll. 295–9)

This figure of Youth has an appropriate expansiveness, but the practical retort of Winner, in Middle Age, has its social force:

'His londes liggen alle ley, his lomes aren solde,
Downn bene his dowfehowses, drye bene his poles;
The devyll wounder the wele he weldys at home,
Bot hungere and heghe horses and howndes full kene!' (ll. 234–7)

For the great mass of the labouring poor, who have no voice in the poem, the choice is one of contrasting evils: the beams of Winner's house may sag beneath the weight of the bacon which hangs from them, but it is the rats, not the poor, or even Winner's own household, who reap the benefit; on Waster's estate, the belly may from time to time be glutted with his lavish bounty, but the price of such plenty is a long future fast, as his lands fall to rack and ruin. The alternatives of regular pittance and irregular dearth present no real choice, for both end in semi-starvation.

---

hodirde covered up *happede* wrapped up *ley* untilled *lomes* tools *dowfehowses* dove-cotes *poles* pools *devyll wounder* devil a wonder!

D

The King, himself a Waster on a national scale, gives even less thought than the disputants to the miseries of the great mass of his subjects, for he reserves the goods of Winner for his own use, and detains Waster in London, rather than returning him to the proper management of his estate.

The poem is curiously oblique, in that it does little to make this implication explicit, and it is interesting to gloss its two disputants, and their arbitrator, Edward III, from Langland's open comments in *Piers Plowman*. Both poets clearly 'holde hym bot a fole that fightis whils flyttynge may helpe', and whilst much of the poetry of the period speaks positively of the conquests in France, Langland overtly, and the poet of *Winner and Waster* implicitly, are distinct in their condemnation.[67] In the army of Winner are assembled the merchants and the major orders of the Church, those who exploit the kingdom, and are exploited in return by the King. The army of Waster is composed more attractively of heroic Youth, but the relative brevity of this second description indicates that the poet has little admiration for any military undertaking; the brave army of Waster, like that of the King, does lay waste.[68] Whether from Winner, Waster or King, the people are bound to suffer.

In *Piers Plowman* Lady Meed, familiar of all wasters, cynosure of all winners, comments disapprovingly on the advice proferred by Conscience to the King during the Normandy campaign:

> 'Sothliche, thou Concience, thou conseildest him thennes,
> To leve that lordschupe for a luitel selver,
> That is the riccheste reame that reyn over hoveth!
>   Hit bicometh for a kyng that kepeth a reame
> To give meede to men that mekeliche him serven.'   (A, III, ll. 199–203)

But Conscience is well aware that no kingdom, based upon bribery and extortion at home and abroad, can protect the interests of the people; the poem as a whole censures equally those, like Avarice, who keep the goods of this world to themselves, and those wasters, to be found on all levels of society, who squander the hard-won fruits of the ploughman's labour. So Piers rebuts wasters who try to excuse themselves from work on his half-acre:

> 'Ye ben wastours, ich wot wel, that wasten and devouren
> That leel land-tylynge men leelliche byswynken.
> Ac Treuthe shal teche yow hus teeme for to dryve,
> Other ye shulle ete barliche brede and of the brok drynke.'
>   (C, IX, ll. 139–42)

---

byswynken work for

In the first dream of the *Visio*, where Meed goes to court, Langland depicts a world closely related to that of *Winner and Waster*,[69] in which the King epitomizes, instead of correcting, those two characteristic failings of his subjects; in which, one way or the other, the wealth of the kingdom is engrossed by those who stand high in society, leaving little for the poor on whom all the burden falls, but who have no voice. Only when, as in the second dream, society is considered, not from the King downwards, but from the ploughman upwards, do the poor find expression in condemning both those who waste and those who win.

Although clearly a secular poem, concerned with a political theme, *Winner and Waster* has as little as the religious voice to say for the vices which characterize Youth, and Middle Age or Elde: although Waster may have his charm, the larger context of *Piers Plowman* clearly shows the vanity of that attraction. *The Parlement of the Thre Ages* is a more abstract poem, because it has no such specific political context, and at first sight the gay figure of Youth may seem to maintain a point of view less vulnerable than Waster's.[70] The active hunt in the May morning introduction is distinct in its naturalness from the courtly and civilized figure of Youth; yet the one reinforces the other. All natural things, in that springtime, co-operate spontaneously in a celebration of returning life: 'And iche foule in that frythe faynere than other/That the derke was done and the daye lightenede' (ll. 15–16). Youth, 'gerede alle in grene, alle with golde by-wevede' (l. 122), substitutes, in his dress, unfading gems for the evanescent colours of the natural world; his figure thus recalls many medieval descriptions of the eternal city of God, and his sanguine confidence in the moment seems for once, not illusion, but truth.[71]

Middle Age, the Winner to Youth's Waster, loses instantly in the comparison. 'Of sexty yere elde', his eyes narrowly fixed upon the goods of this life, he embodies a myopic and joyless materialism:

> One his golde and his gude gretly he mousede,
> His renttes and his reches rekened he full ofte
> . . .
> And alle his witt in this werlde was one his wele one. (ll. 140–1, 149)

The riches of Youth, if carried on his back, at least give pleasure; Middle Age, though less miserly than Waster, treats even his fair parks and fertile pastures as dead acquisitions, sources of those profits 'that his purse mendis'. He is too much occupied with his own concerns to offer much in the debate that follows.

The discussion is thus effectively conducted between Youth, 'thritty

---

frythe woodland *faynere* more joyous *gerede* attired *mousede* mused *wele* wealth

yere of elde', and Age, 'a hundrethe yeris of age',[72] and nothing whatever is done to make the second attractive: far from singing 'under a rede rosere', he addresses Youth with the menacing warning of the three walk- ing Dead of the Legend: ' "Makes youre mirrours bi me, men bi youre trouthe—/This schadowe in my schewere schunte ye no while" ' (ll. 290– 1). It is, moreover, not impossible that the opening hunt, which at first appears to make a positive contribution to Youth's position, should, by an ironic twist, also come to lend its support to Age. In the Legend, the Living are often engaged in hunting when they encounter the Dead, and the predator becomes the prey as he turns from pursuer to pursued[73] (Plate 26). The luckless stag in *The Parlement*, who falls victim to the poacher, prefigures that inescapable point at which all men become prey to time and to mortality. The poise of the poem is thus achieved in a manner very different from that of *Winner and Waster*. In the per- spective of the moment, Youth is undoubtedly the victor; but he is also confined to the moment—the durability of the gems he wears is an illusion, for he is debarred from their physical invulnerability. The perspective of Age, in contrast, extends to the whole of human history, and finds, in its repetition of negative cycles, an image of decline which generalizes his own predicament: not only every man, but exceptional men, are subject to time, as are the empires, the civilizations, that such men construct. The poem thus offers two equally cogent perspectives on life: in the here and now of Youth, the world seems one brilliant eternal Spring; in the before and after of Age, all things are caught in the cycle of decay. The one is a truth of the imagination, the other of the mind; where Youth persuades by his fullness of physical being, Age convinces by his intellectual cogency. The figure of Youth holds the stage when the debate opens; but, as in life, the voice of Age dominates at its close.

This fine balance between two perspectives, equally cogent yet mutually exclusive, is significantly absent from a later debate structured about the three Ages, Dunbar's satiric 'Tretis of the Tua Mariit Wemen and the Wedo'.[74] The Ages, represented by the three unfortunate hus- bands, are uniformly repulsive, and the freshness of the June prologue, in this case, only emphasizes the staleness of the human disputants. The first married woman has ' "an auld wobat carle" ' for a husband, ' "A waistit wolroun . . . ane bag full of flewme" '. The second, yoked to ' "a young man ryght yaip, but nought in youth flouris" ', is no better off, for, worn out by lechery, he is impotent:

> 'He lukis as he wald luffit be, thocht he be litill of valour;
> He dois as a dotit dog that damys on all bussis,
> And liftis his leg apone loft, thoght he nought list pische.'

---

schewere mirror   *schunte* shrink from   *wobat* caterpillar   *carle* man   *wolroun* mongrel
flewme phlegm   *yaip* eager   *dotit* foolish   *damys* makes water

The widow has run the gamut of the Ages, first with an old husband relieved by a young gallant, her ' "lust for to slokyn" ', and secondly with a man of Middle Age.[75] She retains a preference for the well-lined pockets of the last, who is so engrossed with his winnings that he provides her with the comforts she wants from marriage, without examining her use of them too closely. Even better, he is, in due course, so obliging as to succumb to the business worries which plague that period of life, and thus leaves her in the best condition of all—that of a well-endowed widow.

Unlike the two fourteenth-century debates, Dunbar's 'Tretis' intends no complexity of perspective; if his poem achieves a poise, it is a cynical one, parallel with that of a preacher, though its tone is far from religious. All the women are concerned purely with what they can get out of marriage, and their debate arrives at the simple conclusion that, whilst men of all ages are undesirable, their possessions are not. It is a witty and vivid exchange; but its implications, for human nature, are savage. Certainly the 'Tretis' thus becomes a comment of a kind upon the gravity of the abstract debate; but when Chaucer, descending from the grave abstractions of *The Knight's Tale*, dramatizes the tensions of Youth and Age on a more human level, one does not feel that humanity is in any way debased; and this is partly because different perspectives are sustained, not driven to reductive conclusions. It is true that the darker tales are darkly coloured on both sides: if January is repulsive in bed, May sacrifices much of her freshness when she reads Damian's letters in the privy, or copulates awkwardly with him in the branches of a pear tree. Yet neither January nor May wholly alienates our sympathy, for there are perspectives on that story larger than the Merchant's, which admit compassion for the victims, on both sides, of unequal marriage.[76]

In those Tales discussed earlier, in the context of Age, Chaucer exploits the dramatic possibilities of opposition between different generations; in *The Knight's Tale*, where the three Ages are used in the interests of pattern and structure, he emphasizes their relation. The difference, again, is partly one of genre, for most of those stories which, in *The Canterbury Tales*, dramatize the tensions of Youth and Age, are *fabliaux*, and thus, as the mode dictates, distinguish the two sharply.[77] These tales are, however, frequently concerned with the situation of unequal marriage. As the Miller remarks of the gullible, ageing John:

> He knew nat Catoun, for his wit was rude,
> That bad man sholde wedde his simylitude.
> Men sholde wedden after hire estaat,
> For youthe and elde is often at debaat. (ll. 3227–30)

This situation, which Chaucer exploits as comedy, however black, is, for Langland's Wit, a matter of serious moral concern:

'Hit is an un-comely couple, be Cryst, as me thinketh,
To geven a yong wenche to an old feble mon,
Or to wedden an old widewe for weolthe of hire goodes,
That never schal child bere, bote hit beo in hire armes!
    In Ielesye Ioyeles and Ianglynge in bedde
Mony peire seththen the pestilence han pliht hem to-gedere.'

(A, X, ll. 180–5)

Langland's emphasis is upon the indecorum, the unnaturalness, of such relationships, and it will be remembered that the romances, which set a high value on decorum and on the perfection of nature, never marry an ill-matched pair.[78]

This sense of an appropriate, because natural, patterning of human relationships, is often reinforced in such stories by the presence of the three Ages; and although the triad receives unusually overt and detailed elaboration in *The Knight's Tale*, it is a less salient characteristic of much romance writing. Youth, Middle Age and Elde are represented in *Sir Gawain*, in the persons of Gawain, Bercilak and Morgan la Fay, where their complementary pattern, like that of the seasons, makes its contribution to the many-faceted cyclical structure of the whole. It can be detected in the thirteenth-century romance, *Havelock the Dane*, and in the fourteenth-century *Gamelyn*, where the idealism of Gamelyn's young fellow outlaws is supported by the wisdom of the ageing Adam Spencer; Age and Youth here combine in their opposition to Middle Age represented by Gamelyn's elder brother, his world of law and its meanly acquisitive concerns.[79] The romance form has a natural affinity with the intricate relations of decorous pattern.

This potential is nowhere more fully realized than in *The Knight's Tale*, where the three Ages of the human figures are reflected in the celestial pantheon. Their structure may be set out in a simple diagram:

DIVINE		HUMAN
	Age	
Saturn		Egeus
	Middle Age	
Jupiter		Theseus
	Youth	
Venus, Mars, Diana		Palamon, Arcite, Emily

Saturn is clearly a figure of Age; his is its planet, his season that of Winter, his humour melancholy, and his element earth.[80] His effects are grimly anarchic, like those of the Greek Chronos from whom he derives; and his great speech is at once couched in the generalized terms of astrological influence, and, at the same time, has, on a cosmic scale, the ring of disenchanted vindictiveness to be found in the Reeve and the Merchant:

'My cours, that hath so wyde for to turne,
Hath moore power than woot any man.
Myn is the drenchyng in the see so wan;
Myn is the prison in the derke cote;
Myn is the stranglyng and hangyng by the throte,
The murmure and the cherles rebellyng,

. . .

Myn is the ruyne of the hye halles,
The fallynge of the toures and of the walles,

. . .

And myne be the maladyes colde,
The derke tresons, and the castes olde;
My lookyng is the fader of pestilence.'   (ll. 2454–69)

Egeus, the father of Theseus, Saturn's human counterpart, is developed much less fully; yet he gives expression to that ineffective contempt of the world, which is the passive human correlative of Saturn's savagery:

'Right as ther dyed nevere man,' quod he,
'That he ne lyvede in erthe in some degree,
Right so ther lyvede never man,' he seyde,
'In al this world, that som tyme he ne deyde.'   (ll. 2843–6)

These senile tautologies express the impotent and querulous submission characteristic of Elde to the view of life which Saturn imposes.

At the other extreme, the three divine and the three human representatives of Youth form amongst themselves an internally complex pattern. Chaucer's cycle of the Ages appears to begin with the phlegmatic nature, and to end with the melancholic; certainly his three human representatives of Youth are characterless, as appropriate to their amorphous element of water. Their deities, appositely, are Venus and Diana (the Moon); Mars, who properly belongs to the third choleric age, is an intrusion, but in distinguishing man's life into three, instead of four, stages, Chaucer has had to conflate some of their characteristics. His association of Arcite with Mars has a certain appropriateness, however: love and arms are the two passions of the young male, just as chastity is suitable to a maiden. There is little, at any point, to choose between the two knights, and Arcite's divine patron does not, as his song shows, remove him from his appropriate season of Spring: ' "Welcome be thou, faire, fresshe May,/In hope that I som grene gete may" ' (ll. 1511–12).

With the exception of that association with the planet Mars, Theseus is thus enabled to draw upon the resources of the two mid-seasons of a man's life. His deity Jupiter, the planet of the sanguine man, receives only a bare (though significant) mention during the quarrel in heaven,

---

cote cell   *castes* conspiracies

where, until Saturn intervenes, he is 'bisy it to stente'; similarly, Theseus himself does his best to arbitrate bloodlessly between Palamon and Arcite. Since Chaucer wishes to assimilate Jupiter to Aristotle's 'Firste Moevere', whom theologians had come to regard as a prefiguring of the Christian God, this reticence is the more appropriate. It is clear from Theseus' own words that he regards the beneficent planet, Jupiter, as identical with the instigator of providential order:

> 'What maketh this but Juppiter, the kyng,
> That is prince and cause of alle thyng,
> Convertynge al unto his propre welle
> From which it is dirryved, sooth to telle?'   (ll. 3035–8)

Within his temporal kingdom, Theseus too 'is prince and cause of alle thyng'; he is gifted both with the positiveness of the sanguine nature, and the keen-witted practicality of the choleric. Where Youth and Age succumb to the conditions of their life, the one disabled by dreams of the future, the other disappointed in memories of the past, Theseus, who lives in the present, actively accommodates himself to those conditions. Those who surrender can only conceive of life as prey to a negative fate, and the temples of Venus and Mars both participate in the savage anarchy of Saturn[81] (Plate 11).

Youth and Age are not opposed in *The Knight's Tale*; in a sorry sense they complement each other.[82] Unlike the romance of *Gamelyn*, it is a man's middle years, that stage of life to which the Knight himself belongs, which are shown to be positively operative. Yet the passivity of Youth and Age in the face of disaster is not wholly at odds with that accommodation to events in which Theseus excels, and nothing more radical than a difference in emphasis separates the response of Egeus to the death of Arcite—' "Deeth is an ende of every worldly soore" '—from Theseus' more constructive acceptance:

> 'Why grucchen we, why have we hevynesse,
> That goode Arcite, of chivalrie the flour,
> Departed is with duetee and honour
> Out of this foule prisoun of this lyf?'   (ll. 3058–61)

Certainly Theseus intends, by thus urging, to unite Emily with Palamon, but even that is to advance advice based upon the wisdom of Egeus, 'That knew this worldes transmutacioun': ' "To maken vertu of necessitee,/ And take it weel that we may nat eschue." ' Although it takes a Theseus to interpret to practical purposes those apparently senile ramblings, it is Age which has the answer; and one may reflect further that the sanguine confidence which Middle Age seeks to generate in a First

Mover who orders all things in a hidden harmony of love, does not triumph finally over the melancholic perspective of Saturn. Although the continuity and interconnection of the Ages goes some way towards integrating the providential and anarchic visions of *The Knight's Tale*, its world remains a Saturnine creation of malevolent chaos, in which the upright man retains merely the peripheral freedom of adapting himself to its cruel conditions.

The Ages have less structural and dramatic presence in *Sir Gawain*, but their more limited effect is also more positive. I have already suggested, in the discussion of Youth, that one aspect of Sir Bercilak is that of Middle Age, whilst Gawain, and the court he represents, are figures of Youth. Bercilak, like Theseus, is a constructive presence, whose attention is turned to the present; Gawain, who looks to the future with the idealism characteristic of the young, is more sanguine than either Palamon or Arcite; the hazards he anticipates lie in the hands of God, and are the means of testing an untried virtue, where Chaucer's Knights lament a world of melancholy, insuperable menace. In *Sir Gawain* the two first Ages thus combine to defeat the dark designs of Morgan la Fay, whose plot has in it all the meanness and envy characteristic of Elde. Readers have tended to arrive at the Green Knight's elucidation of her plan with a sense of anti-climax: Morgan's first purpose, ' "to assay the surquidré ... of the Rounde Table" ', is apposite enough to the process of the poem, for that is where the testing begins, although much more has been put on trial than the chivalrous ethic; it is the petty and, in the event, wholly irrelevant intention of frightening Guinevere to death which has given readers pause, and seems only explicable by reference to traditions external to the poem.[83] Of all medieval writers, the *Gawain*-poet seems, however, least likely to be guilty of odd ends, and the 'auncian lady' of Bercilak's court assumes a fitness in the tale if treated as a figure of Age, as she is clearly intended to be from the poet's description:

> ... noght was bare of that burde bot the blake browes,
> The tweyne yyen and the nase, the naked lyppes
> And those were soure to se and sellyly blered;
> A mensk lady on molde mon may hir calle,
>   for Gode! (ll. 961–5)

The difference between Morgan la Fay, and the brilliant youth of Sir Bercilak's lady beside her—'More lykkerwys on to lyk/Was that scho hade on lode'—marks a contrast as formal as that between Yowth and

---

surquidré pride *burde* lady *sellyly* exceedingly *blered* bleared *mensk* noble
lykkerwys delicious *lyk* taste *on lode* with her

Aige in Henryson's 'Ressoning'.[84] It alerts one to the recognition that her plot typifies the jealousy and vindictiveness felt by those on the brink of the grave for those who have life before them. Although technically Arthur's half-sister, the poet separates the two by removing them to the extremes of man's life-span.[85] If Morgan's plot is the petty occasion of a series of encounters which become much more complex and profound in implication than her original design, that implied recognition of its unimportance only helps to emphasize the triumph of Youth and Life. The poet is not criticizing the attitudes of the old; rather, he is disarming the image of Age as *memento mori*, just as he disarms that of Death, embodied in the Green Knight flourishing his axe. Properly understood, Age and Death have no menace; for the upright Christian soul, which neither ages nor dies, has nothing to fear from them.

In achieving that triumph of Life over Death, the *Gawain*-poet is fulfilling the true potential of the medieval figures of the Ages, for that victory is a reflection of the whole meaning of the Incarnation.[86] Within the actual Gospel story, where the child of Nazareth triumphs over the doctors in the Temple, where the New Law comes to fulfil the Old, where Christ defeats Death in the Crucifixion, Youth, the figure of Life, invariably triumphs over Age and Death. But this confidence is all too rare in medieval literature. Religious writing itself, because it looks to sinful man in the Pride of Life rather than to the ideal figure of Youth, tends to set the Ages within a purely temporal context, in which the Saturnine and melancholy sense of human existence inevitably prevails. In secular literature, whilst many writers maintain the distinctive virtues and vices of the Ages in opposition, relatively few show them as consistently connected, in their virtues and their imperfections, to form a part of the irrepressible human continuity. Chaucer's harmony of vision, whilst quite different from that of the *Gawain*-poet, is equally exceptional; it is his humane and secular conception that endures into the Renaissance, rather than the spiritual vision of his contemporary.

The renaissance affirmation of Cusanus (1401–64) expresses the highest spiritual reach of this attitude: the face of God is imagined by each of the Ages in the image of its own condition; thus that face can only be truly seen when men cease to envisage it, and reflect instead upon its concept.[87] There is much in this comment to recall the Middle Ages, notably the Realist conviction that the idea lies closer to truth than any experience of the natural world, which is analogical only. But the assumption that the face of God must, in the eyes of Youth, seem young, in those of Age, ancient, with its implication that the Ages are subjective and complementary states of mind, is unusual in the earlier period, though characteristic of the later. Its secular equivalent can be clearly illustrated in Titian's painting, 'The Allegory of Prudence': here each Age is allowed its appropriate and complementary virtue, for the three

periods of man's life—Age, Middle Age, and Youth—express three forms
of time—past, present and future—and the three corresponding faculties,
which together make up the virtue of Prudence: 'Memory, which remembers, and learns from, the past: intelligence, which judges of, and
acts in, the present: and foresight, which anticipates, and provides for
or against, the future.'[88] This concept of Prudence was already available
in medieval England; it is set out clearly, and its origin noted, in Lydgate's poem, 'A Mumming at London':

> For *Senec* seythe, who that can see,
> That *Prudence* hathe eyeghen three,
> Specyally in hir lookynges
> To considre three maner thinges,
> Alweyes by goode avysement:
> Thinges passed and eeke present,
> And thinges affter that shall falle.
> And she mot looke first of alle,
> And doon hir inwarde besy peyne,
> Thinges present for to ordeyne
> Avysely on every syde,
> And future thinges for to provyde,
> The thinges passed in substaunce
> For to have in remembraunce.[89]

It is significant, however, that neither here, nor in his 'Ditty upon Haste',
where he invokes the same image—'of thre mirrouris longyng to provy-
dence/Of tyme passed, ffutur & presence'—does Lydgate relate the
three eyes of Prudence to the three Ages of Man.[90] Although the Ages are
not infrequently connected with perspectives on the past, present and
future, medieval writers do not seem actually to relate the sum of the
Ages to the sum of those virtues which make up Prudence. Even Dante's
personification, who leads the dance of the cardinal virtues in the Pageant
of Revelation, is an improbable abstract of allegory, *ch'avea tre occhi in
testa* (who had three eyes in her head), exceptionally so in a poem of such
consistently vivid humanity.[91]

It seems probable that the medieval mind did not make this connection,
because its Age does not really learn from the past, and its Youth, at
least as the Pride of Life, conspicuously lacks the foresight to provide
for the future. Middle Age, certainly, acts in the present, but his actions
are usually prompted by his own narrow self-interest, and the generous
concerns of Bercilak and Theseus are exceptional. For Titian, the Ages
of Man are complementary, and his allegory carries the motto: *ex prae-
terito/praesens prudenter agit/ni futura actione deturpet* (from the past, the
present acts prudently, lest it should spoil future action).[92] That motto
can well stand for a period which puts much more faith in man's un-

aided capacities than the Middle Ages were wont to do; since only the
unity of human with divine purpose had meaning, the co-operation of
men had, in the earlier period, only limited significance. It is for this
reason that the Ages can, at best, hope to form a tranquil succession in
the stages of man's pilgrimage, whilst more often they oppose each other
as irreconcilable points of view.

Yet a period which does not expect to understand everything may
achieve a greater range of perspectives than one which accepts that
human judgement, properly applied, can arrive at the solution to all
human problems. When, in *Piers Plowman*, Scripture remarks succinctly
to Will—' "For alle that wilneth to wyte the weyes of god almighty,/I
wolde his eye were in his ers, and his fynger after" '—we are prone to
conclude that medieval thought was apt to be confined by medieval
faith.[93] The contrary is at least as often true, for the mind which expects
to find solutions may reach its conclusions prematurely, whilst an
enquiry less confident may attempt a much longer and more arduous
journey. The *Divina Commedia* and *Piers Plowman* testify to this, for
it would be hard, at any period, to find poems which compare with their
exigence and intensity of search. If the medieval imagination often grinds
to a halt in the pettiness of the Pride of Life, the meanness of Middle
Age, and in Elde's fear of the grave, it can also discover those ideal
figures in which the Renaissance had ceased to believe—the golden
Youth of the romances, so close to Christ in selfless aspiration, the constructive personality of a Theseus, devoted to the common good, the
triumphant and serene figures of patriarchs and prophets who look, as
each man should in Age, to the coming of the Lord. In the greatest
writing, of the *Gawain*-poet, of Langland, Elde is brother to 'wanhope';
the imagination, freed from such terrors, achieves the leap from life to
eternal life:

'And thorw the grete grace of god, of greyn ded in erthe
Atte laste launceth up, wher-by we lyven alle.'[94]

IV

Related Views of Temporal Life

[Cognitio] aliter se habet vis cognoscitiva quae sub ordine temporis aliqualiter continetur, aliter illa quae totaliter est extra ordinem temporis.... Si ergo sint multi homines per viam aliquam transeuntes, quilibet eorum . . . habet cognitionem de praecedentibus et subsequentibus . . . Videt eos qui juxta se sunt; . . . eos autem qui post se sunt videre non potest. Si autem esset extra totum ordinem transeuntium, utpote in aliqua excelsa turri constitutus, unde posset totam viam videre, videret quidem simul omnes in via existentes. . . . Quia igitur cognitio nostra cadit sub ordine temporis . . . cadant res sub ratione praesentis, praeteriti et futuri. . . . Sed Deus est omnino extra ordinem temporis, quasi in arce aeternitatis constitutus; . . . cui subjacet totus temporis decursus secundum unum et simplicem ejus intuitum.[1]

(Knowledge which is enclosed by time has a quite different scope from knowledge which is entirely outside time. Thus if many men were for a time travelling the same road, any one of them would know those immediately in front or behind. He would see those right beside him, but those well behind he could not see. If, however, he were totally outside the file of travellers, stationed well up in a tower for instance, from which he could view the whole road, he would see at the same instant everyone on that road. Because, therefore, our knowledge falls under the order of time, things fall into the categories of present, past and future. But God is entirely outside the order of time, at the apex of eternity, as it were; the whole downward course of time lies beneath him in one single, united view.)

Langland's belief 'wher-by we lyven alle' that 'greyn ded in erthe/Atte laste launceth up', may seem, out of context, an easy allusion to the Christian promise of resurrection through death affirmed by Jesus in the *Gospel of St John*: 'Except a corn of wheat fall into the ground and die, it abideth alone: but if it die, it bringeth forth much fruit' (XII, 24). But within that whole weary and exigent pilgrimage, it is a hard-won moment of assurance, and a moment only. The statement of a belief is easily made, but the communication of conviction is the rare reward of tenacious endeavour. It cannot be assumed that a belief, because orthodox, is therefore commonly held; just as the fear of mortality is, in the

95

later Middle Ages, more frequently felt than a confidence in resurrection, so that religious view in which human history forms a stable ladder ascending from time to eternity, is only one, and not the most common, of the perspectives available. The great cycles of the mystery plays, ranging from the simple timelessness of God through the temporal into timelessness again, are clearly informed with that belief that the meaning of human history is to be found in the working out in time of God's eternal plan: 'To Christians history is like Jacob's Ladder, "ascending by degrees magnificent" towards the Eternal City.'[2] But medieval writers more usually look to the span of time itself, than to its ultimate context in God's eternal present; in this scarcely optimistic perspective, the life of man inscribes, individually and universally, that repetition of meaningless cycles which the pagan and classical world had long ago remarked.[3] Even *Sir Gawain*, for all its spiritual hope, adumbrated in the cycle of nature, takes its point of departure in human time from the fall of Troy, and returns to that collapse at its close:

> Thus in Arthurus day this aunter bitidde,
> The Brutus bokes thereof beres wyttenesse;
> Sythen Brutus, the bolde burne, bowed hider fyrst,
> After the segge and the asaute was sesed at Troye,
>   iwysse,
> Mony aunteres here-biforne
> Haf fallen suche er this.[4]

If that pattern of repeated returns to the same collapses, the same saddeningly inevitable decay of human purposes, is so insistent as to find its way into one of the most positive of all medieval poems, it is evidence at least that the moments of affirmation are no easy triumph of a confident faith.

The rarity of such moments in medieval poetry is not, however, mysterious: poetry is experiential, and man's experience of this world is necessarily dominated by time. The ascending ladder is the construct of a divine view; the cycle, that of human observation. In the passage which serves as an epigraph, Aquinas appropriately uses the metaphor of pilgrimage to clarify the distinction. Medieval poetry rarely places man 'at the apex of eternity', that goal towards which those on the road of time are travelling; Dante in the Empyrean, Troilus in 'the holughnesse of the eighthe spere', the Pearl maiden beyond the sparkling river of death, enjoy that perspective. To those (the vast majority) involved in the pilgrimage of time, seeing only those in their immediate vicinity, the detachment of that 'one single, united view' is difficult and alien. What can

---

bowed came   *sesed* ceased   *iwysse* certainly

Troilus' laughter say to the suffering of Criseyde, or the rebuke of the heavenly bride to a father who has lost his infant daughter? Can those in time be convinced by the detachment of Dante's description of this world as *l'aiuolo che ci fa tanto feroci* (the threshing floor that makes us so fierce), when the impact of his afterworld derives from the strength of those fierce temporal convictions?

Medieval writers did not cease to believe in the affirmation of the ladder; rather, they acknowledged that its confidence was only occasionally felt by the traveller in time. Chaucer, Langland and Dante, even the sorrowing father of *Pearl*, are all pilgrims; and the end of each journey is the beginning of a further pilgrimage. Chaucer's company (in design at least), not only journeys to Canterbury, but returns from the shrine of 'The hooly blisful martir' to the ordinary life of the inn at Southwark.[5] For Langland's Will, the affirmation of Christ's Harrowing of Hell is followed by the Vision of Anti-Christ, and the poem closes with the renewed resolution of Conscience:

> 'ich wol by-come a pilgryme,
> And wenden as wide as the world regneth,
> To seke Peers the Plouhman.' (C, XXIII, ll. 380–2)

Even Dante and the poet of *Pearl*, whose dreams transcend the temporal, must return to tread again the circle of this world, before the vision, through release from time, becomes permanently theirs.

If, in this terrestrial perspective, human history is cyclical, one must add that it follows different cycles, and that all are not equally negative. The first, a seasonal rhythm in which the grain must 'fall into the ground and die' if it is to bring 'forth much fruit', is largely felt, for all the rigours of Winter, to offer a positive assurance; for the annual miracle readily comes to symbolize the mystery of resurrection. When the attention shifts from the cycle of Nature to that of human life, in the traditional lament *Ubi sunt qui ante nos fuerunt?* (Where are they that were before us?), the imagination, on the one hand, gathers resignation from the transience of all natural things, and, on the other, discovers an elegiac intensity in the recognition that, where the seasons return, men are forever gone. The third cycle, that of Fortune, which tends to distinguish man sharply from the ordered rhythm of Nature, has in consequence little comfort of any kind to offer. The arbitrary rise and fall of her wheel generates a flux of meaningless mutability in human affairs, quite distinct from the providential harmonies of the natural order. The behaviour of men may infect that order, as Nature complains in the *Roman de la Rose*,[6] but it remains one in which the divine plan is visible, none the less; whilst the presence of Fortune almost always implies the anarchy of separation from God. The distinction already marked in the

Ages between inevitable opposition, and complementary, or at least successive, harmonies, is thus elaborated and extended in the rhythms which characterize these three cycles.

A comparison of the four Ages with the four seasons is perhaps common because it is comforting: it is, in any event, authorized by some of the works most respected in the Middle Ages. Dante, as already mentioned, compares them in the *Convivio*,[7] whilst the *Secreta Secretorum* devotes much attention to their correspondence. In James Yonge's early fifteenth-century translation of the latter, Spring is described thus:

The byrdys syngyth, the nyghtyngall shewyth his organe notis, al the Erthe rescewyth his anournement and his beute, and is like to a fayre yong man that arrayth hym wel of al maner of anournement to shewe hym-Selfe atte the weddynge.[8]

This 'fayre yong man', a bird on his hand, represents April in a bas-relief from the thirteenth century on the west front of Amiens Cathedral (see also Plates 15a, 15b, 16b), whilst in the same series February, an old man, well clothed and seated before a fire, could, but for a change of sex, accord with Yonge's description of Autumn (see also Plates 14b and 16a):

Than semyth the worlde as a woman of grete age, that nowe wox a colde and hade nede to be hote clothyde, for that the yowuthe is Passyde, and age neghyth, Wherfor hit is no mervaile yf beute she hath loste.[9]

Both tendencies in the *Secreta Secretorum*—to relate the seasonal disposition of elements and humours to the human constitution, and to personify the seasons as figures of the Ages—are lovingly developed in the great Calendar series, with their astrological signs, which achieve their finest realization in the *Très Riches Heures* of the Duc de Berry[10] (cf. Plates 16a and b). When the interest in the zodiac later declines in favour of a more energetic realism, the intricate relationships which Dante indicates in the *Convivio* are diminished, as man and the natural world come to assume more specific and more separate identities.[11] Such renderings lack the spiritual dimensions which Mâle describes expressively in thirteenth-century art:

The year, moreover, is formed entirely in the image of man: it presents the drama of life and death. Spring, which renews the earth, is an image of baptism which, at life's beginning, renews man. Summer is a figure; its scorching heat and light make us dream of the light of another world, of charity's radiance in eternal life. Autumn, season of grain and grape harvest, is the formidable symbol of universal judgement, of the great day when we shall reap what we have sown. Winter, lastly, is the shadow of death which awaits man and the world. Thus thought travels in the midst of a forest of symbols, beneath a sky thronging with ideas.[12]

The passage of the year is reassuring because it is preordained, its succession determined. But one is recalled to the *Consolatio*, where Philosophy's proof that man is not excluded from the natural order generates alarm with its reassurance: what then of man's freewill?[13]

All discussions of seasonal harmony and its analogies with man are not pursued so rigorously, however. If the natural world is predestined, it is to positive purpose; there is no sense, as in human affairs, that a determined world is mutable and anarchic; on the contrary, the predictability of Nature is evidence of her unfailing order and harmony. The labours of the months, in which man is identified with her purposes, offer him certain consolations which these practical verses describe:

Januar	By thys fyre I warme my handys;
Februar	And with my spade I delfe my landys.
Marche	Here I sette my thynge to sprynge;
Aprile	And here I here the fowlis synge.
Maij	I am as lyght as byrde in bowe;
Junij	And I wede my corne well I-now.
Julij	With my sythe my mede I mawe;
Auguste	And here I shere my corne full lowe.
September	With my flayll I erne my brede;
October	And here I sawe my whete so rede.
November	At Martynesmasse I kylle my swyne;
December	And at Cristesmasse I drynke redde wyne.[14]

It should be noted that the two months of Winter, December and January, and two of Spring, April and May, describe pleasures rather than labours, an endearing characteristic shared by those who depict this sequence in art.[15] The passing of the seasons is thus seen as a positive process, in which man and the natural world co-operate to produce the food and fuel which will solace the hardships of Winter. It is true that a certain uneasiness may underlie that confidence; medieval poets were only too well aware of those years when the crops failed, and the rigours of the winter months were not mitigated by feast and fire, but threatened with starvation. The harmonies of Nature which Boethius described provided a 'copy book account of cosmic and seasonal equilibrium [which] served the Middle Ages well',[16] but the price of Adam's fall, pronounced by God in *Genesis*, was not only a remembered, but a felt, truth: 'In the sweat of thy face shalt thou eat bread, till thou return unto the ground' (III, 19). The extent of God's sentence, 'cursed is the ground for thy sake', is in debate, for it is unclear whether the natural world suffers the fall of Adam, or whether that fall merely disrupts man's relation with the natural.[17] The afflictions of the earth are, however, most usually seen as the punishment for immediate, rather than original, sin: Hunger is actually summoned by Piers to chastise those who default from labour on his half-acre.[18] The general view inclines more to the harmonies than the hazards of Nature, and the latter are incurred by man, rather than imposed upon him.

The continuity of the year thus offers a rare, positive resource to medieval poets. Its cycle shapes and gives meaning to the experience of *Gawain*, where that of human history does not; whilst, on a smaller scale, delight in the natural world, and the reassurance of its promise of renewal, instills a much-needed confidence into many other poems, both major and minor. At the latter extreme, Lydgate's little 'Ditty upon Haste' bases its faith in the order of human life upon the analogies between the Ages and the hours, days and seasons that make up the year:

> Eche thyng is beeste take in his sesoun,
>   Thend of Auguste disposeth his ventagys,
> Caneculer dayes bryng home venyson,
>   In May & Iune bryddys synge in cagys,
>   Corn at hervest is brought home by cariagys,
> Off hey moneth Iule hath set the tyde,
>   In temperat weder men goon on pylgrymagis,
> He hastuth weel that wysely can abyde.[19]

Of the twenty verses of his 'Ditty', this contented evocation of the natural world and the satisfactions of its seasonal activities makes these lines quite the most persuasive of his general plea, 'That haste is beeste which wysely can abyde'. Although the seasons may impose trials upon men, as they do upon Sir Gawain and upon Langland's poor, their promise of better things to come can give both the courage to persist in that future hope: 'Now, lorde, sende hem somer, and some manere Ioye,/Hevene after her hennes-goynge, that here han suche defaute!'[20] The recurrent mystery of Nature's death and resurrection chimes insistently with that remoter mystery of the soul's immortality.

If the trials of Winter promise a rich harvest to the spirit, the joys of Summer bring delights to the body which are felt with a corresponding intensity. However much attention was given to seasonal renewal, or to those comforts that mitigate winter rigours, the seasons themselves are as sharply distinguished as are Youth and Age. Although, appropriately, they 'flyte' less frequently than men seem to do, the tradition of such debates is well established. In the eighth century Alcuin composes a *Conflictus Veris et Hiemis*, in which those two seasons fall out over the virtues and vices of the cuckoo; where Winter attacks her fecklessness, a vice of the spirit, Spring, significantly, wins the encounter by citing her physical virtue of fertility.[21] *The Owl and the Nightingale* reaches no such decision, although its descent from such debates is sufficiently clear.[22] This poem is both a seasonal 'flyting' and an encounter between Youth and Age; moreover, the arguments advanced by the Owl for a solemn way of life and by the Nightingale for a joyous one imply a further debate on the values of different forms of worship, and, indeed, the nature of love. Yet the poem is by no means pedantic; its lively and witty exchanges are speeded by the vivid exactitude with which the two birds are depicted. The Owl identifies herself with Winter from her seat on an old ivy-covered stump, the Nightingale with Summer from her aerial perch on a blossoming bough; if their debate is concerned with an abstract issue, the respective merits of a solemn and a joyous way of life, these are securely anchored in the realistic detail of the usefulness of the two birds to mankind. The Owl claims that she renders humanity several services; she rids them of mice, warns them of impending disaster, and sings in the dead of Winter when the Nightingale is silent; moreover, where her opponent's song incites men to lechery, she is recognized as the confidante of faithful wives. The single claim of the Nightingale nevertheless wins the debate, or so she asserts, but by a casuistry which, one would have thought, savoured of owlishness. As conclusive evidence of her usefulness, the Owl has observed that, even after her death, she is of service to men; she can therefore be said to give her life for humanity:

'An hwanne heo habeth me ofslahe
Heo hongeth me on heore hahe,
Thar ich aschewele pie an crowe
Fron than the thar is isowe.' (ll. 1611–14)

Her assertion is a curious variation, in the animal world, on Elde's function as a *memento mori*, but her point is disallowed by the Nightingale: ' "Me thuncht that thu forleost that game:/Thu yulpest of thire owe schame." ' Her charge, that the Owl is ruled out on a technicality,[23] meets with avian acclaim; but the matter can only be decided by mankind, and the dreamer, perhaps wisely, awakes before the decision can be referred to a certain Master Nicholas. The opposition of the two points of view is thus unresolved, but the precarious technical victory of the Nightingale wins poetic support from the effective beauty of her voice. Her infectious joy indeed seems adequate justification for doing

---

ofslahe slain   *hahe* hedge   *aschewele* frighten   *the thar is isowe* i.e. newly sown seed
yulpest boast   *owe* own

nothing ' "Bute singen in sumere tide,/An bringe blisse for & wide" ', whilst the Owl's dirge of ' "Wailawai" ' is, as the Nightingale remarks, indubitably ' "grislich to ihere" '.[24]

It is probable, however, that Master Nicholas, were his judgement known, would have urged the view that the two positions were not mutually exclusive, but complementary. We know that the Nightingale has a high regard for his power to discriminate good music from bad, right from wrong, and dark things from bright ones; whilst the Owl is confident that, having put the ardours of youth behind him, their arbiter will arrive at that mature and righteous judgement which will (naturally) exalt her at the expense of her opponent.[25] Where Alcuin's much earlier poem is resolved in favour of Spring, *The Owl and the Nightingale*, like the debates between the Ages, seems likely to achieve a poise between positions; for the perspectives of Summer and Winter, like those of Youth and Age, convince the different faculties of imagination and reason. Aquinas, through Augustine, expresses the distinction in images of dusk and dawn:

In die consueto mane est principium diei, vespere autem terminus; ita cognitio ipsius primordialis esse rerum dicitur cognitio matutina; et haec est secundum quod res sunt in Verbo; cognitio autem ipsius esse rei creatae, secundum quod in propria natura consistit, dicitur cognitio vespertina.[26]

(As in a normal day, dawn is its beginning and dusk its end, so the knowledge of things in their original being, as they are in the Word, is called dawn knowledge; whilst the knowledge of created things, as they are in their own natures, is said to be evening knowledge.)

Morning light is visionary, evening light realistic; the one is ideal, the other experiential. This distinction can be glimpsed, in varying degrees of simplicity and complexity, in the metaphor of other disputes.

At one extreme, the popular debates between the holly and the ivy express, in a very simple form, the essence of the argument between the Owl and the Nightingale:

> Holy hath beris
> As rede as any rose:
> The foster, the hunters
> Kepe hem fro the doos.

> Ivy hath beris
> As blake as any slo:
> Ther com the owle
> And ete hem as she goo.

---

grislich horrible   *foster* forester

Holy hath birdes,
A full faire flok:
The nightingale, the poppinguy,
The gayntil laverock.

Gode Ivy, gode Ivy,
What birdes hast thou?
None but the owlet
That creye, 'How! how!'[27]

Holly, the male principle of life, the independent tree which stands for
joy, shelters the gay birds of Spring; Ivy, the solemn and possibly kill-
joy female, the clinging parasite, harbours the grim bird of Winter.
This simple poem has its sexual connotations, but without the complexity
with which, at another extreme, Malory uses Spring and Winter as
similes for the virtue and vice, the birth and death of love:

For hit gyvyth unto all lovers corrayge, that lusty moneth of May, in som-
thynge to constrayne hym to som maner of thynge more than in ony other
monethe, for dyverce causys: for than all erbys and treys renewyth a man and
woman, and in lyke wyse lovers callyth to their mynde olde jantylnes and
olde servyse, and many kynde dedes that was fortotyn by neclygence.

    For, lyke as wynter rasure dothe allway arace and deface grene summer,
so faryth hit by unstable love in man and woman, for in many persones there
is no stabylité: for we may se all day, for a lytyll blaste of wyntres rasure,
anone we shall deface and lay aparte trew love, for lytyll or nowght, that coste
muche thynge.[28]

Both poem and prose see a virtue in the vital principle, of Holly or
Spring, where little is apparent in Ivy and 'wyntres rasure'; yet the
Ivy, with the Owl, represents a reality, and Malory's second paragraph
certainly has its 'evening light' to shed on the common fate of love.
In the natural world 'grene summer' is not erased permanently, and
the evergreen Holly with his bright berries perpetuates a summer flourish
through the dead of the year. It is the instability of humanity which
leads to permanent 'rasure', and it is no wonder that, just as Malory
exhorts man to 'florysh hys herte' consistently as May does in his garden,
so the Calendar painters should stress that the death of the year is also
the season of Christmas fire and festivity, of Christ's promise through
the Incarnation of resurrection, a time at which men anticipate within-
doors the renewal which Spring will later proclaim without. As Patience
observes in *Piers Plowman*, the poor man who receives no such solace
may plead with his 'rightful Iugge' that, just as birds and beasts, after

---

poppinguy parrot(?)   *laverock* lark

the suffering of Winter, are rewarded with 'her sovereigne Ioye' of returning warmth, so men who in this life 'nevere Ioye hadde' may look to
that everlasting Summer of eternal life.[29]

The complex tensions between affinity and alienation which, in
English poetry, characterize the relationships of man with the natural
world, are less conspicuous in French. As Rosamund Tuve has demon-
strated, the seasons in French literature are largely used as a decorative
motif to embellish and reflect the moods of love; whilst in English
literature, well before Chaucer, they serve a philosophical purpose.[30] The
visionary 'dawn knowledge' of Spring and Youth, which mediates between
natural and supernatural, is explored in many degrees in English poetry;
whilst the delicate artifice of Guillaume de Lorris' spring introduction
to the *Roman de la Rose* is the 'set piece' of much French verse.

> Li bois recuevrent lor verdure,
> qui sunt sec tant come yver dure;
> la terre meïsmes s'orgueille
> por la rosee qui la mueille,
> et oublie la povreté
> ou ele a tot l'iver esté;
>   · · ·
> lors estuet joines genz entendre
> a estre gais et amoreus
> por le tens bel et doucereus.
> Mout a dur cuer qui en may n'aime,
> quant il ot chanter sus la raime
> as oisiaus les douz chans piteus.[31]

Chaucer's understanding of such decorative verse is revealed in the grace
of his rendering of those lines:

> These wodes eek recoveren grene,
> That drie in wynter ben to sene;
> And the erthe wexith proud withalle,
> For swote dewes that on it falle,
> And the pore estat forget
> In which that wynter had it set.
>   · · ·
> Than yonge folk entenden ay
> Forto ben gay and amorous,
> The tyme is than so saverous.
> Hard is the hert that loveth nought
> In May, whan al this mirth is wrought,
> Whan he may on these braunches here
> The smale briddes syngen clere
> Her blisful swete song pitous.[32]

At first sight, these lines may not seem far distant from those which introduce *The Canterbury Tales*, but the detail of that prelude to pilgrimage explores far more than the enamelled surface. The secret course of the rising sap that 'engenders' the flower; the zodiacal passage of 'the yonge sonne' which, from so vast a distance, prompts that rising; the mysterious connection between the stirrings of Nature and those of men, not, in the latter case, 'to ben amorous', but to seek with restless spirit and mixed motives for the divine goal of 'ferne halwes': all these interrelations and distinctions compose an image of Spring more complex than the confident movement of the lines at first suggests.[33]

Not all English poetry is so subtle, nor all French so simple; the romances of Chrétien de Troyes tend, for example, to open upon days signifying rebirth in natural and Christian calendar alike, for it is as appropriate that romance should open with a phrase like *Au jor de Pasque, au tans novel* (On Easter Day in springtime), as that 'Once upon a time' should dispose the listener to expect a fairy story.[34] The writers of English romance, however, love to elaborate the phrase, and a set description of the Spring almost always heralds an adventure. The dream of Herodis in *Sir Orfeo* occurs on one such morning:

> Bifel so in the comessing of May
> (When miri & hot is the day,
> & o-way beth winter-schours,
> & everi feld is ful of flours,
> & blosme breme on everi bough
> Over-al wexeth miri anough).[35]

In *Ywain and Gawain* the song of birds after storm is twice a prelude to adventure; in the *Morte Arthure* Arthur's quest for the Giant leads him first through meadows 'floreschte with flourez fulle many'.[36] The prelude to the fifth part of *Eger and Grime* seems at first no more complex than the verse of de Lorris:

> Early in that May morning
> Merrely when the burds can sing,
>   . . .
> It was a heavenly melodye
> For a knight that did a lover bee
> On the one side to heare the small birds singing,
> On the other side the flowers springing.[37]

It should be remarked, however, that in each of these instances the reassurance of Spring is not merely ornamental; it prefaces events often

---

breme bright

mysterious, and, in contrast to their context, related to death, not life. The sleep of Herodis adumbrates mortality; the birdsong of *Ywain and Gawain* announces the appearance of a strange and deadly opponent; the Giant of the *Morte Arthure*, surrounded by the bones of the innocent children he has eaten, is a figure of death; Grime does not ride to his love, but to the land of Sir Gray-steele with its 'palaces of mickle pride', whose owner seems indestructible and 'ever waches' to destroy all comers.

The Spring openings of many alliterative poems, so vividly captured in the texture of the language, often bear a similar relation to the visions they announce: the embattled armies of Winner and Waster are seen in a dream into which the narrator has been lulled by the Spring song of birds and waters; the vividly sensuous hunt which prefaces *The Parlement of the Thre Ages* has a dramatic relation, already described, to the hunt which follows.[38] It is, however, *Death and Liffe* that consummates the visionary power of 'dawn knowledge', for its brilliantly jewelled landscape marries Eden with Elysium, and moves between the temporal and eternal worlds:

> Thus ffared I through a ffryth where fflowers were manye,
> Bright bowes in the banke breathed ffull sweete,
> The red rayling roses, the richest of fflowers,
> Lanced broad on their branches with their bright leaves,
> & a river that was rich ronn over the greene,
> With still sturring stryndes that streamed fful bright
> Over the glittering ground, as I glode there.
> Methought itt lenghtened my liffe to looke on the bankes.[39]

There is much in this passage to recall the *locus amoenus* (plesaunce) of classical literature; it is an ideal landscape, a natural (not cultivated) meadow, adorned with trees and flowers, enlivened by birdsong and water.[40] But as Matilda, who gathers flowers beside a similar stream in the earthly Paradise, explains to Dante:

> 'Quelli che anticamente poetaro
>   L'età dell 'oro e suo stato felice,
>   Forse in Parnaso esto loco sognaro.
> Qui fu innocente l'umana radice;
>   Qui primavera sempre, ed ogni frutto;
> Nettare è questo di che ciascun dice.'[41]

(Those who of old celebrated in poetry the golden age and its happy state perhaps, on Parnassus, dreamed of this place. Here the root of mankind

---

waches waits   *ffryth* wood   *bowes* boughs   *rayling* opening   *Lanced* Sprang forth
sturring moving   *stryndes* streams   *glode* went

was innocent; here spring, and each fruit, is everlasting; this is the nectar of which everyone speaks.)

The beauties of the spring landscape become everlasting, *primavera sempre*, when vision transforms them into a paradisal garden, of the earth, yet immune from all change and decay. It is no wonder that the forlorn father in *Pearl* would be content to live forever in such a place with his little daughter, abandoning both the temporal garden with its flowering grave, and the prospect of the durable towers of the heavenly Jerusalem. It is possible that Dante, finding his own way (for the first time without a guide) through that paradisal landscape, encounters a similar temptation to linger forever by its sparkling waters. The landscape of *Death and Liffe* has not moved quite so clearly into that of Eden—it affirms the paradisal prospect of Spring rather than being that Paradise itself; but when Dame Liffe achieves her triumph over Death, that promise is redeemed in the resurrection of her slain company.

The visionary light of the Spring morning can both intensify the temporal until it is eternalized, or, as in Langland, render it more abstractly, as a sign 'of things in their original being'. Although *Death and Liffe* often recalls *Piers Plowman*, the joys of its prelude have no counterpart in the earlier poem:

> In a somere seyson, whan softe was the sonne,
> Y shop me in-to shrobbis, as y a shepherde were,
> In abit as an ermite, unholy of werkes,
> Ich wente forth in the worlde wonders to hure,
> And sawe meny cellis and selcouthe thynges.
> Ac on a May morwenyng on Malverne hulles
> Me byfel for to slepe for weyrynesse of wandryng.   (C, I, ll. 1–7)

Langland's stirrings, like Chaucer's, are to pilgrimage, not to love and adventure in the simply human sense; if he has less interest than Chaucer in the seasonal instincts' range from stars to plants, it is because the human and supernatural worlds coexist with such intensity in his poem. On the one hand, he has a realistic awareness that, whilst May will bring 'myrthe' to beasts and to the rich 'that han meoble ynow and heele', the summer season brings little solace to beggars who have no bread. Such social urgency reduces the seasons to symbols of the human condition, and the comfort of those 'A-furst and a-fyngred' is to be found in the May and Summer of heaven, not of earth.[42] The joys of this world do not often detain him, for they are largely seen as the temptations of

---

shop put   *shrobbis* shrubs (i.e. outdoors)   *hure* hear   *cellis* cells   *selcouthe* strange
meoble goods   *heele* health   *A-furst* Very thirsty   *a-fyngred* very hungry

privilege; his May is vision, his Summer beatitude, their temporal light leading him to dream of the unfailing radiance of another world.

The 'evening knowledge' of Winter and Autumn, which sheds its cruelly clear illumination on 'things as they are in their own natures', is rarely softened, as the Calendar sequences are, by the promise of well-earned comforts. As a subject in itself, or as a prelude to vision, Winter has for the poets at an early date much of the cool realistic light which characterizes the Grimani Breviary's later rendering of the seasons in the *Très Riches Heures*.[43] Scenes of Christmas warmth and feast occur in *Sir Gawain*, and Chaucer's hospitable Franklin builds one such vignette into his tale:

> Janus sit by the fyr, with double berd,
> And drynketh of his bugle horn the wyn;
> Biforn hym stant brawen of the tusked swyn,
> And 'Nowel' crieth every lusty man.   (ll. 1252–5) (Plates 13 and 14a)

Both poems are, however, concerned with Winter only as a part of the seasonal cycle: Dorigen and Gawain both face, in the realistic light of December, the execution of those promises made months before, Dorigen's in the optimistic warmth of Spring, Gawain's from amongst the indoor securities of Arthur's court.[44] For both, however, the seed of returning life is buried secretly in the dead heart of the year. Winter, on its own, more usually opens to the eyes of medieval poets prospects already too plain and common.

The themes of Winter, Age and Death become virtually interchangeable in this 'Winter Song' from *The Harley Lyrics*:

> Al that grein me graveth grene,
> nou hit faleweth al bydene;
> Iesu, help that hit be sene,
>   ant shild us from helle,
>   for y not whider y shal ne hou longe her duelle.[45]

The confidence of the natural world—that, in due time, the grain will grow green again—finds no parallel in man's mortality, 'for y not whider y shal ne hou longe her duelle'. Nature does not individualize the grain, but each human creature is distinct, and a communal harvesting cannot be mitigated by the prospect of next year's crop. 'An Autumn Song' in the same collection, which has in it more of the delicate regret of transience, nevertheless sees the season largely as a *memento mori*; the poet places no confidence in the return of other roses and lilies, but looks

---

graveth buries   *faleweth* withers   *al bydene* forthwith

instead to the unfading flower of heaven: 'On o ledy myn hope is,/moder ant virgyne.'[46]

As a prelude to vision, the winter opening seems in England to parody, in a sombre and satiric vein, the promise of the May morning. Such preludes are not uncommon in French love poetry, where they reflect emotions of loss, disillusion and failure;[47] but in English writing they serve a less subjective purpose, corresponding to the insular poets' more conceptual attitude to the seasons as a whole. The dream of Chaucer's *House of Fame* opens on a winter night, though its mention is brief and unelaborated: 'Of Decembre the tenthe day,/Whan hit was nyght, to slepe I lay' (ll. 111–12). Chaucer wastes no more words on the season; the implied contrast between May morning and winter night makes a sufficient point in introducing a poem whose satire does nothing to idealize. Lydgate, whose *Temple of Glas* reflects Venus' 'temple y-mad of glas' in *The House of Fame*, adopts and elaborates Chaucer's winter setting:

> For thought, constreint, and grevous hevines,
> For pensifhede, and for heigh distres,
> To bed I went nou this othir nyght,
> Whan that Lucina with hir pale light
> Was Ioyned last with Phebus in aquarie,
> Amid decembre, when of Ianuarie
> Ther be kalendes of the nwe yere,
> And derk Diane, ihorned, nothing clere,
> Had hid her bemys undir a mysty cloude.[48]

A distressed state of mind, intensified by the dark of the year, issuing in 'dedli slepe', does not promise auspicious dreams; indeed, Lydgate's general view of the lovers in Venus' temple is as discouraging as Chaucer's. This is the 'winter rasure' which experience suggests to be love's end, for the plaintiffs include not only the doomed lovers of legend, but those who have suffered the fate of unequal marriage: 'For it ne sit not unto fresshe May/Forto be coupled to colde 'Ianuari.'[49] Lydgate does not confine himself to the Chaucerian brief for very long, however. With a burst of renewed Spring, the tone of his poem changes: a lady, sovereign in beauty as May is among months, is granted Venus' aid, united with her lover, and endowed with every assurance the goddess can offer of amorous stability. The poem becomes occasional, a celebration of romantic courtship, its harsh beginning either forgotten, or turned to emphasize the compliment to the loves of the living.

Lydgate's retreat into the reassurance of Spring is not beaten in good order; so much emphasis has been placed upon that wintry 'evening knowledge' in isolation from the other seasons, that the abrupt burst of

springtime radiance seems less a genuine continuity than the arbitrary
see-saw of mutability. The latter is felt in another line from the Harley
'Winter Song': 'Nou hit is ant nou hit nys'; when the image of man
engulfs that of the natural world, the signs offered by earth seem only
to reflect his 'lack of steadfastness'. This is the view that Gower sketches
in his *Confessio Amantis*:

> The purest Eir for Senne alofte
> Hath ben and is corrupt fulofte,
> Right now the hyhe wyndes blowe,
> And anon after thei ben lowe,
> Now clowdy and now clier it is:
> So may it proeven wel be this,
> A mannes Senne is forto hate,
> Which makth the welkne to debate.
>
>   . . .
>
> The See now ebbeth, now it floweth,
> The lond now welketh, now it groweth,
> Now be the Trees with leves grene,
> Now thei be bare and nothing sene,
> Now be the lusti somer floures,
> Now be the stormy wynter shoures,
> Now be the daies, now the nyhtes,
> So stant ther nothing al upryhtes,
> Now it is lyht, now it is derk;
> And thus stant al the worldes werk
> After the disposicioun
> Of man and his condicioun.[50]

Human hatred and dissension cause the skies to storm, the weather to
vary; a natural world dictated by 'the disposicioun/Of man and his con-
dicioun' is as uncomfortably mutable as his own fortunes.

This is not the view of Alanus de Insulis in his *Anticlaudianus*; there
Nature, in the role of creator, has instilled harmony and order into
primaeval chaos:

> Scrutatur rerum causas, et semina mundi:
> Quis chaos antiquum vultu meliore redemit,
> Dum formae melioris opem vultusque decorem
> Quaereret . . .
>
>   . . . cur contristata pruinis
> Luget hiems canis, ridet ver, aestuat aestas,
> Effluit autumnus rerum torrente profundo,
> Vel cur terra sedet, fluit amnis, profluit aer,

Senne Sin   *welketh* withers

Flamma volat, reliquisque fidem non invida servat,
Non audens violare fidem, cur foedera terris
Labilis unda tenet, certo contenta meatu.[51]

(She scrutinizes the causes of things, and the seeds of being; she put a better face on ancient chaos, when she sought the beauty of a better form and grace of feature. Hence fierce winter howls, heavy with snow, spring smiles, summer glows, and autumn surges forth in a deep torrent of plenty; thus the earth settles, the river flows, the air streams forth, the flame flies upwards and without envy keeps faith with the rest, not daring to violate its trust; hence the fleeting tide makes treaty with the land, contained within a certain measure.)

The very things which express, to Gower, the infection of man's instability, are evidence, to Alanus, of harmony, order, decorum. Yet the Nature of Alanus agrees with Gower at least in this: it is man in whom her endeavours have so often been frustrated, through whom her name has so often fallen into disrepute. In the *Anticlaudianus* there is only one remedy—to create another perfect human being, who will be a mirror to Nature, reflecting her splendours.[52]

When the world of Nature can retain its separateness from man—not tainted by his mediation, but reaching directly to the divine—it can offer him the ordered context that Alanus describes; and if his relation to that context is complex, its harmonies nevertheless do much to stabilize him. It is easy to forget that *Sir Gawain*, whose impact on the imagination has in it so much of Spring's smile and Summer's glow, should yet begin and end at a time when 'fierce winter howls, heavy with snow'. The poet is, however, at pains to stress that the year in midwinter looks, like the double-faced Janus, equally to birth and death (Plates 13 and 14a). The Green Knight appears in Arthur's court 'Wyle Nw Yer was so yep that hit was nwe cummen', and the second fitt begins: 'This hanselle has Arthur of aventurus on fyrst/In yonge yer, for he yerned yelpyng to here.'[53] The longing for adventure is part of Youth's springtime yearning, but the poem does not let us forget that it is a matter of death as well as life. Gawain, like Dorigen, defers thought of his 'anious viage' until 'Meghelmas mone/Was cumen wyth wynter wage', when the approaching dark of the year recalls him to his tryst with death. He lingers at the court until 'Al-hal-day', a festival which, in the Christian calendar, celebrates the saints of the Church—those who, by definition, have certainly received the reward of eternal life; but November 1st, in an older tradition, is the beginning of Winter, and its festival is that of the dead, not of the eternally living. Gawain feasts with the Christian court on that day, but he leaves for his journey on the day following,

---

yep fresh   *hanselle* gift   *yelpyng* boasting   *wage* earnest

which becomes in the Church's calendar the feast of All Souls, a time
of prayer for those who have died, but who are not yet assured of eternal
life. When, on his last night at Sir Bercilak's castle, Gawain lies listening
to the final moments of the dying year, he (like those souls) sees in the
coming day no comfort of new beginnings, but a presage of his own
mortality:

> Now neghes the Nw Yere, and the nyght passes,
> The day dryves to the derk, as dryghtyn biddes;
> Bot wylde wederes of the worlde wakned theroute,
> Clowdes kesten kenly the colde to the erthe,
> With nyye innoghe of the northe, the naked to tene;
> The snawe snitered ful snart, that snayped the wylde;
> The werbelande wynde wapped fro the hyghe,
> And drof uche dale ful of dryftes ful grete.
> The leude lystened ful wel that ley in his bedde,
> By uch kok that crue he knwe wel the steven.   (ll. 1998–2008)

Yet the tryst at the green chapel, despite the bitter tears of a man's self-
accusation, possesses the more auspicious characteristics of a New Year's
dawn;[54] the Spring of earth will not only return, but, for the repentant
Christian soul, *primavera è sempre*.

The promise of rebirth is felt not only at its close, but at every point
in the poem, for it is reflected in the cyclical form which speaks for so
much more than man's little history. The passage of the year is splendidly
described in the opening of the second fitt, and certain significant
features of the description are worth stressing. The lines, primarily,
are concerned with the seasons: the dispersion of the cold with the
coming of May, the fruitfulness of Summer, Autumn harvests, the fall
of the leaves and the approach of another Winter. But this cycle is
paralleled and reinforced by that of the Christian year: 'After Crysten-
masse com the crabbed lentoun', and so through to Michaelmas, to All
Hallows, and to another Christmas, season of Christ's birth. In the
human imagination, however, the passage of the months, like that of
life, seems to accelerate progressively; time, in obedience to Gawain's
state of mind, becomes more hasty than measured: 'Bot then hyyes
hervest, and hardenes hym sone,/Warnes hym for the wynter to wax ful
rype.' So men must gather in their spiritual harvest, as they read the
signs of their approaching mortality.[55] The passing of the seasons thus
comes to reflect the passage of life, and mirrors in the temporal world
both the uncertainties and the assurance of the eternal. The uncertainties

---

dryghtyn God   *kesten* sent down   *nyye* bitterness   *tene* torment   *snitered* shivered down
snart bitterly   *snayped* nipped cruelly   *wapped* rushed   *leude* knight   *steven* tryst
hyyes hastens   *hardenes* becomes severe

lie with men, with their fears and fallibilities, individually expressed in Gawain, comprehensively in the cycle of human time from Troy. The assurances inhere in the context which contains them, that of the natural world where 'The day dryves to the derk, as dryghtyn biddes'; in the mercy of God, who has created a world of 'wrake and wonder' for man's trial and his salvation.

The *Gawain*-poet does not avoid the darker discoveries of the Middle Ages. The fear of Winter and of death, the recognition that 'blysse' must alternate with 'blunder', that a man knows not how long he will dwell here nor whither he will go hence, are all acknowledged. Yet the promise offered by the seasons, in their miraculous power of regeneration, contains these hazards within its reassurance. The poem, however, is never complacent, for it is not only the regenerative power of the Green Knight that remains mysterious: the renewal of the seasons and of the human soul are also rediscovered as subjects for wonder—and for laughter.

Despite all the difficulties which medieval poets encountered in relating mankind to the natural world, the seasonal cycle is felt as a genuine reassurance, not only by the contentedly superficial (as Lydgate often is), but by the profoundly questioning, such as the *Gawain*-poet, whose confidence is more exigently won. In such poetry the emphasis comes to rest on the necessary sequence of birth to death; Elde's notion— 'This world nys but a thurghfare ful of wo'—is contained in the confidence that its pilgrimage promises 'lyfe that es lely ay lastande'.[56] The rigours of Winter may indeed alternate with the joys of Spring, but this variation is ratified not only because, as Augustine claimed, the world's course is thus made like a *pulcherrimum carmen ex quibusdam quasi antithetis* (most beautiful song from these antithetic figures);[57] it is also because, when the natural world becomes a place of trial for men, it tests them for a divine, and ultimately preservative, purpose.

It is when the attention shifts from his natural context to man himself—to man, moreover, as a purely physical being, removed from his full setting in the divine plan—that a painful sense of humanity's disjunction from natural order, even of its exile from God's harmony, begins to be felt. The imagination then senses that grain and man are not really alike; the seed, like Keats's nightingale, is immortal because neither bird nor plant is ever individualized. Humankind will survive, but that is no comfort when Paris, Dido, Tristram, the musing mind itself, will come no more:

---

wrake distress

> Hwer is paris & heleyne
>> that weren so bryht & feyre on bleo,
> Amadas & dideyne,
>> tristram, yseude and alle theo,
> Ector, with his scharpe meyne,
>> & cesar, riche of wordes feo,
> Heo beoth i-glyden ut of the reyne
>> so the schef is of the cleo.[58]

Even so, that final line has its comfort to offer, for the great are not dissolved in the humiliation of the grave: they are harvested like the sheaf from the hillside.

Ubi sunt, the lament which becomes so popular in medieval poetry, is a theme rather than a figure, a mood rather than an attitude. It does, however, offer its own version of mankind and his cyclical history. Because it is concerned more usually with individual rather than with communal fate, the dead that it mourns and memorializes are generally the legendary great: the prophets of the Christian Church, the heroes and heroines of romance or of classical story. But they may also be exalted figures of immediate memory—Edward II, Richard II, Blanche the Duchess—and may occasionally be personal rather than political, as in Dunbar's 'Lament for the Makaris', which includes contemporaries and friends in its litany of dead poets.[59] All, in one way or another, are irreplaceable figures, where the grain is not.

It occasionally happens that *ubi sunt* becomes detached from particular persons altogether, and develops into a merely generalized lament for the loss of beauty, prowess and riches:

> UUere beth they biforen us weren,
> Houndes ladden and hauekes beren
> And hadden feld and wode?
> The riche leuedies in hoere bour,
> That wereden gold in hoere tressour
> With hoere brightte rode.

Secular regret may, as in this case, shade into political and religious admonition:

> Eten and drounken and maden hem glad;
> Hoere lif was al with gamen I-lad,
> Men keneleden hem biforen,

---

bleo appearance   *meyne* strength   *wordes feo* worldly possessions   *reyne* kingdom
schef sheaf   *cleo* hillside   *tressour* treasure   *rode* face

They beren hem wel swithe heye—
And in a twincling of on eye
Hoere soules weren forloren.[60]

Such poems censure the Pride of Life, but it is more common for the
theme to lament, in the present, the loss of past greatness, than to
prognosticate the future torments of the victims of time. Although concerned with mortality, the *ubi sunt* question is moreover unusual in its
freedom from an obsession with the grave; death is seen as a natural,
not as a macabre, event—men fade like the rose, are harvested like the
grain. Because it is largely a mood, of regret or even of nostalgia, the
theme is most frequently found in lyric poetry; yet its emotion may be
sustained through a larger work, where it becomes an insight into historical process, as in the stanzaic *Morte Arthur*, in Malory's *Morte
d'Arthur*, and to some extent in Lydgate's *Fall of Princes* (Plate 12).
The juxtaposition in *ubi sunt* of life with death, of the living with the
dead, though in essence apparently so simple, nevertheless possesses its
own insights, for it is the dead, not the living, who are regarded as the
possessors of abundant life. Compared with the greatness of the past,
the present lacks vitality; the truly noble are departed, the golden age is
gone. Thus Malory, though concerned with the adultery of Lancelot
and Guinevere, as one of the reasons for the decline of that civilization,
can compare unfavourably the lusts of his own day, 'sone hote sone
colde', with the fidelities of the past: 'than was love, trouthe and faythe-
fulnes.'[61]

It is often difficult to isolate the theme of *ubi sunt* from other motifs
of life and death: it may, for example, become a lament for Age, or,
alternatively, a celebration of Youth; in the religious voice it can serve
as a *memento mori*. But its closest affinity is with the theme of Fortune,
and in the lyric particularly a poet may move between the two with
scarcely perceptible transitions, whilst the major work may use either
or both as its structure. Thus, of the three great English treatments of
the Death of Arthur, whose life and whose civilization form a paradigm
of the great past, the alliterative *Morte Arthure* is structured around the
figure of Fortune, to whose wheel Arthur himself lends his hand in the
Round Table's lust for blood; the stanzaic *Morte Arthur* is written almost
wholly in the elegiac cadences of *ubi sunt*; whilst Malory's account draws
upon both explanations of human disaster.

Even in lyric poetry the transitions between the two can be sensed by
an attentive ear, for the distinction, significantly, can often be established
in terms of rhythm: *ubi sunt* is a mood before it is a concept, much less
an attitude; Fortune a concept, before she is an attitude or mood. The

---

forloren lost

rhythms of the first, in consequence, flow naturally, for they have the musical cadence of ritual lament; those of Fortune chop and change, see-saw arbitrarily, enacting the heady ascent and dizzy drop of her wheel. The contrast could be widely illustrated, but Lydgate's poem, 'That now is Hay some-tyme was Grase', is both pleasing and characteristic.[62] The seventh verse of this poem might come from almost any lyric on the *ubi sunt* theme, and its cadence of regret for the transience, at once natural and inevitable, of *all* created things, is quite distinct:

> Whilome full feyre was Polixene,
>   So was Creseyde; so was Helene
> Dido also of Cartage quene,
>   Whos beaute made many one pleyne;
>   But dethe came laste and can dysteyne
> Their freshenes, and made them full base,
>   Youre remembraunce let not disdeyne,
> That now is heye some tyme was gras.[63]

In the sixteenth verse, the rhythms of Fortune, 'chaungynge of her doublenes',[64] are, in contrast, distinctly *un*natural:

> In this mater lat ws not tarye;
>   Alle stont on chaunge, who list to see,
> Every thynge here dothe chaunge and varye,
>   Nowe feythe, nowe mutabylyte;
>   Nowe upon tweyne, nowe upon thre;
> Who clymbeth hyest gothe ofte base,
>   Ensample in medowes thow mayst se
> That nowe is heye some tyme was grase.

The feminine rhymes, emphatic caesura, the whole movement of the verse is mimetic of giddy vacillation. Yet it would not be true to claim that Lydgate is consciously distinguishing between natural transience and unnatural mutability; the last three lines of that verse combine the arbitrary image of Fortune's wheel with the lament for natural decline, which forms the refrain of the poem, as though there were no difference. Whilst the mind perceives no distinction, the imagination seems to sense one: it can accept transience, as the rhythm implies, but revolts at mutability. In the poetry of *ubi sunt*, more perhaps than anywhere else, the medieval imagination fuses its image of man with that of the natural world: the passing of human life, like that of the seasons, may be reason for sorrow; but life is not rejected on account of its transience, only regretted.

This distinction does not, however, hold true for didactic writing; as the sermons, with typical materialism, repeatedly demonstrate, the transience of an object is evidence of its uselessness. From a divine, eternal perspective that conclusion is unavoidable. Aquinas, who does not disparage human life, nevertheless observes:

Damascenus accipit immortalitatem perfectam, quae includit omnimodam immutabilitatem; *quia omnis mutatio est quaedam mors*, ut Augustinus dicit.[65]

(Damascene is thinking of perfect immortality, which implies complete immutability; for every change is a kind of death, as Augustine says.)

Yet for the secular imagination, this very impermanence may endow an object with a particular poignant beauty. It may be significant that Dante's writers, artists and poets are found, even in the afterworld, chiefly amongst those who are still 'in love with the productions of time'—amongst the damned, who revert with regret and nostalgia to their life upon earth,[66] amongst those who, suffering purgation, recall the sweetness of temporal life with a sense of missed opportunity.[67] The Blessed, for whom beatitude suffices, are mostly Christian philosophers, who refer to mortal life only when it serves a didactic purpose connected with salvation.[68] Not until the Renaissance does temporality cease to be the mark of mortality, and become the definition of that arena in which a man may gain undying reputation.[69] Within the Middle Ages, the theme of *ubi sunt* does, however, confer a poetic immortality upon its heroes, even though the same poem may both celebrate, and, in the religious voice, condemn, the vanity of all such fame.

This duality is apparent very early in the Middle Ages. The 'Lov Ron' of Friar Thomas, already quoted as a typical example of the theme, can lament the passing of such figures as Tristram in the resigned rhythm of transience, but its didacticism quickly leads into the vexed see-saw of mutability:

> This world fareth hwilynde—
>   hwenne on cumeth an-other goth;
> That wes bi-fore nu is bihynde,
>   that er was leof nu hit is loth.

The maid, at whose bidding the song has been written, is finally advised to wed the permanence of Christ, whose colours will outlast even those of precious stones, the most durable of earth's products: 'He is betere an hundred folde/than alle theos in heore culur.'[70] In France, the imagination of Villon, with its mixture of tenderness and irony, can blend scepticism with nostalgia in a sophisticated secular wisdom:

---

hwilynde temporary

Où est le tres sage Heloïs
Pour qui chastré fut et puis moine
Pierre Esbaillart à Saint Denis?
. . .
Mais où sont les neiges d'antan?[71]

(Where is Heloise, so wise, for whom Peter Abelard was first castrated then made monk at Saint Denis? But where are last year's snows?)

This ironic poise is absent in English poetry; even Chaucer, in *The Book of the Duchess*, which is a finely sustained example of this traditional lament, directs his humour towards the naïve dreamer who fails fully to understand the nature of loss, thus enforcing, not mitigating, the elegiac intensities of the Man in Black. In a poet like Lydgate there is a total divorce between religious scepticism and secular nostalgia;[72] in many of his secular poems and in *The Fall of Princes*, he laments tenderly the passing of the great and the changing sweetness of the seasons, yet in the religious poems he affirms that he prefers God's mercies to the deeds of the past, the figure of Mary to the mighty women of old, the song of the Scriptures to that of the poets, for where the rose fades, the roses of Christ's wounds are everlasting, where the seasons change, the sweetness of Mary is unvarying.[73]

Despite such dualities, poems on the theme of *ubi sunt* have a peculiar consistency, for they tend to assume the same formalized patterns; thus, in Chaucer, the complaints amongst his minor poems are more conditioned by technique than any of his other works.[74] One may, for example, move with no sense of interruption from that thirteenth-century 'Lov Ron' to Dunbar's 'Of Man's Mortalitee', written late in the fifteenth century:

Worthye Hector and Hercules,
Forcye Achill and strong Sampsone,
Alexander of grit nobilnes,
Meik David and fair Absolone,
Hes playit thair pairtis, and all are gone
At will of God that all thing steiris;
Think, man, exceptioun thair is none,
Sed tu in cinerem reverteris.[75]

Dunbar's heroes are no longer the maculate figures of romance; that the exalted and various virtue of the classical or biblical great should prove no insurance against death, enforces the universality of his refrain. The question—'UUere beth they biforen us weren'—is discarded in face of the didactic (and materialist) rejoinder—*tu in cinerem reverteris.*

---

steiris steers

His lines, though so similar to those of Friar Thomas, are perceptibly the product of a later period, for the autumnal lament with its resigned cadence has become a dirge for inevitable dissolution; the theme is no longer one of romantic longing for the past, but has come very close to *memento mori*.

The similarity between these two poems, so widely separated in time, is, however, more striking than their difference; the mood, and hence the attitude, have changed, but the conventions of the language are unaltered. The omnipresence of the theme no doubt encourages this formality, for it is the profoundly general that demands its own ritual. Formality, moreover, is no real obstacle to the personal; a convention may assert that an emotion is common to all, and yet, as everyone knows, the discovery of general truth has always, in personal life, the shock of the unforeseen. The point is poignantly made in Chaucer's *Book of the Duchess*, for the fact of his lady's death is both unacceptable to the Man in Black, and reaches the dreamer with a shock that deprives him of speech. Moreover, the lover's description of his lady is charged with life: as in lyric poetry, it is the dead in *ubi sunt* vision who live, whilst the living are without vitality—the colours, black for the living, white for the dead, have their relevance. The life of Dame White is like that of a soul which has animated the body of her lover, but leaves it a shell in absence.[76] Significantly, the dreamer takes love, not death, to be the cause of the speaker's misery, an imputation which the Man in Black rejects indignantly. Only in describing his lady does he recover that vitality of language which love has taught him to sing:

'I sawgh hyr daunce so comlily,
Carole and synge so swetely,
Laughe and pleye so womanly,
And loke so debonairly,
So goodly speke and so frendly,
That, certes, y trowe that evermor
Nas seyn so blysful a tresor.' (ll. 848–54)

In his imagination, the dead lady lives, and it is the uncomprehending dreamer who asks him the insistent question of lament: ' "Where is she now?" '[77]

The Book of the Duchess is not only a fine example of that movement between the general and personal which the theme of *ubi sunt* permits; the poem also indicates that, although the emotion of the genre finds its readiest expression in the brevity of the lyric, it is not confined to that form. For *The Book of the Duchess* is more than a protracted elegy or complaint: it is a debate, and the delicate emotions of loss and regret prove finally more durable than the bracing Boethean consolations that the dreamer offers. Imagination prevails over reason, both in persuading the dreamer that the dead still live, and, through that persuasion, finally rendering his advocacy of resignation irrelevant. If, as Clemen suggests, the conventions which belong to complaint contribute to the dreamer's confusion, it might also be remarked that it is in their nature to promote just that kind of misunderstanding: for poems in this genre the dead, in terms of art, do not die.[78]

This emotion, apparently so frail, perhaps proves so durable because it is rooted in romance imagination, for lyrical nostalgia may sometimes develop into an attitude, or even an ethos. This can be as true for the religious as for the secular voice, as the following passage from a sermon suggests:

But here what David the prophete seys, that oure seyntes ben goyn awey:.. 'good Lord, seyth he, make us save, for seyntes ther is none as ther were,' . . . I shall afferme that yiff this world be an enterludie, as doctors ymagynne, I wote never who shall pley the seynte in oure enterludie. For in comparison that it was som tyme, vertewes morall ben goyn. Feyth, hope, and charite be welnygh exiled, and sewerly with-owte thise vertewes may be no seynt in this liff.[79]

The preacher of this sermon, like the poets of *ubi sunt* lyrics, can conceive of the present only as a decline; the great figures which once sustained men—for such giants are necessary to our moral sustenance—'ben goyn awey', and the present can boast no saints 'as ther were'. The image of life in this world as an 'interlude', an intermediary act inserted in God's great drama which stretches before and after, takes on a special poignancy with the remark that there are no players left suitable to be cast in the great roles. The interlude recurs as an image in Dunbar's 'Lament for the Makaris', where it touches upon a notion essential to lament: that the present is phantasmagoric, because faith in human greatness has been lost; whilst the past, with its great role players, continues to command belief. Even the 'makaris' who compose the dramatic pieces, themselves 'amang the laif/Playis heir ther pageant, syne gois to graif'.[80]

It is never quite possible for the religious imagination to believe as fully in the achievements of the past as the secular poets, particularly those concerned with Arthurian legend, can be shown to do. As the preacher indicates, the note of regret is present in the Old Testament; religion, concerned with the span of divine, not human, history, thus traces decline from the Fall of man and his expulsion from Paradise. In the mystery cycles, the elegiac note echoes through all those scenes

---

sewerly certainly   *laif* rest

which occur within the temporal span; as soon as Adam steps out into the world as we know it, the lament is heard: 'Gone ar my games withowten glee.'[81] Abraham, though initiating a new age of man, nevertheless regrets the great past, as though he were marking a new stage in human decline, rather than a fresh beginning:

> when I thynk of oure elders all,
>   And of the mervels that has been,
> No gladnes in my hart may fall,
>   My comfort goys away full cleyn.[82]

Even the Incarnation does little to arrest this sense of decay, although it reveals that history, after all, has been no recession from Paradise, but a progression from the *felix culpa* of Adam to the triumph of this redeeming birth. Only when the Last Day puts an end to time, does the inescapable sadness of transience at last dissolve. The warning offered to Anti-Christ:

> And as the flowrs now springes,
> falleth, fadeth, and hings,
> so thy ioy now it raignes,
> that shall from thee be rafte—

is redressed at last by the words of the Regina Salvata:

> My flesh that as a flower can flee,
> and Powder was, through thy pitty
> togeather hath brought, as I now se,
> the soule the body too.[83]

Only to the Damned does the image of natural transience remain relevant: 'my flesh as flowr, that all to-flaw,/now tydes a fearly fitt.'[84] For the Saved, the flower loses forever its haunting significance as time is brought to an end.

The mystery cycles are, however, dominated by the ascending ladder of God's eternal plan; when poets look to the passage of purely human events, the cycle of the flower is endlessly repeated. Political verse will often invoke the great analogies of the past; thus Barbour, when attacking the treachery of Edward I to Bruce, instantly invokes the betrayal of Arthur and Alexander.[85] A remembrance of the great and fallen may also serve as a rebuke for present decadence; Richard II and Edward II are, predictably, often recalled for this purpose, in a tone poised between admiration and censure. Here indeed the theme of transience seems to

---

to-flaw flew asunder   *tydes* suffers   *fearly* dreadful

merge with that of mutability, as the cycle of Nature and of the wheel become identified in that form inscribed by tragedy (in the medieval sense):

> Se howe Richard, of Albyon the kyng,
>   Which in his tyme ryche and glorious was,
> Sacred with abyt, with corone, and with ring,
>   Yit fel his fortune so, and eke his cas,
>   That yvel counseyle rewled him so, elas!
> For mys-tretyng lordes of his monarchye,
> He feyne was to resigne and in prysone dye.[86]

A didactic sense that the great are those whose souls stand most in peril, may come to dominate the elegiac cadence: when Elde, in *The Parlement of the Thre Ages*, asks the familiar question—' "Whare es now Dame Dido was qwene of Cartage?" '—his tone is vindictive rather than regretful.[87] Edward IV is particularly subject to such harsh treatment, yet his lament also retains the familiar 'dying fall':

> Where is my gret conquest & vyctory?
>   Where be my Rentis & my Ryall aray?
> Where be my coursors & my horsys so hy?
>   Where is my grett plesure, solas & play?
> As vanite to noughte all ys gon away.[88]

This poem, like Skelton's *Magnificence*,[89] loses its sense of a golden past, since the *ubi sunt* lament, for didactic reasons, is narrowed to a sense of personal loss. It retains the elegiac cadence largely because Edward IV's death, unlike that of his two unhappy predecessors, falls within the natural order—'I ly now in mowlde as it ys naturall . . . I have pleyd my pagent.'

Où sont les neiges d'antan? becomes a cry subject to a variety of interpretations: it can stand as a warning to the proud and presumptuous, or express nostalgia for perished brilliance; it can indicate the vanity of beauty, or suggest that transience is its essence. Yet even the most didactic of these poems carries some trace of romantic recall, a nostalgia to be found, in its most elevated and sustained form, in Arthurian literature. Because these legends recall no actual age, but one which, for imaginative purposes, had to exist, their spell is the more powerful; unhampered by historical fact, the mind is free to idealize the past without impediment. Despite some early sceptics amongst scholars and historians, the need to believe in Arthurian civilization proved stronger, for the greater part of the Middle Ages, than the demand for proof.[90] Thomas Churchyard, writing in 1587, still sustains this conviction, despite renaissance scepticism:

And though we count, but Robin Hood a Jest,
And old wives tales, as tatling toyes appeare:
Yet Arthurs raigne, the world cannot denye,
Such proofe there is, the troth thereof to trye:
That who so speakes, against so grave a thing,
Shall blush to blot, the fame of such a King.[91]

It is significant that those medieval writers—Malory and the poet of the stanzaic *Morte Arthur*—who place the deeds of Arthur most firmly in long-past history, should discover the elegiac tone more fully than those—the author of the alliterative *Morte Arthure*, even the *Gawain*-poet—who treat those deeds as virtually contemporary. The martial spirit and purpose of the *Morte Arthure* has little of that historical sense which sadly marks the decline of even the best of created things; it anchors Arthur's failure firmly to explanation, on the one hand to a dangerous development of the lust for blood and conquest which overtakes the Round Table, on the other to the arbitrary ascent and fall of Fortune's wheel.[92] Malory, who clearly regards himself as an historian, can invoke both the fallibility of men and the inexorability of Fortune, without making either the dominant explanation. At least as important is the effect of the Grail quest, where the best, in the divine plan, destroy the good that human and temporal societies can achieve. Before the knights depart on that sublime and fatal journey, the King already addresses them elegiacally:

'I am sure at this quest of the Sankegreall shall all ye of the Rownde Table departe, and nevyr shall I se you agayne hole togydirs, therefore ones shall I se you togydir in the medow of Camelot, to juste and to turney, that aftir youre dethe men may speke of hit that such good knyghtes were here, such a day, hole togydirs.'[93]

That reiteration of 'hole togydirs' is the more poignant because so many knights fall by the wayside in the spiritual quest; the ethic of errantry no longer suffices, and those, the great majority, who fail spiritually, cannot recover the temporal ideal they once held. Instead they turn upon, and destroy, each other: the internecine brawls of Gawain's family gather impetus, and Arthur's depleted court can no longer contain their violence.

Malory gives many other 'reasons' for the collapse of Arthurian civilization. Lancelot forgets, though not permanently, 'the promyse and the perfeccion that he made in the queste', and resorts again to the queen; cruel accident and coincidence speed Fortune's wheel—when unwittingly he kills Gawain's brothers; when a sword, thoughtlessly drawn to slay an adder in the grass, precipitates the final battle.[94] That fatal jealousy of human distinction, which destroys so many achievements of men, makes its own contribution, as Malory remarks:

He that was the moste kynge and nobelyst knyght of the worlde, and moste loved the felyshyp of noble knyghtes, and by hym they all were upholdyn, and yet myght nat thes Englyshemen holde them contente with hym. Lo thus was the olde custom and usayges of thys londe, and men say that we of thys londe have nat yet loste that custom. Alas! thys ys a greate defaughte of us Englysshemen, for there may no thynge us please no terme.   (pp. 861–2)

The death of Arthur is thus complex and many-faceted, embracing both the secular perspective of time, and the religious, of eternity. It does not merely indicate that all men must die, but affirms the value of man's endeavour: if human fallibility brings low the proud, the good are defeated only by the best, and the achievements of Arthurian society remain those of temporal excellence. Natural transience, though never a dominant explanation, is nevertheless the prevailing tone. It is heard even at the Round Table's foundation, for Merlin constantly prophesies the collapse to come; for a time, in the Quest of the Grail, it is held in suspension; but with the return, in the last two books, to the world of time, it becomes inescapable.[95] It can be felt in the passages already quoted, and reaches its climax in the concluding elegies, spoken by Lancelot over the bodies of Arthur and Guinevere, and by Sir Ector, over Lancelot's body.

A new harmony is reached when Lancelot, from his repentant heart, laments the passing of the great: ' "For whan I remembre of hir beaulté and of hir noblesse, that was bothe wyth hyr kyng and wyth hyr, so whan I sawe his corps and hir corps so lye togyders, truly myn herte wold not serve to susteyne my careful body" ' (p. 880). But where Lancelot speaks for the King and Queen, Sir Ector, in lamenting the proudest of its knights, testifies to the Round Table as a whole. His elegy, in stressing Lancelot's temporal, not ideal, virtue, seems, by implication, to promise salvation to all 'synful' men:

'A, Lancelot!' he sayd, 'thou were hede of al Crysten knyghtes! And now I dare say,' sayd syr Ector, 'thou sir Lancelot, there thou lyest, that thou were never matched of erthely knyghtes hande. And thou were the curtest knyght that ever bare shelde! And thou were the truest frende to thy lovar that ever bestrade hors, and thou were the trewest lover of a synful man that ever loved woman, and thou were the kyndest man that ever strake wyth swerde. And thou were the godelyest persone that ever cam emonge prees of knyghtes, and thou were the mekest man and the jentyllest that ever ete in halle emonge ladyes, and thou were the sternest knyght to thy mortal foo that ever put spere in the reeste.'   (p. 882)

Malory is in love with the greatness of the Arthurian past, and his work brings many other instruments to orchestrate the full range and depth of *ubi sunt* melody. By comparison, the stanzaic *Morte Arthur* is chamber music, and the elegiac note is both more solitary and more lyrical. The common underestimation of this late fourteenth-century poem may indeed result from its exclusion of resonant martial cadence,[96] but if its fidelity to the theme of natural transience confines its range, its realization of that theme has its own mastery. The poem is, from its opening, suffused with a sense of decline and retrospect: the quest for the Grail is over, and all the other great 'Aunturs . . ./Fynisshid and to ende brought'.[97] For four years the court has lived in peace, but its calm, as Guinevere warns Arthur, marks, like that of Age, the onset of decline:

'Syr, your honour by-gynyys to falle,
    That wount was wide in world to sprede,
Off launcelott and of other all
    That evyr so doughty were in dede.' (ll. 25–8)

This note of regret for past greatness, together with an apprehension of imminent death, thus reverberates through the poem; Sir Bedwere's claim that he has seen nothing in the sea ' "But watres depe And wawes wanne" ' captures in a line the moral and emotional landscape of the whole. Disguise and duplicity bring suffering, separation and death to innocent and guilty alike. The tournament that Guinevere has proposed as a cure for the ills of peace, leads eventually to Lancelot's separation from her and from the court, which robs the Round Table of its integrity: 'In the courte was litelle pryde,/So sore they sighyd for his sake.' The innocent Maid of Ascalot anticipates her own death from the moment she falls in love with Lancelot, as Guinevere, in her jealousy of the Maid, does also: ' "I may wofully wepe and wake/In clay tylle I be clongyn cold." '[98] Arthur's lament over Lancelot expresses that conflict of opposed loyalties which lies at the poem's centre:

'Allas!' than sayd the kynge thore,
    'Certes, that were grete pyte,
So As man nad nevyr yit more
    Off biaute ne of bounte
Ne man in worlde was nevyr yit ore
    Off so mykylle noblyte
Allas! full grete duelle it were
    In hym shulde Any treson be. (ll. 1736–43)

The battle with the despicable Mordred, although the actual cause of Arthur's death, is far less painful than his unwilling conflict with

---

duelle sorrow

Lancelot, for the virtues and achievement of the Round Table and those of love are not to be reconciled here any more than in Malory: social and personal integrity are inevitably at odds. This perception again promotes that most poignant of recognitions—that the conflict does not lie finally between the virtuous and the vicious, for it is different forms of virtue which destroy each other.

Le Morte Arthur is, however, by no means a pessimistic poem. Not only is the dead Arthur felt to live, but so too is Lancelot, for whilst the knight is dying, the Archbishop dreams that his body is being borne to heaven by angels. Yet the promise of an afterlife, though allowed to offer comfort at the close, obtrudes very little in the poem. The imagination remains centred on its vision of this world, perceiving both its value and its transience: 'Allas! thys day so sone is goone!' *Le Morte Arthur* is, moreover, a deeply religious poem, in the best, not the conventional, sense; for its profound feeling for inevitable transience neither generates contempt for this life, nor induces horror at the prospect of the grave. The passing of man's brief day, like the passage of the seasons, meets with natural acceptance, just as Autumn can, in ordinary life, be welcomed for its special poetry of sadness. Because transience is accepted as a part of the natural order, it does not make endeavour in human life mere vanity, any more than Winter makes mockery of the previous Summer and Spring.

Although both the seasons and *ubi sunt* may have their darker reaches, the reassurance of the natural cycle, and the resignation of the human, predominate. The medieval belief that Nature was God's special creation may have exacerbated a sense of determinism,[99] but where the revolt against Fortune leads to pessimism, the acceptance of transience invites tranquillity. Whilst religious writing may find hope in the Gospel image of the grain, it can, however, invoke the flower in a darker vein which derives from the Book of Job:

Man that is born of woman is of few days and full of trouble. He cometh forth like a flower and is cut down. He fleeth also as a shadow and endureth not.

This path leads to admonition rather than resignation, so that one medieval preacher gives a savage turn to the question, ' "Where ben all these worldely lovers that were here a litill before with us?" ' when he replies in the words of St Bernard, ' "here sowles ben in hell, and there flessh is geven to wormes to ete" '.[100] The shadow here dominates the fragile flower; but another preacher, less explicitly echoing the elegiac question, comes closer to its spirit when he writes:

Man's lyffe may well be figurde by roosis in iii degreis. ffyrst there is a bud, in the whiche the rosis ben closyd. And aftyr, owte of this bud spryngythe a feyre rose and a swete and a delicius. And sone aftyr, with wyndys and weders the levis fadithe a-wey to the grownde, and so turnethe to erthe.[101]

In lyric poetry, religious and secular, the image of the flower can thus mitigate the horrors of mortality by suffusing death with autumnal resignation:[102]

> Nou skrinketh rose ant lylie-flour
> that whilen ber that suete savour
>   in somer, that suete tyde;
> ne is no quene so stark ne stour
> ne no levedy so bryht in bour
>   that ded ne shal by glyde.[103]

The fate of rose and lily remains distinct from that of human beauty, but the one may relieve the harshness of the other. Lydgate, whose feeling for the natural world is unusually insistent, often tempers his monk's didacticism with a natural image which assuages its severity:

> In large lakys and riveers fressh rennyng,
>   The yelwe Swan famous and aggreable,
> Ageyn his deth melodyously syngyng,
>   His fatal notys pitous and lamentable;
>   Pleynly declare in erthe is no thyng stable,
> His byl, his feet, whoso look ariht,
>   In tokne of moornyng be of colour sable;
> Look in thy myrour and deeme noon othir wiht.[104]

Although his *Fall of Princes* tends, in its later books, to exhibit a deadened, didactic sense of mutability, Lydgate returns in his envoy to the note of natural resignation, and recovers the finest quality of his imagination (Plate 12). Even in the most moralistic writing, the elegiac sense can prove its strength: the Regina Damnata in the Chester Last Judgement expresses less the terror of Hell than regret for the vanished beauties of life.[105]

If, in the most severe religious writing, the flower can still soften the cruelty of mortality, the perilous beauty of its fragile cycle can, in secular and especially Arthurian story, inscribe both the great flowerings of civilization and their inevitable decay. The great dead mark the grand stages of human achievement, and the vulnerability of man may (in certain perspectives, though clearly not in all) render his successes more, and not less, precious.[106] The elegiac motif is far less complex than the medieval concept of Fortune; it is certainly less cerebral, and

---

stark strong

its development less intricate, because it is an intuition of the imagination rather than a dialogue of the mind. Yet the intuitions of the imagination have a profundity of their own; and in their acceptance of the transience of all created things, the perceptions of the poets may sometimes reach beyond the debates of the philosophers.

Unlike the affirmation of seasonal sequence, or the resignation of *ubi sunt* lament, the cycle of Fortune has little reassurance to offer the victims of time, for the rise and fall of her wheel is as arbitrary as it is inevitable, and testifies to a world, distinct from the ordered transience of nature, which is continually prey to the anarchy of mutability. This cruel figure represents, however, the conviction of poets rather than philosophers: as Virgil explains to Dante in the *Inferno*, *Fortuna*, properly understood, is yet another *general ministra e duce* (universal minister and leader), entrusted by God with the distribution of *li ben vani* (empty possessions), so that a rhythm, similar to Nature's own, is established from civilization to civilization—*Perchè una gente impera, e l'altra langue* (hence one people dominates, another languishes).[107] Seen in a timeless perspective, Fortune is neither anarchic nor vindictive; she is an angelic presence, her eyes fixed upon her creator, immune to human recrimination:

> 'Quest' è colei ch' è tanto posta in croce
> Pur da color che le dovrian dar lode,
> Dandole biasmo a torto e mala voce.

> Ma ella s'è beata, e cio non ode:
> Con l'altre prime creature lieta
> Volve sua spera, e beata si gode.' (VII, ll. 91–6)

(This is she who is so much abused, even by those who should praise her, when blaming her wrongly and with foul language. But she is in bliss and does not hear it: joyful amongst the other primal creatures, she turns her sphere, and rejoices in her blessedness.)

The serenity of this description is emphasized by its context—the eternal habitation of those who have irrevocably fallen from that wheel; this is not the earthbound viewpoint, to be found in most English poetry, where Fortune gazes vindictively downwards upon the puppets of her whims. When, in this perspective, she retains a function in the divine order, it is merely because her interventions confirm the vanity of human aspiration; she is a sublunar figure of menace and revenge, who moves in the dark company of Age and Death. Where *ubi sunt* may come to affirm the value, as well as the sadness, of transience, Fortune renders the mutable a mockery.

It is in part the 'substantiality' of this figure which causes her to dominate the medieval mind: she interposes between God and man like a cloud between sun and earth. Nature is an equally specific personification, but, unlike Fortune, she commonly retains her heavenly context; whilst on earth her visible manifestations, as the law which governs seasonal sequence and animal behaviour, are directly expressive of the harmony of divine order. Fortune's effects, however, are as clearly negative as those of Nature are positive, and because her providential function è occulto, come in l'erba l'angue (is hidden, like a snake in the grass), a belief in the constructiveness of that purpose is not easily sustained. It is rare, in English literature, to find a writer who can sense in the rhythms of Fortune the naturalness of the flower's decline; in this darker view, man 'fleeth as a shadow and endureth not', a vision that is without comfort. The conviction is emotional, not rational, for, as Reason observes in the Roman de la Rose:

> '. . . mieuz vaut au genz et profite
> Fortune perverse et contraire
> que la mole et la debonaire.'[108]

> (Ill or contrary Fortune is more valuable and profitable to men than good and favourable.)

But, as Reason has earlier noted of Age, no one welcomes decline on account of its insights; similarly, few would prefer the wisdom of the wheel's base to the ignorance of its apex.

Enfranchisement from Fortune's domination seems, however, to occur in English poetry in rhythm—as an imaginative freedom—before it is achieved conceptually. It may also be significant that the single poet to achieve this freedom, writing in English in the fifteenth century, should be Charles d'Orléans, a Frenchman, captured at Agincourt, and imprisoned in England for twenty-five years. During that period he wrote many poems in the language of his (enforced) adoption, some of them translations of his own French originals, a great number lamenting the undoubted ill-fortune of his lot. Yet, just as Villon brings to the theme of ubi sunt a sophisticated poise rarely found in English, so Charles d'Orléans achieves an equanimity in his treatment of the difficult goddess which cannot be paralleled in England for another century. In the following verse, for example, wit combines with measure to control the troubled oscillation typical of contemporary English verse:

> Toforne love have y pleyd at the chesse
> To passe the tyme with cursid false daungere
> And kepte eche poynt bi good avysynes
> Withouten losse to that as wol ye here

> That fortune came to strengthyn his matere
> O woo worthe she that my game ovyrthrew
> For tane she hath my lady welaway
> That y am matt this may y se and say
> Without so be y make a lady newe[109]

The courtier's wit, which here links the fickleness of Fortune with that of woman in the image of the game, anticipates a moment in Wyatt, where the courtier's grace establishes the same connection in the more traditional image of the wheel:

> Ons in your grace I knowe I was,
>   Evyn as well as now ys he;
>   Tho ffortune so hath tornyd my case,
>   That I am doune, and he ffull hye,
>   Yet ons I was.[110]

The poem is clearly written within the tradition of the medieval figure, but the wheel turns easily within its rhythms, in a manner that assuages even as it bereaves. Moreover, Fortune herself is mentioned by name only once in the full seven verses, and she has little substantial being, for the verses are addressed to Wyatt's fickle lady; by the fusion of the two, the abstract is humanized, and becomes an opponent with whom combat is possible. The movement of the wheel in this case is even a source of adornment and form; yet, only a half century earlier, the dislocating motion, and the darkly substantial goddess, still figure in this representative verse:

> A! mercy, Fortune, have pitee on me,
> And thinke that thu hast done gretely amisse
> To parte asondre them whiche ought to be
> Alwey in on. Why hast thu doo thus?
> Have I offended thee? I? Nay! iwisse.
> Then turne thy whele and be my frende again,
> And send me joy where I am nowe in pain.[111]

Not only are Fortune and her wheel clearly represented in the verse; the poet's address is wholly directed to her, and his rhythms, until the last two lines, are the broken ones of mutability. The wheel turns regularly only when it is felt to ascend.

English literature of the fourteenth and fifteenth centuries treats the subject of Fortune with a grim seriousness from which the saving grace of Wyatt or d'Orléans is wholly excluded. It is the dominant medieval subject, and, even in lyric poetry, its oppression is a felt weight. In part

---

matt mate

this gravity is due to the long history of the theme in those 'treatises' to which de Meun's Reason refers; its intellectual life is, to Chaucer's knowledge, at least a thousand years old when he comes to write *The Knight's Tale* and *Troilus and Criseyde*, both of which draw directly upon its originator, Boethius. Whilst this long history suits the theme to the more ambitious forms of literature, an awareness of its philosophical complexities may become, as in the fourth book of *Troilus and Criseyde*, a burden upon the poetry; the complicated debates on freewill and determinism to which the concept of Fortune leads are not readily assimilable to poetic experience. Nevertheless, *The Knight's Tale* and *Troilus* are amongst the greatest medieval poems, for the attempt to engage with the full complexities of the subject elicits many profound human perceptions; whilst the superficial allusions of many lyrics, where Fortune dwindles to a merely rhetorical figure, and the problems she generates are invoked with a complacence ignorant of their difficulty, obstruct real insight or response. Her reduction to another variant of the grave wisdom of *contemptus mundi* is characteristic of such writing: 'What is this worlde but oonly vanyte?/Who trustith fortune sonnest hath a falle.'[112]

Although Fortune is certainly an obsession with the later Middle Ages, it would be wrong to conclude that it is merely an antiquated interest, peculiar to a period in the past. The issues of freewill and determinism which stem from it have never become irrelevant, although they have often assumed a place less central. We now discuss genetic, economic or environmental determinism, where the medieval writer spoke of divine omnipotence, of Fate, Fortune and the influence of the stars; yet all these terms are only different formulations of that troubling and inescapable sense that, although we would like to believe that we can choose what we are and do, we are all the time determined by influences quite beyond our control. It is because Fortune comes to express such problems that she dominates late medieval poetry; all other figures and themes encounter each other in her eventually, as the great 'Why?' of existence. It is an irony of history that the medieval interest in Boethius should have ended in comfirming man's servitude to Fortune, for the *Consolatio*, as the Elizabethans realized, specifically intends to rid men of the belief that they are prey to an arbitrary force which they cannot control.[113] For the Middle Ages, the arguments that Philosophy displaces prove more durable than those she advances.

One explanation of this curious tendency may lie in the strength of the medieval allegoric imagination; when abstracts are more real than specific individual dilemmas (Boethius' Philosophy seeks to redress that balance in Book II), it is natural to delineate Fortune as a figure, and correspondingly alien to internalize to the mind the problems that figure implies. Where those problems *are* shown to be those of the individual consciousness, as in Henryson's *Testament of Cresseid*, the cosmic complexities of Fortune are distanced and simplified. This solution was always open, for, as Robertson has pointed out, it is possible to read the *Consolatio* itself 'as a fable consisting of a dialogue between two parts of the same person'.[114] Dante certainly attempted to do so, for he asserts in the *Convivio* that Boethius is merely using the dialogue form as a cover for self-justification;[115] yet the Fortune of the *Inferno* remains a figure, even if divine.

The *Consolatio* was not an original work, but few of its sources survived into the Middle Ages, so that it remained the seminal text for nearly all medieval art, thought and literature concerned with Fortune. Its colouring is strongly Neo-Platonic, and its acceptance by the Middle Ages probably owes much to that fact; yet, whilst it contains no doctrines antipathetic to Christianity, it includes none that is strictly Christian. The theories of the *Consolatio* are pagan in origin, and the background of the work is that of Greek and Arab determinism.[116] Although, at the end of the Middle Ages, predestination is a conviction of Calvin and Luther, it is basically at odds with Christian thinking; the soul must earn its reward through its own endeavours, even though these alone will not suffice without God's grace. The *Consolatio*, however, is at root an attempt to confront the determinism of the pagan world with the argument that man is rational and free.

The dialogue between Boethius and Philosophy is conducted in the cell where the author is imprisoned (as he actually was) for his service to the state. His lament, which retains its spell for so many centuries after his cruel execution, is that man alone should seem to be excluded from the harmonious order which visibly governs the rest of the natural world; the wicked flourish, whilst the just suffer. Philosophy first invalidates this complaint (which she says is exacerbated by poetry), by demonstrating that man too is contained within that order; it is as part of this argument that she mentions Fortune, in order to show that her desertion of Boethius is natural, not arbitrary (Plate 17):

'Tu fortunam putas erga te esse mutatam; erras. Hi semper eius mores sunt ista natura. Servavit circa te propriam potius in ipsa sui mutabilitate constantiam.'[117]

(You think Fortune has been fickle to you; you are wrong. Such manners are invariably her nature. She has kept constancy in her bearing to you in her very mutability.)

The case for Socratic detachment is carefully elaborated, but this serves only to cultivate an attitude of mind which can sustain Fortune's blows; it does not justify her place in a providential creation. When Philosophy moves on to that point, she seeks perversely to destroy the vindictive figure she has so indelibly delineated, where Dante, by rendering the

Goddess beatific, can more easily assimilate her to divine harmony. Philosophy's argument is based upon the Neo-Platonic conception of the spiritual cosmos as an orb, with God at its centre, and Fate in control of the circumference.[118] Fortune, Chance and Fate are thus, in a sense, illusions, since they are ministers which a perfect providence employs in order to operate in an imperfect world; they are not, in other words, forces in their own right. As ministers they share to some degree in the imperfections of the world, but man's mistake is to see no further than their distorted forms. If he looks beyond them, as Theseus does in *The Knight's Tale*, he will perceive that the world is not a cruel, anarchic place, but is firmly bound in that 'faire cheyne of love', which operates through the mutable, but emanates from the immutability of God.

Caeci numinis ambiguos vultus (the shifting aspect of the blind Goddess) which Boethius has discovered, is not easily forgotten, however (Plate 19); in endeavouring to destroy her dominance over men, to render her a transparency through which the light of God's providence is visible, Philosophy, paradoxically, succeeds only in establishing the substantial form and entrenched position which Fortune enjoys for so many subsequent centuries.[119] The very humanity of the *Consolatio* leads it to have the opposite effect from the one it intends; for the complaints of Boethius remain more memorable than the counsels he receives, the blind Goddess more substantial than the arguments intended to displace her. Philosophy is less than wise in speaking of Fortune as an actual figure, whom at one point she even endows with speech.[120] When she disproves the existence of Chance her tactics are much more effective, for she employs the Aristotelian argument which disposes of the concept by showing it to be merely a collection of secondary causes.[121] Aquinas, who treats Fortune, Fate and Chance as synonyms, is careful to avoid the personified figure; although he takes from Boethius a number of the observations which relate to Fortune, he relates them as general principles (not specific characteristics) to the explanation from secondary causes.[122] But his arguments leave as little mark upon literature as those of Philosophy, thus confirming the latter's suspicion of the Muses. Only exceptional writers—Dante, Chaucer, the *Gawain*-poet and Langland—can, in their very different ways, prevent the shadow of Fortune from obscuring the light of that providence she serves.

The construction of 'the faire cheyne of love', whilst disposing of Fortune, creates new problems in the *Consolatio*, for Boethius is thence led to ask:

'Sed in hac haerentium sibi serie causarum estne ulla nostri arbitrii libertas an ipsos quoque humanorum motus animorum fatalis catena constringit?'[123]

(But in this coherent series of causes, do we have any free-will, or does the fatal chain bind too the movements of the human mind?)

Philosophy's reply to that question is complex,[124] for it centres upon the argument that necessity is dependent upon time; thus God, to whom all time is contemporaneous, does not impose necessity, and no conflict therefore exists between divine foreknowledge and human freedom. Aquinas, in the image of pilgrimage quoted at the beginning of this chapter, reformulates this argument in terms which, if simplified, are also more accessible.[125] As Nature remarks in the *Roman de la Rose*, the question is not one for *lais genz* (laymen) to resolve; divine foreknowledge and human freedom must be compatible, however, for to deny the first is to impugn God's omnipotence, whilst to negate the second is to claim that men can merit neither reward nor punishment.[126]

Despite Nature's good sense, laymen do, however, continue to puzzle over this apparent paradox, whether with anguish, as in Langland's discussion of predestination,[127] or, like the Nun's Priest, in order to generate amusement at its convolutions:

> Wheither that Goddes worthy forwityng
> Streyneth me nedely for to doon a thyng,—
> 'Nedely' clepe I symple necessitee;
> Or elles, if free choys be graunted me
> To do that same thyng, or do it noght,
> Though God forwoot it er that was wrought.[128]

The argument itself forms a circle in the mind, resembling the wheel; it is only to be resolved if the mind takes off at a tangent, and inspects its preoccupation from an independent standpoint. Where Troilus travels heavenwards, to adopt a timeless perspective, the Nun's Priest comes as firmly down to earth: 'I wol nat han to do of swich mateere;/My tale is of a cok, as ye may heere.'

The conflicting authorities mentioned by the Nun's Priest—Augustine, Boethius and Bradwardine—succinctly suggest the range of medieval positions. Augustine's *De Libero Arbitrio* affirms the existence and importance of human freedom of choice. Boethius, and after him Aquinas, allow it a necessary, but more limited, area of operation; the causality of God may work upon the will, but it is not determined by external agents.[129] Bradwardine agrees with Aquinas in rejecting all minor forms of determinism, such as natural necessity or psychological pressure; but, unlike his predecessors, he does not, on that account, preserve an area of decisive freedom. On the contrary, he denies absolutely the existence of any such freedom, on the grounds that God must will what he foresees, so that the good man is in consequence predestined to be saved.[130] It is not, however, the absolute of divine determinism which figures in medieval literature, but precisely those intermediate or minor forms which all four of those thinkers reject. This tendency to pursue middle

ways is not a reaction to scholastic thought, but a response to the figure
of Fortune, as distinct from the arguments which surround her; the
manifestations of apparently deterministic forces in this world prove more
persuasive to the imagination than the abstracts of divine foresight or
timelessness, whilst man's obstinate tendency to behave as if free,
whilst arguing that he is powerless to choose, endears the paradox at the
expense of its solution.

This characteristic difference between philosophy and poetry may be
briefly illustrated in the Wife of Bath. She is, both physically and
psychically, just what those planets, Venus and Mars, which presided
at her birth, determined that she should be; in this sense, her history
is wholly determined from the moment of her birth.[131] On the other
hand, she so consciously uses that argument as self-justification, whilst
taking so much decisive initiative in the development of her fortunes,
that the impression she gives seems to embody freedom itself. Chaucer's
relish for this paradox, that buoyancy which generates the very impression of freedom, is, however, unusual in medieval literature. Elsewhere,
as in the schools,[132] those writers who stressed the role of the stars (and
most did), were not automatically those who denied freewill; but the
tendencies went together. Thus, whilst so much writing in the later
Middle Ages is religious in tone, and intended to be thoroughly orthodox, the centrality of Fortune and the related figures of the planets tends
to reduce mankind to the status of puppets (Plate 6). Orthodoxy is
preserved only because the implications of this imaginative tendency
are rarely explored: man's lack of freedom is not, for example, allowed
to release him from responsibility for sin; it merely seems to debar him
from the attainment of real virtue.

The dominant theme of the later Middle Ages thus intensifies its
despair, rather than prompting its most distinguished literature. Its
intellectual complexity, moreover, demands expression in some spacious
dramatic structure, but Chaucer alone seems to discover forms adequate
to it. Even in a work conceived on the grand scale, like Lydgate's Fall of
Princes, the wheel of Fortune falls with a predictable thud which quickly
becomes monotonous. Chaucer's own Monk's Tale invites that criticism,
and receives it from the Host: ' "Swich talkyng is nat worth a boterflye,/
For thereinne is ther no desport ne game." '[133] When one has heard
one tale, one has heard them all; there is no room for development. For
these reasons, the possibilities of the theme can best be understood in
Chaucer, its most (and possibly sole) distinguished exponent. The whole
of Chaucer's literary development can, from one point of view, be expressed in terms of his interest in Fortune and the problems which
stem from her. Even the early poems, in which Chaucer's knowledge of
Boethius is still either only superficial or indirect, reveal a mind that is
disposed to the attitudes of the Consolatio, but is nevertheless exercised

by the ambiguities of the total wisdom it purports to offer. At the other extreme, after a period of intense and direct interest in the *Consolatio*,[134] the later *Canterbury Tales*, in their humorous treatment of the problem, suggest a mind finally content to leave these ambiguities unresolved, and to regard Boethean wisdom as personal, not comprehensive. The development of Chaucer's attitude to Fortune, marked by the three distinct stages in his creative life, thus embraces, in a rewarding form, most facets of that theme which, more than any other, obsessed the medieval imagination.

In his writings, Chaucer assumes three personae, of dreamer, scholar and pilgrim, which belong to his early, middle and late periods respectively; these various personae offer different perspectives on his attitude to Fortune, and may be used as a suggestive outline. The dreamer of the early poems[135] is intensely aware of the ambiguities of life; he is a man in search of total wisdom, yet he is an entirely passive recipient of its manifestations. From the beginning, Chaucer casts himself as an observer, and, unlike Boethius, his problem at this stage is not one of detachment but involvement. In *The Book of the Duchess*, for example, he learns from the failure, not the success, of Philosophy's argument for Socratic detachment, which he offers as consolation to the Man in Black:

> 'Remembre yow of Socrates,
> For he ne counted nat thre strees
> Of noght that Fortune koude doo.'
> 'No,' quod he, 'I kan nat soo.'   (ll. 717–20)

It is the rejection of this argument by the Man in Black which stands at the end of the poem, and if the dreamer does not totally abandon Philosophy's point, he certainly finds it insufficient.[136] Yet the balance he seeks is not unlike that of the *Consolatio*, although approached from a different direction: his involvement needs to be strong enough to prompt the search for a solution, and his detachment sufficiently firm to perceive the form that such an answer might take.

'Solution' is never a really apposite word for Chaucer, however, and the early poems particularly offer 'hints and guesses' rather than clear indications.[137] Unlike Boethius, Chaucer is never in danger of becoming imprisoned by a structure of explanation which is too neat and self-contained; as in the later poems, it is the habit of question, rather than the answers, which mainly interest him. As yet, however, Fortune is to him a figure, a literary convention, rather than a complex dramatic issue, and the fall of her wheel is a form rather than a problem. The

---

strees straws

ragedies of the Monk, probably first written at this period, are didactic eiterations of this negative pattern in human affairs. Where Boccaccio, n the original of these tales, *De Casibus Virorum Illustrium*, is deiberately ironic when he pleads for Fortune's help in completing a vork intended to show the vanity of such appeals,[138] Chaucer, who at a later period would certainly have savoured that self-mockery, makes 10 attempt whatever to explore the questions to which the figure gives ise. Nevertheless, the habit of search which characterizes the other early poems, and their receptive awareness of the mystery of life, has ts connection with *The Knight's Tale* and *Troilus and Criseyde*.

It must, however, have been an interest in the problem of Fortune, 10t simply her figure, which led Chaucer to translate the *Consolatio* in he 1380s.[139] It is revealing, in this connection, that his dramatic persona changes in *Troilus and Criseyde*; the scholar of the later poem remains, ike the earlier dreamer, at one remove from his material, for he is the recipient of his 'auctour', as the dreamer is of his dream; but where he latter accepts events as they come and tries to understand their significance, the scholar is fully aware of the form his story must take, and dramatizes his reluctance to accept that predestined shape. The later persona thus has more dramatic effect than the earlier, for he enacts the dilemma of his narrative: he has no freedom to change events, but can choose his own attitude to them, his interpretation of them.[140] Thus, n his own persona, Chaucer goes some way towards challenging that subjection to events which is at the root of the problem of Fortune.

The Knight's Tale, which, in an early version, probably preceded *Troilus and Criseyde*, renders less dramatically the conflict between freewill and determinism. Despite its imaginative vitality, *The Knight's Tale* is statuesque rather than mobile; its visions coexist, they do not cohere. One view, which remains dominant, is thoroughly deterministic; it sees human life as prey to capricious astrological deities, whose interventions precipitate anarchy, despite the order of humane government. Theseus may, for example, seek to resolve the bloody conflict of Palamon and Arcite in a bloodless tournament, but because of the intervention of Saturn, Arcite dies none the less. In the teeth of these forces, man can do so little that he is effectively no more than a cipher. It is not because Chaucer has failed in characterization that Palamon and Arcite are virtually indistinguishable: it is their attitude of mind, in its subservience to event, which renders them identical. Arcite, freed from prison, but banished from Emily, complains to his cousin: ' "Wel hath Fortune yturned thee the dys,/That hast the sighte of hire, and I th'absence." ' Palamon, however, though free to look upon Emily, also abuses the 'crueel goddes' for her indifference to men, especially those who remain ' "in prison and arreest" '; ' "Sith thou art at thy large, of prisoun free," ' he rejoins to Arcite, " 'greet is thyn avauntage/Moore than is

myn." '[141] Chaucer's question, 'Who hath the worse, Arcite or Pala
moun?'[142] both participates in this passive vision, and points the way to
that other, Boethean conception of life which Theseus adopts, and which
coexists with anarchic determinism: man's power to choose lies in his
freedom to adapt himself to whatever Fortune sends. The great speech
on the First Mover, with which the poem concludes, echoes the reason
ing offered by Philosophy in the *Consolatio*, just as the acceptance of a
random determinism by the two young knights reflects the world as the
imprisoned Boethius sees it. In the limited space which he allows to
freewill—' "To maken vertu of necessitee,/And tak it weel that we may
nat eschue" '[143]—Theseus renders the gist of Philosophy's advice. Where
the liberated Arcite and the imprisoned Palamon once lamented alike
the harshness of their lot, Palamon must now (since nothing can bring
Arcite back to life) make the best of a sad occasion by marrying Emily.
It is an additional irony, one which confirms the dominant pessimism
of the poem, that in so doing Palamon is merely enacting the will of
Saturn.

In *The Knight's Tale* Theseus alone achieves stature and dignity
because he alone remains, if not 'master of his fate', at least 'captain of
his soul'. In *Troilus and Criseyde*, this capacity to internalize the problem to the mind of an individual is true, to a varying extent, of all, and
not merely one, of the main characters. When, for example, Troilus is
struck with Cupid's dart,[144] one cannot say that Cupid is a distinct
presence in the poem as Saturn is in *The Knight's Tale*. Similarly, when
Criseyde asks ' "Who yaf me drynke?" '[145] as she sees Troilus ride by,
the answer is clearly no magic love potion, but Pandarus' careful preparation and her own receptive disposition; the responsibility for her
later betrayal of Troilus cannot be squarely placed at the door of events
over which she has no control, as Arcite's loss of Emily clearly can. So
many forces play upon Criseyde, and she permits them so readily to
determine her frail resolution, that it is hard to say just where the fault
lies, and necessary to feel that part, at any rate, resides in the heroine
herself. Troilus, moreover, is rewarded with salvation for his fidelity in
love, whilst it is left to Henryson to save Cresseid; yet even this distinction is ambiguous, for whilst Criseyde must be seen as partly responsible
for her unfaithfulness, it is harder to discern active virtue, as distinct
from passive disposition, in Troilus' fidelity. Just as Palamon and
Arcite are faint figures beside the active Theseus, so Troilus seems
curiously negative when compared with his mobile and fickle lady; at
the least, one is led to ask why his passivity should amount to virtue,
where hers declines into vice.

The poem is thus darkly coloured by determinism, and this tint is
deepened by the comments of the narrative voice. Criseyde's known
betrayal receives a larger resonance from its context in the known fall

f Troy: in anticipating the collapse of that city, Calchas unwittingly
ngineers the fall of the daughter he seeks to save. From its opening
ines, the poem inscribes the rise and descent of Fortune's wheel 'Fro
vo to wele, and after out of joie', and the narrative voice never permits
ts hearers to forget this ominous rhythm: ' "This Troilus is clomben on
he staire,/And litel weneth that he moot descenden." '146 It would,
1owever, be too simple to say that the poem is itself deterministic, for
he inevitability of events is sensed most fully in the words of the reluc-
ant scholar, who keeps reminding us that he cannot alter the statements
)f his authority, however much he would like to do so. Determinism
s thus primarily an artistic predicament, one inherent in the tragic story,
vhilst the position of the actors within that story is more ambiguous.
When, for example, Troilus watches from the walls of Troy for Criseyde's
)romised return from the Greek camp, the reader is well aware, because
)oth tradition and Chaucer have left him in no doubt of it, that Criseyde
vill never come; yet, like Troilus himself, the imagination leaps with
1ope as Troilus exclaims: ' "I se hire! yond she is!" '147 It is possible,
o the very end of the story, to feel that the tragic and inevitable outcome
s somehow resistable, and it is for this reason that, just as Theseus'
iffirmation remains distinct from the anarchic world of *The Knight's
Tale*, so the epilogue of *Troilus and Criseyde* remains a separate vision,
ichieved through a different medium. The temporal world of the greater
)art of the poem is, however, much less simple than that of *The Knight's
Tale*, and is, in consequence, both more baffling and less pessimistic.

The character of Pandarus anticipates the perspective which, in *The
Canterbury Tales*, transforms Chaucer's narrative figure from a scholar,
inhabiting a world of books, to a pilgrim, a participant in a world of
men; for Pandarus is not only intrinsically comic, but gives comic
utterance to almost all the positions in the *Consolatio*. When Troilus is
first love-stricken, Pandarus consoles him initially with an observation
which echoes Philosophy's to Boethius: that none is spared by fickle
Fortune's pride.148 Yet, having stated that ' "Fortune is comune/To
everi manere wight in som degree" ', Pandarus is quick to argue from
this the ' "comfort" ' that ' "as hire joies moten overgoon,/So mote hire
sorwes passen everechon" '.149 This argument, far from being Philosophy's, is found in the words which she attributes to Fortune herself:
'*Quid si haec ipsa mei mutabilitas iusta tibi causa est sperandi meliora?*'
(What if my mutability itself gives you proper reason to hope for better
things?)150 Adeptly, Pandarus then incorporates into his thesis the
earlier rebuke of Philosophy: that it is folly to try to stay the turning
wheel, for if that were possible, Fortune would not be Fortune.151 In
face of this fact, Philosophy counsels resignation, but Pandarus argues
that Troilus' fortunes are now bound to improve: ' "For if hire whiel
stynte any thyng to torne,/Than cessed she Fortune anon to be." '152

When Criseyde leaves Troy, Pandarus abuses Fortune with as much vehemence as do Troilus and Boethius, and even more surprise: ' "O mercy, God, who wolde have trowed this?" ' To judge from his earlier statements, Pandarus should be the last to express amazement at Fortune's abrupt reversals; yet the moral he draws from the event, though verbally parallel with his earlier optimism, is now entirely pessimistic

> 'Swich is this world! forthi I thus diffyne,
> Ne trust no wight to fynden in Fortune
> Ay propretee; hire yiftes ben comune.'[153]

At this point, however, Pandarus, like Theseus, advises Troilus to make a virtue of necessity, although his proposal—' "If she be lost, we shall recovere an other" '—is somewhat less elevated. The problems which so exercise Troilus become material for comedy in Pandarus; like the Wife of Bath, he is free where Troilus is enchained, because he can twist any argument to his purpose. Where good men can only escape the treadmill of this debate by adopting a viewpoint entirely outside the circumference of its circle, ordinary men can win their freedom (if not their salvation) by cheerful chicanery. The questions which appear so deeply to pre-preoccupy Chaucer in his middle period, recede, in *The Canterbury Tales*, where he joins that ordinary company, to a mere aspect of the human comedy. In the context of that pilgrimage, even the gloomy tales of the Monk and the Knight can become humorous comments upon their narrators, and the once total vision of their stories is held up simply as a mirror to the diversity of human attitudes.

The Knight, for example, finds it fitting to relate the ill-fortune of Arcite, yet he cannot stomach the analogous stories which the Monk offers; since, of all the pilgrims, he stands highest on Fortune's wheel, their didactic implication comes painfully home to him. Stories of those that ' "clymbeth up and wexeth fortunat" ' would, he protests, be much more ' "gladsom" ' and ' "goodly for to telle" '.[154] Where now is Theseus' wisdom of detachment? Attitudes to Fortune, Chaucer reminds us, tend to be emotively subjective; the Knight's comment, from a privileged point of view, is entirely reasonable, for only the unfortunate are likely to derive ' "greet solas" ' from hearing of the fall of those more favoured. It is no accident that the tale elicited by the Host to meet the Knight's request for something ' "gladsom" ', should be the Nun's Priest's account of the buoyant Chaunticleer, who, by quick exercise of wit, retains his precarious perch on the top of Fortune's wheel, and escapes the catastrophe that his dreams predicted. It is, however, characteristic of Chaucer's oblique wit that he should win acclaim for his exhaustively

---

propretee individual characteristic or response

tedious version of the theme which once obsessed him, so that the 'doctryne' of the laboured *Tale of Melibee* succeeds, where the 'murthe' of *Sir Thopas* is dismissed by the Host as ineptitude.[155] This is no doubt true to the taste of the time, yet the wit of *Sir Thopas* is infinitely preferable to the weight of *Melibee*; the pilgrim figure is better company than either dreamer or scholar, and common humanity more engaging, and in the end more astonishing, than the literary conventions of the earlier poems, or the anguished speculation of the great works of Chaucer's middle period.

It is interesting that two of the three greatest poets of the English Middle Ages, Langland and the *Gawain*-poet, should pay the figure of Fortune so little attention, when she is elsewhere so dominant. Langland, certainly, is exercised by the problem of predestination,[156] but, although *Piers Plowman* throngs with such abstractions, Fortune's appearances are startlingly few, and then very marginal.[157] The *Gawain*-poet employs the word, but only *as* a word, and then in a very reduced sense: it occurs, for example, in the phrase 'As fortune wolde fulsun hom', when the poet is describing Arthur's pleasure in challenge and tournament.[158] Where the occasion is momentous, 'destiné' or 'wyrde', much stronger words implying 'fate' in the sense of divine decree, are the terms used.[159] When Gawain prepares to depart on his perilous journey, we are told:

> The knyght mad ay god chere,
> And sayde, 'Quat schuld I wonde?
> Of destinés derf and dere
> What may mon do bot fonde?'   (ll. 562–5)

No shadow interposes between man and the providence of God; Gawain is fearless because he can put his trust in divine decree. Both poets, as profoundly religious writers, whose eyes are steadfastly fixed on the world of celestial order and ordinance, place Fortune in a greatly reduced perspective. Chaucer achieves his final emancipation in a different way: by fixing his attention as firmly upon the world of men.

Amongst lesser medieval writers, such freedom is rarely attained; those who become obsessed with the theme, of whom Lydgate is the prime example, fall prisoner to it. This obsession is, however, far more marked in the later than in the early Middle Ages, for, although Fortune makes many earlier appearances, her presence is at first less defined. In the thirteenth century she is already a subject popular with artists, who draw directly upon the *Consolatio*.[160] She can be found, at this period, on the walls of Rochester Cathedral, revolving her wheel, and

---

fulsun help   *wonde* fear   *derf* harsh   *dere* grievous   *fonde* test

with it those figures who cling to its circumference[161] (Plate 18). But she is still, as in the *Consolatio*, a creature men need to be warned against rather than their dominant deity. She is not infrequently mentioned in poetry contemporary with such paintings; yet, if one compares collections of thirteenth-century lyrics with those of the fourteenth, and even more of the fifteenth, it is clear that her appearances greatly increase towards the close of the Middle Ages. Moreover, earlier allusions are more casual; a poem 'Fortune', included in *An Old English Miscellany*, reproaches her chiefly for her neglect of the poor, whilst her desertion of the great, as in the romance of *Sir Orfeo*, is so clearly felt as redemptive opportunity that the 'blind Goddess' recedes entirely.[162] She has yet to join hands with the great abstracts of Death and Love to afflict the human spirit;[163] the wilful principle of mutability, irrevocably interposed between the anarchy of the temporal and the harmony of the eternal, is the creation of a later period.

The consolidation of this grim intermediary may be briefly indicated in late medieval reaction to *The Book of Job*. In the Bible, Job falls prey to Satan, 'going to and fro in the earth, and . . . walking up and down in it'; in poetry of the fifteenth century, however, Job becomes the prototypical victim of the equally ubiquitous Fortune:[164] to this 'newe Iob', 'Fortune hir falsnesse hath overt,/Hir swifte wheel turned up so doun'. This allusion (one of many examples) occurs in Lydgate's 'Fabula Duorum Mercatorum',[165] where, as throughout his writing, he detects in the turning of the wheel the mutable tenor of all human life and history, rather than the dark designs of the tempter whom God permits to try the souls of men. His *Fall of Princes* opens with the original Fall of Man, and traces its pattern through all subsequent history; thus his greatest work becomes another *Cursor Mundi*, written to illustrate this single point:

> And how Fortune kan floure & afftir fade—
> Ioie undir cloude, prosperite in the shade,
> Entirchaungyng off every maner thyng,
> Which that men feele, heer in this world lyvyng.
>
> And in his processe, who-so list beholde,
> Off alle estatis, off hih and louh degre,
> And off pryncis bothe yong and olde,
> Fro the begynnyng, which in this world ha be.[166]

The edges of this dark wisdom are indeed slightly softened by the images of natural transience;[167] although his portrayal of Fortune is protracted and repellent enough,[168] Lydgate is never quite the rigorous moralist he sets out to be. Yet the moral he, along with so many less distinguished poets, draws, is invariable: human life, prey to the law of mutability can offer no securities; these exist only in the unchanging love of God. Chaucer, one may remember, arrives, by a much more complex route in *Troilus and Criseyde*, at the same conclusion in his epilogue, that Christ alone 'nyl falsen no wight'.[169]

'What nedeth feynede loves for to seke?' Chaucer enquires, and such injunctions (though without his redeeming warmth) can be paralleled in poem after poem; so too can that connection between an awareness of mutability, and the adoption of an attitude of contempt for life, as the only real defence man possesses against human misery. It is pre-eminently the great, once Fortune's favourites, who, for obvious reasons, provide most of the examples, and this didactic vein is indubitably strengthened by social indignation, as it is in the Pride of Life. In political verse, Fortune invariably afflicts the enviable, the rich and powerful, the young and beautiful,[170] but the vicious circle she inscribes is illustrated by the fact that she can both afflict and *be* the Pride of Life. Thus, in the play *Mary Magdalene*, the King of the World indulges in the customary vaunts of the Pride of Life, and announces that it is he who controls the wheel of Fortune:

> & I am he that lengest xal Induer,
> and also most of domynacyon;
> yf I be his foo, woo is abyll to recure,
> for the whele of fortune with me hath sett his sentur.[171]

It is doubtful whether, in this play, the writer has any real insight into the complexities of the image he creates; an abyss generally exists between the subtlety of Chaucer's treatment of Fortune, and the mechanic exercise of more ordinary talents. Nevertheless, it is significant that even routine versions of the theme should create their own problems, and if their uninspired didactic authors are led to an apprehension of muddle rather than mystery, that sense of confusion in itself suggests the power of the figure. One typical question—of man's responsibility for the reverses which befall him—is profoundly explored by Chaucer, but is frequently broached by writers who attempt no such investigation. The general law of mutability carries with it, in theory, no intrinsic condemnation of those it afflicts: if 'Fortune is comune/To everi manere wight in som degree', no man can be singled out since none is exempt. When this observation is used as a text from which to preach detachment, it is, however, the proud, those who seem to be her favourites and exceptions from her rule, who become obvious subjects; here the temptation to see their fall as the justified punishment for sin becomes irresistible. Of the fall of princes, Lydgate, quoting his authority Bochas, comments: 'Off ther onhapp, as he doth reherce,/Toward hemsilff the cause doth rebounde.'[172] Yet within the same book, when describing the fall of the virtuous Gracchus, Lydgate places the blame squarely on Fortune:

> How that Fortune is ai fals & onstable,
> Ever double, froward and deceyvable,
> The fall off Graccus declare can ful weel,
> That whilom sat so hih upon hir wheel. (Bk III, ll. 3007–10)

Fortune, it seems, is at once the lot of everyman, and the instrument of God's vengeance on those whose 'gredi etik doth hemsilff confounde'.

As in Chaucer, this leads directly to the related problem of fate and freewill, though again, that question is rarely explored with any profundity. The alliterative *Morte Arthure* has, for example, been praised because it does not simply follow the medieval form of tragedy, the cycle of the wheel,[173] but shows the decay of that civilization, in a way which anticipates renaissance attitude, as the result of its own 'gredi etik'.[174] Nevertheless, the dream in which Arthur joins the other eight Worthies on the inexorable wheel, delineates a Fortune as wilful and fickle as any in medieval literature.[175] The visions coexist, rather than truly cohering. Malory's *Morte d'Arthur* embraces, along with Fortune, a much wider range of explanation for the fall of the great; and the conflict between the conviction that, on the one hand, events must follow an inescapably catastrophic cycle, and, on the other, that man can deflect catastrophe by anticipating what is determined, run irresistibly together, not only in the whole design, but in its detail. Thus Merlin warns Balyn that, because he has been the (innocent?) cause of a woman's death, he will ' "stryke a stroke moste dolerous that ever man stroke, excepte the stroke of oure Lorde Jesu Cryste" '. To this, Balyn retorts: ' "Nay, nat so; for and I wyste thou seyde soth, I wolde do so perleous a dede that I wolde sle myself to make the a lyer." '[176] To the very end of the work, the tragedy to come (so often adumbrated, so often emphasized), seems avoidable; thus the dead Gawain is sent by God to Arthur to tell him how the fatal day may be avoided, ' "for pité of you and many mo other good men there shall be slayne" '.[177] The close connection between those two questions—whether Fortune punishes sin, and whether man has freewill—is subtly sensed in such situations; it is given a startling abstract form in *The Assembly of the Gods*, where Prescience and Predestination reward virtue and vice, as Doctrine explains:

> 'And as for Prescience and Predestinacion,
>   That eche of hem rewardyd aftyr hys desert,
>   Is to undyrstond nomore but dampnacioun

---

froward capricious

To vycyous pepyll ys the verrey scourge smert
Rewarde; for they fro Vertu wolde pervert.
    And endelese ioy ys to hem that be electe
    Rewardyd & to all that folow the same secte.'[178]

Where Doctrine herself is so confused, not to say heretical, it is
scarcely surprising that, save in exceptional cases, these problems are
too thorny to possess great dramatic potential. Yet an impatience with
their intricacies can lead to that internalization of Fortune which is
the first step towards man's triumph over his tormentor. The notion
that a man can somehow anticipate and circumvent the inevitable, even
the search for that detachment which renders tolerable what is inescapable, invites that distinction between event and response to event
which Chaucer explores in Theseus. In the Prologue to the *Confessio
Amantis*, Gower reviews many of the conventionally passive explanations of Fortune—that she, or the stars, or foreknowledge, or the law
of mutability is to blame for human suffering; he comes, however, to
the decisive conclusion that:

> . . . the man is overal
> His oghne cause of wel and wo.
> That we fortune clepe so
> Out of the man himself it groweth.[179]

Although he immediately continues with the conventional remark that
Fortune is she who rewards the good and punishes the wicked, Gower
has gone a good way towards rendering the problem merely mental,
thus escaping the figure's domination.[180]

The struggle to dominate Fortune is not, however, truly won until
the English Renaissance, and then largely because questions of providential order have become less pressing. Perhaps because he is there
concerned with medieval history, Shakespeare, in his early plays, has
much to say of Fortune; yet, although she is still a threat to the inward
peace of men, she can more readily be circumvented in his rendering of
medieval attitudes than was possible in the Middle Ages themselves.
Thus the saintly Henry VI adopts an earlier possibility—'I may conquer
Fortune's spite/By living low, where Fortune cannot hurt me'—whilst
the more worldly Edward IV asserts, with a renaissance flourish:
'Though Fortune's malice overthrow my state,/My mind exceeds the
compass of her wheel.'[181] Shakespeare has a profound understanding
of the Middle Ages, and it is significant that, at the end of his life, he
returned to them in *Pericles*, the most medieval of all his plays. There
he reincarnates Gower, and recaptures the earlier poet's voice in kindly
caricature, as this ancient ghost repeatedly advances Fortune as the
comprehensive explanation of every human event. When Pericles is

wrecked on the shores of Simonides' kingdom where he is to meet Thaisa, Gower relates that 'fortune, tired with doing bad,/Threw him ashore, to give him glad'.[182] When Thaisa is lost at sea, 'fortune's mood/varies again'; whilst, in his final speech, he sums up comfortably:

> In Pericles, his queen and daughter, seen,
> Although assailed with fortune fierce and keen,
> Virtue preserved from fell destruction's blast,
> Led on by heaven and crowned with joy at last.[183]

There are, however, more allusions to these relatively simplistic notions of Fortune in the speeches of Gower than in the play itself. There her apparently random operation is seen to result from man's partial perspective; in the integrated vision of the play's ending, the power of the sea to preserve as well as to destroy is recognized as a means to a providential end. Thus, though the figure of Gower is preoccupied with Fortune, the play is never dominated by her, for her vicissitudes, despite appearances, move with, not apart from, the harmony of nature; they harmonize, moreover, with divine purpose in enabling a providential end. In merging the image of Fortune with that of the sea, Shakespeare marries those forces, natural and unnatural, which, for the Middle Ages, were so often polarized. His point of rest is different from those discovered by the three great medieval writers; but it has, none the less, its contacts with each of them. *Sir Gawain* perhaps comes closest to *Pericles*, for it achieves that integrated perspective within life, and allows the rhythm of nature to dominate that of Fortune. The same perception of providential pattern is, however, reached outside time in the epilogue to *Troilus and Criseyde*, just as it is indicated in the speech of Theseus; whilst Langland, whose eye is always firmly fixed upon man's ultimate end, sees human life from no other point of view with equal clarity.

The profundity of Shakespeare's insight is, however, as exceptional in the sixteenth century as those three poets are in the Middle Ages. The renaissance solution to the problem of predestination was relatively simple: it was to separate omniscience from omnipotence, ascribing the former to Apollo, the latter to Jupiter.[184] Robbed of destinal power, subjugated to man, the gloomy dominance of Fortune gradually waned (cf. Plates 19 and 20). By espousing her with a confidence alien to the Middle Ages, men changed her nature; her name ceased to be synonymous with disaster, and came to mean either 'success' or 'prosperity', or the future outcome of things still unknown.[185] But if the ease of the Renaissance is enviable, the unease of the Middle Ages continues to have its own merit and relevance. ' "The only question is—which

Tandē p̄ stragem hoīm maximā luct̃ ieiunia et
pēnas graues ꝓ proceffionalr̃ cuṅt p romā cuṅt
hinuifa plebe et cl̃ero apparet angelus fanguino
lentū enfe inagina reponēs fup ꝑtacui magr̃

1   Plague

(a)

(b)

(c)

(d)

2   The Pride of Life

3 (a)   (*top, opposite*) Nature at her Forge
3 (b)   (*below, opposite*) Venus Assaulting the Tower of

(a)

(b)

4 Chaucer's Squire

5 Langland's Pride

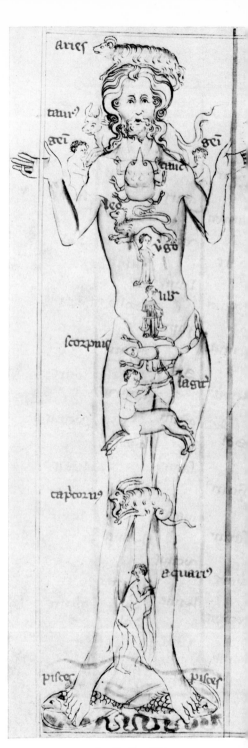

6 Zodiac Man

7   Youth Succeeds to Age

8 Lamech, Adolescens and Cain

10   The Wheel of Life

13   Janus as
Youth and
Age

14 (a)   January

14 (b)   February Warming

15 (a) April

15 (b) May

16 (a) January and Aquarius

16 (b) May and Gemini

17 (*top*) Two-Faced Fortune, Philosophy, the Muses and Boethius

18 (*left*) Open-Eyed Fortune

19 (*above*) Blindfold Fortune

20 (*opposite*) Renaissance Fortune

I MI LASO PORTARE ALA FORTVNA SPERANDO
ALFIN D AVER B NA VENTVRA

21   The Contemplation of Death

22   Lazarus

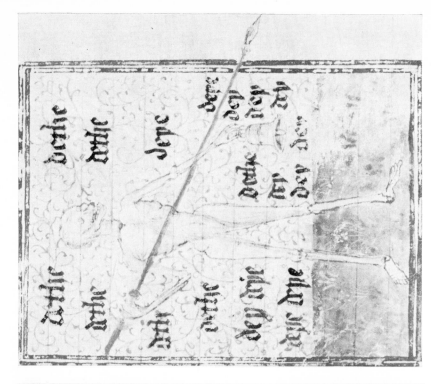

24 'Drerv Dethe'

23 Animate Corpse

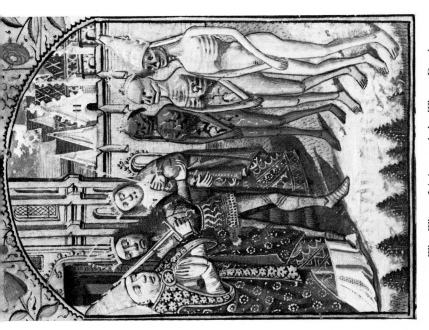

25   The Three Living and the Three Dead

26   Hunting Version

27　Battle for Soul with Dance of Death

(a)   The Expulsion

(b)   Age

(c)   The Knight

(d)   The Child

28   Holbein's Dance of Death

29 Idealized Effigy   30 Heroic Effigy

31 (*left*) Renaissance Tomb

32 (*below*) The Double Tomb

(a)   Planted in Adam's Mouth   (b)   Growing from Adam's Grave

33   The Tree of Life

34   Garden Paradise of the Old Man of the Mountain

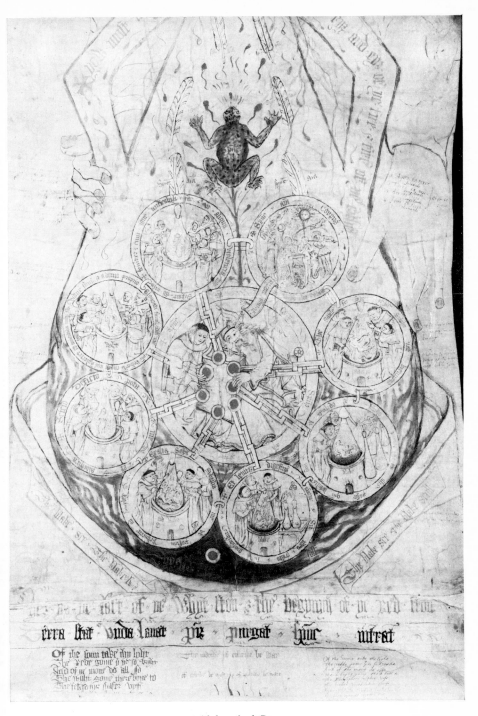

35 Alchemical Scenes

36   The Harrowing of Hell

determines which? Is the man formed by life, or does he, if he has a strong enough personality, shape life around him?" ' This is the voice of a modern Boethius, one of the prisoners in Solzhenitsyn's *First Circle*, and we are no nearer an answer than the Middle Ages were. It is the question of another age which lacks renaissance confidence, which is again uncertain of man's dignity. The twentieth-century prisoner can only affirm that dignity by alluding to 'the image of perfection' which art creates. The medieval image was more spacious, for it could invoke divinity; and if such a standard made the full stature of man less easily attainable, it also gave his potential a more expansive and generous definition.

The three views of temporal life with which this chapter is concerned— the cycles of nature, of transience and of mutability—are placed in a meaningful sequence at the close of the Middle Ages in Henryson's *Testament of Cresseid*.[186] This poem is undoubtedly one of the great achievements of medieval literature, yet, partly because it moves towards a renaissance insight, *The Testament* does not realize fully all the possibilities of these three themes: since Henryson anticipates a literature more secular and humane in character, he refuses to adopt a position outside the temporal, and his poem is in consequence coloured with those darker shades of medieval attitude which tend to obscure its brightest possibilities. In the present context, the interest of his poem is twofold: from his temporal standpoint, he offers an unexpected revaluation of these themes, for Fortune becomes the least, not the most, compelling of the three; moreover, by making all such views inward to the mind of Cresseid, he enables her to achieve a dignity which is tragic in the Shakespearian, not the medieval, sense.

The seasonal cycle is the first to be invoked in the poem, for its Prologue, as already mentioned,[187] elicits the possibilities of the winter prelude more fully than most earlier examples. The evening light of Age and Winter is not only counterpoised, but intertwined, with the 'dawn knowledge' of Youth and Spring.[188] The time of the poem, 'Aries, in middis of the Lent', places it in the first month of Spring, for the sun enters Aries at the vernal equinox. Because, from one point of view, the poem is concerned with the still youthful Cresseid, whose discovery of disinterested love, prompted by her encounter with Troilus, becomes the instrument of her redemption, the work has its claim to dawn vision. But the realistic light of evening is equally strong, for the first line announces 'Ane doolie sessoun', and the first verse describes an abrupt alteration, one which corresponds to the prematurely blighted life of Cresseid, when 'the wedder richt fervent' degenerates into winter chill as 'Schouris of haill gart fra the north discend'. The natural cycle

F

is, moreover, related to the Christian: Lent is the period of penance and repentance which prepares the soul for the spiritual rebirth of Easter, as, in the temporal calendar, the signs of approaching Spring relieve with hope residual winter hardships.

The emphasis of the poem falls more upon hardship than hope, however, for it opens at nightfall, when Venus 'in oppositioun/Of God Phebus' dominates the sky:

> Throw out the glas hir bemis brast sa fair
> That I micht se on everie syde me by;
> The northin wind had purifyit the air
> And sched the mistie cloudis fra the sky.   (ll. 15–18)

This is the cruelly realistic clarity whereby men come 'to a knowledge of things in their own natures', and if the aged narrator can practise a February wisdom by retreating to the warmth of his fire, Cresseid is left outside to endure the bitter blasts of self-knowledge. This bleak exposure is, however, the path to redemption, and the dawn vision of the poem's close is the stronger for having endured the searching light of Winter.[189]

Henryson's dualities go some way towards combining birth and death in a single vision; but because Cresseid and her poet exist in a strictly temporal world, the poem, whilst certainly looking to spiritual regeneration, gives little hint of physical renewal. On the contrary, the hope offered by the grain is the substance of Cresseid's blasphemy, for she has expected, against Nature's order, a perpetual springtime in the physical and temporal, which can only obtain in the eternal and spiritual:

> 'O fals Cupide, is nane to wyte bot thow
> And thy mother, of lufe the blind goddes!
> Ye causit me alwayis understand and trow
> The seid of lufe was sawin in my face,
> And ay grew grene throw your supplie and grace.
> Bot now, allace, that seid with froist is slane,
> And I fra luifferis left, and all forlane.'   (ll. 134–40)

Cresseid's complaint is that of all women who put too much passive confidence in the power of their beauty to elicit the love and protection they consider their due. Certainly that beauty has been prematurely blighted, but those who rely alone on attributes merely physical, should not consider themselves immune to bodily decay.

---

brast burst   *wyte* blame   *supplie* assistance   *luifferis* lovers

Cresseid's view of life, at this point, is the purely passive one of those who think that their history is entirely determined by forces beyond their control. If she invokes 'the blind goddes' of love rather than Fortune, she sees herself equally as the prey of anarchy and mutability. The dominant preoccupation of the Middle Ages is thus presented as the product of immature and egocentric attitude, but this should not suggest that Henryson is unaware of the complexities that relate to Fortune; rather that he resolves them. The descent of the Gods, Cresseid's condemnation, and the sentence of leprosy, all indicate a view of life quite as darkly determined as that in *The Knight's Tale*. Furthermore, Cresseid's fate is not only unavoidably, but actively, cruel; she not only loses her beauty and becomes a prostitute, she also incurs leprosy, an infection then connected with venereal disease, which makes evident the corruption of her moral being.[190] The Gods, who personify planetary influence, intensify the deterministic view, for astrological influences, in assuming personal form, become motivated, not random, actions. Whilst Cresseid's suffering is clearly related to her offence, it is impossible to treat these vengeful figures as instruments of a God who uses them to providential purpose, for, in punishing sin so cruelly, they attach a vindictive grimace to the divine countenance.

Unlike Chaucer, Henryson seeks no answer in displacing an overtly cruel law with the benign order of the First Mover, which it conceals. Instead, he greatly extends Theseus' belief that freedom lies in a man's adaptation to the events that befall him, for he internalizes all views to the mind which conceives them. Cresseid learns not only to adapt to events, but to adopt them as her responsibility; she discovers that salvation lies in regarding her history as that of a free, if culpable, individual, whilst despair lies in viewing it as the unhappy chronicle of a passive, if inoffensive, victim. The Gods, and the leprosy, are no illusions, but only the immature imagination sees no further than their physical form: the deities descend in dream, and their respective characters and qualities—beneficent, malevolent, unstable—also reflect aspects of Cresseid's own disposition; the leprosy, in addition to its ugly physical manifestations, has spiritual significance, for if it points, on the one hand, to Cresseid's guilt, it includes her, on the other, in the company of those especially favoured by God, for they suffer their purgatory in this life.[191] When Cresseid accepts her condition, and exchanges the comfort of her father's house for the miseries of the leper hospital, her complaint is no longer that she, peculiarly gifted, has been peculiarly betrayed. Freed from the prison of her own mind, she senses her community in transience with 'all thing generabill'.

Where once, in easier days, she complained against the mutabilities of a determined world, she expresses her plight in the leper house in the elegiac tones of *ubi sunt*:

> 'Quhair is thy garding with thir greissis gay
> And fresche flowris, quhilk the quene Floray
> Had paintit plesandly in everie pane?' (ll. 425–7)

This courtly vision is the more sharply felt through its recall in 'ane dark corner of the hous allone'; that May morning scene, which can be stiffly formalized in its rich conventional detail, is given a poignant fragility by its dark context, reflected in the weighty tone of the lines which follow:

> 'Thy greit triumphand fame and hie honour,
> Quhair thou was callit of eirdlye wichtis flour,
> All is decayit, thy weird is welterit so.' (ll. 434–6)

In these lines, the delicate image of the flower becomes an ominous reminder of mortality, and its darker connotations are extended in the final verse of this 'Complaint', where many of the themes common to the poem and this book may be detected: not only transience, but the Pride of Life, the apprehension of corruption, the mirror offered by the dead to the living, the insubstantiality of human experience, the *memento mori*, Fortune and mutability:

> 'Nocht is your fairnes bot ane faiding flour,
> Nocht is your famous laud and hie honour
> Bot wind inflat in uther mennis eiris,
> Your roising reid to rotting sall retour;
> Exempill mak of me in your memour
> Quhilk of sic thingis wofull witnes beiris.
> All wealth is eird, away as wind it weiris;
> Be war thairfoir, approchis neir your hour;
> Fourtoun is fikkill quhen scho beginnis and steiris.' (ll. 461–9)

Even here, Cresseid's words are less a personal protest, than an admonitory lament for the common human lot; to move thus from an arbitrary to a natural explanation of life, from individual grudge to general regret, from rebellion to resignation, is undoubtedly a moral advance. In making the lament of *ubi sunt* succeed the complaint against Fortune, Henryson is discriminating between those two common medieval explanations of the vicissitudes of life, and is in favour of that view in which decline is seen as part of the natural order, not a visitation of the unnatural.

Cresseid's full moral maturity is not reached, nor the promise of the

---

pane part   *eirdlye* earthly   *wichtis* creatures   *flour* flower   *weird* destiny
welterit overturned   *inflat* puffed   *roising* rosy   *eird* earth   *steiris* is active

Prologue realized, through either of these views of human life. Both
achievements belong to the moving, and essentially human, scene where
the mounted knight and the leper woman encounter, mutually ignorant
of the other's identity. Some fleeting resemblance in that distorted face
to 'fair Cresseid, sumtyme his awin darling', indeed prompts Troilus to
throw a purse of gold 'For knichtlie pietie and memoriall' into the lap
of the pitiable beggar, before riding silently away.[192] No such memory of
'olde jantylnes and olde servyse' reaches Cresseid, for whom the 'wynter
rasure' of love is complete,[193] for she sits, locked in her own sorrow,
'not witting quhat scho was'.[194] But when he is identified as ' "Troylus . . .
gentill and fre" ', she recognizes, by a sudden detachment from her own
sorrows, both the truth of Troilus' love and her own falsity. Apart from
the writing of her testament, the last words she speaks in the poem are
those of self-accusation and realization: ' "Nane but my self as now I
will accuse." '[195] In taking her destiny so firmly in her own hands,
Cresseid denies the meaningless, deterministic cycles of temporal history
which, for the Middle Ages, did so much to reduce the figure of man;
for the first time in medieval literature, that figure is allowed to achieve
a genuinely tragic stature. As in later tragedies, one is led to feel that the
recognitions afforded by suffering in themselves constitute salvation;
but on this Henryson, like his successors, is silent. His temporal verdict
remains as sparing, in both senses, as Troilus' epitaph:

> 'Lo, fair ladyis, Cresseid of Troy the toun,
> Sumtyme countit the flour of womanheid,
> Under this stane, lait lipper, lyis deid.'   (ll. 607–9)

The Testament of Cresseid is far from being, as some critics have
claimed,[196] a cruel work of unsparing didacticism; Henryson allows
Cresseid a freedom, and thence a dignity, which has no need of the
mitigation that Chaucer offers on Criseyde's behalf. It is interesting,
however, that the rigorous compassion of this poem should repel some
readers, where a Shakespearian tragedy might not, for it indicates the
starkness with which Henryson has delineated the imprisoning circles
which the Middle Ages distinguished as the pattern of temporal life.
His position, certainly, achieves a renaissance dignity, but at the price
of medieval affirmation. He can only suggest that 'greyn ded in erthe/
Atte laste launceth up'; he cannot affirm, through the Triumph of Life
in the Harrowing of Hell, that belief, 'wherby we lyven alle',[197] that man
can break from the dark wheel of the temporal into the timelessness of
eternal light.

---

fre noble, generous

V

Mortality and the Grave

And therfore every gentil wight I preye,
For Goddes love, demeth nat that I seye
Of yvel entente, but for I moot reherce
Hir tales alle, be they bettre or werse,
Or elles falsen som of my mateere.
And therfore, whoso list it nat yheere,
Turne over the leef and chese another tale.[1]

A chapter concerned with medieval attitudes to mortality and the grave
is as aptly prefaced as the bawdy tales of the Reeve and the Miller by
that apology to 'gentil' sensibilities. The darkly detailed images of
sentient physical corruption which proliferate in the last century of that
supposed 'Age of Faith' are indeed much more shocking to the euphemism
of current attitudes to death than outspokenness in sexual matters is
now likely to be. Because the medieval spectrum of beliefs about life
and death was so much wider than ours, it reached to greater extremes:
the strenuous vision, on the one hand, of eternal beatitude, led, on the
other, to the desolation of wanhope, the despair of those many who could
no longer, with confidence, affirm their expectation of immortality. Just
as the meaningless cycle of mutability came, at the close of the Middle
Ages, to dominate the more purposeful rhythms of nature and transience,
so morbid imaginings of the detail of decay displaced the affirmation of
resurrection.

The very strength of the high Middle Ages, their conviction that all
temporal things were no more than reflections of their perfect form in
the mind of God, became a prevailing weakness in their decline. Philo-
sophic realism was never materialist, for it strove to move from the
substantiality of things to the freedom of ideas; but the impulse, on a
simpler level, to buttress a wavering faith by rendering mystery in concrete form, inevitably debased the ideal to the grossly literal.[2] When a
poet, for example, transforms the host into an actual corpse, his crudely
literal handling of the sacrament is no doubt intended to confirm the
doctrine of transubstantiation, but its effect is totally to rob the mass of

spiritual meaning.[3] The veneration accorded to relics is a related phenomenon, for exceptional spiritual power is here reduced to the primitive, concrete superstition that the corpse is somehow possessed of continuing life and influence. Christ himself was not exempt from this macabre merchandise, for the relative merits of the two relics of the circumcision was hotly debated in Christendom.[4] On his death in 1274, Aquinas was decapitated and boiled by his fellow monks at Fossanuova, in order to secure his relics; the bones of St Louis were distributed to guests by his descendant, Charles VI, at a solemn feast in 1392.[5] These crudities leave their mark even on relatively reticent and pious sensibilities. Lydgate is fond of such tales, and relates how five roses sprout from the eyes, ears and mouth of a dead devotee of the Virgin, each one inscribed with her name in gold.[6] These stories may indeed endeavour to correct macabre terrors with the assurance that, if the evil stink in their decay, the good remain incorrupt and sweet-smelling. The body of St Alexius gives off a sweet savour;[7] St Germaine attempts to raise one of his disciples from the grave, but the corpse refuses his invitation, protesting that it finds interment soft and pleasant; St Loy defies decay, and his hair and nails continue to grow;[8] so too, Lydgate notes in devout and level tone, do those of St Edmund:

> Thyn hooly nailles and thy royal heer
> Greuh be myracle, as seith the cronycleer,
> Kept clos in gold and silvere as I reede.[9]

But if such examples gave heart to the faithful, they also did much to confirm the materialist tendency, whose corrupt nature is exposed only by exceptional writers. *The Pardoner's Prologue* and *Tale* is, for example, precisely poised between spiritual insight and physical superstition, for a profound and moving perception of man's mortality seeks its surrogate in the bones of pigs and the paper of indulgences. The paradox that the very spirituality of the Middle Ages begets its own opposite is nowhere dramatized more powerfully.

This hectic endeavour to render mystery in literal, substantial terms inevitably had its effect upon depictions of the final end of man. Indulgences themselves, which measure the timeless in years, and even months and days, are an endeavour to render the unimaginable in gross multiples of time. The image of the bird, which carries away in its beak, grain by grain, a huge mountain of sand, without measuring an instant of eternity, is the invention of Denis the Carthusian[10] and becomes a commonplace in the medieval sermon; Joyce rightly renders it ridiculous in the sermon on Hell in *Portrait of the Artist*, for it destroys exactly that sense of the irrelevance of time and space which it is meant to enforce. Depiction of the afterlife was inevitably subject to such crude imaginings, the more so when one remembers that its geography was a relatively late development in Christian thought.[11] Even the immortality of the soul had not always been accepted by the Fathers of the Church; Tertullian and Cyprian both questioned it, and, though the work of the former seems to have been little read, that of the latter is sometimes found in the library lists of monastic houses at the Dissolution.[12] The torments of Hell, as is clear in Dante's *Inferno*, draw heavily on the more grotesque aspects of displaced beliefs. The detail of purgatorial description, as in the sixth-century account of Pope Gregory VI, or Bede's eighth-century dream of Drihthelm, is also derived from pagan sources.[13] Even the joys of the Christian Paradise were elaborated with the aid of Celtic legend,[14] whilst the metallic and jewelled permanence of St John's heavenly Jerusalem was adorned with the glitter of travellers' tales from the Orient.[15] In so impressionistic and eclectic a context, it is not surprising that more ordinary talents should tend to envisage man's end in the visible, and all too familiar, pit of the grave. There they found torments enough for Hell itself.

The Christian imagination should, of course, move beyond the grave to the eternal destination of the soul, but the invitation to linger there was extended, not only by didactic materialism, but by religious devotion. The practice of meditation upon the corpse or skull was an established means of detaching men from the transient joys of temporal life (Plate 21); one may feel that this custom has reached excess when the author of a fifteenth-century devotional work, *Jacob's Well*, describes with approval how a certain friar cured himself of a liking for kisses by removing to his cell the decaying body of a woman who had once attracted him—yet his action has traditional authorization.[16] To conceive of life merely as 'ane straucht way to deid', which must be unpleasant if eternity is to be pleasant, inevitably exalts the figure of Death, 'quhome vane is to repell', in all its gruesome detail.[17] Although Owst has claimed to find 'something approaching a genuine tragical feeling—certainly more classic than Christian—when preachers reviewed the lot of humanity trembling on the brink of the grave',[18] the term 'tragic', unless used in a strictly medieval sense, has little validity save in exceptional cases such as *Everyman*, for the apprehension of decomposition has little nobility or elevation of feeling to offer.[19]

It has been argued that fear, as a Christian response to death, whilst not evidently right, is nevertheless justified as a transitional emotion, since fear must issue in action and becomes transformed in the process.[20] In the earlier Middle Ages, where the fear of the grave is not only less frequently expressed, but may even, as in the following example, be treated with something approaching a satiric buoyancy, the point may have its validity:

Thanne y schel fflute
ffrom bedde te fflore,
ffrom fflore to here,
from here to bere,
from bere to putte,
and te putt ffor-dut.
thanne lyd min hus uppe min nose,
off al this world ne gyffe ihic a pese.[21]

It is more questionable whether, in the later Middle Ages, this fear could any longer be justly described as transitional; for if the terrors of the pulpit issued in actions which transformed that emotion, these make few appearances in literature. Even the gentle Lydgate, when writing of 'The Fifftene Toknys aforn the Doom', alludes only cursorily to the summoning of the Blessed in his final verse—'Hevene and erthe al newe shal be sene,/And alle bodyes shal that day aryse'—though he dwells attentively on the grim spectacle of corpses upright in their graves:

Ded boonys that day shal aryse,
    And grisly stonde on ther sepulture,
    And shewyn outward a dredful foul figure;
So to stonde al day, with boonys blak and donne;
    Of doom abyde the dredful aventure,
Tyl goyng doun of the bloody sonne.[22]

As a Catholic theologian once remarked, 'It is vain to seek even a single Saint who has taught that the number of the elect forms the majority';[23] when, at the close of the Middle Ages, the thunderous warnings of the pulpit reverberate, it is not surprising that so many should have failed to see further than the narrow walls of the grave, and the repellent processes of dissolution within them.[24]

The fear of annihilation is, after all, quite as natural to man as a confidence in continuing existence. As Aquinas remarks:

Deus potest universam creaturam redigere in nihilum; cujus ratio est, quia creatura non solum producitur in esse Deo agente, sed etiam per actionem Dei conservatur in esse, . . . potest subtrahere suam actionem a rebus conservandis, et hoc ipso omnia in nihilum deciderent.[25]

(God could reduce all creation to nothingness; for this reason, that creation is not only brought forth by God's action, but also preserved in being by it. He could withdraw his sustaining action from things, and everything, as a result, would fall away to nothingness.)

---

fflute go   *here* shroud   *putte* pit   *ffor-dut* shut up   *lyd* lie

To fall into nothingness is the expectation of physical nature; a confidence that God will sustain his creation in being is the achievement of faith. When one considers that even Langland, so urgent a believer, writes in the conviction that God is angry with mankind, that the coming of Anti-Christ is a reality, it is not surprising that so many less courageous writers should have felt that God's sustaining action *had* been withdrawn, and that there was justice in his destruction of the living. Certainly a conviction that Death is God's ally is more frequently found than the view that it is God's enemy; in *Piers Plowman*, Christ defeats Death through the Crucifixion and Harrowing of Hell, but in the vision of Anti-Christ, with which the poem ends, Death is the instrument of divine justice.[26]

One does not need to look to pagan sources for the many heretical superstitions that surround mortality in the later Middle Ages; primitive analogues can easily be found for many of them, but such anomalies as the sentient corpse, the animate skeleton, the effective relic, are more immediately explained by the materialist tendencies of a faltering faith. Even where certain practices seem to have an actively pagan connection, it does not follow that those who adopted them were conscious of that fact. We still close the eyes and fold the hands of a corpse, without consciously intending to deprive the dead of their power to harm us; we still mistrust the number thirteen, but few could explain that this is because it follows the perfect cycle of twelve, and hence represents Death.[27] It is, however, in this area, more than any other, that one feels the strength of the renaissance claim to be an enlightened age. The grave reveals medieval man at his lowest point (in more senses than one), and the craven fear of death clearly distinguishes the period from the detachment of earlier civilizations, or their later imitators. Sects so dissimilar as Stoics and Epicureans treated mortality with evident contempt: the Stoic cry, ' "I suffer not from death, my suffering was life" ', and Epicurus' assertion, ' "Death is nothing with reference to us" (for, where we are, death is not, and where death is, we are not)',[28] both resist any obsession with mortality; so too do the typical tombs of the Renaissance, where the deeds of a man, not his corpse, remain his memorial (Plate 31). But neither the Renaissance nor the ancient world gave such centrality to the figure of an omnipotent creator, and where the mind is not subdued to the Almighty, the generic difficulty of explaining the presence of evil, suffering and death, recedes considerably. The medieval concern with these questions can, at one extreme, debase the figure of man; but it can, at another, exalt him in ways which more 'enlightened' ages cannot parallel.

This chapter is, however, confined to the debasement of man at the darkest extreme, and it is worth noting that this has Old Testament authorization.[29] In itself, this is appropriate enough, for the world of the Old Law is only liberated by the coming of Christ from the shadow of death; yet that shadow, so sharply captured in certain Old Testament phrases, continues to shroud mankind under the new dispensation, especially when humanity seems exiled once more from God's redemptive love. The burden of *Ecclesiastes*, 'All is vanity', has its echo in the medieval conviction that life is merely 'ane straucht way to deid': 'I have seen all the works that are done under the sun; and, behold, all is vanity and vexation of spirit'[30] has its reflection in *contemptus mundi*. 'Then shall the dust return to the earth as it was' is a strain powerfully continued in the liturgy and the lyrics of the Middle Ages;[31] whilst the affirmation of Job, 'And though after my skin worms destroy this body, yet in my flesh shall I see God', continues to be less powerful in its main clause than in the image of corruption which qualifies it.[32] Job's continual prayer is for deliverance from eternal death, his constant horror that of corruption in the grave, 'the house appointed to all living'. The early history of Christianity confirms this dark tradition, for the homilies of the eastern Church do much to emphasize the grave's restrictions, whilst the miseries of stench and corruption constitute the earliest notions of Hell, which acquires its elaborate torments only at a later date.[33]

The word 'hell' itself derives from the Old Norse *hel*, where it is used originally simply to signify death or the burial mound. The Norse imaginings of the other world are, indeed, merely elaborations of what the living mind conceives as the experience of burial.[34] Their conception of the dead is essentially corporeal, without the notion of a liberated soul: those who return from the burial mound behave and respond as in life; they suffer from hunger and cold, exile and loneliness, rejected by those whose life they once shared. They are feared, because it is felt to be unjust that the living should succeed to their property, and are suspected of malevolent designs upon their heirs, as the authors of disease and death. The size of the Norse burial mound may be explained by the expectation that it would serve as a hall in which this reduced life would continue; the dark world of the slain, though elaborated into a gloomy underworld, is in origin merely the grave. The ceremony of the wake originated in a desire to keep its vindictive denizens at a distance; it was not intended to express grief, but to demonstrate the superiority of the survivors to the victim. Although the animate corpse appears frequently in the sagas, there is little emphasis on corruption, for Norse society was, from its beginnings, heroic, and remained so in its attitude to death even after the advent of Christianity.[35]

The identification of the torments of Hell with the miseries of corruption thus has a long history; it is not surprising, for this, and other reasons given earlier, that it should persist so powerfully in the literature of the Middle Ages. Although an incessant strain at their close, it can be found in very early Middle English; a 'Poema Morale' of the late twelfth century describes torments which have more to do with life in the coffin than with Dante's distinct fiery or frozen Inferno:

> Ther beoth neddren and snaken, evete and frute,
>   tha tereth and freteth the uvele speke, the nith fulle,
>   and te prute.
> Nevre sunne ther ne scinth, ne mone ne steorre.[36]

The terror which such poems evoke is powerfully specific;[37] it derives from a sense that the body will be alive enough to experience its own corruption, yet too dead to be able to defend itself from the adder and worm, or to escape the restrictions of coffin and shroud:

> I ligge wounden in a clout,
> In boordis narwe I am nailid:
> Allas that evre I was proud,
> Now alle mi freendis ben to me failid.
>
> In mi riggeboon bredith an addir kene,
> Min eiyen dasewyn swithe dimme:
> Mi guttis rotin, myn heer is grene,
> Mi teeth grennen swithe grymme.
>
> Mi bodi that sumtyme was so gay,
> Now lieth and rotith in the grounde.
> Mi fairhed is al now goon awai,
> And I stynke foulere than an hounde.
>
> Mi faire feet, mi fingris longe,
> Myn eiyen, myn eeren and mi lymes alle,
> Noon wil now with other honge,
> But everech wole from other falle.[38]

No man can know more of the life after death than this wretched image offers, and the uncertainty of anything else is a frequent lament in medieval poetry: 'Whan bodyes stynken under stone,/Where soules been no man can telle.'[39] Even Lazarus, the single figure who lives (in this life) to tell the tale, can only reiterate this dark insight:

> Under the erthe ye shall thus carefully then cowche;
> The royfe of youre hall youre nakyd nose shall towche;
> Nawther great ne small To you will knele ne crowche;
> A shete shall be youre pall, sich todys shall be youre nowche;
> Todys shall you dere

---

neddren adders *evete* newts *frute* toads *freteth* bite *uvele speke* slanderers
nith fulle malicious *prute* proud *riggeboon* back-bone *dasewyn* grow dark
nowche brooch *dere* harm

ffendys will you fere,
youre flesh that fare was here
    Thus rufully shall rote;
In stede of fare colore
    sich bandys shall bynde youre throte.[40]

Possibly Martha's protest, 'Lord, by this time he stinketh: for he hath been dead four days', encouraged the popular belief that Lazarus lived out the rest of his life in continual misery at the thought of having to die again.[41] Certainly the Lazarus of the Towneley Cycle celebrates his escape from corruption, rather than his renewed vitality as evidence of Christ's claim: 'I am the resurrection, and the life' (Plate 22).

The grim visions of literature are fully elaborated before they become a theme in art. Although a concern with decay is more frequent in writing after the Black Death, its depiction in tomb sculpture develops only after that date (Plate 32). Mâle describes an *en transi* at Laon as one of the earliest examples:

A naked corpse that does not decompose, but withers; this pitiful figure, half mummy, half skeleton, hides its nakedness with its bony hands. The anguish, abandonment, annihilation of this death are inexpressible. Who is the sincere man who wished to be represented on his tomb as he was in his coffin? It is a famous fourteenth century physician, Guillaume de Harcigny. . . . He died in 1393.[42]

Earlier examples of this *réalisme funèbre* could certainly be found in painting; certain depictions of the Three Living and the Three Dead antedate the Black Death.[43] But it is from the middle of the fourteenth century that the visual arts join the verbal in contradicting Aquinas' statement:

Non oportet ut semper aliquis cogitet de ultimo fine quandocumque aliquid appetit vel operatur: . . . Sicut non oportet quod qui vadet per viam, in quolibet passu cogitet de fine.[44]

(It is not necessary for one always to be thinking of one's ultimate end whenever one desires or does something: any more than a traveller needs to think of his destination at every step.)

Each step for the traveller through life in the later Middle Ages was a stage in the process of dying; the purpose of pilgrimage, to know God through knowing oneself, eclipsed divine, in the gloomy discovery of human, truth; for man (to paraphrase the language of the time), is

---

fere terrify

begotten in vile matter, in the body more loathsome than any filth, and in the end a mere sackful of dung and meat for worms.[45]

The close connection between the art and literature of this period is exemplified in a fifteenth-century *Disputacione betwyx the Body and Wormes*.[46] The poet, in a 'ceson of huge mortalite,/. . . with the pestilence/ Hevely reynand', enters a church, where he sees 'a towmbe or sepulture/ Ful freschly forgyd, depycte, and depynte'. His eye dwells both on this tomb and its epitaph, which seems to be the verse written below the illustration of a double tomb which precedes the poem:

> Take hede unto my fygure here abowve
> And se how symtyme I was fresche and gay
> Now turned to wormes mete and corrupcone
> Bot fowle erth and stynkyng slyme and clay
> Attend therfore to this disputacione written here,
>
> . . .
>
> To se what thou art and here aftyr sal be.

These lines are the familiar warning of the *memento mori* to the living observer, of the Dead to the Living of the Legend; their burden is still carried by tombs into the eighteenth and nineteenth centuries.[47] The transition from 'a speaking sight' to actual speech is easily made.

The sight of tomb and epitaph thus prompts the poet's dream, in which he hears the dialogue of the body within with the worms which devour it. Body (female) complains that Worms, 'With ane insaciabylle and gredy appetyte', are destroying the beauty of 'a fygure whylom fresche and feete'; Worms retort that their labour is selfless, for who but those deprived of scent and taste would approach carrion so repulsive? They refuse to leave their grim employment 'While that one of thi bones with other wil hange'. Their victim then makes a futile appeal to those knights and squires 'That sumtyme to me offerd your servyse'; but Worms are not deterred, for, as they remark, 'at the utteraunce we hafe to do/With alle that wer myghty', the 'neyne worthy' and the great beauties of *ubi sunt* lament included. They remind her, in a verse which vividly evokes the realities of medieval life, of their 'mesyngers', lice, nits, worms and fleas, which, from the day of her birth, have warned her 'of us to make yow redy'. Body protests that David declares in the Psalms that men will have dominion over the creatures of the earth, but is told that this power terminates with life. She then laments her former, unthinking Pride of Life, offers herself as a warning to the living, and makes peace with her adversaries:

> Let us kys and dwelle to-gedyr evermore,
> To that God wil that I sal agayn upryse
> At the Day of Dome before the Hye Justyse,
>
> With the body glorified to be.

One may recognize here the characteristics of much grave poetry: life, literally, is but the first stage in the process of dying; the authority of the Scriptures and the liturgy lend their support to this view; worst of all, that sentient sub-life in the grave will continue for 'evermore', a word which chimes oddly with the qualification—until the body's resurrection on Judgement Day. 'Evermore' is precise if one takes it as 'until the end of time'; but it is the span of time that weighs upon the imagination, unrelieved by the distant, impossible hope of future glory. To be called then to the 'blis of heven' is the Body's prayer, not her certainty; and no mention is made of the judgement of her soul upon death. Although the Church did not subscribe to the opinion of some early fathers that body and soul awaited that Day in the grave, much devotional literature seems unconsciously to assume that position.

Just as there is a ready connection between the admonition of the *memento mori*, and the dramatization of the words that issue from the tomb, so there is a natural progression from the corpse that talks to one that walks. The animate dead make many appearances in medieval religious writing, where their instructive value is clearly felt to outweigh their unorthodoxy (Plate 23). *The Golden Legend*, in order to encourage prayers for the dead, relates how a man, whose custom it was to recite such prayers each time he passed through the churchyard, fled thence for shelter when attacked by enemies; the grateful bodies instantly rose from their graves, weapons in hand, to defend him.[48] *An Alphabet of Tales* has many stories to tell of corpses, and of those restless in their graves for instructive reasons.[49] The theme is equally popular in sermons; one preacher, in order to demonstrate the actuality of Hell, relates how a dead man rose three times before the eyes of his mourners, his tongue on fire, and his body pitch black from the neck down.[50] In 'The Legend of St Austin at Compton' Lydgate relates how, at the saint's command, a tormented ghost, 'terrible of face', rose from his grave to explain that he had been cursed by his parish priest for his failure to pay tithes; the priest responsible is dug up, the two shades absolve each other, and then return to the ground in hope of better things.[51] Even St Bonaventura was condemned by the popular imagination to spend a period on earth, as a groaning soul, to atone for his opposition to belief in the Immaculate Conception;[52] but save in rare cases, where primitive superstitions attach to some saint (as to St Bertulph), it is unusual for the officially blessed to appear as apparitions in such stories.[53] The miseries actively suffered in the grave are normally reserved for the damned, the unbaptized, or at least the imperfect.

The abstract figure of Death itself, which, with scythe and hourglass, makes so many appearances in renaissance and baroque art, does not seem to develop from these individualized stories of animate corpses within (or without) the grave; it more probably develops from the impersonal motifs of the Legend, and the Dance which succeeds it. It is, however, difficult, in this area, to say with any certainty what precedes and what devolves; the same practices—meditation on the skull, admonition by the *memento mori*—must nourish both strains, and the origins for such customs are so ancient that the search for precedents becomes abortive.[54] The dialogue of the Legend can, for example, be paralleled in Egyptian civilization, where a corpse might be introduced to a banquet with the admonition, 'Behold this image of what you yourselves will be'; the moral drawn from the spectacle—'Eat and drink therefore, and be happy'—was not, however, the one the Christian Church chose to draw.[55] At the close of the Middle Ages, Myrc is still advising parish priests to contemplate dead men's bones as a cure for pride,[56] whilst, before the Legend actually develops, the bones and dust of the buried 'would say' the very words that, two centuries later, the three Dead are actually to speak.[57]

It is easy to find analogues for the Legend, but impossible to tell precisely where it originated, or whether it occurred first in art or in literature. Like the double tomb, it spells out the instruction that bones and dust can offer; for although the tomb is personal, the Legend impersonal, both juxtapose Life and Death to similar effect. Although Panofsky considers that such double tombs express a 'feeling for the collective', not merely a 'general preoccupation with the macabre',[58] the juxtaposition of Living and Dead in literature seems almost always to be prompted by admonitory didacticism; its sense of the collective extends no further than the (sometimes vindictive) wish 'to bring down the mighty from their seats'. Both the Legend and the Dance are rapidly assimilated, in consequence, to the admonitory stock of the medieval preacher.[59]

The Legend may be very simply narrated, for it is essentially the encounter between three living men and three animate skeletons who address the Living with the words: 'What you are, so once were we; what we are, so shall you be.' The core of the Legend never varies, though time adds to it certain embellishments: the Living may, for example, be gaily dressed youths, or kings, or be distinguished into the three Ages; they are often engaged in hunting, occasionally with hounds, but more often with falcons, for falconry was, *par excellence*, the sport of the nobility[60] (Plates 15b and 16b). The Dead are less easily differentiated, at least in painting, but even there the endeavour is sometimes made to suggest what the written word may state explicitly: that they image each man's individual future. In one illumination[61] (Plate 25), the Living are distinguished into Age, mitred and robed, his hands folded in prayer: Middle Age, arrayed in full armour, his sword drawn; and Youth, crowned and bearing a sceptre. Where Age responds to the apparitions with prayer, and Middle Age with aggression, Youth shrinks fearfully away from the horrible sight. The Dead image the Living, for two are crowned and one mitred, but the corpse most newly dead faces episcopal Elde, whilst the grimmest and most withered of the three confronts Youth; the point is possibly that Age, because closest to the grave, least fears it, whilst Youth, from his greater distance, finds its threat the more terrifying. In wall paintings, stages of corruption may reflect in the Dead the various ages of the Living; their bodies may, moreover, be hung with worms, and sometimes with the moths which were supposed to carry plague.[62] A hermit occasionally figures, both in painting and in poetry,[63] who probably represents Macarius, an early saint who seems to have established a curious reciprocity with corpses:

S. Macarius was in a desert, and entered in to a pit or sepulchre, whereas had been buried many bodies of paynims, for to sleep, and he drew out one of these bodies and laid it under his head instead of a pillow. Then came thither devils for to make him aghast and afeard, and said one to another: Come with me to bathe thee. And the body that lay under his head said: I may not come, for I have a pilgrim upon me lying, that I may not move. For all this S. Macarius was not afeard, but he beat the body with his fist, and said: Arise and go if thou mayst.[64]

The life of the corpse, one should note, is a devilish trick, for Macarius, hitting it firmly, shows that it has none; but the later Middle Ages continued obstinately to animate their corpses, even in the presence of the sceptical saint.

The theme first appears in painting in England in the early fourteenth century; after the Black Death, its popularity increases greatly, and no fewer than fifty paintings have been discovered, often on the walls of quite humble churches, executed largely in the late fourteenth and fifteenth centuries. In contemporary writing, only one full version of the Legend exists, in a poem dubiously ascribed to John Audelay;[65] but it is obliquely referred to in numerous other works. The subject, however, seems to originate in France, where it occurs in both paintings and poems at the close of the thirteenth century.[66] The earliest illumination in England illustrates this transmission, for it is attached to a reduced version of one of the five extant French poems.[67] The earliest of the five seems to be that of Baudoin de Condé, minstrel at the court of Margaret, Countess of Anjou, from 1244–80. The anonymous poem which begins *Diex pour trois peceours retraire* appears to derive from it; whilst the version of Nicole de Margival is similarly imitated in another anonymous work, *Conpains, vois tu ce que je vois?* Whilst these four poems all belong to the last decade of the thirteenth century, a fifth, *Se nous vous aportons nouvellez*, is probably fourteenth century; originally the sole example of pure dialogue, it has, in a later manuscript, acquired a narrative introduction and conclusion. Other European poems on the subject exist—four German, one Italian, one Latin—but all except the last, which seems to be based on Italian paintings of the Legend, appear to derive from the French, and all are later in date than the work of Baudoin de Condé.[68]

The most significant limitation of the French poems lies in their inability (or reluctance) to make any significant use of narrative elaboration. Whilst only the fourteenth-century work is conceived as a pure *dit*, additions to the dialogue of the Living and the Dead are of a most perfunctory kind. The poems indicate merely that three fine young men, inevitably proud, and generally noble, encounter three skeletons; from whom, having exchanged words (though 'exchange' is too intimate a term), they part, resolving to amend their ways. One poet who, to judge from his introduction, is particularly anxious to establish the veracity of his story, lends it realism by a churchyard setting,[69] whilst the addition to the fourteenth-century account places the whole episode within the vision of the hermit who relates it. On the whole, however, very little attempt is made to provide circumstantial detail; there is, for example, no mention of the hunting and hawking common in English painting, apart from a single remark of the Dead that hawks and fine clothing should not lead the Living to forget that all men lie cold in the grave eventually.[70] Realism is similarly sacrificed to moralism by a lack of differentiation amongst the participants: for the Living (save possibly in the account of de Condé) are differentiated neither by age nor by attitude; whilst the Dead, though occasionally distinguished by their former rank, as nobility or aberrant clerics, seem intended rather to enforce a general moral point, at the expense of the rich or the Church, than to delineate an individual life. Their speeches are, in consequence, largely repetitive, and could even, in some cases, be spoken by Living or Dead indifferently.

The English poem attributed to Audelay is no work of genius, but the literary tradition of the second quarter of the fifteenth century was clearly a richer one. The boar hunt with which the poem opens offers a resource of poetic meaning which is not available to the original writers.[71] At first sight the hunt appears to have little connection with the events which follow; but its noise, violence, and the narrator's enjoyment of both, is vividly caught:

> Fro the noyse that hit was new til hit was ne nyght,
>   Fro the non bot a napwile, me thoght hit bot noght—
>   Me thoght hit noght but a throw—
>   To se how he throbyt and threw.
>   Honters with hornes thai kowth blow;
>   Thai halowyd here howndys with 'how!'
>   In holtes herde I never soche hew. (ll. 7–13)

---

napwile time for a nap   *throw* brief while

Later in the poem, the violent life of this scene contrasts dramatically
with the chill encounter between Living and Dead; the words of the
second King, ' "What helpis our hontyng with how?' " suggests that the
contrast is deliberate. The encounter with the Dead is a bringing to
bay of the Living; the predators, turned prey, now suffer those emotions
which the narrator witnessed with delight in the boar (Plate 26). This
second hunt occurs in silence and solitude, remote from the comforting
din of an unreflecting life; the active opening retains its independent
force, for the apparitions strike at a different level—to the still, cold
heart, not the exuberant surface—of a related experience.

The superiority of this poem to its French predecessors is partly due
to its elaboration as narrative, which enables it to escape the constricting
symmetry of alternating dialogue, in order to oppose vision to anti-
vision. The vision is of life, to which belong the narrator, the hunt, and
the three kings 'With donyng and tryffylyng and talis thai telde'; to this
the poem returns at its close, with the building of the minster, and the
inscription of the tale upon its walls. In the opposing anti-vision of death,
the narrator/reader significantly has no part, for it is a tale reported of
another time and another country. As mist and rain envelop the bright
wood of the hunt, the kings venture on:

> . . . fotis bot a fewe,
> Thai fonden feldus ful fayre and fogus ful fow.
> Schokyn out of a schawe thre schalkys at ene,
> Schadows unshene . . .   (ll. 40–3)

The reversal is abrupt and dramatic; the tale, itself once matter for
'donyng and tryffylyng', acquires a deathly seriousness. Unlike its
French forbears, the meaning of this poem cannot be expressed in
didactic platitudes. The wood of the hunt is, for example, at first a cheerful, perfectly mappable place, as the world characteristically is to those in
the Pride of Life:

> These wodis and these wastis thai waltyn al to welde,
> Thai waltyn at here wil to ware
> These wodis and these wastis that ther were. (ll. 21–3)

With the appearance of the anti-vision, this familiar landscape alters
dramatically to a place which, in more senses than one, resembles
Dante's *selva oscura*—a state of mind, a landscape of the soul, terrain,
in any event, no longer chartable.

No other English writer explores the Legend for its intrinsic interest,

---

donyng making a loud noise *Schokyn out* Started out *schawe* grove
schalkys men *unshene* ugly *waltyn* chose

but a multitude reflect it obliquely, a number quite directly. Many poems use the mirror image; in 'A Mirror for Young Ladies at their Toilet', the voice of the reflected future develops into that of Death itself:

> O maset wriche, I marke the with my mace.
> Lyfte up thy ieye, be-holde now, and assay!
> Yche loke one me aught to put the in affray;
> I wyll not spare the, for thou arte my pray.[72]

It is hard to say whether the Dead of the Legend, Death in the Dance, or the great abstract itself is speaking; but in other cases the words of the first are directly employed:

> Umthynke the ay of thre
> What we er, and whate we warre,
> And whate that we sall be.[73]

The Legend must, through visual art, have become so familiar that an allusion was sufficient. It is possible that Chaucer's Pardoner relied for effect partly on the assumption that, just as the three rioters expect to discover Death in some physical form which they can challenge, so the listening pilgrims would have awaited, moment by moment, the appearance of three animate corpses. The point of his story—that the warnings of death are offered in plenty by life to those who have eyes to see—is made by arousing more dramatic expectations, whilst refusing to satisfy them.

The final years of the fifteenth century can still provide, in Henryson's 'Thre Deid Pollis', a poem directly modelled on the Legend; one which, moreover, returns in a more refined form to the simplicity of the French originals. Not only has all the circumstantial detail of the hunt disappeared; the Living have no physical presence or voice, other than that sketched by the address of the Dead to 'wantone yowth', 'febill aige', and the objects of Youth's desire:

> O ladeis quhyt, in claithis corruscant,
> poleist with perle, and mony pretius stane;
> With palpis quhyt, and hals so elegant,
> Sirculit with gold, & sapheris mony ane:
> Your finyearis small, quhyt as quhailis bane,
> arrayit with ringis, and mony rubeis reid:
> as we ly thus, so sall ye ly ilk ane,
> with peilit pollis, and holkit thus your heid.[74]

---

maset terrified   *hals* neck   *quhailis* whale's   *peilit* skinned   *pollis* skulls   *holkit* dug out

Henryson's poem is not dramatic in the narrative sense, as Audelay's is, but the vivid sensuality of that verse achieves drama in the stark contrast of the final line; a sense of life is necessary if the menace of death is to be fully felt. Henryson's moral points are, moreover, enlivened by their grim wit: the Dead address the proud at the summit of Fortune's wheel with the sharp, if grisly, question, 'quha was farest, or fowlest, of us thre?/or quhilk of us kin was gentillar?' By embracing the three Ages, his poem also achieves some serenity in its conclusion, for the old, 'drawand neir the dait/of dully deid', are summoned to prayer: 'fall on thy kneis; ask grace at god greit,/with oritionis, and haly salmes sweit.'

As already indicated, it is often difficult to distinguish between the warnings of Age, the voice from the tomb, motifs derived from the Legend or Dance, and the abstract personification of Death itself. The last three were, however, originally distinct, and succeeded each other in that chronological order. The Legend is initially a warning to men to reform in this life; it has its relation to that instructive fear which ends in redemptive action. The Dance, which may possibly develop from it, no longer prompts men to choose, but forces them to submit to the inevitable; it allows, however, for a wider range of social comment than the Legend, for each Death is personal, and arrests individuals in an appropriate form (Plates 27 and 28b, c, d). Thus the poor who have nothing to lose, the good who are at peace with God, the old who are weary for the grave, even the innocent child from whom the skeleton shields its face, do not feel terror at its approach; it is the proud, the rich and the powerful, those who, as Langland would say, enjoy their reward in this life, who feel the full menace of its coming. Death in the Dance is still the adumbration of each man's specific end, not the anonymous abstract which later tugs impartially at the sleeve of every-man. To a modern eye, the distinction may seem unimportant; the personification may even appear preferable to the earlier, personalized figures of corruption. But the later abstract is less fearful largely because it has less to express (Plate 24). The interconnection, and distinction, between the three, may be illustrated from the Cemetery of the Innocents at Paris. An elaborate depiction of the Dance was executed on the walls of the Cemetery itself, between 1424–5. At the same period, the Duc de Berry commissioned a representation of the Legend, to be carved above the church portal. Where the Dance spoke to those who had newly suffered the arrest of Death, the Legend had its injunction to offer the Living who attended their obsequies. When, a century later, the abstract figure of Death was added, the distinction between Dance and Legend was lost, in the dull awareness of universal mortality.[75]

Whilst it is probable that the Dance was, in its extended form, a development from the Legend, its specific origins are obscure. Dances of Death were actually performed in the Middle Ages, and various non-

Christian analogues can be found for them: the revelry of the souls in Elysium was a Roman motif, but it had of course none of the terror and horror of the medieval renderings.[76] The Church's suspicion of these actual dances, and their identification with fairies, witches, and other pagan beliefs, can encourage speculation on originals even more remote.[77] Mâle, without looking quite so far afield, suspects that the Dance is foreshadowed in the twelfth-century verses of Hélinand, and conjectures that these, in their turn, originate in mimed illustration of sermons on Death.[78] Speculation apart, the earliest example, both in art and literature, is that at the Cemetery of the Innocents, where the paintings were accompanied by descriptive and dramatic verses. This is the text which Lydgate translated for a similar scheme, which was executed at St Paul's c. 1430.[79] The English imitation was destroyed when the cloisters were demolished in 1549; but other examples are recorded at Whitehall, the Archbishop's Palace at Croydon, Wortley Hall in Gloucester, and Salisbury Cathedral.[80] It is probable that depictions of the Dance were fairly familiar in the fifteenth century, but many more examples of the Legend have survived from that period; this is doubtless because it was cheaper to execute, rather than more popular. With the exception of the chapel at Haddon Hall, the Legend is to be found in parish churches, for it requires only a single painting; the Dance, on the other hand, demands an extended scheme, few of which were undertaken after the Black Death.

The description of the Dance as the *danse macabre* or *danse des morts* has intrinsic interest. The latter—of the dead, not simply of Death—supports the individualized interpretation already mentioned, which is intensified by the impression that it is the dead, paradoxically, who dance, whilst the living are frozen in fear.[81] The meaning of *danse macabre* is more obscure, for our adjectival use of the word derives from the spectacle itself. In his translation of the Paris text, Lydgate ascribes those lines, which belong in his original to *Ung maistre qui est au bout de la danse*, specifically to 'Machabree the Doctour'. The attempt to identify Dr Machabree has led to much scholarly speculation, ranging from Judas Macchabaeus to more contemporary figures.[82] Douce connected the name with that curious intimate of the dead, St Macarius, but more expert etymologists deny that this is linguistically feasible, whilst their own suggestions are widely scattered from Arabic to fifteenth-century Parisian slang.

Lydgate's composite observation, in the *verba translatoris*, makes a comment upon the sequence which, whilst typical of the author, moves in the direction of the abstract and away from the individual:

Dethe spareth not low ne hye degre
Popes kynges ne worthi Emperowrs

When thei schyne moste in felicite
He can abate the fresshnes of her flowres
Ther bright sune clipsen with hys showres
Make hem plownge from theire sees lowe
Maugre the myght of al these conquerowres
Fortune hath hem from her whele ythrowe.[83]

The harsh, generalized moral, that all men are equal in death, all subject
to the fall of Fortune's wheel, is modified by the natural freshness and
tenderness, equally typical of Lydgate, of those images of transience—
flower, sun, shower and shadow. This duality, of vengeance with compassion, of natural release with unnatural intervention, reflects the
diversity of his original.

It is rewarding to relate the words of Lydgate's translation to Holbein's woodcuts of the Dance. The latter were executed a century later
than the series at the Cemetery of the Innocents, but they are based
upon a sequence at Basel, dating from about 1440, which Holbein must
have studied when he resided in the Swiss city in 1515.[84] His work,
moreover, shows great fidelity to both the spirit and the detail of medieval
art, and since his Dance is the only complete series to survive in England,
it would be a pity to ignore it because it so narrowly post-dates the
Middle Ages.[85] As Clark remarks, 'If it were not for his work the idea
would have died out with the Middle Ages. It was he who expressed it
in a form intelligible to the modern world.'[86] Like Lydgate's general
comment, Holbein's woodcuts move between the general and the personal. Where Death faces a group, as in the case of the Duke or King,[87]
he becomes an anonymous abstract, a 'fell sergeant' who arrests the
former from amongst his followers, a cupbearer at the table of the
second, who, as in the *Ludus Coventriae* Play of Herod, comes to join
the dissipations of the feast. It is in his personal form, where Death
confronts a single figure, that complexities of response, as in Lydgate's
translation, become most apparent.

To the humble at the tail of the Dance, the coming of Death is, in
both verse and woodcut, far from fearful. The words of Death to the
Labourer are tempered with humanity:

Thow laborere which yn sorow & peyne
Haste had thi life in ful grete travaile
Thow most eke daunce ...   (ll. 545–7)

The Labourer's reply mingles regret with resignation: 'I have wisshed
after dethe ful ofte/Al-be that I wolde have fled him nowe.' In Holbein's
woodcut of the Ploughman (XXXVIII), Death urges the horses forward
to drive the last furrow, whilst the sun sets radiantly behind the distant
tower of the church. The following illustration, of Death and the Child,
has similar qualities, for whilst the mother and an older sibling express

their anguish from the fireside where supper is cooking, the toddler
turns back from the door to wave a cheerful and affectionate farewell,
whilst his other hand is grasped protectively by the skeleton who leads
him over the threshold (Plate 28d). In Lydgate's translation, Death's
words to the Child, and the Child's reply, are so touched with tenderness
that they merit full quotation:

> Litel Enfaunt that were but late borne
> Schape yn this worlde to have no plesaunce
> Thow moste with other that gon here to forne
> Be lad yn haste be fatal ordynaunce
> Lerne of newe to go on my daunce
> Ther mai non age a-scape yn sothe ther fro
> Late everi wight have this yn remembraunce
> Who lengest leveth moste shal suffre wo.
>
> A a a a worde I can not speke
> I am so yonge I was bore yisterdai
> Dethe is so hasti one me to be wreke
> And liste no lenger to make no delai
> I cam but now and now I go my wai
> Of me no more no tale shal be tolde
> The wille of god no man with-stonde mai
> As sone dyeth a yonge man as an olde   (ll. 577-92)

To those neither humble nor proud, Death adopts an appropriate
aspect. To the Man of Law, he is litigious—'Sire advocate shorte processe
for to make/Ye mote come plete a-fore the hye Juge'—whilst in Holbein's
depiction of the Advocate, Death participates in the colloquy between
lawyer and defendant, raising his hourglass to allow time for a few coins
to change hands.[88] From Holbein's Rich Man, the skeleton steals money,
undeterred by the owner's protests, whilst Lydgate's Usurer recognizes
too late the ineffectiveness of gold: 'Socowre to fynde I see no maner
weie/Of golde ne silver.'[89] It is, however, noticeable, particularly in their
treatment of the great, that Holbein's comment exhibits a social optimism
which Lydgate's account largely lacks; the former allows for virtue
amongst the powerful, where the latter does not. It is Lydgate's Hermit
who accepts the approach of Death with real equanimity—'And for
my parte welcome be goddes grace'; his detachment, as Death allows,
is appropriate to one who has lived 'longe yn wildernesse/And there
contynued longe yn abstynence'.[90] No corresponding virtue is found in
the dignitaries of the Church, for Lydgate's Bishop regrets the turning
of his feasts into dismal ferials, where Holbein's faces death serenely,
whilst his abandoned flock bitterly laments its loss.[91] The later series
includes the heroism of Knight (Plate 28c) and Nobleman, who attempt
to fight their opponent; an Emperor who meets his end whilst enforcing

justice; an Old Man who steps with relief into his grave, supported by
the skeletal arm beneath his elbow[92] (Plate 28b). It is clear that the Middle
Ages exercised a less liberal compassion, and there is in Holbein no
equivalent for the words, spoken by a 'kynge liggyng dede & eten with
wormes', which, in Lydgate's version, conclude the Dance:

> Ye folke that loken upon this purtrature
> Beholdyng here alle the estates daunce
> Seeth what ye ben & what is yowre nature
> Mete unto wormes not elles yn substaunce
> And have this myrroure ever yn remembraunce
> How I lye here som-tyme crowned kynge
> To al estates a trewe resemblaunce
> That wormes fode is fyne to owre lyvynge.   (ll. 633-40)

One may detect the influence of the Legend here, and possibly its
close connection with the later motif curtailed the extent to which the
latter could express compassion, admiration, or even sympathy. As single
incident or as series, the image of the Dance in other medieval literature
is used primarily as didactic admonition to the proud and mighty; it
is only incidentally a comment on the death of everyman, or on the
relation between that moment and the quality of the life which preceded
it. The Dance may lend its structure to drama: the unfinished morality,
The Pride of Life, promises to be a single confrontation, whilst the Last
Judgement scenes of the Chester cycle represent a composite sequence.
In neither case is the spectrum of comment as wide as that to be found
in Holbein's sequence, or even in Lydgate's translation. Chambers,
while noting that two of the six moralities which can confidently be
assigned to the fifteenth century, 'are based upon a motif akin to that
of the Dance of Death', deduces that its popularity contributed im-
portantly to the development of those abstractions which the moralities
present.[93] Whatever the merit of that suggestion, it does indicate the
simplification of possibilities inherent in the Dance when it was adopted
into another form.

The lyric has many related examples to offer; the following verses level
all ranks, impartially, in death:

> I Wende to dede, knight stithe in stoure,
> thurghe fyght in felde i wane the flour;
> Na fightis me taght the dede to quell—
> weend to dede, soth i yow tell.

> I weende to dede, a kynge I-wisse;
> What helpis honor or werldis blysse?

---

stithe stout   *stoure* combat

Dede is to mane the kynde wai—
i wende to be clade in clay.

I wende to dede, clerk ful of skill,
that couth with worde men mare & dill.
Sone has me made the dede ane ende—
beese ware with me! to dede i wende.[94]

'Beese ware with me!' instantly recalls the injunction of the three Dead
and the voice from the tomb. By conflating several motifs, such lyrics
lose touch with the personal and specific, replacing it with an impersonal,
composite figure. The address of Death in Henryson's 'Ressoning betuix
Deth and Man' is a powerful example:

'O mortall man, behold, tak tent to me,
Quhilk sowld thy mirrour be baith day & nicht;
all erdly thing that evir tuik lyfe mon die:
Paip, emprious, king, barroun, & knyght,
Thocht thay be in thair roall stait and hicht,
may not ganestand, quhen I pleiss schute the derte;
waltownis, Castellis, and towris nevir so wicht,
may nocht risist quihill it be at his herte.'[95]

The vanity of worldly achievements recalls the burden of *Ecclesiastes*;
the 'derte' of Death relates to the iconography of pestilence; the 'mirrour' conjures the reflection of the three Living in the three Dead; whilst
the summons to that series of the mighty comes directly from the
Dance. Such a spectre has power, but the fear it inspires is craven; it
is a force from without which pierces the heart of man, not an inward
condition to which he himself may adjust (Plate 24).

The mighty figure of Death the Leveller is not, however, always
impersonal; as he becomes more distinct, he may even extend to his
victims a weirdly appropriate courtesy. For Dunbar, the figure is clearly
generalized: 'That strang unmercifull tyrand', armed 'with his schour
of mortall haill', imposes on a mutable world the solitary, negative
certainty:

The stait of man dois change and vary,
Now sound, now seik, now blith, now sary,
Now dansand mery, now like to dee;
    Timor mortis conturbat me.[96]

In 'Lament for the Makaris', the Dance, though never explicitly mentioned, is felt in the rhythm of each verse which captures the negative
declension of *vado mori*, and in the sequence of the whole which opens

---

mare ruin   *dill* benumb   *tent* care   *waltownis* walled towns

with the mighty—'Princis, Prelotis, and Potestatis'—whilst it ends with
figures familiar to Dunbar—the Roulls of Aberdene and Corstorphin:
'Two bettir fallowis did no man se.' Where the mighty encounter
superior might, those at the centre of the Dance meet their match: to
the Knight, Death is 'Victour . . . at all mellie'; to the wise, intelligence
is not defence, 'Thame helpis no conclusionis sle'; nor is their art to the
doctors, 'Thame self fra ded may not supple'. But to Dunbar's intimates
Death comes with courtesy: 'he hes done roune' with 'Maister Robert
Henrisoun', and 'enbrast' 'Schir Johne the Ros'.

Both the Dance and the Legend have often been criticized as examples
of late medieval obsession with the macabre: Caiger-Smith, writing on
wall paintings, contrasts unfavourably the later, more elaborate renderings of the Legend with the contemplative simplicity of the first examples,
and remarks that 'the tale turned into a dramatic episode of almost
entirely negative significance'. On the Dance, he is even more severe,
describing it as 'a powerless process and dull awareness of man's lot',[97]
yet the variety of meanings which both motifs can sustain, in the better
poetry and painting, does not justify so negative a judgement. The varied
perceptions and tone of Lydgate's translation, Holbein's woodcuts, or
Dunbar's 'Lament', render Death irresistible without declining into
'powerless process', whilst their complex awareness of man's lot is never
'dull'. If the Renaissance is free from these obsessions, it is in part
because such complexities have diminished: both Legend and Dance
can be traced as motifs, but their presence is faintly felt because they
are now *merely* acknowledgements of 'powerless process'. The dying
Hamlet alludes to the latter when, struggling to impart his last wishes
to Horatio, he laments that 'this fell sergeant, Death,/Is strict in his
arrest'.[98] Pericles, viewing the heads of previous unsuccessful claimants
for the hands of Antiochus' daughter, spells out the Legend's moral with
a calm detachment which recalls its earliest versions:

> Antiochus, I thank thee, who hath taught
> My frail mortality to know itself,
> And by those fearful objects to prepare
> This body, like to them, to what I must;
> For death remembered should be like a mirror,
> Who tells us life's but breath, to trust it error.[99]

The injunction of Richard II, 'For God's sake let us sit upon the ground,/
And tell sad stories of the death of kings', is often related to those
repetitive medieval tragedies, traceable through Boccaccio's *De Casibus
Virorum Illustrium*, Chaucer's *Monk's Tale*, Lydgate's *Fall of Princes*, to

---

mellie conflict   *supple* help   *done roune* held converse

the Elizabethan *Mirror for Magistrates*; whilst its image of Death is frequently connected with Holbein's depiction of the Emperor:

> ... within the hollow crown
> That rounds the mortal temples of a king,
> Keeps Death his court, and there the antic sits,
> Scoffing his state and grinning at his pomp.[100]

Certainly, its medieval antecedents are powerfully sensed in this play, but again, the anguish and perplexity of those who die are absent. One must turn to the soliloquy of Hamlet for that 'dread of something after death', or to the tormented cry of Claudio, 'Ay, but to die, and go we know not where,/To lie in cold obstruction, and to rot'.[101] For the Middle Ages, this lacerating apprehension was not only private, but communal, for it had its root in the recurrently troubling question, Who created Death?

From its inception, Christian thinking was far from settled in its answers, and a return to *Genesis* indicates the source of this uncertainty. The warning addressed by God to Adam—'the tree of the knowledge of good and evil, thou shalt not eat of it: for in the day that thou eatest thereof thou shalt surely die'[102]—gives no clue to its origin, and a study of the Bible as a whole provides no solution. The Old Testament explicitly declares that God did not create death, but does not explain who did;[103] whilst the New, though describing it as demonic in origin, does so in contexts too mythologic to sustain an exact aetiological interpretation.[104] It is, moreover, unclear whether death is the punishment for original or specific sin; *Genesis* is not explicit on that point,[105] whilst St Paul, though clearly stating, 'as by one man sin entered into the world, and death by sin', sees it also as the price paid for individual offences.[106] God's words in *Genesis*, 'cursed is the ground for thy sake', seem to remove the possibility of explaining death as natural process, by implying that nature fell with man; whilst the New Testament never admits this neutralizing explanation.[107] Augustine, however, held that death was contrary to the laws of nature;[108] whilst Aquinas, though agreeing with the earlier Father, that death was not God's creation,[109] nevertheless sees it as conformable with natural law, and the direct result of original sin:

... in morte tria sunt consideranda: scilicet causa naturalis; et quantum ad hoc ex conditione naturae statutum est hominem semel mori, inquantum componitur ex contrariis. Secundo donum inditum; et quantum ad hoc in conditione datum est homini beneficium originalis justitiae, per quam anima continebat corpus, ut posset non mori. Tertio meritum mortis; et sic homo peccando meruit illud beneficium amittere, et sic mortem incurrit.[110]

(Three things should be considered about death: namely, as to its natural

cause; here from the condition of his nature, inasmuch as he is composed
of contraries, it is established that man should once die. Secondly, as to his
appointed gift; and here man was given the gift of original integrity, through
which the soul so contained the body that it was able not to die. Thirdly, as
to deserving death; and thus man, by sinning, deserved to lose his gift, and
thus incurred death.)

The care with which Aquinas treads this disputed ground, in formulat-
ing his three considerations, suggests why less subtly theological minds
should have continued to ask the old blunt questions. Was Death God's
messenger or Satan's? Was it a natural, or an unnatural, phenomenon?
Did man incur it through original sin, or through individual offence?[111]
Most medieval literature is agreed at least that death is the penalty
paid by man for original sin. In Holbein's Dance the skeleton first
appears when Adam is banished from the garden (Plate 28a), but thereafter is never absent: it plays the fiddle as the angel flourishes his sword
above the unhappy pair, labours beside Adam as he tills the ground (but
no doubt with different intent), and thenceforward dogs the steps of all
men, from the highest to the low.[112] This assumption is linked with
a (less general) conviction that Death is natural; thus, Lydgate writes:

> Twene me [Death] and kynde ther ys a knot y-knet
> That in thys worlde every lyvyng creature
> For Adams synne must dye of nature.[113]

Yet even such plain statements are not without their internal problems
and contradictions. In *Everyman*, for example, where Death makes a
claim identical, even to its wording, with Lydgate's 'Warning', it has
stated as explicitly, some lines earlier, that it punishes specific, not
merely original, sin: 'Every man wyll I beset that lyveth beestly/Out of
Goddes lawes, and dredeth not foly.'[114] It seems that Death is conflating
the mortality of the body with the damnation, or moral death, of the
soul: 'He that loveth richesse I wyll stryke with my darte,/ His syght to
blynde, and fro heven to departe.'[115] It is all too easy for the two to
become identified; like the fall from Fortune, the death of everyman is
both the common lot and specific punishment. The finer writers or
artists subtly distinguish the two, for it is sudden death, the hope of
the pagan but the terror of the Christian (since it allows no time for
repentance), which is the punishment allotted to the wicked, whilst
death in the due course from natural causes is felt to be a different matter.
The Dance itself makes that distinction, for it is the unprepared who
take their leave with terrified reluctance, whilst the old, who have spent
their time well, are grateful; the child, who has had no time to offend,
is tranquil (Plates 28b and d). This difference is vividly dramatized in
The Pardoner's Tale, where the Old Man longingly seeks the grave which

the rioters rightly fear; to them, the unprepared, the event signifies mortality of body and soul together.

To serene Elde it is unnatural *not* to die; to those in the flower of life, it is 'agayn the ordre of nature'. One fifteenth-century poet thus laments the death of his mistress, in language which, in its emphasis on growth, asserts the right of the gifted and beautiful to live out their time:

> Of lordis lyne & lynage sche was, here sche lyse!
> Bounteuus, benigne, enbleshed wyth beaute,
> Sage, softe and sobre an gentyll in al wyse,
> fflorishyng ant fecunde, wyth femenyn beaute,
> Meke, mylde and merciful, of pite sche bar the prise.
> Comely, kynde and curteis, in nobleye of nurture,
> Vernant in alle vertu, plesaunt and demure.[116]

One might explain this poet's general statement, that Death is invariably 'contrarious to creatures in kynde', as a reflection of the emotions arising from that single, premature loss; but many others seem to doubt that 'knot y-knet' between Death and Kind which Lydgate and *Everyman* assert so confidently. In the *Roman de la Rose*, Nature labours perpetually to preserve the species against the ravages of Death, who '*ne les peut aconsivre,/ja tant ne savra corre aprés*'[117] (can never catch them up, no matter how fast he runs). The alliterative English poem, *Death and Liffe*, remarks the same opposition when Liffe complains that she and Nature cannot bring up their people properly because of her opponent's interference.[118] Death, even in the natural course, is not always, or even usually, accepted as part of the natural order, whatever relation it may bear to the original sin of Adam. In *Death and Liffe*, she advances that argument without avail;[119] for once (and it is a relief to say so), Life's victory over Death is decisive.

It is not surprising that, in this unusually positive poem, the origin of Death should be quite clear: she is ' "Dame Daughter of the Devill" ', and the destruction of that gay company of the living is ' "a deed of the devill" '.[120] This is invariably the explanation given in writing concerned with the Harrowing of Hell, for the mythic context here permits an acceptance, as aetiology, of those visionary New Testament statements 'that through death [Christ] might destroy him that had the power of death, that is, the devil'.[121] All accounts of the Harrowing derive ultimately, however, from the apocryphal *Gospel of Nicodemus*, where three Rabbis testify to meeting 'a great multitude of men in white garments who had died aforetime'. To the question, 'How are ye which were dead remaining in the body?' they reply:

We arose with Christ out of hell, and he raised us up from the dead. And hereby may ye know that the gates of death and darkness are destroyed, and the souls of the saints are taken out thence, and have ascended into heaven with Christ the Lord.[122]

They themselves are in the body only that they may testify to the chosen amongst the living; for the Harrowing of Hell does not signify physical resurrection, which must await the Last Day, but the release of the soul from that moral death which is damnation. It is, however, possible that these 'men in white garments', testifying in the body to that supreme hope, acted as precedents for that cavalcade of corpses who seem so often to enunciate the opposite truth. In any event, the confidence inspired by the Harrowing is rarely allowed to extend outside it.[123] If Christ vanquishes Death in Langland's account of the Passion, it is summoned with Kind, pestilence and Elde in the Vision of Anti-Christ, when Conscience despairs of winning the wicked to reform in any other way.[124] In Everyman, God himself describes Death as his 'myghty messengere', and, like Conscience, summons it to 'do iustyce' on his ungrateful people.[125] When, in The Speculum of Guy of Warwick, Death is described as a deceiver, and men are urged to fear God instead, advice is offered of which the medieval imagination clearly stood in need;[126] but there is much evidence that it went unheard. Like Fortune, the dark figure of Death came to eclipse the divine light, and although men remained sufficiently certain of Christ's conquest, they also felt profoundly excluded from its reassurance.

The creation of Death as abstract personification, whilst it makes its appearance in several of the texts already mentioned, is strictly a late development of the much older debate over its origin (Plate 24). The appearance of its grim and vengeful figure near the close of the Middle Ages must to some extent have been staged by the prevalence of sudden death in time of pestilence; for the inexplicable collapse of men who an hour before walked apparently whole and sound, together with the arbitrariness of a visitation which spared some communities and destroyed others totally, must clearly have suggested, in the absence of a better explanation, an unseen and deliberate hand. A telling illustration of the process which led to the figure's formation can be found in the choice of St Sebastian as one of several saints who came to be invoked for protection from the plague; the arrows which figure in his martyrdom were interpreted as the darts of Death itself, which thus acquired its armoury: 'I wyll stryke with my darte.'[127] It is certainly true that this objectified image of fear often loses the capacity to speak to the inward heart of personal experience, which is retained in the conception of both Legend and Dance, although banal renderings of both may diminish that potential. The personification has certain analogies with the late medieval tendency to ignore the actual body in favour of the tomb or monument, a shift in attention which seems to suggest a deadening of sensibility in response to Death's ubiquity.[128] One may actually come to miss the over-real, over-graphic quality of that earlier tradition of meditation upon the corpse, perceptible in so much poetry concerned with the grave; such an experience of death is at least vividly felt, whereas the later, generalized treatments, in redeploying established insights without extending them, too often allow them to decay into enervated convention. This enervation is by no means identical with renaissance detachment: man does not see his mortality in perspective; rather, he allows its shadow to obliterate meaningful distinctions.

When Death appears at Herod's feast in the *Ludus Coventriae*, his entrance, because exceptional in mode, is dramatic and terrifying. In *The Castle of Perseverance*, which, as morality, is peopled with such figures, it has degenerated into a cliché, conflated with the Pride of Life:

> Ye schul me drede everychone;
> Whanne I come ye schul grone;
> My name in londe is lefte alone:
>   I hatte drery Dethe.[129]

Death is not only just one amongst many abstractions; a loss of inwardness and complexity accompanies this development. *Everyman*, too, is a morality, but its skeletal figure not only expresses very various connections with the divine on the one hand, the human on the other; it is a chill voice that speaks to the heart of each man's essential solitude:

> No, Everyman; and thou be ones there,
> Thou mayst never more come here,
> Trust me veryly.[130]

In the *Roman de la Rose*, half a century before the plague's arrival, Death speeds across the variously colourful stage of life like a rapacious shadow:

> Mort, qui de nair le vis a taint,
> queurt apres tant qu'el les ataint,
> si qu'il a trop fiere chace.[131]

> (Death, whose face is dyed black, runs after them so fast that, however cruel the chase, he captures them.)

But, for Jean de Meun, there are many truths about human life of more importance than this single figure; there are, moreover, perspectives that circumvent it, even in the temporal world; for the human race, like the phoenix, survives in the species, if not in the individual:

> Ceste maniere neïs ont
> tretoutes les choses qui sont

desouz le cercle de la lune
que, s'il an peut demourer l'une,
s'espece tant en li vivra
que ja Mort ne l'aconsivra.[132]

(All things that are beneath the circle of the moon, are born in such manner that, if only one remains, the species so lives on in it, that Death can never overtake the race.)

The cycle of Nature still includes, and thus offers its solace, to its human members. When one moves from de Meun to *The Assembly of Gods*, the rude figure of Atropos has destroyed that possibility. He reminds the Gods that he was appointed their officer: ' "All tho with my dart fynally to chastyse/That yow dysobeyed or wold your law dyspyse." '[133] Nature no longer fights a narrowly victorious battle with Death; because the two are discontinuous, Atropos can even call her as a witness in his defence:

'And that can Dame Nature well testyfy;
Yef she be examynyd she woll hit nat deny.
   For when she forsaketh any creature,
   I am ay redy to take hym to my cure.'[134]

Death is undoubtedly 'dreary' here, as in Gower's *Confessio Amantis*,[135] because its powers are too well defined, too absolute, displacing all other truths.

This is not, however, the impression given by the greatest medieval literature. In *Piers Plowman* the abstract figure, because an extreme remedy and hence a rare visitant, intervenes with a power that startles and horrifies:

So Kynde thorgh corupcions culde ful menye.
Deth cam dryvyng after, and al to douste paschte
Kynges and knyghtes, caysers and popes;
Lered ne lewide, he lefte no man stande;
That he hitte evene sterede nevere after.[136]

The alliance of Death with Kind is for the moment only; both are come to defend the faithful against Anti-Christ, 'for Peers love the Plouhman', for when men are wicked, they bring upon themselves visions of evil. Elsewhere in the poem, Kind is the careful creator who studies to distinguish the 'flekede fetheres' and 'fele colours' of 'wonderful foules'; whilst Death's origin is demonic, for the 'lord of lyf' tells Lucifer, 'doctour of deth', to swallow the draught which he himself prescribed.[137] Chaucer and the *Gawain*-poet both avoid the figure (though not the subject); they can afford to laugh at Death as the construct of man's

G

fears, because the one understands the human heart so fully, whilst the other fears God, not mortality. The fox of *The Nun's Priest's Tale*, 'who wold han maad areest' upon Chaunticleer, is shrewdly outwitted and rendered ridiculous; the Green Knight, supporting his weight on the blade of the levelling axe, himself laughs at the figure he has assumed in Gawain's mind: far from being the hollow 'last laugh' of the spectre, it is, simultaneously, a recognition both of the courage of the knight who attempts to fight off death, and of his folly in failing to recognize his own security.

There is laughter too, of a grimmer kind, in *Death and Liffe*, for the approach of 'One of the uglyest ghosts that on the earth gone', is coloured by the apprehensive imagination of the dreamer: 'The ground gogled for greeffe of that grim dance;/I went nere out of my witt for wayling care.'[138] Death, as Liffe later points out, is damned, and, like medieval devils, her figure is grotesquely comic:

> Shee was naked as my nayle, the navele above;
> & below she was lapped about in linnen breeches;
> A more fearffull face no freake might behold,
> For shee was long & leane, & lodlye to see;
>
> . . .
>
> Her eyes farden as the fyer that in the furnace burnes;
> They were hollow in her head, with full heavye browes;
> Her leres were leane, with lipps full side;
> With a marvelous mouth, full of main tushes;
> & the nebb of her nose to her navell hanged,
> & her lere like the lead that latelye was beaten.[139]

This poet is clearly capitalizing on those materialistic renderings of the metaphysical which characterize his age; as one realizes with the personification allegory of Langland's Deadly Sins, the extremely detailed realization of an abstract may, if carried far enough, lead the reader to reject, with horrified laughter, such exaggerated literalism. The huge burnished blade, running with blood, which Death brandishes in one hand, the implement like the leg of a vulture which she holds in the other, so clearly have gross designs upon the body that they leave the spirit free. To an imagination still in touch with the finer possibilities of the Middle Ages, its opposite extremes may become positive advantages.

Many genuine enthusiasts for the period have felt that, in its latter years, there is progressively less to be said for the prevalent preoccupation with Death and its appurtenances, that it calls for excuse, or, at the

---

gogled shook *farden* behaved *leres* cheeks *full side* wide-spreading *main* strong
tushes tusks *nebb* tip *lere* countenance

.

least, a polite turning of the leaf. It is certainly true that much minor literature concerned with the subject, in the century previous to the Reformation, makes dispiriting reading; but this is more because Death is too remotely, rather than too vividly, felt. The personification is often unsuccessful precisely because it appears at a moment when the culture is so sated with an awareness of its final end that the entry of Death itself is a virtual anti-climax. Such writing is often horrifying, but not in the direct sense: it is not Death which appalls so much as the lack of any real sense of purpose, much less nobility, in human life. The figure of Mankind, in the play of that name, carries a spade as a weapon:[140] a view which is reflected by the child in *Mundus et Infans*:

> Fourty wekes my moder me founde,
>   Flesshe and blode my fode was tho;
> Whan I was rype from her to founde,
>   In peryll of dethe we stode bothe two.
>
> Now to seke dethe I must begyn,
>   For to passe that strayte passage;
> For body and soule that shall than twynne
>   And make a partynge of that maryage.[141]

In this speech, life becomes an inverted birth, an attempt to return through 'that strayte passage' to the womb of the earth in which the living creature will be unmade; the world which surrounds this unhappy traveller, in his gravebound journey, offers only those temptations which threaten, with every step, to quench the feebly struggling light that promises him future beatitude. Nor do his fellow-travellers have any comfort to offer, for the hostility of the living to the dying is a recurrent theme at the end of the Middle Ages.

At an earlier period, the Fathers of the Church had distinguished two kinds of fear, *servilis* and *castus*; the latter fear, of losing God's love, is compatible with loving God; the former, of Hell, is not. For the later Middle Ages, to which Hell has become the grave, the fear that surrounds it is not only *servilis*, but, because every man must endure burial, it cannot even encourage constructive action, as the threat of damnation can.[142] Even if, as has been suggested, such literature is properly related to those manuals on the art of dying which abound in the later Middle Ages, such an emphasis does little to correct that sense of hopelessness. Hoccleve's contribution, 'How to Learn to Die', conforms, for example, to most of the attitudes and assumptions hitherto described;[143] whilst frequent invocations of the Virgin and certain saints, as intercessors who are expected to be more merciful than God is likely to prove, do little to alter the sense of man as a craven degenerate.[144] So subject a creature, helplessly dependent upon its creator for the reward its feeble endeavours can never earn, is a world away, not only from renaissance confidence, but from that earlier medieval vision of man implied in the rebuke of Hugh of St Victor: 'If you consider well the nature of man you will not wonder at the great things he can do, but rather at the little things to which he devotes himself.' 'Thou makest all unboolde' writes one fifteenth-century poet of Death; his words are an apt verdict on the enervated perception of mortality typical of his time.

If, however, one distinguishes between that dulling of response and the vivid apprehension of mortality, the fifteenth century can, as has been shown, provide many exceptions; it is indeed possible that this distinction is infrequently made, because the whole subject of death is offensive to modern taste. In any event, it seems significant that, after the end of the Middle Ages, the Dance declined into unthinking morbidity (a failing only of the medieval second-rate), whilst the Legend decayed into a sentimentality of which the Middle Ages were never guilty. After the Council of Trent in 1570, the remaining Catholic countries of Europe not only preserve the emphasis on Death, but, stimulated by the reforming zeal of the Jesuits, actually extend it.[145] More representations of the Dance have survived from the Europe of the sixteenth and seventeenth centuries, than from the Middle Ages, and in these examples Death gradually loses its earlier, individualized character; thus in France, after 1570, it is readily displaced by comparatively inert Italianate representations of Death, based upon the skulls and bones of Jesuit meditation, which are simply *memento mori*, as the Dance never was.[146]

The Legend, too, eventually finds its way into a tradition not unlike that of Baroque art, where the skull serves merely to intensify the splendour of Arcadia. Panofsky describes Dr Johnson's reaction, in the eighteenth century, to Reynolds's latest painting of two beautiful ladies, contemplating the inscription on a tombstone, *Et in Arcadia Ego*:

'What can this mean?' exclaimed Dr Johnson. 'It seems very nonsensical—I am in Arcadia.' 'The King could have told you,' replied Sir Joshua. 'He saw it yesterday and said at once: "Oh, there is a tombstone in the background: Ay, ay, death is even in Arcadia." '[147]

Johnson's assumption, that the corpse declares itself to be in Arcadia, is as inapposite as the meaning we now attach to that inscription—that the dead, in a vein resembling *ubi sunt*, remind us that they too once enjoyed happiness. The more stringent reading of George III is correct, for it derives ultimately from the Legend's rigorous warning.[148]

Post-medieval art thus indicates that, whilst the medieval obsession with death survived into the Renaissance and beyond, many of its insights were sacrificed by a decrease in intensity. It may be right to disparage the servile element betrayed by the more routine medieval treatments of mortality; but it is surely wrong, or self-delusive, to ignore the power of the profoundly sentient works of less commonplace imaginations. Because they were willing (as we are not), to face the fact of death, their response to it was much more complex, varied and profound; because they did not attempt to coat with sugar the bitterness of the pill all had to swallow, they could detect in it more flavours than an ersatz sweetness. They gave unsparing expression to the common nightmare of sentient burial—and it is sometimes more helpful to know that a nightmare is shared, than to be told that it does not exist. They were haunted by images of physical corruption, but by animating and confronting these figures, they brought themselves face to face with their own fears, and learnt what they could from them. They studied painfully the different ways in which Death came to each man, and by acknowledging the horror of that moment to the many, they came to a genuine understanding of the hard-won serenity of the few. With the vehemence of those to whom life is really precious, they railed against the unnaturalness of mortality; then, arrested by the spectacle of autumnal calm or winter stillness, they wondered whether it was not, after all, part of Nature's merciful order. Even the fear that God had abandoned mankind had its reward to offer, for it could lead, as in *Piers Plowman*, to the exigent reassessment, not only of the individual life, but of human society as a whole. Through all this, the most courageous could win to laughter, for it is only those who really endure who can truly laugh. Their affirmation of Resurrection, though occasional, was so because it had genuinely to be won. At its best, medieval belief is no panacea, no evasion of reality; it is the hard-won vision occasionally glimpsed by those who persist courageously in facing their own despair.

VI

Christ and the Triumph of Eternal Life

[Deus] volens ut nascendi, occidendique mutuae relationis circuitu per instabilitatem stabilitas, per finem infinitas, per temporabilitatem aeternitas rebus occiduis donaretur.[1]

([God] wishing that, by the cycle of birth's inter-relationship with death, there should, to perishable things, be given stability through instability, infinity through impermanence, eternity through transience.)

When comparing the products of the later Middle Ages with the great synthetic achievements of the thirteenth century, it is natural to feel that an age of despair, dominated by the insistent sense that 'in the midst of life, we are in death', has succeeded to an epoch of confident faith. The range of the original Gothic cathedrals, with their assured advance from temporality to timelessness; the comprehensive *Summae*, which express so clear a conviction that the structure of faith can answer all questions connected not only with man but with God; the *Divina Commedia*, with its monumental clarity, and ultimate trust in the justice of divine decision—these commanding works of the high Middle Ages have no equivalents in the later fourteenth and fifteenth centuries.[2] *The Canterbury Tales* or *Piers Plowman* possess no comparable certainty of structure; they are distinguished rather by the complexity and contrariety with which they image the divergent, and often bewildered, impulses of human life.

If, as the Middle Ages were traditionally disposed to do,[3] one marshals the forces of Life against those of Death, it seems, in this later period, that the first can have little chance of victory. Despite the promise of Youth, the persistence of Nature, the reassurance of the seasonal cycle, and (as a last resort) the resignation of *ubi sunt*, Life's army in review seems pitifully vulnerable. Venus and the Pride of Life are camp-followers only; their narrow conception of Life merely as temporal advantage makes them apt, at the crucial moment, to desert to the forces of destruction.[4] The company of Death, on the other hand, is grimly formidable: there is Elde, and his darkly final words in the debates of the Ages; the wheel of Fortune, which gives the lie to those more positive cycles of Nature and transience; and the many forms that Death itself assumes, in the grave, the animate corpse, the skeleton. All these, in the temporal struggle between Living and Dead, have, by definition, the final advantage.

One may wonder at the rift that seems to exist between the Triumph of Life in some of the finest productions of the later Middle Ages—in the radiant calm of the Ghent altarpiece, or the ultimate confidence of *Gawain* and *Pearl*—and its chaotic and morbid context in a civilization which comes to see Death as the sole, omnivorous reality.[5] Yet the two are not discontinuous, for such serenity may only be won from a world in chaos—may indeed be actively dependent upon it. Its particular quality is not so conspicuous in the achievements of the thirteenth century, for these, though the products of faith and vision, rest at the pinnacle of a massive structure of assurance largely rational in nature. Comparable certainty, when that structure is shaken and its confidence so much harder to come by, has a more mobile and various quality than the rational can offer. It can be expressed in a distinction between 'eternal' and 'perpetual', for the former excludes movement, where the latter implies it.[6] The thirteenth-century syntheses have an eternal quality which is literally monumental: even in the *Divina Commedia*, the occasional anguish of Dante the traveller, when confronted with the results of divine decision, is placed as a myopia consequent on temporal being.[7] It is, however, no accident that many of Dante's readers feel most at home in the 'perpetual' world of the *Purgatorio*, for there time still exists and change remains meaningful. Where the eternal joys of the *Paradiso* seem difficult, not only of attainment, but in their challenge to sublunar understanding, the serenity of the *Purgatorio* is won from a context familiar in its mingling of pain with hope, of present sorrow with the prospect of future joy. Not only do the attitudes of its sinners, *contenti nel fuoco* (contented in the fire), reflect the consolations of the temporal—in their courtesy and affection, or their delight in poetry and song—but their context preserves a cyclical variation to which the imagination is insistently recalled, in the promise of dawn, the repose of dusk, the freedom of the stars by night, the confident circuit of the sun by day. The universal darkness of the *Inferno*, and the blazing light of the Empyrean, afford no comparable variety.

The 'dapple' of life, for the medieval poet as for Hopkins, constitutes one of its chief beauties. As the shadow of Death intensifies, the approach of 'time's vast, womb-of-all, home-of-all, hearse-of-all night', encouraged many secular writers to preserve, in the magical and mysterious worlds of their imagining, the 'skeined stained veined variety' of life, from the decisive judgement of 'two spools . . . two flocks, two folds'. These imaginings often find expression in the romances, where they are sustained by the persistence of a heroic attitude to Death; they are particularly frequent in those of the Grail, where, in alliance with Christianity, they form a temporal mysticism of death and resurrection. Such largely secular impulses thus foster the affirmations of religious faith: the heroic tradition informs the conception of Christ as a valiant knight who, in the Crucifixion and Harrowing of Hell, jousts with Death and secures the victory; whilst the magical and mysterious worlds of imagination provide the material from which are built the earthly paradise and heavenly Jerusalem.[8] None the less, only the greatest religious poetry really inhabits a perpetual world which can offer a cogent and convincing perspective to those who live in time. The Harrowing of Hell in Langland, the vision of the dreamer in *Pearl*, mark, in very different forms, that lonely achievement; and it is significant that both should retain the quality of movement, the variety of light with shadow, that delight the reader of the *Purgatorio*. The reversals brought about by Christ's Descent, in which Youth succeeds to Age, and Life to Death, are achieved through a titanic struggle; and that combat, though ultimate, has continually to be fought again, just as, in the Mass, the Crucifixion perpetually recurs. The process of *Pearl* is different, for eternal life is there continuous with the temporal, not its reverse; Youth achieves in Youth its perfect form, and the brevity of earthly existence is compensated in a land where *primavera è sempre*. It is, however, equally a poem of struggle; and its impulse—that all things are in movement towards their perfect form—is as dynamic as any in *Piers Plowman*.

It is only in that eternal perspective, where sequence becomes meaningless, that Life can triumph over Death as surely as, in the world of time, the dead must succeed to the living. Beyond the grave, Life finds her champion in Christ, the wounded knight, in the bleeding lamb with 'glentes gloryous' of *Pearl*.[9] Where, in Langland's temporal vision of Anti-Christ, Lyf leaps to his 'lemman' Fortune, in the timeless context of Christ's Descent she leaps instead to her 'Lord' who gathers her up.[10] It is surely explicable that, in the uncertain climate of the time, affirmations as powerful as these should be occasional only. In literature it is more natural for the imagination to look to the vulnerable productions of time, than to an eternal world of remote conjecture, and the emphasis of the age inevitably fell upon vulnerability, rather than creativity. It is perhaps less surprising that so many writers should have succumbed to despair, than that so large a minority should have persisted in the search for hope. *Piers Plowman* and *Pearl*, though exceptional poems, have many antecedents and some successors; in more humble ways, many writers sought to preserve the various wonders of life from the grotesque armed with bloody blade and vulture talons.

---

glentes looks

The persistence, until the very end of the Middle Ages, of a heroic attitude to Death, is one instance of the imagination's resistance to that universal darkness. This attitude has, of course, an ancient origin, for 'the antique belief in immortality is "heroification" ';[11] in English art before the Black Death, its enduring image is found in those dramatic effigies of struggling knights, which have sometimes been described as 'dying Gauls'.[12] The finest and earliest example of these, the crusader's tomb at Dorchester in Oxfordshire, is at once an agonizing and a triumphant sight, for the struggle to draw the sword, to stand upright, is perpetuated in the stillness of stone (Plate 30). Such tombs belong largely to a more confident period than that marked by the decline of the Middle Ages; but even when the *en transi* appears, the heroic tradition is continued in the knights of the Dance. Where other men submit to the 'fell sergeant', avert their eyes, or attempt to flee, the warriors fight on; the hopelessness of their resistance to Death, 'Victour . . . at all mellie', only intensifies their heroism. In Holbein's Dance, Death's triumph is cowardly, for the skeleton thrusts the knight's own lance into his back; whilst the warrior, even in his last agony, attempts to turn and retaliate with his sword upon his treacherous assailant (Plate 28c).

In romance, too, the heroic attitude persists, although again it is more conspicuous before the mid-fourteenth century. The carelessness of death, characteristic of the romance hero, has already been described in the context of Youth; in *Sir Orfeo*, where the land of the dead is actually entered, it is given an enduring form. Orfeo's opposition to the loss of Herodis seems, at first, as futile as that of the knights in the Dance; when he surrounds the Queen with his company of armed warriors, he quickly learns that arms have no effect against the faint company of the underworld, with their 'dim cri' at the hunt, their 'Queynt pas & softly' at the dance, and their mysterious vanishing, 'No never he nist whider thai bi-come'.[13] But the death of Herodis, because untimely, is a cruel enchantment, not an irreversible event; that long sleep underground—'& thought dede, & nare nought'—is a spell which may be broken by love and by art, if not by arms. The legend is, of course, classical, but it is fertilized, in this instance, by Breton *lai* and Celtic myth.[14] The land of the dead which Orfeo enters is neither the Christian Hell nor its Heaven, but a mingling of the Celtic afterworld with the classical underworld. It has a Celtic radiance, 'As bright so sonne on somers day', and the castle set in its midst has all that brilliance of precious stone and metal which one finds in the heavenly Jerusalem: Orfeo, indeed, first takes it to be 'The proude court of Paradis'.[15] But its dazzling light is unnatural, for it is the stones in the castle which create this permanent noonday,[16] whose brilliance contrasts unfavourably with the fertile colours of the natural world from which Herodis has been taken, where 'everi feld is ful of flours,/& blosme breme on everi bough'.[17] The strangeness of this world, which both attracts and repels, differs from the castle's interior, which is both closer to the classical underworld and to the condition of burial:

> Sum stode with-outen hade,
> & sum non armes nade,
> & sum thurth the bodi hadde wounde,
> & sum lay wode, y-bounde,
> & sum armed on hors sete,
> & sum astrangled as thai ete;
> & sum were in water adreynt,
> & sum with fire al for-schreynt.[18]

From this grim company of those prematurely dead, Orfeo rescues Herodis, for the tale, in this medieval version, restores them both to the temporal world to live out their appointed span. Death comes in due course, but without lament or resistance;[19] the company of the 'fairy' is an image of the chill that shadows happiness, the apprehension of the unnatural division of those who love, and, as such, opens upon mysterious worlds, from which, for the heroic, escape is possible.

The late fifteenth century, in Henryson's *Orpheus and Eurydice*, has its own version of the tale, and the difference between its emphases and those of the early romance of *Sir Orfeo* is characteristic of the time. The mysterious brilliance of that otherworld is gone; the miseries of the grave and the torments of Hell are synonymous, and no escape is possible from 'hiddouss hellis houss', to which Orpheus is led by 'a stynk rycht odiuss'.[20] The tale, as one could predict, closes in classical manner, with Orpheus left lamenting ' "Bot for a Luke my Lady is forloir" ', but the lengthy moral drawn from the story has all the dark wisdom of its time.[21] In a world where death is ubiquitous, Orpheus has no justification for casting his 'myndis E,/Blindit with lust' upon his beloved queen; this moral allegory of the vanity of human affections refuses to accommodate either heroism or love.

Few traces of the heroic tradition remain at the close of the Middle Ages, but these few are still to be discovered in romance. The macabre may carry its infection even into this robustly hopeful genre,[22] as it does into *The Squire of Low Degree*, where the lady, mistaking the body of another man for that of her lover, disembowels the corpse, embalms the remainder, and, enclosing it in a carefully locked receptacle, sets it at the head of her bed where she can kiss it daily.[23] The Squire, however,

---

breme bright   *wode* mad   *adreynt* drowned   *for-schreynt* shrivelled   *Luke* Look
forloir lost

is no true aristocrat, but an aspiring bourgeois; Shakespeare and Scott were mistaken in taking this tale as a typical medieval romance, though their choice is perhaps expressive of the attitudes of their respective periods. More usually, as in the Dance, the warriors of romance are resolute in resisting Death. In *Eger and Grime*, for example, the hero, inspired by love, fights with and defeats Sir Gray Steel, whose land of the dead is a more natural variation on the unnatural brilliance of Orfeo's underworld.[24] In Malory, the macabre is reserved for the pagan, as in the case of the 'felownse knyght', Sir Corsabryne:

Than [sir Palomydes] smote of his hede. And therewithall cam a stynke of his body, whan the soule departed, that there myght nobody abyde the savoure. So was the corpus had away and buryed in a wood, bycause he was a paynym.[25]

Yet even this pagan refuses to yield, and the wicked Christian is similarly capable of a final heroism. In the last tragic battle, Mordred not only 'ded hys devoure that day and put hymselffe in grete perell', but, in precisely the manner of Holbein's knight, inflicted a fatal wound upon his father, by thrusting himself through on Arthur's spear, when he 'felte that he had hys dethys wounde'.[26]

It is no wonder that those strange otherworlds, which have little to do with a Christian destination, should so often be found in literature which retains its admiration for the heroic. It is difficult to damn even a Mordred, when his treachery is transformed by such evident bravery; and the notion of a different destination for those who, in some way or other, stand outside the Christian ethic, recurs until the end of the Middle Ages. *Guy of Warwick* includes an elvish castle, in which none grow old, and whose ruler is virtually impervious to wounds.[27] Thomas of Erceldoune, in the romance of his name, is summoned by a mysterious lady to leave the earth and pass under Eildon Hill; they travel three (symbolic) days in darkness, and the lady shows him three roads, to Heaven, Purgatory and Hell, together with a fourth destination:

> 'Seese thou yitt yone faire castelle,
> That standis over yone heghe hill?
> Of towne & towre, it beris the belle;
> In erthe es none lyke it un-till.
> ffor sothe, Thomas, yone es myne awenne,
> And the kynges of this Countree.'[28]

Nor is this fairy's territory exceptional: *Partonope of Blois* sports such enchanted lands and castles, which form an escapist image of human needs;[29] whilst even a work so orthodox as *The Golden Legend* occasionally reveals the same impulse to preserve some at least from the stark alternatives of beatitude and damnation. St Brandon, in his travels, comes upon a 'fair island full of flowers, herbs, and trees', one of which is so thronging with birds 'that unnethe any leaf of the tree might be seen'.

And then anon one of the birds fled from the tree to S. Brandon, and he with flickering of his wings made a full merry noise like a fiddle, that him seemed he heard never so joyful a melody. And then S. Brandon commanded the bird to tell him the cause why they sat so thick on the tree and sang so merrily; and then the bird said: Sometime we were angels in heaven, but when our master Lucifer fell down into hell for his high pride, we fell with him for our offences, some higher and some lower after the quality of the trespass, and because our trespass is but little, therefore our Lord hath set us here out of all pain, in full great mirth and joy after his pleasing, here to serve him on this tree in the best manner we can.[30]

As in so many instances of this kind, the voyages of St Brandon, and his discovery of this island of half-fallen angels, have their origin in the Celtic *immram*.[31] The Celtic otherworld, unlike the Norse Hel, is a place of promise, for possibly no other race has taken such pleasure in imagining it. Death is conceived as the departure for a better destination, and the going, though hazardous and strange, is free from the terrors of burial. Birds may appear to the living, bearing branches from that further land as an earnest of its existence. The fact that the Dead of the Legend bear such sprays of foliage in their teeth, in the painting that still survives on the walls of the chapel at Haddon Hall, may have no real connection with this Celtic tradition; but skeleton and spray accord so strangely that they exemplify mysteriously those divergent impulses, towards the hope of renewed life, and the terror of interment. The promise of the Celtic otherworld is, however, less easily assimilable to the orthodox Christian Heaven, where the Norse Hel, with its fear of the grave, forms a broad path to Christian notions of damnation. The story of St Brandon is unusually accommodating, and the exclusion of the Celtic otherworld from orthodox eschatology is vividly illustrated in a late fourteenth-century work, *Guecino detto il Meschino*. In one such magic otherworld, the hero is offered earthly riches and paradisal pleasures; but he sensibly elects for the greater security of the Christian afterlife, and asks absolution of the Pope.[32]

The impulse which fostered such unorthodox destinations is vividly expressed in the twelfth-century French romance, *Aucassin et Nicolette*. When Aucassin is threatened by the Count of Biaucaire with the torments of Hell if he becomes Nicolette's lover, his spirited retort is expressive of all that youthful gaiety which makes this romance so attractive:

En paradis qu'ai je a faire? Je n'i quier entrer, mais que j'aie Nicolete ma tresdouce amie que j'aim tant; c'en paradis ne vont fors tex gens con je vous dirai. Il i vont ci viel prestre et cil viel clop et cil manke qui tote jor et tote

nuit cropent devant ces autex et en ces viés creutes, et cil a ces viés capes
ereses et a ces viés tatereles vestues, qui sont nu et decauc et estrumelé, qui
moeurent de faim et de soi et de froit et de mesaises; icil vont en paradis:
aveuc ciax n'ai jou que faire. Mais en infer voil jou aler, car en infer vont li
bel clerc, et li bel cevalier qui sont mort as tornois et as rices gueres, et li
buen sergant et li franc home: aveuc ciax voil jou aler; et s'i vont les
beles dames cortoises que eles ont deus amis ou trois avoc leur barons, et
s'i va li ors et li argens et li vairs et li gris, et si i vont herpeor et jogleor et
li roi del siecle: avoc ciax voil jou aler, mais que j'aie Nicolete ma tresdouce
amie aveuc mi.[33]

(What should I do in Paradise? I don't seek to enter there, but to have Nicolette, my most sweet friend whom I love so much. For to Paradise go only
such people as I shall describe. There go old priests, old cripples and those
maimed, who all day and all night crouch in front of altars and in old crypts,
and those who have ragged old coats and tattered old rags, who are naked,
without boots or shoes, who die of hunger and thirst, cold and misery. These
go into Paradise, and I've nothing to do with them. But I want to go to Hell,
for to Hell go the fair clerks, and the handsome knights who have died in
jousts and fine wars, and the good men-at-arms and the nobles. I would like
to go with those. And there go gracious and beautiful ladies, who have two
or three lovers along with their husbands. And there go the gold and the silver
and the furs, pied or grey; and there go the harpers and the tumblers and the
kings of the world. With these I want to go, so long as I have with me Nicolette,
my most sweet friend.)

There is nothing exceptional about Aucassin's division of the saved from
the damned; many religious writers would make identical discriminations. What is unusual is his outrageously sensible conviction that the
quality of the afterlife will be determined by the tone of the company.
Just as in life he enjoys the companionship of those who (as Langland
would say) have their heaven on earth, whilst avoiding those others to
whom earthly existence is misery and burden, so in the afterlife he is
willing to leave the latter to their belated reward, provided he can continue his carefree association with the former. This strain of irrepressible humanity rarely finds such buoyant expression in the context of
'the four last things'; but a persistent wish to preserve those qualities,
both in men and in objects, which make the temporal so pleasurable,
does much to explain the recurrence in romance of strange and enchanted
lands.

Such territories do not invariably originate in Celtic legend; as in the
case of *Sir Orfeo*, analogues may be numerous, and direct antecedents
few. Classical imaginings of Elysium make their contribution, whilst
travellers' tales from the east do much to sustain the proximity of the
magical and marvellous. The notion that the west was a region of death
and the east of life may be owed to the interpretation of *occidere* as 'kill'

rather than 'set'; but the connotations of sunset and sunrise lend this idea their support. In *Genesis*, moreover, 'The Lord God planted a garden eastward in Eden', and it is in extension of these geographical polarities that Eve is described as travelling westward in search of death, where she bears Cain; she then follows Adam eastward and gives birth to Abel, the prototype of Christ.[34] It is not surprising that men should have looked to the literal east for lands which resembled Eden, and that the wonders reported by such actual travellers as Marco Polo should have confirmed their expectations (Plate 34). The stories of Alexander, the Epic of Gilgamesh, and Mandeville's travels all include journeys through darkness to gardens brilliant with the permanence of precious stones.[35] When Mandeville comments on the Tartar belief that the next world is made in the image of the present, he is echoing the aspirations of an Aucassin; he fosters, moreover, the hope that this earth itself may provide a land free from death, or beyond it, one which his own accounts go far towards rendering specific.[36]

Whatever the origin of these various myths of unorthodox afterlife or terrestrial resurrection, their acceptance or rejection by the Christian consciousness seems to obey no general rule. Aucassin's afterworld is a youthful joke at the expense of the Count of Biaucaire, yet lands which relate to it are treated with gravity in Arthurian romance. Geoffrey of Monmouth's dead Arthur is taken to an island which, despite touches of classical learning, seems chiefly to derive from the Celtic Elysium;[37] whilst it is in the story of the Grail, the most elevated and Christian of all the various quests, that such mysterious territories appear most frequently.[38] Unlike Arthur's island, however, these seem to be regions of trial rather than solace; there is nothing bright or benign about the *terre gaste* through which men seek the Grail, any more than the Joy of Court, in Chrétien's more secular tale of Erec, proves a pleasant experience. Yet, whether the Christian imagination embraces these territories or holds them at a distance, their notions of death and immortality remain curiously distinct from orthodoxy. Lovelich's *History of the Holy Grail* exemplifies this tendency in a religious context, for he not only recurs to the incorrupt or resurrected corpse, but devotes much attention to the mysterious Tree of Life (Plates 33a and b). This grows from a branch of the Tree of the Knowledge of Good and Evil, which Eve takes with her from Paradise and plants in the ordinary world. There it grows white at first, foreshadowing that second Eve, the Virgin, but when Adam and Eve have intercourse, it becomes green and bears flowers and fruit. On Abel's murder, it turns red, grows large, but becomes infertile; when Solomon's wife cuts it, it bleeds. In furnishing the wood for the cross, the tree achieves its final apotheosis. Significantly, Eve calls it the Tree of Death, but by God's command it is named the Tree of Life. The *History* thus contains an imaginative mysticism of death and resurrection, which dissociates it from the literalism of macabre didacticism, permitting instead an intuitive spaciousness of the imagination which allows certain unorthodox freedoms.[39]

Heroic tradition, and the mysterious worlds of non-Christian experience and imagining, thus combine to offer their antidotes to despair, by preserving in a dimension, earthly yet everlasting, the variety of life which ultimate Christian judgement can seem to exclude. It is, however, no accident that they make their contribution to the great, if relatively rare, affirmations of Christian poetry. This is true not only of such a poem as *Pearl*, which preserves the continuity of this life with the next; but, even more strikingly, of those writings based upon the Harrowing of Hell, which embrace the division between the things of time and those of eternity. If the otherworlds of eastern travel and Celtic legend help to form the garden in which the Pearl maiden walks as she speaks with her living father, and that more remote heavenly city where she rejoices as the Bride of the Lamb, the heroic tradition not only lends its knightly image of human valour to the victorious Christ who jousts with Death; it preserves, in the Harrowing of Hell, the conviction that joy and sorrow, light and darkness, must alternate and intermingle:

'After sharpest shoures,' quath Pees, 'most sheene is the sonne;
Ys no weder warmer than after watery cloudes,
Nother love levere, ne levere freondes,
Than after werre and wrake, whanne love and pees beon maistres.'[40]

In the Harrowing of Hell, and in those religious perceptions which relate to it, the darkest aspects of medieval sensibility are contained by the most positive (Plate 36). The didactic admonition that Life is Death, so familiar from the obsession with mortality, is here balanced by the corresponding affirmation that Death is Life. The two can indeed be found to complement each other in the earliest medieval poetry. The author of the twelfth-century 'Poema Morale' prepares for this affirmation when he remarks, 'Ech Mon scal him solf demen to dethe other to live';[41] in giving Life and Death their eternal, not their temporal, connotations, he anticipates that ultimate reversal of terrestrial experience, where:

Ther is blisse a buten treye & lif a buten deathe
the eure scullen wunien ther blithe muwen ben ethe

---

sheene beautiful   *levere* dearer   *scal him solf demen* shall judge himself   *a buten* without *treye* torment   *the eure scullen wunien ther* they that live there forever   *ethe* eternally

> Ther is yeoyethe bute ulde & hele a buten un helthe
> nis ther sorewe ne sor, ne nevre nan un sealthe.[42]

Some two centuries later, Dan Michel explores the same paradoxical proposition, when he complains in the *Ayenbite of Inwyt* that the wise of this world are blind, because what they describe as life is really death; whilst what they regard as death and see as the end is, for the good (the wise of the next world), the end of evil and the beginning of every blessing.[43] Rolle, writing at much the same period, recalls this insight to its context in the Incarnation, when he calls upon death as the release into eternal life, declaring that Christ alone is true life, and death, therefore, man's gain.[44] In dying, Christ redeems the Fall, thus releasing mankind from that eternal death consequent upon it; in carrying his cross along the road to Calvary, he 'bereth hys owne deth, and bereth thy lyfe'.[45] To celebrate his Resurrection, is to rejoice in the promised resurrection of all mankind:

> On leome is in this world ilist,
> ther-of is muchel pris;
> a-risen is god & that is rist
> from dethe to lif.
> Al for ure redempciun
> He tholede pine & passiun,
> Derne wnden & greve;
> He broutte to salvaciun
> the world that was ibrot adun
> thuru adam & eve.[46]

It is, however, in the Harrowing, rather than the Resurrection, that Christ most resonantly assumes his role as Lord of Life, and Satan his as Prince of Death. That uneasy alliance between Death and God's order is at an end; the macabre is ranged firmly alongside the forces of evil, whilst Life, in the triumph of Christ over Satan, is at last victorious over her dark antithesis. The later Middle Ages were disposed to dwell upon the lamentations of Mary over the suffering flesh of her son; yet one such poem of Lydgate's, whilst stressing this ultimate pathos in its detail, its refrain and its conclusion, still recovers the cadence of courage and hope in the single verse concerned with the Harrowing:

> Thus deth with deth was outraied and brouht lowe,
> Mankyndys quarel maad vyctoryous,
> For than leviathan was bounde and over-throwe,

---

yeoyethe youth   *ulde* age   *hele* health   *un helthe* disease   *un sealthe* misery   *leome* light
ilist kindled   *tholede* suffered   *pine* torment   *derne wnden* hidden wounds

Whan with his tryumphes most synguler glorious,
My sone had faught with his blood precyous
Conqueryd the dragoun for al his ffel pouste,
And dryve hym hom to his Infernall hous,
Whan first my sone was naylled to a tre.[47]

The Harrowing of Hell becomes the ultimate battlefield for those dualities which conflict in medieval imagination; it is the sole arena where the
forces of Life achieve their proper victory. Whilst the notion of struggle
is formative, and basic to the period,[48] Christ's descent is the major,
and almost the solitary, event which can resolve its conflicts.

Legendary descents into Hell are, of course, classical before they are
Christian; and the myths of Orpheus and Proserpina, even Aeneas,
may in their turn be rooted in far earlier rituals of death and rebirth.
Dante, whose journey is a redemption from spiritual death, links St
Paul with Aeneas as analogous travellers.[49] Certainly the Church very
early accepted Christ's Descent as fact, though there was some controversy over its purpose; from the fifth century the story, crystallized
in the *Gospel of Nicodemus*,[50] spread rapidly, and, by describing the
empty tombs of the patriarchs, left no doubt of the connection between
Christ's death and a general resurrection, a literal fulfilment of the
Gospel promise: 'he that believeth in me, though he were dead, yet shall
he live: and whosoever liveth and believeth in me shall never die.'[51]
This work was disseminated both directly, by translation, and indirectly,
by accounts based upon it, as in *The Golden Legend*, where the sons of
Simeon are 'adjured and sworn . . . that they should tell and say what
Jesus did in Hell.'[52] By the fifteenth century the event is so thoroughly
domesticated to the Christian story, that the Devil can plead with
Christ for permission to return to heaven and be merry once more,
since he has, after all, already served a four-thousand-year sentence of
banishment.[53]

The theme, predictably, comes into its own most fully in the drama,
where it crowns the Passion sequence in the four complete cycles, and
is adumbrated well before, particularly in plays concerned with Lazarus.
Since, in the grand design, the latter incident can carry its taint of the
macabre,[54] because it contrasts the fate of man with that of God, its
implications are more fully explored in contexts less inclusive. In the
play of *Mary Magdalene*, the liberation of the soul in this life is given,
in Mary, a prominence which the subsequent physical resurrection of
her brother merely underwrites. Her gratitude for conversion interprets
the significance of the later miracle (where the writer allows the Gospel
words to speak simply for themselves):

---

pouste power

Cryst, that is the lyth and the cler daye,
He hath on-curyd the therknesse of the clowdy nyth.
Of lyth the lucens and lyth veray,
Wos prechyng to us is a gracyows lyth,
Lord, we be-seche the, as thou art most of myth,
Owt of the ded slep of therknesse de-fend us aye![55]

Christ's own encounter with death, in contrast with the raising of Lazarus, is reported indirectly by a resentful devil, whose enthusiastic poetry seems to make him of God's party without knowing it:

ower barres of Iron ar all to-brost! stronge gates of brasse!
the kyng of Ioy enteryd In ther-at, as bryth as fyrys blase!
for fray of his ferfull baner, ower felashep fled asondyr;
whan he towcheyd it, with his toukkyng they brast as ony glase,
and rofe asonder, as it byn with thondor.
now ar we thrall, that frest wher fre,
Be the passon of his manhede.
On a crosce on hye hangyd was he,
whych hath dystroyd ower labor and alle ower dede.[56]

Man's salvation and God's triumph are enabled, through a difference in mode, to sustain a significance at once equal and separate; the fate of Lazarus is not, as in the cycles, a poor contrast with the death of Christ. In the same manuscript, *Christ's Burial and Resurrection* 'reports' the Harrowing to similar effect: rather than dramatizing an event, it develops a series of eschatological images, which contrast life and death, burial and resurrection. In the Burial, played on Good Friday, the finality of Death is powerfully rendered:

The sonne hinge, & the moder stood,
And ever sho kissid the droppes of blood
That so fast ran down.[57]

The lament of Mary, with its poignant contrast of living, beloved child and torn, disfigured corpse, makes the confident affirmation of Joseph—'the thride day aryse he shall'—an incomprehensible act of faith. But the Resurrection, played on Easter morning, is a jubilant reversal of that intensely human despair: 'Her was sorow & mournyng, lamentacion & wepinge;/Now is Ioy & gladnesse, & of comfurth plentee.'[58]

In the cycles, where the confrontation of Christ with Death is directly dramatized, there is some loss of symbolic implication; the enacted scene is inevitably humanized, but its life and energy can compensate for the

---

lyth light   *lucens* brightness   *to-brost* shattered   *rofe* split   *frest* before

decline in metaphoric strength. The Devil, if no power of darkness, is shown as amusingly venal; he rallies his faltering followers with a Pride of Life swagger:

> ffy, fature! wherfor were ye flayd?
>   have ye no force to flyt him fro?
> loke in haste my gere be grayd,
>   my self shall to that gadlyng go.[59]

This failing, he resorts to argument with Christ, quoting Job's assertion 'That nawder freynde nor fo/shall fynde relese in hell'. In the last resort, he is reduced to pleading:

> Whi, and will thou take theym all me fro?
>   then thynk me thou art unkynde;
> Nay, I pray the do not so;
>   Umthynke the better in thy mynde;
> Or els let me with the go,
>   I pray the leyffe me not behynde![60]

Such Satanic venality is kept distinct from the voices of those souls redeemed from death, who draw upon all that poetry of pain and hope which adumbrates the coming of Christ in the Old Testament; for these, unlike Satan, Hell is no place of domestic discord, but real torment: 'suffre thou never thi sayntes to se/The sorow of thaym that won in wo.'[61] Nevertheless, the implications of Christ's descent are largely reserved for later scenes, where, for example, he explains to the doubtful Thomas: 'My saull and my cors have knytt a knott that last shall ay;/ Thus shall I rase, well thou wytt, ilk man on domesday.'[62] Death can no longer affirm that fatal 'knot y-knet' with Kind; through the dual nature of Christ, body and soul are promised ultimate reunion.

The finest realization of the Harrowing of Hell, that in *Piers Plowman*, retains the immediacy of the cycles without sacrificing that power of universalized image which one finds in the single plays. Moreover, because this scene is the culmination of Will's arduous search, it is not only a crucial incident in the pageant of Christian history; its meaning, whilst comprehensive, is also a quite personal revelation of the meaning of life. Although, in the drama, Christ's Descent clearly has meaning for all mankind, the Redeemer remains a figure quite distinct from those he redeems: in *Piers Plowman*, because the enigmatic figure of Piers is, at this point, identified with the human nature of Christ, the death and descent are assimilated to the experience of everyman. This visionary identification, of the human leader with the incarnate God, is beyond the

---

grayd prepared   *gadlyng* fellow   *Umthynke* Meditate   *won* dwell

scope of the drama's more literal rendering. The relation of Piers to Christ is far from simple, but it is carefully prepared; it is Piers who teaches the young Christ 'lechecraft, his life for to save', and the success of this teaching is evidenced in the raising of Lazarus.[63] When, on Palm Sunday, Christ rides into Jerusalem, he is 'semblable to the Samaritan, and some-del to Piers the Plowman'; through the mediating figure of that compassionate outcast, the angry ploughman of the half acre is related to the victorious God. The reply of Faith to the dreamer's question—'who sholde Iouste in Iherusalem'—makes that relation quite explicit:

> 'Iesus,' he seyde,
> 'And fecche that the fende claymeth, Piers fruit the Plowman.'
> 'Is Piers in this place?' quod I, and he preynte on me,
> 'This Iesus of his gentrice wole Iuste in Piers armes,
> In his helme and in his haberioun, *humana natura*.'[64]

The divine and human natures of Christ are at times distinct in the Gospels: the human nature weeps with Mary for the death of Lazarus, whilst the divine affirms to Martha, 'Thy brother shall rise again'; the former suffers the despair and desolation of the cross, 'my God, my God, why hast thou forsaken me', whilst the latter assures the good thief, 'Today thou shalt be with me in Paradise'. Piers, whilst relating to this human nature on the one hand, retains, on the other, a potent connection with everyman. In common with the human Christ, he receives no reassurance from divine omniscience, but must, like all men, seek through uncertainties, even to the suffering of death itself, for the meaning of life.

The chivalric language in which Langland's Christ is described[65] helps to emphasize his humanity, and its connection, through Piers, with that human courage which is the prize of fear. On Palm Sunday, Christ:

> Barfote on an asse bakke, boteless cam prykye,
> Wyth-oute spores other spere spakliche he loked,
> As is the kynde of a knyghte that cometh to be dubbed,
> To geten hem gylte spores, or galoches ycouped.   (B, XVIII, ll. 11–14)

The emblems of knighthood, 'helme' and 'haberioun', are conferred by *human* nature upon this untried bachelor, 'That on the Fryday folwynge, for mankynde sake/Iusted in Ierusalem, a Ioye to us alle'.[66] Like any

---

lechecraft medical skill   semblable like   preynte glanced   gentrice noble nature
haberioun coat of mail   prykye riding   spakliche lively   galoches shoes
ycouped cut down

such encounter, the battle is ultimately with Death, who 'seith he shall fordo and adown brynge/Al that lyveth or loketh in londe or in watere'.[67]

God's reversal of the natural order is already implied in this conflict, for victory, the slaughter of the foe, lies paradoxically through the knight's own death. The transmutation of Death into Life is insistently developed throughout the passus. As 'The lorde of lyf and of lighte . . . leyed his eyen togideres' the familiar animate corpses rise from their graves:

> 'For a bitter bataille' the ded bodye sayde;
> 'Lyf and Deth in this derknesse her one fordoth her other;
> Shal no wighte wite witterly who shal have the maystrye,
> Er Sondey aboute sonne-rysynge,' and sank with that til erthe.[68]

Once the outcome is known, these apparitions lose their power to terrify: Mercy draws a very different meaning from the eclipse of the sun: 'that man shal fro merkenesse be drawe,/The while this lighte and this leme shal Lucyfer ablende.'[69]

The negative paradox, that life is death, now receives its affirmative antithesis in many forms:

> 'That man shal man save thorw a maydenes helpe,
> And that was tynt thorw tre, tree shal it wynne,
> and that deth doun broughte, deth shal releve.'   (B, XVIII, ll. 139–41)

Truth dismisses Mercy's statement as 'a tale of Waltrot!'; it does not accord, as she observes and Lucifer later protests, with Old Testament statement. But Christ, curiously arguing from the ethic of the Old Law, an eye for an eye, justifies the claim of Peace:

> 'So lyf shal lyf lete, ther lyf hath lyf anyented,
> So that lyf quyte lyf, the olde lawe hit asketh.
> *Ergo*, soule shal soule quyte and synne to synne wende,
> And al that man mys-dude, ich, man, to amenden hit;
> And that that deth for-dude, my deth to releven,
> Both aquyte and aquykye, that was aqueynt thorw synne.'[70]

The legalism of this argument has a local appropriateness, in that Christ is responding to the quibbling of Lucifer. But that urgent sense that a paradox requires its antithesis is more than mere rhetoric; it indicates a necessity at once imaginative and spiritual.

This conviction—that the darkest aspects of temporal existence

---

witterly certainly   *leme* brightness   *ablende* blind   *tynt* lost   *lete* permit
anyented destroy   *for-dude* destroyed   *aquykye* quicken   *aqueynt* quenched

actually *engender* their antithesis—is developed and emphasized in the
C text's version of the speech of Peace. No medieval poet is more
sensitively aware than Langland of the misery of the many upon earth;
his certainty, in the context of the Harrowing, that ' "here wo in-to
wele wende mote atte laste" ', is the more commanding:

> 'For hadde thei wist of no wo, wele hadde thei nat knowe;
> For wot no wight what wele is that nevere wo suffrede,
> Ne what is hot hunger that hadde nevere defaute.
> Ho couthe kyndeliche with colour discrive,
> Yf alle the worlde were whit, other swan-whit alle thynges?
> Yf no nyght ne were, no man, as ich leyve,
> Sholde wite witerly what day were to mene.
> Ne hadde god suffred of som other than hymselve,
> He hadde nat wist wyterly whether deth wer soure other sweyte.
> For sholde nevere right riche man, that lyveth in reste and hele,
> Ywyte what wo is, ne were the deth of kynde.'   (XXI, ll. 211–21)

The suffering of the poor is thus a means to savour joy; death, for the
fortunate on earth, is the only path to such understanding; even God
himself may learn from experience of ' "the deth of kynde" '. As Christ
releases the patriarchs from a death that is no longer eternal, that knowledge turns from sour to sweet. Peace, meanwhile, appropriately pipes
'of poetes a note', recalling in temporal imagery the brilliance of sun
after rain, the intensity of love after discord.

The poem does not, however, end in affirmation; this opening upon
eternity is for the moment only, and Langland returns his readers to
the world of time thereafter. Because the Harrowing of Hell relates,
on the one hand, to the Crucifixion re-enacted daily in the mass, and,
on the other, to the pilgrimage through death that every man must take,
it is an event which, in time, must recur and be rediscovered, however
final Christ's victory in an eternal dimension. Hence, although Death
has, in that second context, been ultimately defeated, it returns in the
Vision of Anti-Christ, not only as an active figure, but as an ally of
Nature and of God. In the temporal sphere, the knot tied between
Nature and Death has not been loosened; although that other, knit by
Christ between soul and body, sets a period to the dominance of the
grave. Similarly, whilst Christ, as Lord of Life, gives the word the new
meaning of spiritual life through physical death, 'Lyf', personified in
the Vision of Anti-Christ, represents spiritual death in physical life:

> Lyf tho leep asyde and lauhte hym a lemman,
> 'Hele and ich,' quath he, 'and hihnesse of herte

---

discrive describe   *lauhte* took

Shall do the nat drede neither Deth ne Elde,
And to for-gete youthe and gyve nauht of synne.' (C, XXIII, ll. 152–5)

It is *Death and Liffe* which transposes Langland's affirmative perceptions into a world which mediates between eternal and temporal. Here Nature and Liffe are allies in defending the gay company of those whom so much medieval literature condemns:

Blyth bearnes of blee, bright as the sunn,
Sir Comfort that kerf when the court dineth,
Sir Hope & Sir Hind, thee hardye beene both,
Sir Liste & Sir Likinge, & Sir Love alsoe,
Sir Cunninge and Sir Curtesye, that coint were of deeds.[71]

Liffe herself could be mistaken, in *Piers Plowman*, for Meed or Peronelle Proude-herte, whilst in many other poems her appearance could fit both Venus and the Pride of Life:

& the price of her perrye can no person tell;
& the colour of her kirtle was carven ffull lowe,
That her blisfull breastes bearnes might beholde;
With a naked necke she neighed ther-till,
That gave light on the land as leames of the sunn. (ll. 88–92)

Yet, as she movingly describes her triumph with Christ in the Harrowing of Hell, Liffe is perfectly assured that she is the beloved of the Saviour:

'Then I leapt to my Lord, that laught me upp soone,
& all wounded as hee was, with weapon in hand,
He fastned ffoote upon earth, & ffolowed thee [Death] ffast,
Till he came to the cave that cursed was holden;
He abode before Barathron, that bearne while he liked,
That was ever merke as midnight, with mourninge & sorrowe;
He cast a light on the land as leames of the sunn.
Then cryed that King with a cleere steven,
"Pull open your ports, you princes with-in!
Here shall come in the King, crowned with ioy,
Which is the breemest burne in battell to smite." ' (ll. 401–11)

Death may fell her company, but, as she reassures them:

Shall do the nat drede Shall cause you not to fear (i.e. his mistress, Fortune)
blee visage *coint* skilled *perrye* jewellery *colour* collar *neighed* approached
leames rays *laught* took *steven* voice *ports* gates *breemest* most renowned

'Therefore bee not abashed, my barnes soe deere,
Of her ffauchyon soe ffeirce nor of her ffell words.
Shee hath noe might ne no meane no more you to greeve,
Nor on your comelye corsses to clapp once her hands.'   (ll. 430–3)

Liffe 'crosses the companye with her cleare ffingers'; the dead rise and follow her over the hills, 'Fairer by two-ffold then they before were'.

This dream is a vision, in time, yet free from it; its allegory of death and resurrection belongs both to this world and the next. It may in part be for this reason that the poet assumes, so unusually, that the riches, pleasures and beauties of this world will, under Liffe's leadership, find their way over the hills into the next. Where death opens upon further life, temporal existence is not seen as a form of mortality; the poem celebrates the affirmative paradox, and splendidly ignores its antithesis.

Death and Liffe mediates between those poems which reverse the laws of this life through the severance of death, and those for which the process of the temporal is continued into, and fulfilled in, the eternal. This second type of religious perception is less frequent than the first, though it too can be found in commonplace, as well as distinguished, writing. Though so different in approach, both views result from that characteristic medieval tendency to look in all things for their ultimate, rather than their immediate, meaning: thus, for example, the adder is never a 'yellow-brown slackness soft-bellied', but always a sign, though its meaning may vary between the contradictory extremes of Christ's body and the serpent of Eden.[72] In ordinary writing, significations so various may simply invite confusion, but in the greatest poetry they become a source of insight. Where the imagination senses severance between this life and the next, contradictions are polarized to either side: thus the robe of Meed, rich 'with ribanes of red gold', intimates temptation to sin in the temporal court, whilst the 'cleare clothes . . . of cleane gold', worn on eternity's threshold by Liffe and her company, are indications of future salvation.[73] In the imagination which sees this life as continuous with the next, the signs offered by the temporal world are incomplete, rather than contradictory; they are imperfect suggestions which eternity will render as perfect realities. Thus in *Pearl* the temporal child is described by that recurrent emblem of transience, 'a rose/That flowred and fayled as kynde hyt gef'; but beyond the river of death she flowers perpetually, whilst the process of decay remains, as her father comments, the mark of those living who inhabit time:

---

ffauchyon sword

'I am bot mokke and mul among,
And thou so ryche a reken rose,
And bydes here by thys blysful bonc
Ther lyves lyste may never lose.'[74]

The vision of continuity is necessarily positive, for the imperfection it perceives in the creations of time anticipates their perfection in eternity; for the poetry of severance, the transience of created things implies their uselessness, the decay inherent in their fallen nature, which only Christ's intervention can reverse.

If heroic impulse and terrestrial otherworlds provide the Harrowing of Hell with a context in secular aspiration, the more complex images and insights of alchemy offer their language to this other form of religious perception (Plate 35). Intrinsically, alchemy is a development of Aristotle's notion that all created things are in motion towards fulfilment in their perfect form; hence base metals, when gestated in the earth, finally develop into gold. The material alchemist exploits nature, by seeking to accelerate the process of maturation in metals for the purpose of monetary gain; but for the spiritual alchemist, gold signifies the life of the soul, and he expedites its perfection by seeking to perfect himself.[75] Thus, *The Canon Yeoman's Tale*, as Muscatine observes, 'expresses . . . a distinction between false alchemy and true, between men's alchemy and God's. The body of the poem . . . is an exposure of alchemy without God, of faith in earth.'[76] Because the alchemist assumed the image of the creator, his art was condemned by the Church; but its metaphor, as spiritual truth, was assimilated to Christian thought. In material alchemy, the philosopher's stone, 'sometimes known as the Elixir or Tincture, . . . was credited not only with the power of transmutation but with that of prolonging human life indefinitely'.[77] One medieval preacher, whilst firmly stating, 'ther be no suche stonnes', accepts it as an image of confession, which 'all turneth to gold', an interpretation with which the spiritual alchemist would sympathize.[78]

Many writers were, however, less sceptical, and less categorical in distinguishing material from spiritual meaning. *The Book of Quinte Essence*, translated towards the close of the fifteenth century, explains this elixir as 'quintessence', the incorruptible matter of which the stars are made, which is present, in some degree, in all created things. God's great secret, the writer claims, lies in his power to restore old men to their first youth; but men, too, can make the water of life, which will keep dead flesh from rotting. He describes how a distillation can be made from gold, human blood (or almost anything else), the essence of which—spirit, alcohol—should then be matured in dung or in a horse's

---

mokke filth   mul dust   among mingled   reken fresh   lyste joy   lose be lost

belly.[79] This process both sounds, and is, crudely material; yet it is an image of burial and resurrection, related to the Christian mystery. This is the 'lechecraft' that Christ learns from Piers, the 'witchcraft' of which he is accused through the raising of Lazarus.[80] To the believer, such power testifies to divinity, just as the incorruptibility of the saints evidences their undying virtue.

Divine alchemy, then, is a fulfilment, not a reversal, of the natural order. It is present not only in the lives of the saints but in some romances, particularly those which explore the mysterious otherworlds of this earth. The theme of the resurrected body recurs in Lovelich's *History of the Holy Grail*, both in its account of the miraculous tree, and of the ability of Joseph and Hypocras to raise the dead to life.[81] *Huon of Burdeux*, with its strange mixture of Christian and fairy, explores both the enchanted world, and the mysterious tree of life with its powers of rejuvenation[82] (Plates 33a and b). *St Erkenwald*, describing an incident in the saint's life, vividly traces the continuity between natural and supernatural. As a Christian missionary, reputedly Bishop of London from 675–93, Erkenwald tactfully conflates some aspects of paganism with the new religion: 'He hurlyd owt hor ydols & hade hym in sayntes,/ & chaungit chevely hor nomes, & chargit hom better.'[83] Whilst workmen are transforming St Paul's from heathen temple to Christian cathedral, they open a tomb in which they discover 'a blisfulle body':

> . . . wemles were his wedes, with-outen any tecche,
> Other of moulynge, other of motes, othir moght-freten,
> & als bryght of hor blee, in blysnande hewes,
> As thai hade yepely in that yorde bene yisturday shapen;
>
> & als freshe hym the face & the fleshe nakyde,
> Bi his eres & bi his hondes that openly shewid,
> With ronke rode as the rose, & two rede lippes,
> As he in sounde sodanly were slippide opon slepe.   (ll. 85–92)

The suggestion that this is the work of the *Gawain*-poet has been much debated, but, whatever the merits of the theory, it is intrinsically revealing to compare this description (which is not fully quoted) with that of the Green Knight on his first appearance. In both cases the eye is drawn from an acceptance of detail to a revelation of mystery, greenness in the one case, incorruptibility, a related wonder, in the other. St Erkenwald's tolerance of the old dispensation further recalls the *Gawain*-poet's ability to see the Green Knight's power of renewal as continuous with the Christian mystery.

---

chevely primarily   *wemles* spotless   *tecche* blemish   *moulynge* mould   *motes* spots
moght-freten moth-eaten   *yepely* recently   *yorde* yard   *ronke* abundant   *rode* red colour
sounde health

The body in the grave pre-dates Christ's birth by more than three centuries, and the workmen deduce, from the splendour of its burial, that it must once have been a king's. Under St Erkenwald's questioning, however, the corpse identifies itself as that of a just judge, highly honoured for his integrity. The intact body thus evidences the incorruptibility of the man; but, as a pagan, although physically untouched, his soul suffers the dissolution of damnation:

> '& ther sittes my soule that se may no fyrre,
> Dwynande in the derke dethe, that dyght us oure fader,
> Adam, our alder, that ete of that appulle
> That mony a plyghtles pepul has poysned for ever.' (ll. 293–6)

He pleads with Erkenwald for the grace of baptism, and when the tears of the saint's compassion have conferred that sacrament:

> . . . sodenly his swete chere swyndid & faylide,
> And alle the blee of his body wos blakke as the moldes,
> As roten as the rottok that rises in powdere.

> For as sone as the soule was sesyd in blisse,
> Corrupt was that other crafte that covert the bones;
> For the ay-lastande life, that lethe shalle never,
> Devoydes uche a vayne glorie, that vayles so litelle. (ll. 342–8)

'That other crafte', which is replaced by the spiritual alchemy of baptism, is in no sense an evil magic, which crumbles before divine power. The miracle which has preserved the body from disintegration is fulfilled in that larger mystery which secures the soul; the first only then becomes a 'vayne glorie', an imperfect image of the true glory of 'ay-lastande life'. In this poem, death is genuinely seen as liberation, for it cannot imprison the souls of the saved; the natural process of corruption is ratified, as a sign of man's renewal, and is a necessity to it, as the discarded chrysalis is to the butterfly.

This continuity, of the natural with the supernatural, is realized even more finely and fully in *Pearl*. Individual preference may well find in other English writing works more clearly major; yet, in the context of those figures of Life and Death with which this book is concerned, it is *Pearl* that crystallizes the finest possibilities of an imagination that is distinctively medieval. The intense awareness, peculiar to the time, of the complexities of moral life, which so often engenders a despair of salvation, is not only acknowledged in all its darker detail in this poem,

---

fyrre further *Dwynande* Pining *dyght* appointed *alder* ancestor *plyghtles* blameless *chere* expression *sywndid* vanished *blee* colour *moldes* earth *rottok* decayed thing *sesyd* established *lethe* cease *Devoydes* Expels *vayles* avails

but persists into redemptive vision. The confidence of *Pearl*'s achievement should not be allowed to conceal the difficulty of its task, for it is, in a literal sense, a confrontation between the Dead and the Living. The company of Death is indeed fully represented, but its members are so subtly transformed (as, moreover, are those of Life) that a first reading may scarcely register the shadow of mortality.[84] Yet a fidelity to the realities of common human experience is as basic to this poem as to *Sir Gawain*: whilst it explores many further areas of meaning, it does so through charting, with great accuracy and sensitivity, the peculiar and painful stages through which a man may learn to live with irrevocable loss. Unlike the Dance and Legend, it is ultimately the Dead who live, and the bereaved father who, in his sadness of heart, inhabits the 'doel-doungoun' of this world.

Pearl begins in the garden of earth, with its little grave to which the father returns so insistently, whose vivid summer flowers cannot prevent his imagination from picturing 'hir color so clad in clot'. An obsession with the charnel aspects of mortality is, however, firmly placed by Pearl herself, when she observes that death, the torment of those who live in time, is the hope of those possessed of perfect understanding:

> 'Althagh oure corses in clottes clynge,
> And ye remen for rauthe wythouten reste,
> We thurghoutly haven cnawyng;
> Of on dethe ful oure hope is drest.'[85]

No path but the grave can lead her father to that paradisal garden; when he longs to cross the river and join her, she warns him: ' "Er moste thou cever to other counsayle:/Thy corse in clot mot calder keve." '[86] The account she offers of Death's origin is familiar enough: the body was corrupted in Eden through Adam's sin, and 'drwry deth' became an unavoidable stage in the recovery of joy, forfeited by 'oure forme fader'. The stated continuity of damnation with death is equally conventional: ' "To dyye in doel out of delyt/And sythen wende to helle hete." '[87] It is Pearl's unusual confidence in man's redemption, her ability to see death as a means merely, which is exceptional. Nor is this assurance dryly doctrinal, for the longing of the dreamer to believe in his child's survival is captured in the urgent cadence of her own comment on those whose labour in the vineyard is as brief as her own:

> 'Anon the day, with derk endente,
> The niyght of deth dos to enclyne:

---

doel sorrow *clot* clay *clynge* waste away *remen* cry out *rauthe* grief
cnawyng understanding *drest* set *Er* First *cever* attain *calder* colder *keve* sink down
endente inlaid

That wroght never wrang er thenne thay wente,
The gentyle Lorde thenne payes hys hyne.
Thay dyden hys heste, thay wern thereine;
Why schulde he not her labour alow,
Yys, and pay hem at the fyrst fyne?
For the grace of God is gret innoghe.' (ll. 629–36)

The wish to believe and the certainty of belief meet in the natural image of nightfall; for evening in the vineyard marks the time at which rest follows labour, and 'the niyght of deth' will give way to dawn. The language of the natural world encounters that of the supernatural, bridging the river of death that lies between. Images of mortality are not avoided, but transformed: the scythe of the skeletal reaper is glimpsed as the instrument of harvest plenty, 'In Auguste in a hygh seysoun,/ Quen corne is corven with crokes kene'; Fortune appears, but as a strictly sublunar figure, obedient to the providential decree of that Lord ' "That lelly hyghte your lyf to rayse,/Thagh fortune dyd your flesch to dyye" '.[88]

In the temporal aspect of the poem, the forces of Life thus play their own part in combating Death's menace, though aided by those of supernatural life. The child herself is, in her father's memory, a figure of innocent Youth, whose unfulfilled promise makes resignation so difficult. But the child he knew, who 'lyfed not two yer in our thede', who could not yet recite her prayers,[89] is, beyond the river, a figure whose promise is realized; her 'dawn knowledge' is an articulate reality. The dreamer himself, in presuming prematurely to Paradise, exhibits that 'Maysterful mod and hyghe pryde' which characterizes the Pride of Life;[90] yet the aspiration of his human affections is ultimately sanctioned, as the longing of a father for his small lost daughter develops into the desire of a soul to return to the creator from which it came. The positions of the Ages are reversed in the dialogue across the river;[91] authority, the final word, becomes the privilege of eternal Youth, producing a discomfort, verging on humour, in her erstwhile father: ' "Thyself in heven over hygh thou heve,/To make the quen that watz so yonge." '[92] A sensitivity to the seasons enhances these perspectives; the poem is set in August, a month which recalls the springtime of the year, as the dreamer remembers the youth of his child, whilst standing himself, as does the month, midway between life and death, illuminated by the one, shadowed by the harvest judgement and winter chill of the other. The persistence of Nature and the assurance of the seasonal cycle offer their comfort, however, from the poem's beginning, as the father, gazing on his daughter's grave, argues from it:

---

hyne labourers   *at the fyrst fyne* at once   *lelly* faithfully   *hyghte* promised   *thede* land
Maysterful Arrogant   *mod* temper   *heve* exalt

That spot of spyses mot nedes sprede,
Ther such ryches to rot is runne;
Blomes blayke and blwe and rede
Ther schynes ful schyr agayn the sunne.
Flor and fryte may not be fede
Ther hit doun drof in moldes dunne;
For uch gresse mot grow of graynes dede;
No whete were elles to wones wonne.
Of goud uche goude is ay bygonne;
So semly a sede moght fayly not,
That spryngande spyces up ne sponne
Of that precios perle wythouten spotte.   (ll. 25–36)

That the child should be presented as a pearl, not a flower, her
father as jeweller rather than gardener, has its significance, nonetheless, for the poem is 'lapidary' in more senses than one. Of all earth's
riches, it is precious metals or stones which seem most readily to span
the natural and supernatural worlds; for, in Aristotle's terms, they have
achieved in temporal life that perfection of being to which their permanence testifies. It is no wonder that medieval lapidarists should have
attributed to such stones effective virtues,[93] or that St John should have
built from these materials the Heavenly Jerusalem of *Revelation*. It is
possible that the poem exhibits its own lapidary lore in the notion that a
pearl may be buried in earth to restore its colours; it is certain that the
poet of *Cleanness* knew that a pearl could be cleansed by washing in
wine.[94] The spiritual death consequent on Adam's sin necessitates
rejuvenation through burial; the 'on dethe' of Christ's blood provides
mankind with the redemptive cleansing of sacramental wine. Yet
'lapidary', in the sense of monumental inscription, retains a meaning
more immediate, for the poem is primarily an epitaph, whose art belongs
to this world as well as to the next. The jeweller's craft, imaged in the
finely wrought verbal detail and pattern, secures the pearl in all the
brilliant gold of its paradisal setting; but his words also remain a com-
memorative headstone to the grave in the flowering garden.

In building his *Paradiso*, Dante relied particularly on those manifestations in the temporal world, which may be perceived through the senses,
but which operate immaterially. Light and number are his major resources, for both express unfailing truths which the intelligence may
apprehend through sensible experience, but which are not confined by
material being. Solomon describes the condition of the resurrected body
in one such simile:

---

schyr bright   *fede* faded   *drof* sank   *dunne* dull brown   *wones* dwellings
sponne spring

'Ma sì come carbon che fiamma rende,
E per vivo candor quella soperchia
Sì, che la sua parvenza si difende,
Così questo fulgor, che già ne cerchia,
Fia vinto in apparenza dalla carne
Che tutto dì la terra ricoperchia.'   (*Par.*, XIV, ll. 52-7)

(But like coal that produces flame, which it outshines with its white glow, so that its shape is preserved; so this radiance that now surrounds us will be outshone by the form of that flesh which the earth still covers.)

For the *Pearl* poet, not only light and number, but the properties of jewels, and possibly the lore of alchemy, are all means of capturing that continuity of immaterial with material being.

The earthly Paradise across the river, where the Pearl first appears, establishes that connection between the things of earth and those of heaven. Its landscape, like the *Purgatorio*'s, has the movement and life of this earth, though immune from temporal change and decay. The leaves on the trees are everlasting 'As bornyst sylver', but they quiver and flash 'Wyth schymeryng schene ful schrylle'. Birds fly through this brilliant woodland, but their song is of a sweetness that the instruments of earth, citole and cithern, cannot equal. The river itself rushes over the precious stones which gleam in its bed with the clear voice of a mountain brook: 'Swangeande swete the water con swepe,/Wyth a rownande rourde raykande aryght.' The gems shine through the water:

As glente thurgh glas that glowed and glyght,
As stremande sternes, quen strothe-men slepe,
Staren in welkyn in wynter nyght.   (ll. 114-16)

Whilst the first simile puts the vision directly in the way of our experience, the second, despite its brevity, movingly suggests the distance between earth and heaven, as it invokes the immense distance of the stars, in the wide skies of a clear winter night.

Like Dante's Purgatory, this garden, mediating between the two worlds, is perhaps more moving to earthly imagination than the remote, emblematic perfection of the jewelled Jerusalem. The poet is, in the latter case, pedantically faithful to the description in *Revelation*, no doubt recalling the Divine's warning: 'If any man shall add unto these things, God shall add unto him the plagues that are written in this book: and if any man shall take away from the words of the book of this prophecy, God shall take away his part out of the book of life.'[95] Yet

---

schene bright   schrylle dazzlingly   Swangeande Swirling   rownande whispering
rourde murmur   raykande flowing   glente beam of light   glyght glinted
stremande streaming   sternes stars   strothe-men earthly men   welkyn the heavens

there is much in the poem to prepare us for the enigmatic detail of St John's description. Since the child is clearly the dreamer's way to Paradise, it is the more appropriate that 'every several gate' of the heavenly city should be 'of one pearl'. That 'the city had no need of the sun, neither of the moon, to shine in it: for the glory of God did lighten it and the Lamb is the light thereof', is an anticipated wonder; for the earthly paradise, whose light outshines the sun, has, like the otherworlds of Celtic legend, no natural source for its radiance which derives from the brilliance of precious metals and stones. But St John's account may take on a further significance, if one recalls the relation of Pearl to the moon, of the Lamb to the sun, with those alchemical connotations which Patricia Kean states with appropriate tact: 'I would merely suggest that [the poet] would not have used the symbols in quite this way if he had been unaware of the fact that the equations pearl–moon and gold–sun played an important part in traditional descriptions of a process leading, through "death" and "putrefaction", to "resurrection" and perfection.'[96] Moreover, this single verse, though strictly translated, is one of the few to receive elaboration:[97] beyond the grave, the sunlight and moonlight of earth, the 'blank day' of temporal loss, are superseded by that divine light, at once inward and outward, of love and understanding.

The poem is 'educative', both in its detail and in its process, for it is characterized throughout by this movement between natural and super-natural perception. In its detail, the jeweller's artifice links each verse and section through reiterated words, which develop a higher from a lower meaning. Thus the 'spot' of Part I means 'blemish' in the final line of each verse—'My privy perle wythouten spotte'—whilst in each initial line it indicates 'place', specifically the grave: 'That spot of spyses.' The jeweller feels that his spotless pearl will be blemished in the grave—'O moul, thou marres a myry iuele'—yet it is from the grave that the second section leaps into the freedom of vision: 'Fro spot my spyryt ther sprang in space.' Because the child is indeed spotless, the grave, far from defacing her, has liberated her spirit. The process of the poem may be as specifically traced. In its first line—'Perle, plesaunte to prynces paye', the pearl is a material jewel of monetary value, the Prince an earthly potentate, his 'paye' the self-centred delight of the possessor. In the final section, where 'paye' reappears as the link word, it has developed the subsidiary meaning of 'payment', elaborated in the centre of the poem where the Lord's wages to his labourers are discussed. Its primary meaning is still 'pleasure', but in no selfish sense; the Prince is now the Prince of Life, and the jeweller's pleasure is identified with God's: ' "Now al be to that Prynces paye." ' Because he has learnt to relinquish specious values, pleasure and payment are no longer anti-

privy own

:heses; in willingly losing his life, by entrusting his Pearl to God, he
1as found the prospect of life eternal. The human longing for his dead
daughter has been transformed into the love of God, thus fulfilling the
Gospel analogy between the pearl of great price and the Kingdom of
Heaven.

As in the *Commedia*, it remains true that human love (of Beatrice, the
girl in Florence; of Pearl, the child who could barely speak) forms the
way to heaven. In the eyes of Beatrice, Dante sees the light of God's
ove reflected, until he eventually acquires the strength to gaze on it
directly; in the brilliant figure of Pearl, the jeweller comes to understand
the generosity with which the Lord of the vineyard pays his labourers.
But he never enters the heavenly Jerusalem, as Dante does; he glimpses
t distantly from a hillock on the earthly side of the river, one which may
recall the little grave in the temporal garden. Where Dante is encouraged
o pass through Lethe, the *Pearl*-poet loses his vision, because he at-
empts that passage before his time. In returning to this world, he thus
endures a new bereavement; and the pain of his loss, 'For pyty of my
perle enclyin', is as deeply felt in the final as in the first verse. But the
anguished extremes of human feeling—' "My blysse, my bale, ye han ben
bothe" '—are set at rest; this second loss is acceptable because, under the
child's guidance, anguish has been educated into serenity, and the
jeweller has learnt to find his comfort in the suffering, and promise, of the
cross:

> And sythen to God I hit bitaghte
> In Krystes dere blessyng and myn,
> That in the forme of bred and wyn
> The preste uus schewes uch a daye.
> He gef uus to be his homly hyne
> Ande precious perles unto his pay.   (ll. 1207–12)

Thirteen signifies Death because it exceeds the perfect number twelve.
The poet, with evident deliberation, introduces an additional verse into
Part XV, which prevents his lines from achieving the grander sum of
1,200; to this divine total is added the small, but still perfect and human,
figure of twelve. Temporal life may indeed be flawed, but it mirrors
divinity nonetheless. It may seem a slight, not to say pedantic, mode
of announcing the Triumph of Life; but the humility of its gesture
marks the achievement of medieval perception, of those insights which
are pre-eminently the product of their time, not those one values from
the past because they are familiar. The anguished dichotomies of the
Middle Ages are all too easily recognized in the present; *Pearl* is fully

---

enclyin lying prostrate   *bale* sorrow   *bitaghte* committed   *hyne* household servants
H

aware of them. But the capacity to unite and transcend them demands a rigour that modern ease may find repellent. When Dante is at last reunited with Beatrice, when the dreamer once more sees the little daughter for whom he has mourned so deeply, the response of those beloved figures is unexpectedly chill: ' "Sir," ' says the child severely, ' "ye haf your tale mysetente." '[98] The affirmations of *Gawain*, of *Piers Plowman*, and of Chaucer's poetry, no less than those of *Pearl* and the *Commedia*, are the vision which lies at the end of an arduous pilgrimage; one which, moreover, cannot endure in the world of time. Will must set out again in search of Piers; Dante returns to life to pay the price of his salvation, the poem itself; whilst the father of Pearl must leave his child, until the long day's labour is complete. If the tale is not to be 'mysetente', the search must be unremitting; but the Triumph of Life is always there to be found.

---

mysetente not given proper attention to, told wrongly

Notes*

Introduction

1. *The Vision of William concerning Piers the Plowman*, ed. W. W. Skeat, 1886, 1954, 2 vols; C Text, Ps. XXI, ll. 184, 194–5, 214–17.
2. D. W. Robertson, *A Preface to Chaucer*, Princeton, 1963; p. 51.
3. Edgar Wind, *Pagan Mysteries in the Renaissance*, 1958, 1960; p. 191.
4. *The Stones of Venice*, 1851–3, 1893, 3 vols; Vol. I, p. 237.

Chapter 1: The Figures' Context

1. Jaroslav Pelikan, *The Shape of Death*, 1962; p. 80.
2. This is true even in the Old Testament. Sheol, the realm of the dead, is polymorphous in origin, and is confined to poetic works; elsewhere Old Testament writers 'were engaged in such a persistent struggle with the cult of the dead' that they 'resisted its positive incorporation into the religion of Yahweh'. Rudolph Bultmann, *Life and Death*, 1965; pp. 8–11.
3. *Metalogicus*, Pat. Lat. 199; pp. 823–56. Richard de Bury, *Philobiblon*, ed. E. C. Thomas, 1960; pp. 124–8.
4. cf. Ernst Cassirer, *The Individual and the Cosmos in Renaissance Philosophy*, 1927, New York, 1964; pp. 76–7.
5. *De Civitate Dei*, Pat. Lat. 41; p. 332.
6. *De Trinitate*, Pat. Lat. 42; p. 949.
7. *Gothic Architecture and Scholasticism*, 1951, New York, 1963; pp. 13–14.
8. *De Consolatione Philosophiae*, Bk II, pr. 1; Loeb Classical Library, 1918, 1962; pp. 132 and 174.
9. *Summa Theologiae*, 1a, i, 9; ed. Thomas Gilby, 1963—; Vol. I, pp. 32 and 34.
10. *Metalogicus* (I 3); p. 827.
11. *Trattatello in laude di Dante*, ed. Pier Giorgio Ricci, *La letteratura italiana*, Vol. IX, Milan and Naples, 1965; p. 621.
12. *The Works of Geoffrey Chaucer*, ed. F. N. Robinson, 1933, Boston (2nd revised ed.), 1957; *The Wife of Bath's Tale*, l. 1125; *The Clerk's Prologue*, ll. 31–3.
13. Chaucer's tendency to 'medievalize' Boccaccio is discussed by C. S. Lewis in 'What Chaucer really did to *Il Filostrato*', *Essays and Studies*, XVII, 1932.
14. This separation holds true even in the world of thought: 'Oxford to a great extent belonged to itself; Paris belonged to Christendom'. Gordon Leff, *Paris and Oxford Universities in the Thirteenth and Fourteenth Centuries*, 1968; p. 187.

---

* Full reference is given the first time a work is mentioned; thereafter, the reader is referred to the original entry by Chapter and Note number, thus: *Piers Plowman* (Intro. 1). Details of EETS publications are given as they occur in the EETS check list.

15. cf. G. G. Coulton, *Medieval Panorama*, 1938, New York, 1957; pp. 493–506. May McKisack, *The Fourteenth Century 1307–1399*, 1959; pp. 312–48. David Knowles, *The Religious Orders in England*, Vol. II, 1955; pp. 8–13. George Deaux, *The Black Death 1347*, 1969; pp. 117–44. Philip Ziegler, *The Black Death*, 1969; pp. 117–279. E. F. Jacob, *The Fifteenth Century 1399–1485*, 1961; pp. 367–85.

16. Quoted by Deaux, *Death* (I 15); p. 142.

17. *Religious Pieces in Prose and Verse*, from R. Thornton's MS., ed. G. G. Perry, EETS OS 26, 1867; p. 88.

18. *Death* (I 15); p. 11.

19. *Decameron*, ed. Enrico Bianchi, *La letteratura italiana*, Vol. VIII, Milan and Naples, 1952; p. 11.

20. *Le Prince Noir*, ed. Francisque-Michel, 1883; ll. 317–22.

21. *Historical Poems of the XIVth and XVth Centuries*, ed. Rossell Hope Robbins, New York, 1959. Compare Nos. 74, 75, 77 and 93 with 32 and 33 which, in their celebration of Agincourt, express the contrary heroic view of death.

22. cf. T. D. Kendrick, *British Antiquity*, 1950; pp. 4–9. R. M. Wilson, *Early Middle English Literature*, 1939, 1951; pp. 30–1.

23. Charles Homer Haskins, *The Renaissance of the 12th Century*, 1927, New York, 1958; p. 260. Kendrick, *Antiquity* (I. 22); p. 14.

24. cf. Kendrick, *Antiquity* (I. 22); p. 38. J. D. Mackie, *The Earlier Tudors 1485–1558*, 1952; p. 27.

25. cf. McKisack, *Fourteenth Century* (I 15); p. 251.

26. cf. Walter F. Schirmer, *John Lydgate*, 1952, 1961; pp. 42 and 68–9.

27. *Mum and the Sothsegger*, ed. Mabel Day and R. Steele, EETS OS 199, 1934; Ps. I, ll. 1–2.

28. *Lydgate's Minor Poems*, ed. H. N. MacCracken, Pt I, *Religious Poems*, EETS ES 107, 1910; p. 143.

29. *Death* (I 15); p. 184.

30. cf. Gordon Leff, *Heresy in the Later Middle Ages*, 2 vols, 1967; I, pp. 308–407; II, pp. 494–605.

31. cf. W. A. Pantin, *The English Church in the Fourteenth Century*, 1955; pp. 1–5.

32. cf. Leff, *Heresy* (I 30); p. 259. The heresy of the Free Spirit exemplifies the dangers of an uncontrolled mysticism.

33. *The English Works of John Gower*, ed. G. C. Macaulay, EETS ES 81 and 82, 1900 and 1901, 1957; *Confessio Amantis*, Prologue, ll. 346–51.

34. *Dicts and Sayings of the Philosophers*, ed. C. F. Bühler, EETS OS 211, 1939, 1961; Introduction, pp. ix and xiii.

35. *Palladius on Husbondrie*, ed. Barton Lodge, EETS OS 52 and 72, 1872 and 1879; Preface, p. xv.

36. Nicholas Love, *The Mirrour of the Blessed Lyf of Jesu Christ*, 1908.

37. *Lydgate's Minor Poems*, ed. H. N. MacCracken, Pt II, *Secular Poems*, EETS OS 192, 1933; p. 702.

38. *Selections from Early Middle English*, 2 vols, ed. Joseph Hall, 1920; p. 2.

39. *Meditacyuns on the Soper of our Lorde*, ed. J. M. Cowper, EETS OS 60, 1875; ll. 475–82, 512–28, 653–70, 991–1006.

40. *Religious Lyrics of the Fifteenth Century*, ed. Carleton Brown, 1939, 1962; p. 13.

41. cf. Eric G. Millar, *La Miniature Anglaise du XIVᵉ et du XVᵉ siècle*, Paris, 1928; pp. 28–9 and 35. Margaret Rickert, *Painting in Britain: the Middle Ages*, 1954; pp. 168–9.

42. C. J. P. Cave, *Roof Bosses in Medieval Churches*, 1948; pp. 11 and 12.

43. E. W. Tristram, *English Wall Painting of the Fourteenth Century*, 1955; p. 3.
44. cf. Joan Evans, *English Art 1307–1461*, 1949; p. 74. Deaux, *Death* (I 15); pp. 206–7.
45. *L'Art religieux de la fin du Moyen Age en France*, 1908, Paris, 1925; pp. 347–8.
46. *Tomb Sculpture*, 1964; p. 63.
47. *Bosses* (I 42); p. 17.
48. *English Medieval Mural Paintings*, 1963; p. 74.
49. *The Poems of William Dunbar*, ed. W. Mackay Mackenzie, 1932, 1950, pp. 2 and 142.
50. *Pearl*, ed. E. V. Gordon, 1953, 1958; ll. 1203–4.
51. *Works* (I 12); p. 265.
52. cf. Robinson, *Works* (I 12); p. 773.
53. For a useful discussion of the value of such writing, cf. Derek Pearsall, *John Lydgate*, 1970; pp. 1–18.
54. Leff, *Universities* (I 14); pp. 4–5.
55. Gordon Leff discusses the development of scepticism in *Medieval Thought*, 1958; pp. 255–303.
56. Leff, *Universities* (I 14); pp. 75–115, describes Oxford's early history.
57. cf. Wilson, *Literature* (I 22); pp. 89–91. Basil Cottle, *The Triumph of English 1350–1400*, 1969; pp. 15–27.
58. *A Middle English Reader*, ed. Oliver Farrar Emerson, 1905, 1908; pp. 224–5.
59. cf. *Le opere di Dante Alighieri*, ed. E. Moore and Paget Toynbee, 1904, 1963; *De Vulgari Eloquentia*, pp. 381–2; *Inferno*, XXXI, ll. 76–8; *Paradiso*, XXVI, ll. 124–38.
60. *Middle English Reader* (I 58); pp. 13 and 10.
61. *John Metham's Works*, ed. H. Craig, EETS OS 132, 1906; *Amoris and Cleopes*, l. 2207; *George Ashby's Poems, etc.*, ed. Mary Bateson, EETS ES 76, 1899; p. 2.
62. *Hoccleve's Regement of Princes*, ed. F. J. Furnivall, EETS ES 72, 1897; ll. 801–1029. *Lydgate's Siege of Thebes*, re-ed. A. Erdmann, EETS ES 108, 1911; Prologue, ll. 66–95.
63 *Lydgate's Fall of Princes*, ed. H. Berger, EETS ES 121, 122, 123 and 124, 1918 and 1920, 1967; Bk IV, ll. 1–210.
64. *Poems* (I 49); p. 21.

Chapter II: Youth and its Mentors

1. Aquinas, *Summa*, 1a–2ae, xlvi; ed. cit. (I 9); Vol. XXI, pp. 16–18.
2. *Augustini Opera*, 10 vols, Paris, 1555; *Confessionum*, Vol. I; p. 16.
3. Aquinas, *Summa*, 1a–2ae, xxvii, 1 ad. 3; *Opera Omnia*, 25 vols, Parma, 1852–73; Vol. II; p. 101.
4. cf. Guillaume de Lorris and Jean de Meun, *Le Roman de la Rose*, ed. Felix Lecoy, 3 vols, Paris, 1970; ll. 15861–974. *Lydgate's Reason and Sensuality*, ed. E. Sieper, EETS ES 84 and 89, 1901 and 1903; ll. 407–36.
5. According to the *OED* entry, the word could be used in this sense in Old English. In the thirteenth and fourteenth centuries it was used to describe a young man awaiting knighthood, as well as an infant.
6. *Floris and Blancheflour*, pp. 823–55 in *Middle English Metrical Romances*, ed. W. H. French and C. B. Hale, 1930, New York, 1964; Vol. II, ll. 29–30.
7. cf. J. Huizinga, *The Waning of the Middle Ages*, 1924, 1955; p. 137.
8. Chastellain, quoted by Huizinga, *Waning* (II 7); p. 69.
9. *Le Prince Noir* (I 20); ll. 69–72.

10. It is, for example, significant that painting in Florence and Siena, which in the early part of the fourteenth century frequently celebrates Youth, should cease to do so after the Black Death, until, a century later, the renaissance *putti* become a popular motif. cf. Millard Meiss, *Painting in Florence and Siena after the Black Death*, Princeton, 1951; p. 61.

11. cf. *The Prose Life of Alexander*, ed. J. S. Westlake, EETS OS 143, 1911; pp. 73–4, 77–88.

12. In French and Hale (II 6); Vol. I, pp. 25–70; ll. 2–10.

13. In French and Hale (II 6); Vol. I, pp. 423–55; ll. 917–21.

14. In French and Hale (II 6); Vol. II, pp. 721–55; ll. 221–6.

15. *King Horn*; ll. 29–82. *Sir Degaré* (early fourteenth century), in French and Hale (II 6); Vol. I, pp. 287–320; ll. 1179–232. *Emaré*; ll. 229–76, 583–600.

16. *Gamelyn*, in French and Hale (II 6); Vol. I, pp. 209–35.

17. *Sir Perceval of Galles*, in French and Hale (II 6); Vol. II, pp. 531–603; ll. 293–6.

18. cf. the stories of Mary Magdalen and St Pelagius in *The Golden Legend* translated by William Caxton, 7 vols, 1922; Vol. IV, pp. 76–82, and Vol. VII, pp. 131–3. The play *Mary Magdalene* in *The Digby Plays*, ed. F. J. Furnivall, EETS ES 70, 1896, 1967; pp. 109–30. Her story in Gower's *Confessio Amantis* (I 33), as that of Apollonius of Tyre; Vol. II, pp. 393–440. *Amis and Amiloun*, ed. MacEdward Leach, EETS OS 203, 1935.

19. By A. C. Gibbs, in his introduction to *Middle English Romances*, York Medieval Texts, 1966; p. 37.

20. *Sir Launfal*, in French and Hale (II 6); Vol. I, pp. 345–80; ll. 739–43.

21. cf. ll. 488–92, 558–66, 572–5, 628–30, for conspicuous anti-semitism.

22. See Chaucer's opening verse, ll. 2407–14, where Dante does not specify ages; and his touching interpolated speech for the 'yonge sone, that thre yeer was of age,' ll. 2431–8, where Dante's Anselm says simply, *'Tu guardi sì, padre! che hai?'* (You look so, Father! What's the matter?), *Inf.* XXXIII, l. 51.

23. 'Queynte', for the Squire, means simply 'artful', 'ingenious', although the objects, sword and ring, to which it applies, are innately sexual; cf. ll. 234, 239, 369, 433. For the Wife, it either means simply 'cunt', *Prologue*, ll. 332 and 444, or plays on both senses, l. 516, 'a queynte fantasye'.

24. Sword, ll. 156–67; mirror, ll. 132–6. See also the ring, which restores understanding of the natural world, a capacity lost with the Fall, ll. 146–55; and the horse which moves in freedom from space and time, ll. 115–31.

25. e.g. the Man in Black and his Lady in *The Book of the Duchess*, Troilus, and the Good Women of the *Legend*. His nerveless rendering of Palamon and Arcite in *The Knight's Tale*, whilst in part a response to the *Teseida*, may also register an increasingly sceptical sense of Youth.

26. cf. Alisoun, Nicholas and Absolon in *The Miller's Tale*; Aleyn and John in *The Reeve's Tale*; May and Damyan in *The Merchant's Tale*; Jankyn in *The Wife of Bath's Prologue*; Aurelius in *The Franklin's Tale*.

27. It is interesting that a critic of Chaucer, Wolfgang Clemen, should claim that the notion of 'trouthe' is central to his author (*Chaucer's Early Poetry*, 1963; p. 87), whilst John Burrow (*A Reading of Sir Gawain and the Green Knight*, 1965) makes a similar claim for his theme; pp. 42–50.

28. cf. *Sir Gawain and the Green Knight*, ed. J. R. R. Tolkien and E. V. Gordon, 1925, 1952; ll. 901–27, 1508–34.

29. Gawain is, in Auerbach's term, a *figura*, a protagonist in whom an ideal receives, not an abstract, but a heightened human, fulfilment; not merely an individual or a personification. cf. *Scenes from the Drama of European Literature*, New York, 1959; pp. 11–76.

30. The distinction is made even more clearly in *The Parlement of the Thre Ages*, ed. M. Y. Offord, EETS OS 246, 1959. The poacher of its prologue, ll. 1–99, is vividly attuned to the natural world, where the figure of Youth, whom he sees in dream, echoes that world chiefly in the artifice of his dress; ll. 109–34.

31. Tolkien and Gordon translate 'first age' and 'hyghe eldee' impartially as 'in the prime of life', whilst Burrow explains 'olde' as an off-hand colloquialism, op. cit. (II 27); pp. 69–70. But the prime of Sir Bercilak is that of the fully set man of middle age, 'hyghe eldee', the prime of Arthur's court that of youth, 'first age'. Burrow is not, however, unsympathetic to the relevance of the figure of Youth to the poem (pp. 1–30), and a more extended claim for that reading is made by Charles Moorman in his essay, 'Myth and Medieval Literature: *Sir Gawain and the Green Knight*', in *'Sir Gawain' and 'Pearl': Critical Essays*, ed. Robert J. Blanch, Indiana, 1966; pp. 209–35.

32. op. cit. (II 27); pp. 12–28, 123–49.

33. op. cit. (II 27); pp. 14–16.

34. *The Works of Sir Thomas Malory*, ed. Eugène Vinaver, 1954; p. 791.

35. Aquinas, *Evangelium Mathei*, v, lect. 2; *Opera* (II 3); Vol. X, p. 49.

36. Aquinas, *Summa*, 2a–2ae, xxxv, 4 ad. 2; ed. cit. (I 9); Vol. XXV, p. 32.

37. cf. Burrow, op. cit. (II 27); pp. 179–85, for an interesting discussion of the mixture of styles and the comic element in *Sir Gawain*.

38. In *Non-Cycle Plays and Fragments*, ed. Norman David, EETS SS 1, 1970; pp. 90–105; ll. 17–32.

39. *Speculum Guidonis de Warwyk*, ed. G. L. Morrill, EETS ES 75, 1898; ll. 857–8.

40. Guy's secular life is elaborated in the fifteenth-century version, *Guy of Warwick*, ed. J. Zupitza, EETS ES 25 and 26, 1875 and 1876. cf. ll. 809–20 with 7119–84 (repentance) and 7701–837 (anonymity).

41. As the sin of Lucifer, cf. *Middle English Sermons from MS. Roy. 18 B. xxiii*, ed. W. O. Ross, EETS OS 209, 1938; pp. 49–50, 107–8. As the root of all sins, cf. *Middle English Sermons*, pp. 68, 293, and *Dan Michel's Ayenbite of Inwyt*, ed. R. Morris and P. Gradon, EETS OS 23, 1866; p. 16 ff. In visual art pride is shown as the head of the tree of the 7 Deadly Sins, a motif particularly popular in the late fourteenth century; cf. Caiger-Smith, op. cit. (I 48); pp. 49–53. The representation of Pride as a figure, usually female, from which the other sins sprout, is largely fifteenth century; a clear example survives in the parish church at Raunds, Northants.

42. Aquinas, *Summa*, 1a–2ae, 77, v; ed. cit. (I 9); Vol. XXV, p. 176. cf. also the discussion of pride as the beginning of every sin, 1a–2ae, 84, ii; Vol. XXVI, pp. 64–6.

43. In the Thornton MS, ed. cit. (I 17); p. 24.

44. Cassirer, *Individual and Cosmos* (I 4); p. 69.

45. Dante, *Epistola X*, *Opere* (I 59); p. 416.

46. *The Conversion of St Paul* is included in *The Digby Plays*, as is *Mary Magdalene* (II 18).

47. *The Pride of Life* and *Dux Moraud* are included in *Non-Cycle Plays* (II 38), and *Mundus et Infans* in *Specimens of the Pre-Shakespearian Drama*, ed. John Matthews Manly, Vol. I, 1900.

48. *Paradiso*, XVI, l. 1; *Inferno*, X, ll. 22–94. Whilst Dante's pride in his poem is manifest, the proud of the *Purgatorio* are nevertheless artists, who labour beneath the weight of the inflated self, and reflect upon the brevity of fame (XI, ll. 115–17).

49. *The Chester Plays*, Pt I, re-ed. H. Diemling, EETS ES 62, 1892, 1959;

Pt II, re-ed. J. Mathews, EETS ES 115, 1914, 1959. *Ludus Coventriae*, ed. K. S. Block, EETS ES 120, 1917, 1960. *The Towneley Plays*, ed. G. England and A. W. Pollard, EETS ES 71, 1897, 1952. *York Plays*, ed. Lucy Toulmin Smith, New York, 1963. Examples here are mostly taken from York and Towneley, because their Lucifers are most clearly expressive of the Pride of Life.

50. In didactic prose, though not in the mystery plays, Lucifer's offence is sometimes seen as a refusal to worship man in the image of God; he claims to be the fairer, and that man should worship him. cf. *The Wheatley MS.*, ed. Mabel Day, EETS OS 155, 1917; p. 84. This is an interesting variation on the Pride of Life theme, but the dramatists characteristically prefer the absolute (and thus more expressive) gesture of rebellion against God himself.

51. ed. cit. (I 63).

52. cf. E. K. Chambers, *The Medieval Stage*, 2 vols, 1903, 1954; Vol. II, p. 57: 'I find a parallel reaction of the turbulence of the Feast of Fools upon the *Stella*, in the violence of speech and gesture which permanently associated itself at a very early stage with the character of Herod.'

53. *The Gospel of Nicodemus* or *Acts of Pilate*, in *The Apocryphal New Testament*, trans. M. R. James, pp. 94–146; cf. pp. 96–103.

54. De Voragine lived in the second half of the thirteenth century. Caxton's translation of *The Golden Legend*, ed. cit. (II 18): *Gospel of Nicodemus* cited as authority for Passion, Vol. I, p. 66; the wickedness and cruelty of Pilate, Vol. I, pp. 80–6; represented as the friend of Judas, whom he marries to the latter's mother, Vol. III, pp. 56–7.

55. cf. *The Harrowing of Hell*, and *The Gospel of Nicodemus*, re-ed. W. H. Hulme, EETS ES 100, 107; Introduction, pp. xix and xvii and pp. 23–60.

56. V. A. Kolve, *The Play Called Corpus Christi*, 1966, p. 232.

57. *Pageant of the Shearmen and Taylors*, in *Two Coventry Corpus Christi Plays*, re-ed. H. Craig, EETS ES 87, 1902; p. 18.

58. ed. cit. (II 18); Pt I, ll. 470–4 and 480.

59. This is particularly noticeable in the Chester Last Judgement (XXIV) where many of the themes with which this book is concerned find their place— not only Youth and the Pride of Life, but the lament of *ubi sunt* (Ch. IV), the theme of Fortune (Ch. IV), and the Dance of Death (Ch. V).

60. Émile Mâle, *L'Art religieux du XIIIᵉ siècle en France*, Paris, 1908, 1925; pp. 347–8.

61. Pantin, *English Church* (I 31); p. 129.

62. cf. Leff, *Heresy* (I 30); Vol. II, pp. 544–5.

63. cf. Walter Ullmann, *A History of Political Thought: the Middle Ages*, 1965; pp. 11–18 and 159–73.

64. Rendered by Owst from *Jacob's Well*, *Literature and Pulpit in Medieval England*, 1933, 1961; p. 264.

65. *Death and Liffe*, ed. Israel Gollancz, *Select Early English Poems*, 1930. This point is more fully discussed in Ch. VI, p. 201.

66. ed. cit. (I 27).

67. cf. *Secreta Secretorum*, three prose Englishings, one by Jas. Yonge, 1428, ed. R. Steele, EETS ES 74, 1898.

68. op. cit. (II 11); pp. 54–6, 73–4, 77–88.

69. *Cleanness*, in *Early English Alliterative Poems*, ed. R. Morris, EETS OS 1, 1864; ll. 393–402 (Flood), ll. 1157–356 (unrighteous king).

70. cf. *Twenty-six Political and other Poems* from Digby MS. 102, ed. J. Kail, EETS OS 124; No. 2. *Historical Poems* (I 21), No. 22.

71. The coincidence of Youth, the Pride of Life and Waster is best exemplified in the alliterative debate poem, *Wynnere and Wastoure*, ed. Israel Gollancz, *Select Early English Poems*, 1930. Since it is a poem in which the Ages confront each other, it is discussed in Ch. III, pp. 83–5. It may well be the work of the author of *The Parlement of the Thre Ages* (II 30), and belongs, like that poem, to the second half of the fourteenth century; Gollancz dates *WW* 1352–3, and Offord, *Parl* between that date and 1370.

72. These attitudes are dispersed through *The Parlement* ed. cit. (II 30). Youth's delight in hawking and hunting, ll. 208–45; his fine clothes, ll. 117–29; characterized as a waster by Middle Age, ll. 183–93; Elde expresses the religious censure of Youth, ll. 270–6. A covert sympathy for Youth is implied by the appreciative language in which he is described, ll. 109–35—'the semelyeste segge that I segh ever'. Youth's zest for life is energetically felt in his speeches, ll. 174–81, 195–256.

73. *Sermons* (II 41); pp. 156–7.

74. For debates, see Ch. III, pp. 82–3; for Legend, see Ch. V, pp. 162–7.

75. ed. cit. (I 27); l. 123 and ll. 260–2.

76. ed. cit. (II 38); ll. 123–4.

77. Included in *A Select Collection of Old English Plays*, ed. W. Carew Hazlitt, Vol. II, 1874, from *Dodsley's Old English Plays*, 1744.

78. *Philobiblon* (I 3); pp. 156–8.

79. *Corpus Christi* (II 56); p. 224.

80. cf. E. W. Tristram, *English Medieval Wall Painting; The Thirteenth Century*, 2 vols, 1950; Plates 71 and 159.

81. These poems, in both versions, are collected in *Erthe upon Erthe*, ed. Hilda Murray, EETS OS 141, 1911, 1964.

82. *Mundus et Infans* (II 47). *The Castle of Perseverance* (early fifteenth century) in *The Macro Plays*, re-ed. Mark Eccles, EETS OS 262, 1969.

83. *The Dialogues of Plato*, trans. B. Jowett, 1892, 2 vols, New York, 1937; Vol. I, p. 309.

84. cf. *The Parlement of Foulys*, ed. D. S. Brewer, 1960; Introduction, pp. 30–2.

85. *Pat. Lat.*, No. 210, pp. 430–82.

86. *Teseida*, in *Tutte le Opere di Giovanni Boccaccio*, ed. Vittore Bianca; Vol. II, 1964; Bk VII, vs. 59, l. 5; vs. 61, ll. 1–2.

87. *Roman de la Rose* (II 4); ll. 3402–3 and 19313.

88. *Ibid.*, ll. 20653–766.

89. cf. Bk III, ll. 1–42, with *Consolatio*, Bk II, m. 8. The echo of Boethius comes by way of Boccaccio, for many of Chaucer's lines here are directly based upon the opening of Bk III of the *Teseida*.

90. cf. *Parliament*, ll. 113–19 and l. 260. Brewer (II 84), pp. 31–2, comments usefully on Cytherea.

91. *Lydgate's DeGuilleville's Pilgrimage of the Life of Man*, ed. F. J. Furnivall, EETS ES 77 and 83, 1899 and 1901; ll. 13063–276.

92. *Reason and Sensuality* (II 4); ll. 3385–90.

93. *Ibid.*, ll. 3203–4, 3193–4, 3189.

94. *Ibid.*, ll. 1490–4, 1499–502.

95. *Roman de la Rose*, ll. 20238–652. *Reason and Sensuality*, ll. 3897–900.

96. In DeGuilleville's *Pilgrimage*, Nature attacks Grace-Dieu for interfering in sub-celestial matters, and for contravening her laws by turning wine to blood, bread to flesh, water to wine and virgin to mother. ll. 3344–638.

97. *Lydgate's Assembly of the Gods*, ed. O. L. Triggs, EETS ES 69, 1896, 1957; l. 1271. *Reason and Sensuality*, ll. 672–4. For the spurious attribution of the *Assembly* to Lydgate, cf. Pearsall, *Lydgate* (I 53); p. 60. *Reason and Sensuality*,

though certainly Lydgate's, is largely a translation from the French; cf. Pearsall, p. 115.

98. Debates between body and soul can be found in Old English and throughout medieval literature. In one fifteenth-century example, the Body complains that the Soul has fallen out with him and hates his fashionable dress because she insists on obedience to Christ; Digby MS, ed. cit. (II 70); No. 20.

99. These questions are explored throughout the *Consolatio* of Boethius.

100. Cassirer, *Individual and Cosmos* (I 4); p. 145.

101. On the early Cistercian settlements, cf. David Knowles, *The Monastic Order in England*, 1940, 1950; pp. 211 and 216. Illuminations of the Flight into Egypt provide many examples of the second point; the *Très Riches Heures* of the Duc de Berry has a fine example, f. 57r. The human figures, and the obedient tree which bows to feed the Virgin, engross the viewer's attention, whilst rocky scarp and blue distant mountains serve largely to give the composition balance and depth. Little more than a century later, the paintings of Pieter Brueghel (d. 1569) encourage the eye to scan vast landscapes in search of such spiritual events.

102. cf. also Coulton, *Panorama* (I 5); pp. 103–18.

103. See also C, XV, ll. 157–66.

104. A related uncertainty is evident in plays concerning Abraham's sacrifice of Isaac; God is accused of un*kind*ness in making, of a father, a demand which transgresses both divine and natural bonds. cf. Kolve (II 56); p. 261. Two non-cycle plays should be included as relevant examples: *The Northampton Abraham* and *The Brome Abraham*, included in *Non-Cycle Plays* (II 38).

105. ed. cit. (II 85); p. 432, pr. I.

106. *Ibid.*, pp. 456–60, pr. V.

107. *Poems* (I 49); p. 109, ll. 71–7.

108. *Roman de la Rose* (II 4); ll. 18989–92.

109. Lydgate, *Minor Poems I* (I 28); pp. 46 and 47, ll. 113–14, 119–20.

110. *Incendium Amoris, The Fire of Love*, tr. by Richard Misyn, ed. W. R. Harvey, EETS OS 106, 1896; p. 41.

111. It is significant that, in the Renaissance, the beautiful draws closer to the true than does the good, and thus acquires greater autonomy. cf. Cassirer, *Individual and Cosmos* (I 4); p. 163.

112. cf. Etienne Gilson, *The Spirit of Medieval Philosophy*, 1936, 1950; p. 376. In the *Roman de la Rose*, however, Nature complains specifically of man's tendency to regard himself as predestined; ll. 17029–844.

113. *Reason and Sensuality* (II 4); ll. 558–68 (microcosm), 931–2 (beauty of the world). For man as microcosm, cf. *Roman de la Rose*, ll. 19022–3.

114. cf. Marjorie Hope Nicolson, *Mountain Gloom and Mountain Glory*, Cornell, 1959, New York, 1963; pp. 72–112.

115. *De Trinitate* (I 6); p. 949.

116. Quoted by Chambers, *Stage* (II 52); Vol. II, p. 80.

117. *Genesis and Exodus*, ed. R. Morris, EETS OS 7, 1865, New York, 1969; ll. 183–98.

118. *Cursor Mundi*, ed. R. Morris, EETS OS 57, 59, 62, 66, 68, 99, 1874–92; ll. 1776–96, 11629–730, 12333–86.

119. Classical tradition possessed both a 'hard' and a 'soft' notion of primitivism, a barbarous as well as an idyllic Arcadia; cf. Panofsky, *Meaning in the Visual Arts*, 1955, 1970; pp. 340–67. Pastoral motifs were constantly being re-discovered in the Middle Ages 'because the stock . . . was bound to no genre and to no poetic form'. cf. Ernst Robert Curtius, *European Literature and the Latin Middle Ages*, 1948, New York, 1963; p. 187. The barbarous alterna-

tive was of course ignored because if Arcadia was the secular Eden, it could only be idyllic.

120. *Inferno*, XIV, ll. 94–120.
121. It is striking that the first three lines of the *Parliament* appear at first sight to describe the hardships of composition, and that the following half-line, 'Al this mene I by Love', should come as a surprise; the syntax has been suspended to allow entrance to the ambiguity. It is an ambiguity that arises from deficient feeling: 'I knowe nat Love in dede', the poet complains; and since love is the great resort of such poetry, the difficulties of the would-be poet are sufficiently clear.
122. J. A. W. Bennett, *The Parlement of Foules*, 1957; p. 193.
123. *Ibid.*, pp. 16–17. C. S. Lewis, in *The Discarded Image*, 1964, offers a useful note (pp. 34–40) on the medieval idea of Nature, tracing it back beyond Alanus to Statius and Claudian. cf. also George D. Economou, *The Goddess Natura in Medieval Literature*, Cambridge, Massachusetts, 1972.
124. Bennett, *Parlement*, p. 18.
125. *Ywain and Gawain*, ed. Albert B. Friedman and Norman T. Harrington, EETS OS 254, 1963; l. 1525–44. *Eger and Grime*, in French and Hale (II 6); Vol. II, pp. 671–717; ll. 315–464.
126. *Vita Nuova*, *Opere* (I 59); p. 233.
127. *Sermons* (II 41); p. 78.
128. *Ancrene Wisse*, ed. J. R. R. Tolkien, EETS OS 249, 1960; pp. 198–200.
129. *Medieval English Lyrics*, ed. R. T. Davies, 1963; p. 272, cf. note, pp. 363–4.
130. This continuity can be traced in other formative figures of positive meaning, such as Anima; Piers himself is the outstanding example, for the humble ploughman is ultimately recognized as the human nature of Christ.

Chapter III: Age and its Perspectives
1. Reason in *Le Roman de la Rose* (II 4); ll. 4399–404, 4433, 4447, 4461–4.
2. *Parlement of the Thre Ages* (II 30); ll. 152–65.
3. *The Harley Lyrics*, ed. G. L. Brook, 1948, 1956; pp. 46–8. Dunbar, *Poems* (I 49); pp. 26–7.
4. *Selections* (I 38); pp. 2–3. *Cursor Mundi* (II 118); ll. 3555–88.
5. *Ars Poetica*, in *Satires, etc.*, Loeb Classical Library, 1926, 1970; ll. 158–78. The Elegies of Maximian are discussed by Rosemary Woolf in *English Religious Lyric in the Middle Ages*, 1968; pp. 102–5.
6. *English Lyrics of the Thirteenth Century*, ed. Carleton Brown, 1932, 1953; p. 100.
7. Aquinas, *Summa*, 3a, lxxii, 8; ed. cit. (I 9); Vol. LVII, p. 212. See also *Rohan Hours*, f. 159, where the corpse is aged, the soul that of adolescent Youth.
8. Aspects of the renaissance attitude in tomb sculpture are enumerated by Panofsky, *Tomb Sculpture* (I 46); p. 73.
9. *The Complete Works of John Webster*, ed. F. L. Lucas, 4 vols, 1927, 1966; Vol. II, *Duchess*, Act IV, Sc. ii, ll. 151–9.
10. Thus one preacher, whilst remarking that the 4th commandment enjoins respect for age, denies that privilege to the old men of his day, because their viciousness can occasion no reverence: 'Cursed is the child of an hundreth yere old'. Another, alleging that old men boast of their former sins and pervert Youth by singing lecherous songs, confirms this opinion. *Sermons* (II 41); pp. 119–20 and 236.
11. e.g. Age is given to avarice, because he seeks, with the aid of his goods, to keep a hold on the living. A preacher recounts how an old man, who in-

advisedly gave all his wealth to his son-in-law in advance of his death, and was reduced to beggary where he expected to be treated with gratitude, managed inventively to regain the young man's friendship by pretending to count money in a basket. *Sermons* (II 41); pp. 89–90.

12. There are exceptions: Audelay, the blind and deaf Capellanus of Haghmont Abbey, and Lydgate, the ageing Benedictine at Bury, can write in the earlier fifteenth century as though such contemplative poetry were the proper product of bodily decrepitude; to an extent unusual in the Middle Ages, their meditations have the tone of present and personal experience. cf. Lydgate, *Minor Poems* I (I 28); 'A Prayer in Old Age', pp. 20–1; 'The Testament of Dan John Lydgate', pp. 329–62. *The Poems of John Audelay*, ed. Ella K. Whiting, EETS OS 184, 1930; No. 50, p. 210.

13. The edition of Denton Fox, Nelson's Medieval and Renaissance Library, 1968, is particularly valuable; it is the text used here.

14. cf. Panofsky on the purpose of Age in Titian's Allegory of Prudence, *Visual Arts* (II 119); p. 184.

15. cf. Woolf, *Religious Lyric* (III 5); pp. 78–82.

16. *Political Poems* (II 70); No. 26, pp. 143–9.

17. *Sermons* (II 41); p. 85.

18. *Everyman*, in *Chief Pre-Shakespearian Dramas*, ed. Joseph Quincy Adams, Cambridge, Massachusetts, 1924, 1952; pp. 288–303, ll. 184–6, 192–5.

19. *Pilgrimage* (II 91); ll. 24127–328. Age here is the 'courier' of Death; female, ugly, but full of wisdom.

20. C, XXIII, ll. 95–6.

21. Neither the Merchant nor the Reeve appears in the *General Prologue* specifically as a figure of Age; if anything, both tend rather to suggest prosperous middle years. The crabbed vision of Elde which they express in the remarks prefatory to their tales, and in the tales themselves, thus comes as a surprise which emphasizes the observation that the attitudes of Elde and of *contemptus mundi* are primarily those of a state of mind, and not purely of a physical condition.

22. *The Reeve's Prologue*, ll. 3879–80.

23. *The Reeve's Prologue*, ll. 3884, 3885, 3891–2.

24. *The Merchant's Prologue*, l. 1228, ll. 1243–4; *The Merchant's Tale*, l. 1685.

25. *The Squire's Tale*, ll. 202–3; *The Merchant's Tale*, ll. 1469–70, 1546–8.

26. cf. Woolf, *Religious Lyric* (III 5); p. 102.

27. *The Pardoner's Tale*, ll. 780 and 700. *The Pride of Life* (II 38); ll. 451–68.

28. *Religious Lyrics 15th C.* (I 40); p. 235.

29. John merely shares with Alisoun and Nicholas in the rough justice of the *fabliau*, cf. ll. 3850–4.

30. *Towneley Plays* (II 49); III, ll. 163–71.

31. cf. Kolve, *Corpus Christi* (II 56); p. 249.

32. In *Apocryphal N.T.* (II 53); pp. 38–49, p. 42.

33. cf. Kolve, *Corpus Christi* (II 56); pp. 247–53. Huizinga, *Waning* (II 7); pp. 170–1.

34. Quoted by Huizinga, *Waning* (II 7); p. 171.

35. cf. *Ludus Coventriae* (II 49); X. Betrothal of Mary; XII. Joseph's return; XIV. Trial of Mary and Joseph; XV. Birth of Christ.

36. *York Plays* (II 49); XVIII, ll. 173–83, 193–9.

37. Hoccleve, in *Regement* (I 62), professes his love for the old, and his prologue consists in an admonitory address from beggared Elde to his own wasted youth; ll. 113–2009. Capgrave, in his account of St Augustine, remarks on the care taken by the saint of the old, and on his exhortations to the other

monks of his community to do likewise; *Capgrave's Lives of St Augustine and St Gilbert of Sempringham*, ed. J. Munro, EETS OS 140, 1910; p. 49.

38. In *Cursor Mundi* (II 118), Lamech is described as the last man of the first world who died at the age of 777; ll. 1487–9.

39. *LC* (II 49), IV, ll. 142–97.

40. In Genesis Lamech is the descendant of Cain, by five generations; he is the father of Noah, and lives to the age of 777. The cryptic sentence which generates this episode is Lamech's statement: 'I have slain a man to my wounding, and a young man to my hurt' (IV, 23). The distinction between the meaningless cycles of human history, and the meaningful progress of divine design, is explored in Chap. IV, pp. 96–7.

41. *Herod's Killing of the Children*, in *Digby Plays* (II 18); l. 456.

42. *Ibid.*, ll. 388, 397–8, 501–2, 505–6.

43. *Inferno*, XIV, ll. 97–9.

44. In DeGuilleville's *Pilgrimage* (II 91), ll. 3344–62, Nature, though old and in a bad temper, is redeemed by the brightness of her large eyes; in *Reason and Sensuality* (II 4), she appears 'sempt flouryng in youthe' but is 'ful fer y-ronne in age'; ll. 334 and 336.

45. ll. 2847–8.

46. It is interesting that the Franklin in *Mum and the Sothsegger* (I 27), which has, at the least, concerns in common with Langland's, should be presented as a venerable and venerated figure, who seems, in many ways, to personify a humanized Nature; cf. Ps. IV, ll. 952–65.

47. *The Poems and Fables of Robert Henryson*, ed. H. Harvey Wood, 1933, 1958; pp. 185–6.

48. *Ibid.*, pp. 179–81.

49. *The Owl and the Nightingale*, ed. Eric Gerald Stanley, 1960.

50. See Chap. IV, pp. 101–2.

51. In religious writing, for example, an old man without belief and a youth without obedience are seen as parallel anomalies in the early thirteenth century; cf. *Old English Homilies*, ed. R. Morris, Series I, Pt I, EETS OS 29, 1867; p. 109. Almost two centuries later, another preacher, in similar vein, rebukes the old for leading the young astray by singing lecherous songs and boasting of their past youth; *Sermons* (II 41); p. 236.

52. *Works* (II 34); p. 118.

53. *Prose Life* (II 11); p. 86.

54. Rendered from MS. Bodl. 649, fol. 120b, by Owst, *Literature and Pulpit* (II 64); pp. 534–5.

55. *Minor Poems* I (I 28); pp. 20–1.

56. This sense of life as accelerating decline is succinctly expressed in another of his lyrics, 'Timor Mortis Conturbat Me', *Minor Poems* II (I 37); pp. 828–32; ll. 97–104.

57. *Mundus et Infans* (II 47). 'The Mirror' is included in *Hymns to the Virgin and Christ; The Parliament of Devils, etc.*, ed. F. J. Furnivall, EETS OS 24, 1867; pp. 58–78.

58. *Ibid.*, pp. 83–5.

59. *Minor Poems* II (I 37); pp. 759–64; ll. 49–56.

60. *Convivio*, Bk IV, Chap. 23; *Opere* (I 59); p. 327. Because sext and none are rung at the same time—the hours before noon (prime, terce and sext) being rung at the end of their period, the hours after (none, vespers and compline) being rung at the beginning of theirs—Dante reduces the five intervals to four.

61. cf. Klibansky, Saxl and Panofsky, *Saturn and Melancholy*, 1964; pp. 4, 9–11.

62. *Ibid.*, pp. 127–33, 292–3, 369.

63. *Minor Poems* II (I 37); pp. 734–8.
64. *Stage* (II 52); Vol. I, pp. 80–1.
65. For date and edition of *Winner and Waster*, cf. (I 71). The MS. is incomplete, but little seems to be lost, insufficient at least to make a substantial difference to the ambiguities of the King's lengthy decision.
66. In Dante's *Inferno* (VII, ll. 16–66), both sins are punished in the same mode in the same circle; they simply roll their weights in contrary directions.
67. *Winner and Waster*, l. 154. *The Poems of Laurence Minot*, ed. Joseph Hall, 1897, provide a striking contrast; of eleven poems in this volume three celebrate Edward III's conquests in Scotland, and the other eight his victories, on land or at sea, over the French, Flemish and Spanish.
68. Waster's army is described ll. 193–6.
69. The relation of the two poems is explored by Nevill Coghill in *The Pardon of Piers Plowman*, British Academy Lecture, 1945.
70. References to Offord edition (II 30).
71. cf. comments on Squire, p. 29, and on Youth in note (II 30). Descriptions of the jewelled Heavenly City derive from *Revelation*, Ch. XXI.
72. For further remarks on the Elde of *The Parlement*, see above, pp. 63 and 67.
73. For a discussion of the Legend, and particularly of the poem attributed to Audelay, which enforces the reverse of the hunt of life by the pursuit of Death, see below, pp. 164–5. In visual art, the point is vividly made in a Book of Hours of the Virgin, Flemish, late fifteenth century; BM, MS. Add. 35313, f. 158v. Here a hunt of the living is disrupted by three pursuing skeletons (see also Plate 26).
74. *Poems* (I 49); pp. 85–97. The poem has other kinds of richness, however, which are amply explored in *A Midsummer Eve's Dream*, by A. D. Hope, 1971.
75. First married woman: ll. 89–91. Second: ll. 170, 185–7. Widow: l. 283.
76. In Chaucer's Tales the complementary nature of the Ages is not perceived as a difference of mode, of intellect against imagination, as in the debate poems; as in the Wife of Bath, first a young woman who exploits and abuses her elderly husbands, then in her own old age the victim of the youthful Jankyn, the two aspects are seen as a genuine part of the human continuity.
77. cf. Charles Muscatine, *Chaucer and the French Tradition*, Berkeley and Los Angeles, 1957, 1964; 'The romance . . . tends to describe its ladies, knights, and *vilains* according to the conventional physiognomy for each group; in contrast the fabliau, where it distinguishes at all, does so sharply, with widely disparate traits dictated by the point of the story.' (p. 62.)
78. No one in the romances, who is not a villain, would behave like the knights and squires of Langland's day, who will neglect a young woman of beauty and high birth on account of her poverty, in favour of an ill-born and unprepossessing heiress; cf. C, XI, ll. 257–83.
79. *Havelock the Dane*, in French and Hale (II 6); Vol. I, pp. 73–176. *Gamelyn* (II 16).
80. cf. Klibansky, Saxl and Panofsky (III 61); pp. 159–95, on Saturn in Medieval Literature. For a discussion of planetary influence in *The Knight's Tale*, cf. Walter Clyde Curry, *Chaucer and the Mediaeval Sciences*, 1926, 1960; pp. 119–63.
81. The temple of Mars is more actively cruel than that of Venus, and its scenes of carnage relate more directly to the chill vision of Saturn; cf. ll. 1995–2023, 2453–69. Venus has her attraction, but the catalogue of those catastrophes which follow in the wake of love is long, and could be longer; cf. ll. 1918–35. The death of 'Attheon' in the temple of Diana, which could

well have been treated with a related emphasis, is treated relatively casually; cf. ll. 2065–8.

82. The connection of Youth's outlook with that of Age is explicitly made in ll. 1372–9, where the lover Arcite is shown to behave like a man under the influence of the 'humour malencolik'.

83. cf. notes to Tolkien and Gordon edition (II 28), on this passage, ll. 2452–66.

84. The contrast is also a rhetorical device; cf. Derek Pearsall, 'Rhetorical "Descriptio" in "Sir Gawain and the Green Knight" ', *Modern Language Review*, Vol. L, No. 2, 1955; p. 131.

85. Tolkien and Gordon, in their note to l. 2460, relate this difference to the notion in *Le Roman de Merlin* that Morgan became ugly and old when she took to witchcraft; this complements, rather than contradicts, the patterning of the Ages.

86. cf. Kolve, *Corpus Christi* (II 56); p. 156, where he discusses the 'notion of youth overcoming age' in the context of the drama, 'a theme pervasive in the religious life of the Middle Ages'.

87. Quoted by Cassirer, *Individual and Cosmos* (I 4); pp. 32–3.

88. Panofsky, *Visual Arts* (II 119); p. 184.

89. *Minor Poems* II (I 37); pp. 682–91; ll. 147–60.

90. *Minor Poems* II; pp. 759–64; ll. 20–1.

91 *Purgatorio*, XXIX, ll. 130–2.

92. Quoted by Panofsky, *Visual Arts* (II 119); p. 184.

93. B, X, ll. 122–3.

94. *Piers Plowman*, C, XIII, ll. 184–5. Skeat argues that this speech belongs to Recklessness, being distinguished by an inverted comma, l. 88, from the words of Trajan. But it is tempting to wonder whether it does not, more properly, belong to Trajan, the great exception to the Christian notion that no pagan could be saved from eternal death. cf. *Paradiso*, XX, ll. 43–8.

Chapter IV: Related Views of Temporal Life

1. Aquinas, Commentary on *Perihermenias*, Bk I, Lect. xiv; *Opera* (II 3); Vol. XVIII, 1865; p. 35.

2. C. A. Patrides, *The Phoenix and the Ladder*, 1972; p. 9.

3. *Ibid.*, p. 9. 'The meaningless cycles of flux and reflux in the Graeco-Roman attitude towards history are like the legendary phoenix, dying periodically in order to revive again.' The phoenix seems too positive an image for the repetition of 'meaningless cycles', whilst the ascending ladder is by no means the only view of history current in the Christian Middle Ages.

4. Burrow, op. cit. (II 27); pp. 172–3, emphasizes that the reference to Brutus, because it is regarded by the poet as fact, not legend, serves as 'one manifestation of his "levelling" realism'. To place the reference within the negative cycle of human history is to extend, rather than to contradict, this observation.

5. cf. *General Prologue*, ll. 790–801.

6. *Roman de la Rose* (II 4); ll. 18967–9024.

7. Quoted in Chap. III, p. 81.

8. *Secreta Secretorum* (II 67); pp. 243–4.

9. *Ibid.*, p. 245.

10. The personification of the months as figures is classical in origin, and is still frequently employed by illuminators in the fourteenth and fifteenth centuries. cf. Derek Pearsall and Elizabeth Salter, *Landscapes and Seasons of the Medieval World*, 1973; pp. 130–1.

11. cf. *Landscapes and Seasons* (IV 10); pp. 155–6, on the zodiacal setting of the *Très Riches Heures*, and p. 158 for comments on the Calendar of the *Grimani Breviary*, which was directly based upon the earlier work.

12. Mâle, *XIIIᵉ Siècle* (II 60); p. 31.

13. The relation of man to the natural order is chiefly explored in the *Consolatio*, Bk I, M. and P. v and vi, M. vii; its harmony is recurrently celebrated in the verses. Boethius raises the question of freewill in Bk V, pr. ii, ed. cit. (I 8); pp. 154–70 and 370.

14. *Secular Lyrics of the XIVth and XVth Centuries*, ed. Rossell Hope Robbins, 1952, 1955; p. 62.

15. In Calendar sequences, such as the *Très Riches Heures*, January is usually devoted to feasting, February to warming, and December to hunting, the duty and pleasure of the nobleman; cf. *Piers Plowman*, C. IX, ll. 19–34. Where the rhyme describes the labourer's year, the illuminators often depicted the months as they affected the wealthy whose commissions they executed.

16. Pearsall and Salter, op. cit. (IV 10); p. 125. For a discussion of the hardships of the natural world, cf. pp. 120–9.

17. cf. Chap. II, p. 57, and note 118, on the power of the unfallen Adam and of Christ to communicate with the natural world.

18. C, IX, ll. 164–204.

19. *Minor Poems* II (I 37); p. 762.

20. *Piers Plowman*, B, XIV, ll. 164–5.

21. Rosamund Tuve, *Seasons and Months*, Paris 1933; pp. 15–16.

22. ed. cit. (III 49). cf. Introduction, pp. 25–33, for the tradition of such debates, and a synopsis in the Appendix, pp. 167–8, of a Latin dialogue between Winter and Summer (where Theologia reconciles the disputants). cf. also Wilson, *Middle English* (I 22); pp. 159–60.

23. The technicality is complex, and seems to include both the notion that the Owl has conceded her opponent's charge in l. 1138, and that, since living birds only are under debate, a claim to be useful when dead is a fatal mistake. For the genesis of such *cautelae* in legal cases, cf. ed. cit., Introduction, p. 27.

24. ll. 709–10, 220, 224.

25. ll. 187–214.

26. *Summa*, 1a, lviii, 6; ed. cit (I 9); Vol. IX, p. 162.

27. *Lyrics*, ed. Davies (II 129); p. 176.

28. *Works* (II 34); pp. 790–1.

29. B, XIV, ll. 108–24.

30. Tuve, *Seasons and Months* (IV 21); pp. 97–122, 170–92.

31. *Roman de la Rose* (II 4); ll. 53–8, 78–83.

32. *Works* (I 12); Romaunt, ll. 57–62, 82–9.

33. For a more sustained discussion of this passage, cf. Arthur W. Hoffman, 'Chaucer's Prologue to Pilgrimage: The Two Voices', *Chaucer: Modern Essays in Criticism*, ed. Edward Wagenknecht, New York, 1959; pp. 30–45.

34. *Erec et Enide*, ed. Mario Roques, *Les Romans de Chrétien de Troyes*, Vol. I, Paris, 1968; l. 27. cf. also *Le Chevalier de la Charrette*, Vol. III, which opens on Ascension Day (l. 30), and *Yvain*, Vol. IV, which chooses Pentecost (l. 6).

35. *Sir Orfeo* (*c.* 1330), ed. A. J. Bliss, 1954, 1966; Auchinleck MS, ll. 57–62.

36. *Ywain and Gawain* (II 125); l. 389 ff. and 625 ff. *Morte Arthure* (late fourteenth century), ed. Edmund Brock, EETS OS 8, 1871, 1961; l. 920 ff.

37. *Eger and Grime* (II 125), ll. 919–20, 925–8.

38. See Chap. III, p. 86.

39. *Death and Liffe* (II 65); ll. 22–9.
40. cf. Curtius, *European Literature* (II 119); pp. 195–200.
41. *Purgatorio*, XXVIII, ll. 139–44.
42. C, XVII, ll. 10–16.
43. cf. Pearsall and Salter, *Landscapes and Seasons* (IV 10); p. 158.
44. *Ibid.*, pp. 150–1.
45. *Harley Lyrics* (III 3); p. 53.
46. *Ibid.*, p. 61.
47. Tuve, *Seasons and Months* (IV 21); pp. 109–10.
48. *Lydgate's Temple of Glas*, re-ed. J. Schick, EETS ES 60, 1891; ll. 1–9.
49. *Ibid.*, ll. 184–5.
50. *English Works* (I 33); *Confessio Amantis*, Prologus, ll. 921–8, 933–44.
51. *Pat. Lat.* 210; p. 492, Bk I, Ch. V.
52. *Ibid.*, pp. 487–9, Bk I, Ch. I.
53. ed. cit. (II 28); l. 60 and ll. 491–2.
54. Just possibly, that cock recalls the trials of Peter; Gawain has betrayed his 'trouthe' not thrice, but once only; as Christ, on a more solemn occasion, forgave his disciple, so the Green Knight brings Gawain to confess and be forgiven.
55. cf. the comment, ll. 494–9, on Gawain's agreement with the Green Knight; these lines could well read as the rational verdict of Elde upon the visionary undertakings of Youth.
56. *Knight's Tale*, l. 2847. *York Plays* (II 49); I, l. 77.
57. *De Civitate Dei, Pat. Lat.* 41; p. 332.
58. *13th C. Lyrics* (III 6); 'Friar Thomas de Hales' Lov Ron', p. 70.
59. *Poems* (I 49); pp. 20–3.
60. *13th C. Lyrics* (III 6); 'Ubi Sount Qui Ante Nos Fuerount', p. 85.
61. *Works* (II 34); p. 791.
62. *Minor Poems* II (I 37); pp. 809–13.
63. There are marked rhythmic affinities between this verse and the fourth, whose images are explicitly those of the natural world.
64. l. 35. It should also be remarked that the perception of the natural world in the verses which follow those which describe the decline of humanity (12–15) is very like Gower's, being clearly infected with 'mannes senne', where the natural world of verse 4 is not.
65. *Summa*, 1a, l, 5, ad. 1; ed. cit. (IV 26); Vol. IX, pp. 26–8.
66. *Inferno*, X, is one of many examples; for Farinata, the continuing reality is the politics of Florence; for Cavalcante, the fate of his son is his dominant concern.
67. Thus, for example, Arnaut Daniel regrets his past and entreats Dante's prayers for his salvation; *Purgatorio*, XXVI, ll. 142–7.
68. e.g. Aquinas, on the decadence of the Dominicans, and Bonaventura on that of the Franciscans; *Paradiso*, XI and XII.
69. Brunetto Latini, who asks Dante '*Siati raccomandato il mio Tesoro/Nel quale io vivo ancora*' (May my Treasure, in which I still live, be recommended to you), displays a renaissance attitude, but is amongst the damned; *Inferno*, XV, ll. 119–20.
70. *13th C. Lyrics* (III 6); p. 70 and p. 73.
71. *The Penguin Book of French Verse*, Vol. I, ed. Brian Woledge, 1961; p. 315.
72. cf. Schirmer, *Lydgate* (I 26); 'The theme of the transitoriness of this earthly life was not only Lydgate's favourite topic but also that of the age in which he lived.' (p. 206.) cf. Huizinga, *Waning* (II 7); pp. 140–1.

73. cf. *Minor Poems* I (I 28); Nos 13, 15, 20, 21 and 64. *Minor Poems* II (I 37); No. 62. This distinction can be generalized, cf. Woolf, *Religious Lyric* (III 5); p. 71.

74. 'The complaint of Mars', Anelida's complaint in 'Anelida and Arcite', *The Legend of Good Women*, are obvious examples, cf. Clemen, *Early Poetry* (II 27); p. 172. Complaint, though more comprehensive than *ubi sunt*, includes the latter; the coincidence of the two suggests that a sense of ritual may well contribute to the remarkable consistency of the lament.

75. *Poems* (I 49); p. 149.

76. cf. ll. 599–615.

77. John Lawlor, 'The Pattern of Consolation in *The Book of the Duchess*', *Chaucer Criticism*, ed. Richard Schoeck and Jerome Taylor, Vol. II, Indiana 1961, 1963; pp. 232–60, gives a sympathetic and sensitive account of this movement in the poem.

78. *Early Poetry* (II 27); p. 46.

79. *Sermons* (II 41); pp. 251–2.

80. *Poems* (I 49); p. 21.

81. *York* (II 49); VI, l. 87.

82. *Towneley* (II 49); IV, ll. 33–6.

83. *Chester* (II 49); XXIII, ll. 414–17, XXIV, ll. 145–8.

84. *Ibid.*, Iusticarius Damnatus, XXIV, ll. 295–6.

85. *Barbour's Bruce*, ed. W. W. Skeat, Pt I, EETS ES 11, 1870; ll. 511–64.

86. Lydgate, *Minor Poems* II (I 37); 'Of the Sodein Fal of Princes in Oure Dayes', p. 660. Note also v. 1, on Edward II.

87. *Parlement of the Thre Ages* (II 30); l. 626.

88. *Religious Lyrics 15th C.* (I 40); 'The Lament of the Soul of Edward IV' (possibly by Skelton), p. 252.

89. *Magnificence, John Skelton's Complete Poems*, 1460–1529, ed. Philip Henderson, 1931, 1966; pp. 165–244.

90. Alfred of Beverley, Giraldus Cambrensis, William of Newburgh, all questioned the authenticity of Geoffrey's *Historia Regum Britanniae* at the close of the twelfth century; with the exception of Higden (rebuked by Trevisa) in the fourteenth century, such views are not expressed again until the close of the Middle Ages. cf. Kendrick (I 22); pp. 11–15.

91. Quoted by Kendrick (I 22); p. 40.

92. The first war against Rome, and the last, against the usurper, Mordred, are justified as the intervening campaigns are not; the Philosopher, who interprets Arthur's dream of Fortune's wheel (ll. 3218–393), remarks that his fall results from the 'schame' of his company (ll. 3393–400). *Morte Arthure* (IV 36).

93. *Works* (II 34); p. 633.

94. *Ibid.*, p. 744, 865 (Arthur's dream of Fortune), 831–5 (Gawain's brothers), 867 (the adder).

95. *Ibid.*, pp. 35, 41, 71 (Merlin's prophecies); Lancelot generalizes the process of decay from his personal life to human history, mingling the strains of Fortune with those of *ubi sunt*, pp. 847–8.

96. e.g., Roger Sherman Loomis, *The Development of Arthurian Romance*, 1963; p. 139. The ballad-like simplicity of the work seems mistaken for banality; cf. his comment on Ector's lament in Malory, p. 174.

97. *Le Morte Arthur*, re-ed. J. C. Bruce, EETS ES 88, 1903; ll. 11–12.

98. *Ibid.*, ll. 3465 (Sir Bedwere), 630–1 (Lancelot), 1065–7 (Maid), 750–1 (Guinevere). cf. also 1072–9, where the Maid bitterly parodies *ubi sunt*.

99. cf. Gilson, *Medieval Philosophy* (II 112); pp. 368–9.

100. *Sermons* (II 41); pp. 98–9.
101. Quoted by Owst, *Pulpit* (II 64); p. 534.
102. Religious writing rarely celebrates the great dead; it invokes them as instances of the vanity of human aspiration. cf. *Piers Plowman*, B, XII, ll. 41–9; *Death and Liffe*, ll. 326–43. Langland's Imaginatyf does not, however, disprize the gifts of the great, and Death is vaunting her power in a context which greatly modifies her point.
103. *Harley Lyrics* (III 3); 'Autumn Song', p. 60.
104. *Minor Poems* II (I 37); p. 766. cf. also p. 809, 'That Now is Hay Sometyme was Grase', and p. 780, 'As a Mydsomer Rose'.
105. *Chester* (II 49); XXIV, ll. 261–92. cf. Huizinga, who remarks that the female version of the Dance of Death becomes a lament for lost beauty, *Waning* (II 7); p. 148.
106. In *The Parlement of the Thre Ages*, for example, Elde brings the long history of the Nine Worthies to bear merely on the didactic point that only death is certain; ed. cit. (II 30); ll. 634–5.
107. *Inferno*, VII, ll. 67–96.
108. *Roman de la Rose* (II 4); ll. 4814–16.
109. *English Poems of Charles of Orleans*, ed. R. Steele and Mabel Day, EETS OS 215 and 220, 1940 and 1944, 1970; p. 72. On his life, see Introduction, pp. xii–xiv; b. 1394, imprisoned 1415–40.
110. *Collected Poems of Sir Thomas Wyatt*, ed. Kenneth Muir and Patricia Thomson, 1969; p. 167. Wyatt's dates: 1503?–42.
111. *Lyrics*, ed. Davies (II 129); p. 243.
112. *Religious Lyrics 15th C.* (I 40); p. 260.
113. The *Consolatio* remained quite as popular in the sixteenth century; Queen Elizabeth was herself one of its many translators. But the Renaissance subordinates Fortune herself to the service of man; see Chap. I, p. 3.
114. *Chaucer* (Intro. 2); p. 359. He quotes Trivet in support of this point.
115. *Opere* (I 59); p. 239 (Bk I, Ch. 2).
116. The origins of the *Consolatio* are explored by Pierre Courcelle in *La Consolation de Philosophie dans la tradition littéraire*, Paris, 1967; pp. 112–34 (Fortune), 161–76, 203–31.
117. *Consolatio*, ed. cit. (I 8); Bk II, P. 1, p. 174.
118. *Ibid.*, Bk IV, P. 6.
119. Erwin Panofsky's essay, 'Blind Cupid' (*Studies in Iconology*, New York, 1939, 1962; pp. 95–128), has some interesting comments to make on those three blind figures, Love, Fortune and Death, transitively blind where they act at random, intransitively, where they personify 'an unenlightened state of mind'. pp. 112–13.
120. *Consolatio*, Bk II, P. 2.
121. *Ibid.*, Bk V, P. 1.
122. *Summa*, 1a, cxvi (all four articles).
123. *Consolatio*, Bk V, P. 2, p. 370.
124. *Ibid.*, Bk V, P. 3–P. 6.
125. In *Troilus and Criseyde*, where this argument is most fully (and dryly) reflected, Troilus stops short of Boethius' conclusion and thus, perhaps deliberately, misses the point. The timeless perspective has its place in the Epilogue, as a comment on human history, but its relation to the problem of freewill is by then oblique. (Troilus' speech, Bk IV, ll. 958–1085.)
126. *Roman de la Rose* (II 4); ll. 17071–170.
127. A, XI, ll. 250–303; B, X, ll. 372–474; C, XII, ll. 199–303. In A and B the question is raised by Will; in C, significantly, by Recklessness. It is also

worth noting that these passages follow a description of Will's suffering at the hands of Fortune.

128. *Nun's Priest's Tale*, ll. 3243–8.
129. cf. I *Summa contra Gentiles*, 67, *Opera Omnia* (II 3); Vol. V, pp. 47–8.
130. See Gordon Leff, *Bradwardine and the Pelagians*, 1957; pp. 85–6.
131. cf. Curry's discussion of the Wife, *Mediæval Sciences* (III 80); pp. 91–118.
132. See Leff, *Paris and Oxford* (I 14); pp. 236–7.
133. *Prologue to Nun's Priest's Tale*, ll. 2790–1.
134. Chaucer's translation of the *Consolatio*, and the two great poems—*The Knight's Tale* (in an early version) and *Troilus and Criseyde*—which directly relate to it, were probably all written 1380–6. cf. Robinson, ed. cit. (I 12); Introduction, p. xxix.
135. These include, in Robinson's chronology, before 1372, *The Book of the Duchess*; 1372–80, *Monk's Tale, House of Fame*; *Parliament of Fowls* he places in the middle period, 1380–6, but notes that it may be a little earlier than the others in that group.
136. The narrator clearly finds the detachment of Scipio's dream unsatisfying in *The Parliament* (ll. 29–81); in *The Book of the Duchess* it is the elegiac force with which the Man in Black recreates the image of his lady which renders the consolation futile that the dreamer proffers; see above, pp. 119–20.
137. If the consolations of Philosophy are shown to be inadequate in *The Book of the Duchess*, a wisdom very relevant to the dreamer's earlier condition of insentience is reached through that recognition; *The Parliament* does not establish the nature of love, but rather suggests its diversity; *The House of Fame* does not confirm the deterministic world entailed in the predictive power of dreams, but the House itself is an ironic comment on such beliefs.
138. *De Casibus Illustrium Virorum*, Facsimile of Paris edition of 1520, Florida, 1962; pp. 141–2. Opening dialogue of Bk VI.
139. This translation has a number of inaccuracies, which imply incomprehension of the argument; cf. B. L. Jefferson, *Chaucer and the Consolation of Philosophy of Boethius*, Princeton, 1917; pp. 16–24. Chaucer's interest in the subject is a writer's, not a philosopher's; as Jefferson remarks (pp. 79–80), he uses aspects of the *Consolatio* to promote discussion, rather than accepting its solutions.
140. Note, for example, Bk III, ll. 1814–20 ('disese' attributed to his 'auctour'); Bk IV, ll. 1–8 (ruthlessness of Fortune); ll. 15–21 (ruthlessness, possibly culpable, of his authorities). The scholar, plainly, would temporize, mitigate, prevent the tragic outcome if he could. cf. M. W. Bloomfield's article on 'Distance and Predestination in *Troilus and Criseyde*' in *Chaucer Criticism* (IV 77); Vol. II, pp. 196–210.
141. *Knight's Tale*, Arcite; ll. 1237–9; Palamon; ll. 1303, 1310, 1292–4.
142. *Ibid.*, l. 1348.
143. *Ibid.*, ll. 3042–3.
144. Bk I, ll. 206–10; the dart is later identified with Criseyde's glance, ll. 295–308.
145. Bk II, l. 651.
146. Bk I, ll. 215–6.
147. Bk V, l. 1158.
148. *Consolatio*, Bk II, M. 1, l.1.
149. *Troilus*, Bk I, ll. 843–7.
150. *Consolatio*, Bk II, P. 2, ll. 43–5.
151. *Ibid.*, Bk II, P. 1, ll. 59–62.
152. *Troilus*, Bk I, ll. 848–9.

153. *Troilus*, Bk IV, ll. 383–5, 390–2.
154. *Prologue to Nun's Priest's Tale*, ll. 2767–79.
155. cf. link between *Sir Thopas* and *Melibee*, ll. 920–35.
156. See note 127.
157. Her major appearance is in C, XII, ll. 166–97, where she is used to indicate a synoptic (and secular) account of an extended period of Will's life. She reappears, but fleetingly, in the Vision of Anti-Christ, C, XXIII, ll. 110–13, 156–7.
158. *Gawain*, l. 99.
159. cf. P. M. Kean, '*The Pearl*: an Interpretation, 1967; pp. 237–42.
160. cf. Mâle, *XIIIe Siècle* (II 60); pp. 89–93, where he discusses the precise delineation of Philosophy; the description of Fortune is more general in the *Consolatio*.
161. cf. Tristram, *13th Century* (II 80); Plates 133–5.
162. *An Old English Miscellany* (mid-thirteenth century), ed. R. Morris, EETS OS 49, 1872; p. 86. *Sir Orfeo* (IV 35); it is significant chiefly that his loss, beggary and exile are *not* attributed to Fortune.
163. cf. Panofsky, *Iconology* (IV 18); pp. 112–13.
164. e.g. *Political Poems* (II 70); Nos 24 and 25, pp. 107–43.
165. *Minor Poems* II (I 37); p. 503.
166. *Princes* (I 63); Bk I, ll. 123–30.
167. i.e. *ibid.*, ll. 123–4; cf. ll. 57–63.
168. *Ibid.*, Bk VI, ll. 18–77.
169. *Troilus*, Bk V, l. 1845.
170. e.g., *Historical Poems* (I 21); compare Nos 55–63 with Nos 71–6.
171. ed. cit. (II 18); Pt I, sc. vii, ll. 309–12.
172. *Princes* (I 63); Bk III, ll. 134–5.
173. See Ch. I, p. 36, for Dante's definition of tragedy. cf. also Chaucer's Monk's uninspiring definition; *Prologue of the Monk's Tale*, ll. 1973–7.
174. e.g. by John Finlayson, in the Introduction to his edition of the *Morte Arthure*, York Medieval Texts, 1967, 1971; pp. 14–20. See above, p. 123, and note 92.
175. *Morte Arthure* (IV 36); ll. 3250–391.
176. *Works* (II 34); p. 54. See also p. 92, where Arthur advises Merlin to profit by his foresight, and circumvent the inevitable; to which Merlin responds, ' "hit woll not be" '.
177. *Ibid.*, p. 866.
178. *Assembly* (II 97); ll. 1842–8.
179. *Confessio Amantis* (I 33); Prologus, ll. 546–9.
180. Langland achieves the same end more perfectly by a different means; his mentions of Fortune are slight partly because he merges her with Lady Meed and her 'gredi etik'. In the revisions of his text, he is careful to distinguish 'Fals', Meed's father, from 'Amendes', her mother. She is thus a figure of dual possibilities; it is men who make her an abomination. Compare A, II, ll. 87–8; B, II, ll. 118–20; C, III, ll. 120–6.
181. *The New Shakespeare*, ed. J. Dover Wilson, 1921 ff.; *Henry VI*, Pt III; IV, vi, ll. 19–20 and IV, iii, ll. 46–7.
182. *Ibid.*, *Pericles*, Pro. to Act II, ll. 37–8.
183. *Ibid.*, Pro. to Act III, ll. 46–7; V, iii, ll. 88–91.
184. cf. Cassirer, *Individual and Cosmos* (I 4), p. 80.
185. cf. entries in the *NED*. The last example of fortune in the sense of disaster is 1627; the first given of its use in an absolute, positive sense is from Gower, *c.* 1390.

186. ed. cit. (III 13).
187. See Ch. III, p. 66.
188. Aquinas' terms; see Ch. IV, p. 102, and note 26.
189. For a discussion of the seasonal implications of this Prologue, see Denton Fox's Introduction to *The Testament* (III 13); pp. 49–55 and relevant notes to text. The interruption of a hot spring sun by hail and cold may be paralleled in *The Floure and the Leafe*; D. A. Pearsall in his edition, Nelson's Medieval and Renaissance Library, 1962, regards this occurrence as an 'allegory of uncontrolled passion'; see note to l. 368, and Introduction, pp. 33–4.
190. See introduction, ed. cit. (III 13); pp. 27–30.
191. *Ibid.*, pp. 40–1.
192. *Ibid.*, ll. 405 and 519.
193. Malory, *Works* (II 34); p. 790.
194. *Testament*, l. 497.
195. *Ibid.*, l. 574.
196. A. C. Spearing, *Criticism and Medieval Poetry*, 1964, p. 144, offers a modified version of this position.
197. *Piers Plowman*, C, XIII, ll. 184–5.

Chapter V: Mortality and the Grave

1. Chaucer, *The Miller's Prologue*, ll. 3171–7.
2. cf. Huizinga, *Waning* (II 7); p. 220.
3. *Minor Poems of the Vernon MS.*, ed. C. Horstmann and F. J. Furnivall, EETS OS 98 and 117, 1892 and 1901; 'The Six Miracles of Christ's body', pp. 198–221 (first miracle).
4. e.g., *Golden Legend* (II 18); Vol. I, p. 40.
5. Huizinga, *Waning* (II 7); p. 168; on the practice of boiling bodies, and the Church's interdiction, see p. 145.
6. *Minor Poems* I (I 28); 'Legend of Dan Joos', p. 313.
7. *Adam Davie's 5 Dreams about Edward II, etc.*, ed. F. J. Furnivall, EETS OS 69, 1878; ll. 940–2 and 1093–104.
8. *Golden Legend* (II 18); Vol. III, p. 207 and p. 266.
9. *Minor Poems* I (I 28); 'To St Edmund', p. 126.
10. Huizinga, *Waning* (II 7); p. 222.
11. See Ch. I, pp. 1–2.
12. cf. Gilson, *Medieval Philosophy* (II 12); p. 462 (note 4); Knowles, *Religious Orders* II (I 15); p. 335.
13. cf. R. Alger, *A Critical History of the Doctrine of a Future Life*, New York, 1878; pp. 409–12.
14. cf. H. R. Patch, *The Other World*, Harvard, 1950; pp. 27–59.
15. Pearsall and Salter, *Landscapes and Seasons* (IV 10); pp. 56–75.
16. *Jacob's Well*, ed. A. Brandeis, EETS OS 115, 1900; p. 219. As Huizinga points out—*Waning* (II 7), p. 140—the practice was originally intended for those who had already turned from the world; it is revealing that the later Middle Ages should generalize the propriety of this rejection to all men. This practice has ancient analogies, cf. Mircea Eliade, *Myths Dreams and Mysteries*, 1957, 1968; pp. 82–4.
17. Dunbar, *Poems* (I 49); 'Of Lyfe', p. 151.
18. *Pulpit* (II 64); p. 527.
19. It is not surprising that, in the face of such traditions, Chaucer should often prefer an agnostic silence. In *The Knight's Tale* he refuses to comment on

the final destination of Arcite (ll. 2809–16), reserving the description in the *Teseida* (Bk XI, vv. 1–3) for the epilogue to *Troilus* (Bk V, ll. 1807–27) where *Il Filostrato* has no comparable passage. The anarchic world of *K's T* cannot accommodate this positive vision; but the macabre is also rare in Chaucer; it occurs in the description of the dying, but not the dead, Arcite, see ll. 2743–60.

20. Woolf, *Religious Lyric* (III 5); p. 68.
21. *13th C. Lyrics* (III 6); p. 130.
22. *Minor Poems* I (I 28); pp. 120 and 119.
23. Godts, quoted by Coulton, *Medieval Panorama* (I 15); p. 418.
24. Huizinga mentions a popular belief, current in the late fourteenth century, that no one, since the Great Schism, had entered Paradise. *Waning* (II 7); p. 30.
25. *Opera Omnia* (II 3); Vol. IX, p. 510, *Quodlibet*, IV, 4.
26. Compare C, XXI, ll. 96–114, with C, XXIII, ll. 74–105.
27. cf. Panofsky, *Tomb Sculpture* (I 46); p. 9; Pennethorne Hughes, *Witchcraft*, 1952, 1965; p. 120.
28. Quoted by Panofsky, *Tomb Sculpture*; pp. 27 and 18.
29. cf. Bultmann, *Life and Death* (I 2); the notion of a further life is deliberately excluded save for a 'joyless shadowy existence' in the grave, 'in no way whatever comparable to even the most wretched life on earth' (p. 8).
30. *Ecclesiastes*, I, 14.
31. *Ecclesiastes*, XII, 7; cf. burial service, and 'Earth upon Earth' poems (II 87).
32. *Job*, XIX, 26; cf. medieval reaction to Lazarus, see Ch. V, p. 158–9.
33. cf. Patch, *Other World* (V 14); pp. 80–133.
34. cf. Reidar Christiansen, *The Dead and the Living, Studia Norvegica*, II, Oslo, 1946; pp. 30–9, 90–6. H. R. Ellis, *The Road to Hel*, 1943; pp. 83–7.
35. cf. G. Turville-Petre, *Origins of Icelandic Literature*, 1953; pp. 8–14. It should, however, be added that Teutonic tradition, especially when crossed with Christianity, emphasizes both punishment and corruption; cf. Patch, *Other World* (V 14); pp. 60–79.
36. *Selections*, ed. Hall (I 38); p. 46, ll. 273–5.
37. They can be found in the thirteenth century; e.g. 'The Latemest Day' in *13th C. Lyrics* (III 6); pp. 46–54, 'When Turf is Thy Tower', p. 54. In the late fourteenth century, Chaucer's gentle Parson preaches as though the grave were the single and final reality, an emphasis that must have been typical of the time.
38. Rosemary Woolf prints these fifteenth-century verses for the first time, *Religious Lyric* (III 5), p. 318, with the comment, 'it is perhaps too repellent in content and too inadequate in style to deserve inclusion in any anthology'.
39. *Wheatley MS.* (II 50); 'Seven Penitential Psalms', p. 21.
40. *Towneley Plays* (II 49); XXXI, ll. 135–44.
41. *John*, XI, 39. For popular tradition, cf. Huizinga, *Waning* (II 7); p. 148.
42. *Fin du Moyen Age* (I 45); p. 348.
43. The illumination in Arundel 83, folio 127, and the paintings at Wensley, Yorkshire, and Tarrant Crawford, Dorset, antedate the Black Death by some twenty years.
44. *Summa*, 1a–2ae, i, 7, ad. 3; ed. cit. (I 9), Vol. XVI, p. 24.
45. *Religious Pieces* (I 17); 'The Mirror of St Edmund', p. 16. *Michel's Ayenbite* (II 41); p. 216. The first translates the OE of Edmund Rich; the second quotes St Bernard; but the sentiments are continuous with those of the later Middle Ages.

46. I am indebted to Dr John Conlee for his transcription of this poem from BM Addit. 37049; he is hoping to include it in a much needed collection of debate poems, to be published in York Medieval Texts.

47. As in the old churchyard, Pateley Bridge, Yorkshire: 'Stand and read as thou goes by/As thou art now so once was I/As I am now so must thou be/ Prepare thy self to follow me' (Tomb of John Bake, d. 1766).

48. *Golden Legend* (II 18); Vol. VI, p. 117.

49. *An Alphabet of Tales*, ed. M. M. Banks, EETS OS 126 and 127, 1904 and 1905; e.g. No. 17, p. 15. Value of contemplating corpse, No. 517, p. 350.

50. *Sermons* (II 41); pp. 176–7.

51. *Minor Poems* I (I 28); pp. 197–203.

52. cf. B. Hauréau, 'Mémoire sur les Récits d'Apparitions dans les Sermons du Moyen Age', *Mémoire de l'Académie des Inscriptions et Belles Lettres*, XXVIII, 1876; Pt II, pp. 239–63.

53. Huizinga, *Waning* (II 7); p. 169.

54. e.g. many primitive races believe in a *mort qui vive*, often in relation to a remnant of the corpse; see Christiansen, *Dead and Living* (V 34); pp. 6–7. The contemplation of the skeleton as evidence both of death and resurrection, long before the advent of Christianity and the assimilation of death to the natural order, is also common in such cultures; see Eliade, *Myths, etc.* (V 16); pp. 82–4.

55. See F. Douce, *The Dance of Death*, 1833; pp. 2–3.

56. *Myrc's Duties of a Parish Priest*, ed. E. Peacock, EETS OS 31, 1868; ll. 1667–78.

57. *Twelfth Century Homilies in MS. Bodley 343*, ed. A. O. Belfour, EETS OS 137, 1909; XII, p. 124.

58. *Tomb Sculpture* (I 46); p. 63.

59. cf. Beryl Smalley, *English Friars and Antiquity*, 1960; p. 254.

60. In fourteen of twenty-one wall paintings in England still clearly visible, the Living are crowned; most of these show them on foot, carrying birds, though in four they are on horseback. Seven paintings (and an eighth recorded) differentiate the figures into Ages; four (and a fifth recorded) clearly do not; the rest are in too bad a state for this to be clear. Those that differentiate are earlier in date, belonging to the early or mid-fourteenth century. On the popularity of falconry, cf. McKisack, *Fourteenth Century* (I 15), p. 242; Coulton, *Panorama* (I 15), pp. 593–4; Schirmer, *Lydgate* (I 26), p. 5.

61. Codex Harley, 2917, Brit. Mus., f. 119.

62. Ages of corruption are distinguished at Tarrant Crawford, Dorset; at Peakirk, Northants, the Dead appear against a background of moths, newts and other insects, as well as being hung, themselves, with worms.

63. e.g., in the wall painting at Raunds, Northants.; the famous Italian work at the Camposanto, Pisa; the fourteenth-century French poem, *Se nous vous aportons nouvellez*, ref. below, 67.

64. *Golden Legend* (II 18); Vol. II, p. 218.

65. *Poems* (III 12); No. 54, pp. 217–23. The editor argues against the ascription of this poem to Audelay, because it is more highly alliterative, and contains 160 words which do not occur in his other verses; see Introduction, pp. xxiv–xxviii.

66. Arundel Psalter, Arundel 83, Brit. Mus., f. 127.

67. These five poems, and the fragment of a sixth, are edited by S. Glixelli, *Les Cinq Poèmès des Trois Morts et des Trois Vifs*, Paris, 1914.

68. *Ibid.*, Introduction, pp. 14–19. It is clear that England acquires the theme from France, but just possible that one of the German poems (published in *Bragur. Ein litterarisches magazin der deutschen und nordischen Vorzeit*, I,

Leipzig, 1791) influenced Audelay, for both identify the Dead as the parents of the Living. It is equally probable, however, that he took the idea from a painting with inscription, for he describes one in the last lines of the poem. Some English murals carry script; Belton, Suffolk, and Wensley, Yorkshire.

69. *Diex pour trois peceours retraire.*
70. *Conpains, vois tu ce que je voi?*, ll. 73–6.
71. cf. comments on *Parlement of the Thre Ages*, pp. 85–6 and note (III 73).
72. *Religious Lyrics 15th C.* (I 40); p. 241.
73. Rolle's 'Moral Poem', *Religious Pieces* (I 17); p. 89.
74. *Poems* (III 48); pp. 205–7.
75. cf. Huizinga, *Waning* (II 7); p. 150.
76. On actual dances, see Beatrice White's introduction to her edition with Florence Warren of Lydgate's translation of the French *Dance of Death*, EETS ES 181, 1929, 1931; pp. xii–xv. On early analogues, cf. Douce, *Dance* (V 55); pp. 5–13.
77. cf. Hughes, *Witchcraft* (V 27); pp. 23–4, 173.
78. *Fin du Moyen Age* (I 45); pp. 360–4.
79. See *Dance of Death* (V 76); Introduction, pp. xxi–xxiv.
80. cf. E. Carleton Williams, 'The Dance of Death in Painting and Sculpture in the Middle Ages', *Journal of the British Archaeological Association*, 3rd series, I, 1937; pp. 229–57.
81. cf. figs 200–12 in Mâle, *Fin du Moyen Age* (I 45).
82. *Dance of Death* (V 76); Introduction, pp. xvi–xviii.
83. ll. 9–16 (all quotations taken from Ellesmere MS).
84. See Hans Holbein, *The Dance of Death*, introduction and notes by James Clark, 1947; pp. 10–12.
85. *Ibid.*, pp. 16–18.
86. *Ibid.*, p. 36.
87. Nos VIII and XIII.
88. ll. 465–6 and No. XIX.
89. No. XXVIII and ll. 403–4.
90. ll. 620, 609–10. cf. the Carthusian, 'dede longe a-gon', ll. 353–60.
91. cf. ll. 209–16 with No. XII.
92. Nos. XXXI, XVI, VII, XXXIII.
93. *Stage* (II 52); Vol. II, pp. 153 and 155. He is thinking of *Everyman* and *The Pride of Life*, which is now given an earlier date in the fourteenth century. The point stands, however, since the majority of moralities are sixteenth century.
94. *Religious Lyrics 15th C.* (I 40); pp. 248–9.
95. *Poems* (III 48); p. 211.
96. *Poems* (I 49); 'Lament for the Makaris', pp. 20–3.
97. *Mural Paintings* (I 48); p. 48.
98. *The New Shakespeare*, ed. J. Dover Wilson; *Hamlet*, V, ii, ll. 334–5.
99. *Ibid.*, *Pericles*, I, i, ll. 41–6.
100. *Ibid.*, *Richard II*, III, ii, ll. 155–6 and 160–3. Holbein's Emperor, No. VII.
101. *Ibid.*, *Hamlet*, III, i, l. 78. *Measure for Measure*, III, i, ll. 117–18.
102. *Genesis*, II, 17.
103. cf. *Ezekiel*, XVIII, 32 (God has no pleasure in death) and *Book of Wisdom*, I, 14 (God did not create death, but created all things that they might be). The second passage, whilst included in the Vulgate canon, is regarded as apocryphal by the translators of the King James Bible. Many medieval thinkers give it centrality, however; cf. Aquinas, *Quodlibet*, IV, art. iv, where he quotes it via Augustine; *Opera* (II 3); Vol. IX, p. 510.

104. cf. I *Corinthians*, XV, 26 (Christ will vanquish death the enemy); *Revelation*, VI, 8 (horseman), XX, 13 (Hell gives up the dead); *Hebrews*, II, 14 (the devil has power of death).
105. cf. Bultmann, *Life and Death* (I 2); pp. 3–4: 'the purport of the curse was not death but life and its embitterment. Thus the OT knows nothing of death as being in itself the wages of sin.'
106. *Romans*, V, 12; see also Bultmann's comment, *ibid.*, pp. 87–90.
107. *Genesis*, III, 17; see above, p. 56. On NT, cf. Bultmann, *ibid.*, pp. 86–7.
108. cf. Ullmann, *Political Thought* (II 63); pp. 172–3. See also Alger, *Future Life* (V 13); pp. 394–426.
109. See above (V 103).
110. Commentary in *Epistolam ad Hebraeos*, Ch. IX, lect. 5; *Opera* (II 3); Vol. XIII, p. 744.
111. The first death in the world is of course that of Abel, at the hands of his brother Cain; the first murderer is thus, paradoxically, the first-born of Eve, 'the mother of all living', and this death, clearly, is the result of specific sin, though on the murderer's part.
112. Compare Nos I and II with III and IV.
113. *Minor Poems* II (I 37); 'Death's Warning', p. 656.
114. *Everyman* (III 18); compare ll. 143–5 with 74–5.
115. *Ibid.*, ll. 76–7.
116. *Religious Lyrics 15th C.* (I 40); 'On the Untimely Death of a Fair Lady', pp. 241–3.
117. *Roman de la Rose* (II 4); ll. 15870–1.
118. *Death and Liffe* (II 65); ll. 247–53.
119. *Ibid.*, ll. 264–77.
120. *Ibid.*, ll. 235 and 301.
121. *Hebrews*, II, 14.
122. *Apocryphal N.T.* (II 53); p. 119, Latin B, I (XVII).
123. Life's point of reference in *Death and Liffe* is the Harrowing; she wins the debate on its evidence. See also *Cursor Mundi* (II 118); l. 17979 ff., where Satan, in the context of the Descent, is described as 'duke of Death'.
124. cf. for example, C, XXI, ll. 28–34 with C, XXIII, ll. 74–105.
125. *Everyman* (III 18); ll. 22–63.
126. *Speculum* (II 39); l. 879 ff.
127. *Everyman* (III 18); l. 76.
128. cf. Woolf, *Religious Lyric* (III 5); pp. 309–10.
129. ed. cit. (II 82); ll. 2787–90.
130. *Everyman* (III 18); ll. 150–2.
131. *Roman de la Rose* (II 4); ll. 15915–7.
132. *Ibid.*, ll. 15969–74.
133. *Assembly* (II 97); ll. 447–8.
134. *Ibid.*, ll. 452–5.
135. *Confessio Amantis* (I 33); Bk I, ll. 2125–257. Death here is thoroughly impersonalized, as a 'Trompe' to which there is 'no resistence'.
136. C, XXIII, ll. 99–103.
137. C, XIV, ll. 137–8; C, XXI, ll. 406, 405.
138. *Death and Liffe* (II 65); ll. 152, 147–8.
139. *Ibid.*, ll. 159–63, 165–70.
140. *Mankind*, ed. Adams, *Chief Pre-Shakespearian Dramas* (III 18); pp. 304–24. Adams dates it *c.* 1475. Mankind enters l. 180.
141. *Mundus et Infans* (II 47); ll. 32–9.
142. See Woolf, *Religious Lyric* (III 5); p. 72.

143. *Hoccleve's Minor Poems*, I, ed. F. J. Furnivall, EETS ES 61, 1892; No. 23, pp. 178–215.
144. The Virgin's interference with the scales is a good example; see Caiger-Smith, *Mural Paintings* (I 48); pp. 60–2.
145. See Mâle, *L'Art religieux du XVIIe siècle*, 1908, 1951; pp. 206–16.
146. *Ibid.*, pp. 222–7.
147. *Visual Arts* (II 119); p. 340. The Legend itself was not depicted beyond the Middle Ages, cf. E. H. Langlois, *Essai historique, philosophique et pittoresque sur les Danses des Morts*, Rouen, 1851; pp. 116–63.
148. *Ibid.*, pp. 355–6.

Chapter VI: Christ and the Triumph of Eternal Life
 1. Alanus de Insulis, *De Planctu* (II 85); p. 453, P. IV.
 2. Panofsky, *Architecture and Scholasticism* (I 7); cf. pp. 8–20
 3. The allegory of battle between Virtues and Vices, based on the *Psychomachia* of Prudentius, is a popular literary form in the Middle Ages; Langland's Vision of Anti-Christ, for example, draws upon this notion.
 4. cf. *Piers Plowman*, C, XXIII, ll. 143–57, where Lyf absconds with his 'lemman' Fortune.
 5. cf. Huizinga, *Waning* (II 7); pp. 244–74, on the contrast between art and life.
 6. See Panofsky, *Tomb Sculpture* (I 46); p. 45.
 7. Beatrice is no more moved by the misery of the damned than she is harmed by the fires of Hell; see *Inf.* II, ll. 88–93.
 8. The finest example of the first is found in *Piers Plowman*; of the second, in *Pearl*. They are discussed in Ch. VI, pp. 197–201, 205–12.
 9. *Pearl* (I 50); ll. 1135–44.
10. Compare *Piers Plowman*, C, XXIII, ll. 152–6, with *Death and Liffe* (II 65); l. 401.
11. Curtius, *European Literature* (II 119); p. 170. On its persistence into the Middle Ages, see pp. 167–70.
12. cf. Panofsky, *Tomb Sculpture* (I 46); p. 56.
13. ed. cit. (IV 35); ll. 285, 300, 288 (cf. ll. 194 and 296).
14. *Ibid.*, Introduction, pp. xxvii–xli.
15. *Ibid.*, ll. 352, 355–68, 376.
16. In the heavenly Jerusalem of *Revelation*, 'the Lord God giveth them light' (XXII, 5); in *Pearl* 'God was her lombe-lyght [lamplight],/The Lombe her lantyrne', ll. 1046–7; the eternal light of God's presence illuminates Dante's Empyrean, *Par.*, XXX, ll. 100–23.
17. *Sir Orfeo* (IV 35); ll. 370–2, 60–1.
18. *Ibid.*, ll. 391–8.
19. *Ibid.*, ll. 595–6.
20. *Poems* (III 48); pp. 129–48, ll. 307, 306; cf. also ll. 310–16.
21. The three heads of Cerberus, for example, represent three kinds of death which correspond to the three Ages; see ll. 460–7.
22. It is very rare to find the macabre in Arthurian romance at any date; there is one exception in *The Awntyrs of Arthure*, where a walking corpse reverses a courtly hunt. This poem (probably early fifteenth century) is included in *Scottish Alliterative Poems*, ed. F. J. Amours, STS, Ser. I, 27 and 38, 1897, 1966; pp. 116–71; ll. 83–325.
23. ed. cit. (II 14); ll. 683–700.
24. ed. cit. (II 125); ll. 919–1090.
25. *Works* (II 34); p. 496.

26. *Ibid.*, pp. 867–8.
27. ed. cit. (II 40); ll. 11377–520.
28. *The Romance and Prophecies of Thomas of Erceldoune*, ed. J. A. H. Murray, EETS OS 61, 1875; ll. 217–22 (*c.* 1400).
29. *Partonope* (fifteenth century), re-ed. A. T. Bödtker, EETS ES 109, 1911; e.g. ll. 831–1716.
30. *Golden Legend* (II 18); Vol. VII, pp. 52–3.
31. See Wilson, *Middle English* (I 22); p. 63.
32. Described by Patch, *Other World* (V 14); pp. 263–5.
33. *Aucassin et Nicolette*, ed. Mario Roques, Paris, 1973; p. 6, VI, ll. 24–39.
34. *Wheatley MS.* (II 50); No. 13, 'The Life of Adam and Eveve', pp. 85–7.
35. cf. Kean, *'Pearl'* (IV 159); p. 100.
36. *Mandeville's Travels*, ed. P. Hamelius, Pt I, EETS OS 153, 1916; p. 167.
37. See Loomis, *Arthurian Romance* (III 96); pp. 39–40.
38. See Pauphilet's fine formulation, quoted by Loomis, *ibid.*, p. 103.
39. *Lovelich's History of the Holy Grail*, ed. F. J. Furnivall, EETS ES 20, 24, 28, 30, 1874, 1875, 1877, 1878; Chs 29 and 30, pp. 366–404.
40. *Piers Plowman*, C, XXI, ll. 456–9.
41. *Selections*, ed. Hall (I 38); 'Poema Morale', pp. 30–53, l. 115, Lambeth MS.
42. *Ibid.*, ll. 371–4, Egerton MS.
43. *Ayenbite* (II 41); p. 72.
44. *Incendium Amoris* (II 110); pp. 37–9.
45. *Meditacyuns*, trans. Robert Manning of Brunne (I 39); l. 574.
46. *13th C. Lyrics* (III 6); p. 34.
47. *Minor Poems* I (I 28); p. 328.
48. cf. Chambers, *Stage* (II 52); Vol. II, pp. 153–4.
49. *Inferno*, II, l. 32.
50. James, *Apocryphal N.T.* (II 53), indicates accounts from the second century on; p. 95.
51. *John*, XI, 25–6.
52. *Golden Legend* (II 18); Vol. I, p. 98.
53. 'The Devilis Parlement', in *Hymns*, ed. Furnivall (III 57); pp. 41–57.
54. See Ch. V, pp. 158–9.
55. ed. cit. (II 18); ll. 768–73.
56. *Ibid.*, ll. 966–74.
57. *Christ's Burial and Resurrection*, in *Digby Plays* (II 18); pp. 169–226, ll. 176–8.
58. *Ibid.*, ll. 1623–4.
59. *Towneley Plays* (II 49); XXV, ll. 225–8.
60. *Ibid.*, ll. 301–2, 315–20.
61. *Ibid.*, ll. 394–5.
62. *Ibid.*, XXVIII, ll. 342–3.
63. B, XVI, ll. 104, 106–18.
64. B, XVIII, ll. 10, 19–23.
65. Such language does not occur in the drama, though it can be paralleled in religious prose; see Ch. V, p. 61.
66. B, XVI, ll. 162–3.
67. B, XVIII, ll. 29–30.
68. B, XVIII, ll. 59, 64–7.
69. B, XVIII, ll. 136–7.
70. C, XXI, ll. 389–94. B is a more human, C a more expository text; I move between the two for that reason, but it should be pointed out that some passages in B, notably XVIII, ll. 19–23, are omitted from C.
71. *Death and Liffe* (II 65); ll. 99–103.

72. *Michel's Ayenbite* (II 41); p. 203. *Cursor Mundi* (II 118); l. 723 ff. In *Old English Homilies* (III 51), the adder symbolizes: (1) the old Adam, Ser. I, Pt II, OS 34; pp. 151–5. (2) The good Christian, Ser. II, OS 53; pp. 197–9. (3) The slanderers and enemies of Christ, Ser. I, Pt I, OS 29; pp. 51–3.
73. *Piers Plowman*, B, II, l. 16. *Death and Liffe*, l. 62.
74. *Pearl* (I 50); ll. 905–8.
75. cf. Eliade, *Myths, etc.* (V 16); p. 172.
76. *French Tradition* (II 77); p. 215.
77. E. J. Holmyard, *Alchemy*, 1957; p. 13. He further comments that the belief that the discovery of the stone was dependent on divine favour led to the development of spiritual alchemy.
78. *Sermons* (II 41); p. 286.
79. *The Book of Quinte Essence*, ed. F. J. Furnivall, EETS OS 16, 1866; pp. 1–2, 4–6, 11, etc.
80. *Towneley Plays* (II 49); XXI, ll. 100–3.
81. ed. cit. (VI 39); Joseph, Ch. 41, pp. 237 ff.; Ypocras, Ch. 36, p. 21. For discussion of Tree, see above, pp. 192–3.
82. *Huon of Burdeux*, in *Charlemagne Romances*, 7, 8, 9, ed. S. L. Lee, EETS ES, 40, 41, 43, 1883–4; pp. 65–81 (Chs 22–6), 370–86 (Chs 109–11), 434–6 (Chs 121 and 122).
83. *St Erkenwald* (late fourteenth century), ed. Israel Gollancz, *Select Early English Poems*, 1932; ll. 17–18.
84. Critics have even denied that the Pearl is a child, the jeweller a bereaved father; see Sister Mary Vincent Hillman, *The Pearl*, Interpretation, pp. xix–xxi, and notes to l. 233 and l. 484.
85. *Pearl* (I 50); ll. 857–60.
86. *Ibid.*, ll. 319–20.
87. *Ibid.*, ll. 642–3.
88. *Ibid.*, ll. 39–40, 305–6. On fortune and *wyrd*, see above, p. 141.
89. *Ibid.*, ll. 483–5.
90. *Ibid.*, l. 401.
91. This is also true of the parable of the labourers in the vineyard, where those who have laboured through the long day of life (the old), complain at the speedy reward accorded to those whose toil, like Pearl's, is brief; see sections 9–11.
92. *Pearl* (I 50); ll. 473–4.
93. cf. *English Mediæval Lapidaries*, ed. Joan Evans and Mary Serjeantson, EETS OS 190, 1932; *passim*.
94. See Kean, *'Pearl'* (IV 159); p. 24. *Cleanness* (II 69); ll. 1124–8.
95. *Revelation*, XXII, 18–19.
96. Kean, *'Pearl'* (IV 159); p. 145.
97. See ll. 1069–76.
98. *Pearl* (I 50); l. 257.

Index

Bold type indicates main references